APEX ACADEMIC RESOURCES

Scholastic Aptitude Test (SAT) Success

*5 Full-Length Tests, 750+ Practice Questions &
Detailed Answer Explanations for Guaranteed
First-Attempt Success*

First edition

This book was professionally typeset on Reedsy.
Find out more at reedsy.com

Contents

I

Introduction

Purpose of the Book

Goals and Objectives

Welcome to your SAT study guide! We're here to help you succeed on your SAT exam, and we believe this book can be the only resource you need to achieve your goals. Here's what we aim to accomplish together:

1. Boost Your Confidence

Preparing for the SAT can feel overwhelming, but with the right tools and strategies, you'll build the confidence you need to tackle the test head-on. We want you to feel prepared and self-assured when test day arrives.

2. Provide Comprehensive Content Review

This book covers everything you need to know for the SAT, from the basics to the more challenging concepts. We've included thorough explanations and examples to make sure you understand each topic inside and out.

3. Offer Practical Test Strategies

Knowing the material is just part of the battle. We'll share effective test-taking strategies to help you manage your time, approach different types of questions, and avoid common pitfalls. These strategies will help you work smarter, not just harder.

4. Include Ample Practice Opportunities

Practice makes perfect. We've included six full-length practice tests to give you plenty of opportunities to apply what you've learned. Each test is designed to mimic the actual SAT experience, so you'll know exactly what to expect.

5. Provide Detailed Answer Explanations

Understanding why an answer is correct is crucial for learning. For every practice question, we've provided detailed explanations that break down the reasoning behind the right answer. This way, you can learn from your mistakes and improve.

6. Help You Develop a Study Plan

Consistency is key in preparing for the SAT. We'll guide you in creating a study schedule that fits your life, helping you stay on track and make the most of your study time.

7. Reduce Test Anxiety

Feeling nervous is normal, but we want to help you minimize anxiety so you can perform your best. We'll share tips on how to stay calm and focused before and during the test.

By the end of this book, our goal is for you to feel fully prepared and confident in your ability to excel on the SAT. Remember, you're capable of achieving great things, and we're here to support you every step of the way. Let's get started!

How to Use This Book Effectively

We're excited to help you ace the SAT, and we want to make sure you get the most out of this book. Here are some tips on how to use it effectively:

1. Start with the Basics

Before diving into practice tests and advanced strategies, make sure you have a solid understanding of the SAT's structure and format. Read through the introductory chapters to get familiar with what to expect on test day and how the SAT is scored.

2. Create a Study Schedule

Consistency is key when preparing for the SAT. Use the study plan guide in Chapter 1 to create a schedule that fits your life. Set aside regular time for studying, and stick to your plan as much as possible. This will help you cover all the material without feeling rushed.

3. Focus on One Section at a Time

The SAT is divided into specific sections, so it's helpful to focus on one section at a time. Start with the chapter on the Reading Test, then move on to the Writing and Language Test, and so on. This approach will help you build a strong foundation in each area before moving on to the next.

4. Practice, Practice, Practice

The practice tests in this book are your best friend. Take them under timed conditions to get used to the pace of the actual test. After each practice test, review your answers and the detailed explanations to understand where you went wrong and how to improve.

5. Use the Strategies Provided

In addition to content review, we've included a wealth of test-taking strategies. These tips can help you approach questions more effectively and manage your time during the test. Make sure to read through the strategy sections and apply them during your practice tests.

6. Review and Reflect

After completing each chapter or practice test, take some time to review your progress. Reflect on what you did well and where you need improvement. Use this insight to adjust your study plan and focus on areas that need more attention.

7. Take Care of Yourself

Preparing for the SAT isn't just about studying. Make sure to get plenty of rest, eat well, and take breaks when needed. A healthy mind and body are crucial for doing your best on test day.

8. Stay Positive and Persistent

It's normal to find some sections or questions challenging. Don't get discouraged. Keep a positive attitude and remind yourself that improvement comes with practice. If you find yourself stuck, revisit the relevant chapters or seek additional help if needed.

Overview of the SAT

Structure and Format

Understanding the structure and format of the SAT is crucial for effective preparation. Let's break it down so you know exactly what to expect on test day.

1. The Basics

The SAT is divided into four main sections:

- **Reading Test**
- **Writing and Language Test**
- **Math Test (No Calculator)**
- **Math Test (Calculator)**
- **Optional Essay** (some schools require it, others don't)

Each section is designed to test different skills, and knowing the format will help you manage your time and approach each part with confidence.

2. Reading Test

- **Time**: 65 minutes
- **Questions**: 52 multiple-choice questions
- **Content**: This section includes passages from literature, historical documents, social sciences, and natural sciences. You'll answer questions about the content, meaning, and structure of these passages.

3. Writing and Language Test

- **Time**: 35 minutes
- **Questions**: 44 multiple-choice questions
- **Content**: You'll be given passages with deliberate errors in grammar, punctuation, and style. Your task is to identify and correct these errors, improving the overall clarity and effectiveness of the writing.

4. Math Test

- **No Calculator Section**
- **Time**: 25 minutes
- **Questions**: 20 questions (15 multiple-choice and 5 grid-in)
- **Content**: This section focuses on algebra, problem-solving, and data analysis. You'll solve problems that test your ability to understand and work with mathematical concepts without the aid of a calculator.
- **Calculator Section**
- **Time**: 55 minutes
- **Questions**: 38 questions (30 multiple-choice and 8 grid-in)
- **Content**: This section covers a broader range of math topics, including advanced math and some trigonometry. You can use a calculator for these problems, which often involve more complex calculations.

5. Optional Essay

- **Time**: 50 minutes
- **Content**: You'll be given a passage and asked to analyze how the author builds their argument. This section tests your reading, analysis, and writing skills. While it's optional, some colleges may require it, so check the requirements of the schools you're applying to.

6. Total Test Time

- **Without Essay**: 3 hours
- **With Essay**: 3 hours and 50 minutes

7. Test Format

- **Multiple-Choice Questions**: Most of the SAT consists of multiple-choice questions with four answer choices.
- **Grid-In Questions**: In the Math sections, some questions require you to calculate and write in your answer.
- **Essay**: If you choose to take the Essay, you'll write a single, structured response analyzing a provided passage.

Understanding this structure helps you know what to expect and how to pace yourself. Each section has a specific focus and format, so practicing under timed conditions will give you a good sense of how to manage your time effectively.

Scoring

Understanding how the SAT is scored will help you set realistic goals and track your progress as you prepare. Here's a straightforward explanation of the SAT scoring system.

1. Total Score

Your total SAT score ranges from 400 to 1600 points. This score is the sum of your scores from the two main sections:

- **Evidence-Based Reading and Writing (EBRW)**
- **Math**

Each of these sections is scored from 200 to 800 points.

2. Section Scores

Evidence-Based Reading and Writing (EBRW)

- This section combines your Reading Test and Writing and Language Test scores.
- Each test is scored from 10 to 40 points, and these scores are then added together and multiplied by 10 to give you your EBRW score.

Math

- The Math section score is based on your performance in both the No Calculator and Calculator sections.
- Like the EBRW, the Math section score ranges from 200 to 800 points.

3. Subscores and Cross-Test Scores

The SAT also provides more detailed feedback through subscores and cross-test scores.

Subscores (1 to 15 points each)
These give you insight into your strengths and weaknesses in specific areas.

Subscores are provided for:

- Command of Evidence
- Words in Context
- Expression of Ideas
- Standard English Conventions
- Heart of Algebra
- Problem Solving and Data Analysis
- Passport to Advanced Math

Cross-Test Scores (10 to 40 points each)

These scores show your performance on questions across the entire test that relate to specific skills.

The two cross-test scores are:

- Analysis in History/Social Studies
- Analysis in Science

4. Essay Score (Optional)

If you take the Essay, you'll receive three scores, each ranging from 2 to 8 points:

- **Reading**: How well you understood the passage.
- **Analysis**: How well you analyzed the author's argument.
- **Writing**: How well you expressed your ideas and used standard written English.

These scores are reported separately and do not affect your total SAT score.

5. How the Scores Are Calculated

- **Raw Scores to Scaled Scores**
- Your raw score for each section is the number of questions you answered correctly. There is no penalty for incorrect answers, so it's always worth guessing if you're unsure.
- The College Board then converts your raw scores to scaled scores using a process called equating. This ensures that scores are comparable across different test dates and versions of the SAT.

6. Score Reports

When you receive your SAT score report, you'll see:

- Your total score (out of 1600)
- Your section scores (EBRW and Math, each out of 800)
- Your test scores (Reading, Writing and Language, and Math, each out of 40)
- Your subscores and cross-test scores
- Your Essay scores (if applicable)

Understanding your SAT scores can help you identify areas for improvement and track your progress. Aim to focus on both your strengths and areas that need more practice as you prepare.

Registration and Test Day Logistics

Getting registered and knowing what to expect on test day can make your SAT experience much smoother. Here's a simple guide to help you through the process.

1. Registering for the SAT

a. Online Registration

- **Create a College Board Account**: Head to the College Board website and create an account if you don't already have one. This account will be your hub for everything SAT-related.
- **Choose a Test Date**: The SAT is offered several times a year. Pick a date that gives you enough time to prepare but also fits well with your other commitments.
- **Select a Test Center**: Find a convenient test center close to your home or school. You'll need to enter this information during registration.
- **Upload a Photo**: You'll need to upload a clear, recent photo of yourself. This will appear on your admission ticket and help verify your identity on test day.
- **Pay the Fee**: You'll need a credit card or fee waiver to pay for the test. Fee waivers are available for eligible students, so check if you qualify.

b. Registration Deadlines

- **Regular Registration**: Be sure to register by the regular deadline to avoid late fees.
- **Late Registration**: If you miss the regular deadline, you can still register during the late registration period, but there's an additional fee.
- **Check Dates**: Always check the College Board website for the most up-to-date information on registration deadlines and test dates.

2. Preparing for Test Day

a. What to Bring

- **Admission Ticket**: Print your admission ticket from your College

Board account and bring it with you.

- **Photo ID**: Bring a valid, government-issued photo ID (e.g., driver's license, passport). School IDs are acceptable if they meet College Board requirements.
- **No. 2 Pencils and Erasers**: Bring at least two No. 2 pencils with good erasers. Mechanical pencils are not allowed.
- **Approved Calculator**: Make sure your calculator is on the approved list. Bring extra batteries just in case.
- **Snacks and Water**: Pack a snack and water bottle to keep your energy up during breaks. These must be stored away during the test but can be accessed during breaks.

b. What Not to Bring

- **Electronic Devices**: Leave your phone, smartwatch, and other electronic devices at home or turn them off and leave them in your bag.
- **Books and Notes**: You can't use any books, notes, or study aids during the test.
- **Unapproved Calculators**: Check the College Board's list of approved calculators to make sure yours is allowed.

3. On Test Day

a. Arrival Time

- **Get There Early**: Plan to arrive at the test center at least 30 minutes before the test starts. This gives you time to check in and get settled.
- **Check-In Process**: Show your admission ticket and photo ID. The test center staff will check these against their records.

b. During the Test

- **Follow Instructions**: Listen carefully to the proctor's instructions. They'll guide you through the process and let you know when to start and stop each section.
- **Stay Focused**: Keep an eye on the time, but don't stress if you don't finish every question. It's better to move on and come back if you have time.
- **Breaks**: Use breaks to relax, eat your snack, and use the restroom. Remember, you can't access your phone or study materials during breaks.

c. After the Test

- **Submitting Your Answer Sheet**: Make sure all your answers are filled in correctly and submit your answer sheet as instructed.
- **Collect Your Belongings**: Gather all your belongings and leave the test center quietly. Others may still be testing, so be respectful.

4. Getting Your Scores

- **Score Release**: Scores are typically released about two weeks after the test date. You'll receive an email notification when they're available.
- **Accessing Scores**: Log into your College Board account to view your scores. You can also send your scores to colleges directly from your account.

II

Getting Started with SAT Preparation

Understanding the SAT

The Importance of the SAT in College Admissions

The SAT is a significant part of the college admissions process, and understanding its role can help you see why preparing for it is so important. Here's why the SAT matters:

1. Standardized Measure of Academic Readiness

Colleges receive applications from students all over the country (and the world), each with different high school experiences and grading systems. The SAT provides a standardized measure that helps colleges compare applicants' academic readiness on an even playing field.

2. Predicts College Success

Research has shown that SAT scores can be a good predictor of how well students will perform in their first year of college. Admissions officers use your SAT scores to gauge your potential for success in college-level courses, especially in areas like critical reading, math, and writing.

3. Complements Your High School Record

Your high school GPA and coursework are crucial parts of your application, but they don't tell the whole story. The SAT adds another dimension to your academic profile, showing your ability to perform under standardized testing conditions. Together, your GPA and SAT scores provide a more comprehensive picture of your academic abilities.

4. Scholarships and Financial Aid

Many colleges and scholarship programs use SAT scores as part of their criteria for awarding financial aid and scholarships. A higher SAT score can increase your chances of receiving merit-based scholarships, which can significantly reduce the cost of your college education.

5. Holistic Admissions

While some colleges have moved toward a test-optional policy, many still consider SAT scores as part of a holistic admissions process. This means they look at your SAT scores alongside other factors like your personal statement, letters of recommendation, extracurricular activities, and interviews. Strong SAT scores can enhance your application and make you a more competitive candidate.

6. Meeting College Requirements

Some colleges have minimum SAT score requirements for admission. Even if a school doesn't have a strict cutoff, higher scores can improve your chances of being accepted, especially at more competitive institutions.

7. Showing Subject Mastery

The SAT Subject Tests (though recently discontinued) were once used to demonstrate your strength in specific academic areas. While the main SAT doesn't replace these, a high score in certain sections can still show colleges your proficiency in those subjects.

8. Personal Achievement

Taking the SAT and doing well is a personal achievement that reflects your hard work, dedication, and readiness for the next step in your academic career. It's an accomplishment you can be proud of and a milestone in your college preparation.

Breakdown of Each Section

The SAT is designed to test a range of skills across several sections. Understanding what each section covers and how it's structured will help you know what to expect and how to prepare effectively.

1. Reading Test
  Time: 65 minutes
  Questions: 52 multiple-choice questions

- **Content**: This section includes passages from literature, historical documents, social sciences, and natural sciences. Each passage is followed by a series of questions that test your ability to understand, analyze, and interpret the text.
- **Skills Tested**: You'll need to identify main ideas, understand words in context, interpret data from charts and graphs, and analyze how an author's choices affect the passage.

2. Writing and Language Test
  Time: 35 minutes
  Questions: 44 multiple-choice questions

- **Content**: You'll work with passages that have deliberate errors in grammar, punctuation, and style. Your task is to find and fix these errors to improve the clarity and effectiveness of the writing.
- **Skills Tested**: This section tests your knowledge of standard English conventions, including grammar, usage, and punctuation, as well as your ability to improve the expression of ideas.

3. Math Test
The Math Test is divided into two parts: one where you can use a calculator and one where you cannot.
  No Calculator Section

Time: 25 minutes

Questions: 20 questions (15 multiple-choice and 5 grid-in)

- **Content**: This section focuses on algebra, problem-solving, and data analysis. You'll encounter linear equations, inequalities, functions, and other algebraic concepts.
- **Skills Tested**: Your ability to solve problems quickly and accurately without a calculator is key here.

Calculator Section

Time: 55 minutes

Questions: 38 questions (30 multiple-choice and 8 grid-in)

- **Content**: This section covers a broader range of math topics, including advanced math concepts and some trigonometry. You can use your calculator to help solve these more complex problems.
- **Skills Tested**: You'll work on problems involving linear equations, systems of equations, and data interpretation. The use of a calculator can assist with more intricate calculations.

4. Optional Essay

Time: 50 minutes

Content: You'll be given a passage and asked to analyze how the author builds an argument to persuade the audience. This section is optional, but some colleges may require it.

- **Skills Tested**: This essay tests your reading comprehension, analytical skills, and writing ability. You'll need to read the passage, identify the author's argument, and explain how the argument is constructed using evidence from the text.

Test-Taking Tips

- **Timing**: Each section has a strict time limit, so practice pacing yourself to ensure you can answer all the questions within the allotted time.
- **Answering Strategies**: Use process of elimination on multiple-choice questions, and don't be afraid to make educated guesses—there's no penalty for wrong answers.
- **Review and Practice**: Regular practice with sample questions and full-length practice tests will help you get comfortable with the format and improve your performance.

Setting Up a Study Plan

Creating a Realistic Study Schedule

Creating a study schedule that you can stick to is crucial for effective SAT preparation. Here's how to build a plan that works for you:

1. Assess Your Current Schedule

Start by looking at your weekly commitments. Identify the times when you're busy with school, extracurricular activities, work, and other responsibilities. This will help you find the free time you can dedicate to studying.

2. Set Clear Goals

Decide what you want to achieve with your study sessions. Break down your goals into specific, manageable tasks. For example, aim to complete a certain number of practice questions each week or master a particular topic.

3. Allocate Study Time

Based on your free time, decide how many hours you can realistically dedicate to studying each week. It's better to have shorter, consistent study sessions than to cram all your studying into a few long sessions. Aim for at least 2-3 hours of focused study time per week, and increase this as the test date approaches.

4. Create a Weekly Plan

- **Divide Your Study Sessions**: Allocate time for each section of the SAT (Reading, Writing and Language, Math, and, if applicable, the Essay). This ensures you're covering all areas and not neglecting any part of the test.
- **Incorporate Variety**: Mix different types of activities within your study sessions. For example, combine reading practice with vocabulary building, or switch between math problem sets and grammar exercises.

5. Set Milestones

Break your overall study plan into smaller milestones. For example, aim to complete a full-length practice test by the end of the month or master algebra by a specific date. Milestones help you stay on track and provide a sense of accomplishment as you progress.

6. Be Flexible

Life can be unpredictable, so it's important to stay flexible. If something comes up and you miss a study session, don't stress. Adjust your schedule as needed and get back on track as soon as possible.

7. Take Breaks

Avoid burnout by scheduling regular breaks. Short breaks during study sessions can help maintain your focus, while longer breaks during the week can keep you refreshed and motivated.

8. Review and Adjust

At the end of each week, review your progress. Did you meet your study goals? Are there areas where you need more practice? Use this reflection to adjust your schedule for the following week.

Sample Study Schedule

Here's a sample weekly study schedule to give you an idea of how to structure your time:

- **Monday**: 1 hour of Reading practice (reading passages and answering questions)
- **Tuesday**: 1 hour of Math practice (No Calculator section problems)
- **Wednesday**: 1 hour of Writing and Language practice (grammar exercises)
- **Thursday**: 1 hour of Math practice (Calculator section problems)
- **Friday**: Review notes and practice questions from the week (30 minutes)
- **Saturday**: Full-length practice test (timed conditions)
- **Sunday**: Rest day or light review (30 minutes)

By creating a realistic study schedule tailored to your life, you can make steady progress without feeling overwhelmed. Remember, consistency is key, and every bit of practice helps you get closer to your goal. Let's get started and make your study time effective and manageable!

Time Management Tips

Managing your time effectively is essential to ensure you cover all the material you need to study for the SAT without feeling overwhelmed. Here are some practical tips to help you make the most of your study time:

1. Prioritize Your Tasks
Start by identifying the most important tasks and focusing on those first. Break down your study goals into smaller, manageable chunks and tackle the most critical areas where you need the most improvement.

2. Use a Planner or Digital Calendar
Keeping track of your schedule in a planner or digital calendar can help

you stay organized. Schedule specific study times and stick to them as much as possible. Seeing your plan laid out can also help you balance your study time with other commitments.

3. Set Specific Study Goals

Before each study session, set a clear goal for what you want to accomplish. Whether it's completing a set number of practice questions, reviewing a particular topic, or writing an essay, having a goal will keep you focused and motivated.

4. Use the Pomodoro Technique

The Pomodoro Technique is a time management method that involves studying for 25 minutes, then taking a 5-minute break. After four cycles, take a longer break of 15-30 minutes. This technique can help you maintain focus and prevent burnout.

5. Minimize Distractions

Find a quiet, comfortable place to study where you won't be easily distracted. Turn off notifications on your phone or computer, and let others know that you need uninterrupted study time. Creating a distraction-free environment can significantly boost your productivity.

6. Break Down Large Tasks

Large tasks can be daunting, so break them down into smaller, more manageable pieces. Instead of trying to study an entire math section in one go, focus on specific topics or types of problems one at a time.

7. Use Study Aids Wisely

There are many tools and resources available to help you study more efficiently. Flashcards, online quizzes, and study apps can be great for reinforcing concepts and making the most of your study time.

8. Stay Consistent

Consistency is key when preparing for the SAT. Try to study at the same time each day or each week to build a routine. Regular, shorter study sessions are often more effective than sporadic, long sessions.

9. Review Regularly

Set aside time to review what you've learned. Regular review sessions can help reinforce your knowledge and ensure you retain the information. This can be as simple as spending the last 10 minutes of each study session reviewing notes or practice questions.

10. Take Care of Yourself

Effective time management also includes taking care of your well-being. Make sure you get enough sleep, eat well, and exercise regularly. A healthy body supports a healthy mind, which is crucial for effective studying.

Balancing Study with Other Responsibilities

Balancing SAT prep with school, extracurricular activities, work, and personal life can be challenging. Here are some tips to help you manage your time effectively and maintain a healthy balance.

1. Assess Your Priorities

Take a look at your current commitments and determine which ones are most important to you. While studying for the SAT is crucial, you don't want to neglect other important areas of your life. Identify where you can make adjustments to fit in your study sessions.

2. Create a Flexible Schedule

Build a study schedule that accommodates your other responsibilities. Use a weekly planner to map out your commitments and find time slots for SAT prep. Flexibility is key – be prepared to adjust your schedule if something unexpected comes up.

3. Combine Activities When Possible

Look for opportunities to combine study time with other activities. For example, you could listen to SAT prep podcasts or review flashcards during your commute. Multitasking in this way can help you maximize your time without sacrificing other responsibilities.

4. Set Realistic Goals

Be realistic about how much time you can dedicate to studying each week. Setting overly ambitious goals can lead to burnout and frustration. Start with smaller, achievable goals and gradually increase your study time as needed.

5. Use Downtime Effectively

Utilize small pockets of free time throughout your day for quick study sessions. Even 10-15 minutes of review can be beneficial. Carrying study materials with you, such as flashcards or practice questions, can make it easier to fit in study time during breaks.

6. Delegate and Share Responsibilities

If you have responsibilities at home or work that can be shared, don't hesitate to ask for help. Delegating tasks to family members or coworkers can free up some of your time for studying. Remember, it's okay to ask for support when you need it.

7. Prioritize Self-Care

Taking care of yourself is essential for maintaining balance. Make sure you're getting enough sleep, eating well, and taking breaks to relax. Stress management techniques, such as exercise, meditation, or hobbies, can help you stay focused and energized.

8. Communicate with Others

Let your family, friends, and teachers know about your SAT prep schedule. Communicating your goals and commitments can help them understand your availability and provide support. They might even offer helpful advice or resources.

9. Stay Organized

Keep your study materials and schedule organized. Use tools like planners, apps, or calendars to track your progress and deadlines. Staying organized can help reduce stress and ensure you're making the most of your study time.

10. Be Kind to Yourself

Balancing multiple responsibilities is challenging, and it's important to be kind to yourself. If you have an off day or miss a study session, don't get discouraged. Focus on getting back on track and celebrating your progress, no matter how small.

III

Effective Test Strategies

General Test-Taking Tips

Time Management During the Test

Managing your time effectively during the SAT is crucial for ensuring you can answer as many questions as possible. Here are some practical tips to help you stay on track:

1. Know the Timing for Each Section
Familiarize yourself with the time limits for each section of the SAT:

- **Reading Test**: 65 minutes for 52 questions
- **Writing and Language Test**: 35 minutes for 44 questions
- **Math Test (No Calculator)**: 25 minutes for 20 questions
- **Math Test (Calculator)**: 55 minutes for 38 questions
- **Optional Essay**: 50 minutes

Understanding how much time you have for each section will help you pace yourself.

2. Practice with Timed Tests
Regularly practice with timed tests to get a feel for the pacing. This will help you build a sense of how long you can spend on each question and train you to manage your time effectively under pressure.

3. Use a Watch

Bring an analog watch to the test center (digital watches are not allowed). This will help you keep track of time without relying on the clock in the room. Set it to 12:00 at the start of each section so you can easily see how much time has passed.

4. Allocate Time for Each Question

Roughly divide your time per question:

- **Reading Test**: About 75 seconds per question
- **Writing and Language Test**: About 45 seconds per question
- **Math Test (No Calculator)**: About 75 seconds per question
- **Math Test (Calculator)**: About 85 seconds per question

These are just averages. Some questions will take less time, allowing you to spend more time on harder ones.

5. Answer Easier Questions First

Quickly skim through each section and answer the questions you find easiest first. This ensures you get the maximum number of points in the least amount of time. Mark the tougher questions and return to them if you have time.

6. Keep Moving

If you're stuck on a question, don't spend too much time on it. Mark it and move on to the next one. You can always come back to it later if you have time remaining.

7. Use Process of Elimination

Even if you're unsure of the correct answer, eliminate the choices you know are wrong. This increases your chances of guessing correctly if you need to make an educated guess.

8. Manage Your Breaks

Use your breaks wisely to relax and recharge. Eat a snack, drink some water, and take a few deep breaths. This will help you stay focused and maintain your energy levels throughout the test.

9. Stay Calm and Focused

Keep an eye on the time, but don't let it stress you out. Stay calm, and maintain a steady pace. Panicking will only waste precious seconds and affect your performance.

10. Review if Time Allows

If you finish a section early, use the remaining time to review your answers. Check for any questions you may have skipped or rushed through. This is your chance to catch any mistakes and make corrections.

Handling Test Anxiety

Feeling nervous before and during the SAT is completely normal. Test anxiety can be managed with the right strategies, helping you stay calm and focused. Here's how to handle test anxiety effectively:

1. Prepare Thoroughly

One of the best ways to reduce anxiety is to feel prepared. Follow a consistent study plan, practice with timed tests, and review your materials regularly. The more prepared you feel, the more confident you'll be on test day.

2. Practice Relaxation Techniques

Learn and practice relaxation techniques that you can use before and during the test. Deep breathing exercises, visualization, and progressive muscle relaxation can help calm your nerves. Try taking a few deep breaths, imagining a peaceful place, or tensing and relaxing different muscle groups.

3. Get Plenty of Sleep

Make sure to get a good night's sleep before the test. Lack of sleep can heighten anxiety and make it harder to focus. Aim for at least 7-8 hours of sleep the night before the test.

4. Eat a Healthy Breakfast

On test day, eat a nutritious breakfast that includes protein, whole grains, and fruits. Avoid too much sugar or caffeine, which can make you feel jittery. A balanced meal will provide steady energy and help you stay focused.

5. Arrive Early

Give yourself plenty of time to get to the test center. Rushing can increase stress levels. Arriving early allows you to settle in, find your room, and get comfortable before the test starts.

6. Stay Positive

Maintain a positive mindset. Remind yourself of your preparation and the hard work you've put in. Positive self-talk can boost your confidence and reduce anxiety. Replace negative thoughts with affirmations like, "I am prepared," or "I can handle this."

7. Focus on the Present

Concentrate on the question in front of you rather than worrying about past questions or future sections. Taking the test one question at a time can make it feel more manageable and less overwhelming.

8. Take Short Breaks

Use the breaks between test sections to stretch, take deep breaths, and relax. Step outside if possible, get some fresh air, or have a quick snack. These short breaks can help you recharge and maintain focus.

9. Manage Your Time

Effective time management can reduce anxiety during the test. Keep an eye on the clock, but don't let it stress you out. If you get stuck on a question, move on and come back to it later if time allows.

10. Accept Some Anxiety

A little bit of anxiety can actually be helpful, keeping you alert and focused. Accept that feeling nervous is normal and use that energy to stay motivated. Recognize the signs of anxiety and use your relaxation techniques to keep it in check.

11. Seek Support

Talk to friends, family, or teachers about your anxiety. They can offer support, encouragement, and helpful tips. Sometimes, just sharing your feelings can make a big difference.

12. Practice Mindfulness

Mindfulness involves staying present and fully engaging with the task at hand. Practicing mindfulness can help you stay calm and focused. Techniques like deep breathing, body scans, or mindful walking can be practiced regularly to reduce overall anxiety.

Answering Strategies (e.g., Process of Elimination, Educated Guessing)

When it comes to the SAT, having effective answering strategies can significantly boost your performance. Here are some tips to help you tackle questions confidently and efficiently:

1. Process of Elimination

Using the process of elimination can increase your chances of selecting the correct answer, even if you're unsure at first.

- **Eliminate Clearly Wrong Answers**: Read the question and eliminate any choices that are obviously incorrect. This narrows down your options and makes it easier to focus on the remaining choices.

- **Compare Remaining Choices**: Look closely at the remaining options and compare them to each other. Determine which ones fit best with the question's requirements.
- **Look for Traps**: Be aware of common traps, such as answers that are too broad, too specific, or contain absolute terms like "always" or "never."

2. Educated Guessing

When you're not sure of the answer, making an educated guess is better than leaving a question blank. Here's how to improve your guessing:

- **Use Clues from the Question**: Sometimes the question itself can provide hints or context that can help you make an educated guess. Pay attention to key terms or concepts mentioned.
- **Eliminate Unlikely Answers**: Even if you don't know the correct answer, you can often identify one or two choices that are less likely to be correct.
- **Make an Informed Choice**: With fewer options, base your guess on what seems most logical or aligns best with the information provided.

3. Answering All Questions

There is no penalty for wrong answers on the SAT, so it's in your best interest to answer every question, even if you have to guess.

- **Don't Leave Blanks**: Ensure you fill in an answer for every question, especially if you're running out of time.
- **Use Remaining Time Wisely**: If you finish a section early, go back and review any questions you were unsure about. Use this time to make educated guesses if needed.

4. Handling Multiple-Choice Questions

Multiple-choice questions can be tricky, but with the right approach, you can improve your accuracy:

- **Read Carefully**: Carefully read the question and all answer choices. Sometimes answers can be very similar, so pay attention to detail.
- **Answer in Your Head First**: Before looking at the choices, try to think of the answer on your own. Then see which choice matches your answer.
- **Look for Keywords**: Identify keywords or phrases in the question that are critical to finding the correct answer. Match these with the answer choices.

5. Handling Grid-In Questions

Grid-in questions on the Math sections require you to calculate and write in your answer. Here's how to approach them:

- **Double-Check Your Work**: Since there are no multiple-choice options to fall back on, double-check your calculations to ensure accuracy.
- **Use Estimation**: If you're running out of time, use estimation to arrive at a reasonable answer. This can be better than leaving it blank.
- **Practice Grid-In Formatting**: Make sure you're familiar with how to enter your answers in the grid format to avoid any mistakes on test day.

6. Time Management During Answering

Managing your time while answering questions is crucial. Here's how to stay on track:

- **Pace Yourself**: Keep an eye on the clock and pace yourself to ensure you have enough time to answer all questions. Don't spend too much time on any one question.

- **Skip and Return**: If you encounter a particularly challenging question, skip it and return to it later if you have time. This prevents you from getting stuck and running out of time.

Section-Specific Strategies

Reading Test Strategies

The Reading Test on the SAT can seem challenging, but with the right strategies, you can improve your comprehension and accuracy. Here are some tips to help you tackle this section effectively:

1. Understand the Passage Types

The Reading Test includes passages from different genres: literature, historical documents, social sciences, and natural sciences. Familiarize yourself with these types so you know what to expect. Each genre has its own style and focus, so recognizing these can help you better understand the content.

2. Skim First, Then Read Thoroughly

Start by quickly skimming the passage to get a general sense of the topic and structure. This initial skim can help you identify key themes and the passage's main idea. Then, read the passage more thoroughly, focusing on understanding the details and how they support the main idea.

3. Take Notes While Reading

While reading, jot down brief notes or underline key points. Mark important details, such as names, dates, and concepts. This can help you quickly locate information when answering questions and improve your comprehension.

4. Pay Attention to the Questions

Read each question carefully before looking at the answer choices. Identify what the question is asking—whether it's about a specific detail, the author's tone, or the main idea. This focus will help you avoid being misled by tricky wording.

5. Refer Back to the Passage

Always refer back to the passage to find evidence for your answers. Don't rely solely on your memory. The text contains all the information you need, so use it to support your choices.

6. Manage Your Time Wisely

Pacing is crucial. Spend no more than 4-5 minutes reading each passage and about 1 minute on each question. This helps ensure you have enough time to answer all questions without rushing.

7. Answer General Questions Last

Answer specific detail questions first, as they often help you understand the passage better. General questions about the main idea or author's purpose can be easier to answer once you've worked through the detailed questions.

8. Be Cautious with Extreme Answers

In multiple-choice questions, be wary of answers with absolute terms like "always," "never," or "completely." These are often incorrect because they leave no room for exceptions. Look for more nuanced or balanced options.

9. Practice Active Reading

Engage with the text by asking yourself questions as you read. Consider why the author included certain details, how the passage is structured, and what the main argument is. Active reading helps you stay focused and retain more information.

10. Use Context Clues

If you encounter an unfamiliar word, use context clues from the surrounding sentences to infer its meaning. Understanding the overall context of the passage can often help you decipher difficult vocabulary.

11. Don't Get Stuck

If you're stuck on a question, move on and come back to it later if you have time. Spending too much time on one question can hurt your performance on the rest of the test.

12. Practice, Practice, Practice

The more you practice reading passages and answering questions, the more comfortable you'll become. Use practice tests to hone your skills and develop a strategy that works best for you.

Writing and Language Test Strategies

The Writing and Language Test on the SAT is designed to assess your ability to revise and edit passages for clarity, grammar, and effectiveness. Here are some strategies to help you excel in this section:

1. Understand the Passage Context

Each passage has a specific context and purpose. Read the introductory blurb (if provided) to understand the setting and main idea. This will help you make more informed decisions about edits and improvements.

2. Focus on Clarity and Conciseness

When you see an underlined section, think about how you can make it clearer and more concise. The SAT values straightforward, effective writing. Eliminate any unnecessary words or redundant phrases to improve readability.

3. Know Your Grammar Rules

Brush up on fundamental grammar rules, including subject-verb agreement, verb tense consistency, pronoun clarity, and parallel structure. Many questions will test your ability to spot and correct common grammatical errors.

4. Pay Attention to Punctuation

Punctuation can change the meaning of a sentence. Make sure you know how to use commas, semicolons, colons, and dashes correctly. Be especially mindful of comma splices and run-on sentences.

5. Look for Consistency

Ensure that the passage maintains a consistent tone, style, and point of view. If the passage is written in a formal tone, make sure your revisions match that tone. Consistency is key to effective writing.

6. Improve Sentence Structure

Sometimes, a sentence can be made clearer by restructuring it. Look for ways to combine sentences or break long sentences into shorter ones. This can help improve the flow and readability of the passage.

7. Answer Questions in Context

Always consider the broader context of the passage when answering questions. A change that improves one sentence might not fit well with the surrounding sentences. Make sure your revisions enhance the overall passage.

8. Use Process of Elimination

For multiple-choice questions, use the process of elimination to narrow down your options. Eliminate choices that are clearly incorrect or do not improve the passage. This increases your chances of selecting the correct answer.

9. Address All Parts of the Question

Some questions may ask you to consider multiple aspects, such as grammar and clarity. Make sure your answer addresses all parts of the question. For example, if you're asked to improve both grammar and style, ensure your choice accomplishes both.

10. Practice Editing Passages

The more you practice, the better you'll get at spotting errors and making effective revisions. Use practice tests to familiarize yourself with the types of passages and questions you'll encounter. Review explanations for answers to understand why certain choices are correct.

11. Be Mindful of Word Choice

Choose words that are precise and appropriate for the context. Avoid overly complex or technical language unless it suits the passage's tone and subject matter. Aim for clarity and effectiveness in your word choices.

12. Manage Your Time

Pacing is important. Don't spend too much time on any one question. If you're unsure, make your best guess and move on. You can always come back if you have time at the end.

13. Use the Contextual Clues

Look for clues within the passage that can help you answer questions. Contextual clues can often guide you toward the correct answer, especially for questions about word choice or sentence structure.

Math Test Strategies (No Calculator and Calculator Sections)

The Math Test on the SAT is divided into two sections: one where you can use a calculator and one where you can't. Here are some strategies to help you excel in both sections:

No Calculator Section

1. Master Mental Math and Simple Calculations

Practice doing calculations in your head or on paper without a calculator. This will help you save time and avoid mistakes in this section.

2. Understand Key Concepts

Focus on understanding the fundamental concepts of algebra, geometry, and basic trigonometry. Know how to manipulate equations, work with functions, and solve for variables.

3. Simplify the Problem

Simplify complex problems by breaking them down into smaller, more manageable steps. Look for ways to combine like terms and reduce fractions before solving.

4. Use Estimation

If a question seems complicated, use estimation to get a rough idea of the answer. This can help you narrow down multiple-choice options and save time.

5. Check for Shortcuts

Look for patterns or shortcuts that can help you solve problems more quickly. For example, knowing common algebraic identities or geometric properties can speed up your calculations.

6. Practice Grid-In Questions

Since some questions in this section require you to write in your answer, practice gridding in correctly. Make sure you're comfortable with the format and how to avoid errors.

Calculator Section

1. Know When to Use the Calculator

- Use your calculator for complex calculations or when it can save you time. However, don't rely on it for every problem. Sometimes, simple mental math can be faster.

2. Familiarize Yourself with Calculator Functions

- Make sure you know how to use the functions on your calculator, including trigonometric functions, exponents, and memory functions. Practice using your calculator to solve different types of problems.

3. Double-Check Your Work

- Use your calculator to double-check your answers, especially for questions involving multiple steps. This can help catch any errors you might have made in your calculations.

4. Manage Your Time

- Don't spend too much time on any one question. If a problem is taking too long, move on and come back to it later if you have time.

5. Work Backwards for Multiple-Choice Questions

- For multiple-choice questions, consider plugging in the answer

choices to see which one works. This can be a quick way to find
the correct answer.

6. Use the Process of Elimination

- If you're unsure about an answer, eliminate the choices that are
  clearly incorrect. This increases your chances of guessing correctly
  if needed.

7. Understand Graphs and Tables

- Be comfortable interpreting and analyzing information from graphs
  and tables. These types of questions often appear in the calculator
  section and can be answered more quickly with a calculator.

General Math Test Strategies

1. Read Each Question Carefully

- Make sure you understand what the question is asking before you
  start solving. Misreading the question can lead to simple mistakes.

2. Write Down Your Steps

- Writing down your steps helps keep your work organized and makes
  it easier to review your answers. It also reduces the likelihood of
  making errors.

3. Practice, Practice, Practice

- The best way to improve your math skills is through practice. Use
  practice tests to familiarize yourself with the types of questions you'll
  encounter and to refine your problem-solving techniques.

4. Review Your Mistakes

- After practicing, review any mistakes you made and understand why you got them wrong. This will help you avoid similar errors in the future.

Optional Essay Strategies

The Optional Essay on the SAT gives you the opportunity to demonstrate your reading, analysis, and writing skills. Here are some strategies to help you craft a strong essay:

1. Understand the Prompt

Before you begin writing, read the prompt carefully. The essay task typically asks you to analyze how the author builds an argument to persuade their audience. Focus on identifying the author's use of evidence, reasoning, and stylistic elements.

2. Plan Your Essay

Take a few minutes to outline your essay before you start writing. Organize your thoughts and decide on the structure. A typical essay structure includes an introduction, three body paragraphs, and a conclusion.

3. Craft a Strong Thesis Statement

Your thesis statement should clearly state your analysis of the author's argument. It should outline the main points you'll discuss in your essay. Make sure it's specific and directly addresses the prompt.

4. Use Specific Evidence

Support your analysis with specific examples from the passage. Quote or paraphrase parts of the text to illustrate how the author uses evidence, reasoning, and rhetorical techniques. Be sure to explain how each example supports your thesis.

5. Analyze, Don't Summarize

Focus on analyzing how the author's techniques contribute to their argument rather than simply summarizing the passage. Discuss the effectiveness of the author's methods and their impact on the audience.

6. Stay Organized

Each paragraph should have a clear main idea that supports your thesis. Start each paragraph with a topic sentence, followed by evidence and analysis. Use transition words and phrases to maintain a logical flow between paragraphs.

7. Write Clearly and Concisely

Use clear and concise language. Avoid overly complex sentences that might confuse the reader. Make sure your writing is easy to follow and free of grammatical errors.

8. Vary Your Sentence Structure

To keep your essay engaging, vary your sentence structure. Use a mix of short and long sentences and incorporate different sentence types. This will make your writing more dynamic and interesting to read.

9. Maintain Formal Tone

Keep a formal and objective tone throughout your essay. Avoid using slang, contractions, or overly casual language. Your essay should be professional and academic.

10. Manage Your Time

Keep an eye on the clock to ensure you have enough time to write, review, and revise your essay. Aim to spend the first few minutes planning, the majority of the time writing, and the last few minutes reviewing and editing.

11. Proofread Your Work

If time allows, quickly proofread your essay for any spelling, grammar, or punctuation errors. Small mistakes can detract from the overall quality of your essay, so it's worth taking a moment to catch them.

12. Practice Regularly

Practice writing essays under timed conditions to get comfortable with the format and time constraints. Review sample essays and scoring guidelines to understand what graders are looking for.

IV

In-Depth Review: Evidence-Based Reading and Writing

Reading Test

Types of Passages and Questions

The SAT Reading Test includes a variety of passages designed to assess your reading comprehension skills. Knowing what types of passages and questions to expect can help you feel more prepared and confident. Here's a breakdown of what you'll encounter:

1. Types of Passages

The Reading Test features five passages, each followed by a set of questions. These passages come from different genres and disciplines:

- **Literary Passages**: These are excerpts from classic or contemporary works of fiction. They focus on character development, themes, and narrative techniques.
- **Historical Documents**: These passages include primary source texts from the United States' founding documents or the Great Global Conversation. They might include speeches, essays, or historical writings.
- **Social Science Passages**: These passages come from fields like sociology, psychology, and economics. They discuss concepts, research findings, and theories relevant to social sciences.
- **Natural Science Passages**: These excerpts are from areas like biology, chemistry, physics, and Earth science. They present scientific

theories, experiments, and discoveries.

- **Paired Passages**: Occasionally, the test includes two shorter passages that are related in theme or subject matter. You'll need to compare and contrast the viewpoints or information presented in these passages.

2. Types of Questions

After each passage, you'll encounter a variety of question types. Understanding these can help you know what to look for as you read:

- **Detail Questions**: These questions ask about specific information stated in the passage. They often start with phrases like "According to the passage…" or "The author states that…". To answer these, you'll need to find and understand specific details.
- **Inference Questions**: These require you to read between the lines and make logical conclusions based on the information provided. They often include words like "suggests," "implies," or "infers."
- **Vocabulary in Context Questions**: These ask about the meaning of a word or phrase as it is used in the passage. The meaning might not be the most common definition, so context is key.
- **Function Questions**: These questions focus on why the author included a particular detail, sentence, or paragraph. They often ask about the purpose or role of a specific part of the passage.
- **Main Idea Questions**: These questions ask you to identify the central theme or main point of the passage. They require you to understand the overall message the author is conveying.
- **Author's Tone and Attitude Questions**: These questions ask about the author's tone (e.g., serious, humorous, critical) or attitude towards the subject. You'll need to interpret the author's choice of words and style to answer these.
- **Evidence-Based Questions**: These pairs of questions require you to choose an answer to the first question and then identify the specific part of the passage that supports your answer. The second question

asks you to find the evidence that backs up your response to the first.

· **Comparative Questions**: For paired passages, these questions ask you to compare and contrast the two passages. You might need to identify how the authors' perspectives differ or how they would respond to each other's arguments.

Strategies for Active Reading and Annotating

Active reading and annotating are essential skills for tackling the SAT Reading Test. These strategies help you engage with the text, improve comprehension, and make it easier to answer questions. Here are some tips to enhance your active reading and annotating:

1. Preview the Passage

Before you dive into the passage, take a moment to preview it. Read the title and any introductory information. This gives you a sense of what the passage is about and helps you set a purpose for reading.

2. Read with a Purpose

As you read, keep the questions in mind. Think about what the author is trying to convey and why they wrote the passage. This focus helps you stay engaged and retain important information.

3. Annotate Key Points

Use simple annotations to highlight key points. Here are some effective ways to annotate:

· **Underline or Highlight**: Mark main ideas, important details, and key phrases. This helps you quickly locate information when answering questions.
· **Circle Vocabulary Words**: Circle unfamiliar words or important terms. Look for context clues to understand their meanings.
· **Write Marginal Notes**: Jot down brief notes in the margins. Sum-

marize paragraphs, note the author's tone, or write down questions that come to mind.

4. Identify the Main Idea and Supporting Details

Determine the main idea of the passage or each paragraph. Underline or highlight the sentence that best captures this idea. Then, identify the supporting details that back up the main idea. This helps you see the structure of the argument or narrative.

5. Pay Attention to Author's Tone and Purpose

Notice the author's tone and purpose. Are they trying to inform, persuade, entertain, or describe? Is the tone formal, casual, critical, or enthusiastic? Annotating these elements helps you answer questions about the author's attitude and intent.

6. Look for Transitions and Logical Flow

Identify transition words and phrases that show how ideas are connected (e.g., however, therefore, in addition). This helps you understand the logical flow of the passage and how different points relate to each other.

7. Summarize Each Paragraph

After reading each paragraph, write a brief summary in the margin. This practice forces you to process and condense the information, making it easier to remember and review later.

8. Ask Questions

Engage with the text by asking questions as you read. For example, "Why did the author include this detail?" or "What is the author's main argument here?" This keeps you actively thinking about the passage.

9. Predict Questions

As you read, try to predict the types of questions that might be asked.

This anticipatory reading helps you focus on details that are likely to be important.

10. Review Your Annotations

After reading the passage, quickly review your annotations. This reinforces your understanding and helps you locate information more efficiently when answering questions.

11. Practice Regularly

The more you practice active reading and annotating, the more natural it will become. Use practice passages to refine your skills and develop a system that works best for you.

Sample Passages with Detailed Explanations

Practicing with sample passages is one of the best ways to prepare for the SAT Reading Test. Here, we'll go through a sample passage and provide detailed explanations for each question. This will help you understand how to apply the strategies we've discussed and improve your reading comprehension skills.

Sample Passage

Read the following passage and answer the questions that follow:

In recent years, researchers have increasingly turned their attention to the field of regenerative medicine, which aims to repair or replace damaged cells, tissues, and organs. The promise of regenerative medicine is immense: it offers the potential to treat conditions that are currently incurable, such as certain types of heart disease and neurodegenerative disorders.

One of the most exciting developments in regenerative medicine is the use of stem cells. Stem cells have the unique ability to develop into different types of cells, making them invaluable for repairing damaged tissues. Researchers have already made significant strides in using stem cells to regenerate heart tissue, which could lead to new treatments for heart attack patients.

However, the field is not without its challenges. Ethical concerns about the use of embryonic stem cells have led to strict regulations in many countries. Additionally, there are technical hurdles to overcome, such as ensuring that the new cells integrate properly with the existing tissue and do not cause adverse reactions.

Despite these challenges, the future of regenerative medicine looks promising. Ongoing research and technological advancements are paving the way for new therapies that could revolutionize the way we treat a variety of medical conditions.

Questions and Explanations

1. What is the main purpose of the passage?
A. To explain the ethical concerns surrounding stem cell research
B. To describe the potential and challenges of regenerative medicine
C. To argue against the use of regenerative medicine
D. To provide an overview of different types of stem cells

Explanation:
The main purpose of the passage is to describe both the potential and challenges of regenerative medicine. The author discusses the promise of regenerative medicine, particularly the use of stem cells, and addresses the ethical and technical challenges involved. Therefore, the correct answer is **B**.

2. According to the passage, why are stem cells considered invaluable for repairing damaged tissues?

A. They are easy to harvest from adult tissues

B. They have the ability to develop into different types of cells

C. They do not cause any ethical concerns

D. They integrate seamlessly with existing tissues

Explanation:

The passage states that stem cells are invaluable for repairing damaged tissues because they "have the unique ability to develop into different types of cells." This ability makes them essential for regenerating various types of tissue. Therefore, the correct answer is **B**.

3. Which of the following is mentioned as a challenge facing regenerative medicine?

A. The high cost of stem cell treatments

B. The lack of interest from the medical community

C. Ethical concerns and technical hurdles

D. Limited availability of research funding

Explanation:

The passage mentions both ethical concerns and technical hurdles as challenges facing regenerative medicine. Ethical concerns are specifically related to the use of embryonic stem cells, and technical hurdles involve ensuring proper integration and avoiding adverse reactions. Therefore, the correct answer is **C**.

4. In the context of the passage, what does the phrase "the promise of regenerative medicine is immense" suggest?

A. Regenerative medicine is currently ineffective

B. Regenerative medicine has the potential to be very beneficial

C. The costs of regenerative medicine are very high

D. The ethical issues of regenerative medicine are insurmountable

Explanation:

The phrase "the promise of regenerative medicine is immense" suggests that regenerative medicine has the potential to be very beneficial, offering new treatments for currently incurable conditions. Therefore, the correct answer is **B**.

5. The author's attitude toward the future of regenerative medicine can best be described as:

A. Skeptical

B. Optimistic

C. Neutral

D. Pessimistic

Explanation:

The author acknowledges the challenges facing regenerative medicine but ultimately describes the future as promising, with ongoing research and advancements paving the way for new therapies. This indicates an optimistic attitude. Therefore, the correct answer is **B**.

6. Which of the following best describes the tone of the passage?

A. Enthusiastic

B. Critical

C. Informative

D. Persuasive

Explanation:

The passage provides information about regenerative medicine, discussing both its potential and challenges in a balanced manner. Therefore, the tone is best described as **C. Informative**.

7. The author mentions "heart disease and neurodegenerative disorders" in the passage primarily to:

A. Highlight the types of conditions that are incurable

B. Provide examples of diseases that could be treated with regenerative medicine

C. Criticize the current treatments for these diseases

D. Explain why regenerative medicine is controversial

Explanation:

The author mentions these conditions as examples of diseases that could potentially be treated with regenerative medicine, illustrating the promise of this field. Therefore, the correct answer is **B**.

8. The passage implies that one reason why there are ethical concerns about stem cell research is because:

    A. Stem cells are difficult to obtain

    B. Stem cells are expensive to use

    C. Embryonic stem cells involve the use of embryos

    D. Adult stem cells are not effective

    Explanation:

The ethical concerns mentioned in the passage are specifically related to the use of embryonic stem cells, which involve the use of embryos. Therefore, the correct answer is **C**.

9. According to the passage, one of the technical challenges in regenerative medicine is:

    A. Finding funding for research

    B. Integrating new cells with existing tissue

    C. Training medical professionals

    D. Conducting clinical trials

    Explanation:

The passage states that a technical challenge in regenerative medicine is ensuring that the new cells integrate properly with the existing tissue and do not cause adverse reactions. Therefore, the correct answer is **B**.

10. What can be inferred about the future of regenerative medicine from the passage?

    A. It will likely face more ethical challenges than technical ones

    B. It has the potential to revolutionize medical treatments

    C. It is not yet a viable option for most patients

    D. It will replace all current medical treatments

Explanation:

The passage suggests that despite the challenges, ongoing research and technological advancements make the future of regenerative medicine promising, with the potential to revolutionize the way we treat various medical conditions. Therefore, the correct answer is **B**.

Writing and Language Test

Grammar and Usage Rules

Understanding grammar and usage rules is essential for doing well on the SAT Writing and Language Test. Here are some key rules to keep in mind as you prepare:

1. Subject-Verb Agreement
Ensure that subjects and verbs agree in number. A singular subject requires a singular verb, and a plural subject requires a plural verb.

- **Example**: The dog (singular) runs (singular) fast. / The dogs (plural) run (plural) fast.

2. Verb Tense Consistency
Maintain consistent verb tenses throughout a sentence or paragraph. This helps clearly convey the sequence of events.

- **Example**: She **was** walking (past tense) when she **saw** (past tense) a bird.

3. Pronoun-Antecedent Agreement
Pronouns must agree with their antecedents in number and gender. The antecedent is the noun that the pronoun replaces.

- **Example**: Each student (singular) must bring **his or her** (singular) own book. / All students (plural) must bring **their** (plural) own books.

4. Proper Use of Commas

Commas are used to separate items in a list, after introductory elements, to set off nonessential information, and before conjunctions in compound sentences.

- **Example**: I bought apples, oranges, and bananas. / After the movie, we went to dinner. / My friend, who lives nearby, is coming over. / I wanted to go, but I was too tired.

5. Avoiding Comma Splices

A comma splice occurs when two independent clauses are joined by a comma without a conjunction. To fix a comma splice, you can use a period, a semicolon, or add a conjunction.

- **Example**: Incorrect: I went to the store, I bought milk. / Correct: I went to the store. I bought milk. / I went to the store; I bought milk. / I went to the store, and I bought milk.

6. Use of Semicolons and Colons

Semicolons link closely related independent clauses and separate items in a complex list. Colons introduce lists, explanations, or quotes.

- **Example**: I have a big test tomorrow; I can't go out tonight. / There are three things I need: bread, milk, and eggs.

7. Parallel Structure

Parallel structure means using the same grammatical form for similar elements in a sentence. This improves readability and balance.

- **Example**: She likes reading, writing, and swimming. (not: She likes reading, to write, and swimming.)

8. Proper Placement of Modifiers

Modifiers should be placed next to the word they modify to avoid confusion.

- **Example**: Incorrect: She almost drove her kids to school every day. / Correct: She drove her kids to school almost every day.

9. Pronoun Clarity

Ensure that pronouns clearly refer to a specific noun. Avoid ambiguous pronouns that could refer to more than one antecedent.

- **Example**: Incorrect: When Sarah met Jane, she was happy. / Correct: Sarah was happy when she met Jane.

10. Correct Use of Apostrophes

Apostrophes show possession or form contractions. Do not use them for plural nouns.

- **Example**: The cat's toy (one cat) / The cats' toy (multiple cats) / It's raining (it is) / The dog wagged its tail (possessive).

11. Consistent Point of View

Maintain a consistent point of view within your writing, whether it's first, second, or third person.

- **Example**: Incorrect: One must be careful with your words. / Correct: One must be careful with one's words. / You must be careful with your words.

12. Avoiding Double Negatives

Using two negative words together creates a positive statement, which is often incorrect in standard English.

- **Example**: Incorrect: I don't need no help. / Correct: I don't need any help.

Common Types of Questions and Errors

On the SAT Writing and Language Test, you'll encounter a variety of question types that test your ability to spot and correct errors in grammar, usage, and style. Here's a breakdown of the most common types of questions and errors you should be prepared for:

1. Sentence Structure Questions

These questions focus on the construction of sentences, ensuring they are clear and grammatically correct.

Common Errors:

- **Run-On Sentences**: Two independent clauses joined without proper punctuation or conjunctions.
- **Sentence Fragments**: Incomplete sentences that lack a subject or verb.
- **Comma Splices**: Two independent clauses joined by a comma without a coordinating conjunction.

Example:

- Incorrect: She loves reading she often visits the library.
- Correct: She loves reading, and she often visits the library.

2. Agreement Questions

These questions test your understanding of subject-verb agreement and pronoun-antecedent agreement.

Common Errors:

- **Subject-Verb Agreement**: Ensuring the subject and verb agree in number (singular/plural).
- **Pronoun-Antecedent Agreement**: Ensuring pronouns agree with their antecedents in number and gender.

Example:

- Incorrect: Each of the students must bring their own book.
- Correct: Each of the students must bring his or her own book.

3. Verb Tense Questions

These questions ensure that verb tenses are consistent and correctly used within sentences and paragraphs.
Common Errors:

- **Tense Shifts**: Inconsistent verb tenses within a sentence or passage.
- **Incorrect Tense Usage**: Using the wrong tense for the context.

Example:

- Incorrect: She was walking to the store and buys some groceries.
- Correct: She was walking to the store and bought some groceries.

4. Pronoun Usage Questions

These questions test your ability to use pronouns correctly, ensuring they are clear and refer to the correct antecedents.
Common Errors:

- **Ambiguous Pronouns**: Pronouns that could refer to more than one antecedent.
- **Pronoun Case**: Using the wrong pronoun form (subjective, objective, possessive).

Example:

- Incorrect: When John met Peter, he was happy.
- Correct: John was happy when he met Peter.

5. Punctuation Questions

These questions focus on the correct use of punctuation marks such as commas, semicolons, colons, and dashes.
Common Errors:

- **Comma Misuse**: Using commas where they aren't needed or omitting them where they are necessary.
- **Semicolon/Colon Usage**: Incorrect use of semicolons and colons.

Example:

- Incorrect: She wanted to go to the store but, she didn't have a car.
- Correct: She wanted to go to the store, but she didn't have a car.

6. Parallelism Questions

These questions ensure that elements in a list or series are in parallel structure, making the sentence clearer and more balanced.
Common Errors:

- **Non-Parallel Structure**: Mixing different grammatical forms in a list.

Example:

- Incorrect: He likes running, to swim, and biking.
- Correct: He likes running, swimming, and biking.

7. Diction Questions

These questions focus on the correct word choice, ensuring words are appropriate for the context and meaning.

Common Errors:

· **Incorrect Word Choice**: Using a word that sounds similar but has a different meaning.
· **Formal vs. Informal Language**: Using language that is too casual for the context.

Example:

· Incorrect: The principle of the school gave a speech.
· Correct: The principal of the school gave a speech.

8. Logical Flow and Organization Questions

These questions test your ability to organize sentences and paragraphs logically and cohesively.

· **Common Errors**:
· **Disjointed Sentences**: Sentences that do not logically follow each other.
· **Misplaced Modifiers**: Modifiers that are not placed next to the word they modify.

Example:

· Incorrect: She found a coin walking to school.
· Correct: Walking to school, she found a coin.

Practice Questions with Detailed Explanations

Practicing with real SAT-style questions is crucial for understanding the kinds of errors you'll need to correct on the Writing and Language Test. Here are some sample questions along with detailed explanations for each answer.

Question 1: Subject-Verb Agreement

Each of the students (A) **was** asked to submit (B) **their** homework by (C) **Friday**. (D) **No error**

Answer Choices:
  A. was
  B. their
  C. Friday
  D. No error

Explanation:
  The error is in part B. The pronoun "their" should agree with the singular noun "Each" (of the students). The correct sentence should use the singular pronoun "his or her."

Corrected Sentence:
  Each of the students was asked to submit **his or her** homework by Friday.

Question 2: Parallel Structure

She likes **(A) running**, **(B) to swim**, and **(C) biking** in the morning. **(D) No error**

Answer Choices:

A. running

B. to swim

C. biking

D. No error

Explanation:

The error is in part B. The verbs should be in the same form to maintain parallel structure. "To swim" should be changed to "swimming."

Corrected Sentence:

She likes **running, swimming,** and **biking** in the morning.

Question 3: Pronoun-Antecedent Agreement

The committee members could not agree among (A) **themselves** about (B) **its** decision on the new policy. (C) **No error**

Answer Choices:

A. themselves

B. its

C. No error

Explanation:

The error is in part B. "Its" should be "their" because "committee members" is plural.

Corrected Sentence:

The committee members could not agree among themselves about **their** decision on the new policy.

Question 4: Comma Usage

My favorite authors are **(A) J.K. Rowling (B) J.R.R. Tolkien** and **(C) George R.R. Martin**. **(D) No error**

Answer Choices:
  A. J.K. Rowling
  B. J.R.R. Tolkien
  C. George R.R. Martin
  D. No error

Explanation:
  The error is the lack of a serial (Oxford) comma after "J.R.R. Tolkien" for clarity.

Corrected Sentence:
  My favorite authors are **J.K. Rowling, J.R.R. Tolkien**, and **George R.R. Martin**.

Question 5: Verb Tense Consistency

When the alarm **(A) rang**, he **(B) jumps** out of bed and **(C) ran** to the door. **(D) No error**

Answer Choices:
  A. rang
  B. jumps
  C. ran
  D. No error

Explanation:
  The error is in part B. The verb "jumps" should be in the past tense "jumped" to maintain consistency with "rang" and "ran."

Corrected Sentence:

When the alarm **rang**, he **jumped** out of bed and **ran** to the door.

Question 6: Misplaced Modifier

Driving to work, a deer suddenly appeared in **(A) the road** and caused **(B) him** to **(C) swerve** suddenly. **(D) No error**

Answer Choices:

  A. the road

  B. him

  C. swerve

  D. No error

Explanation:

The modifier "Driving to work" is misplaced. It incorrectly suggests that the deer was driving to work. It should be placed closer to the noun it modifies, which is "he."

Corrected Sentence:

While **he was driving** to work, a deer suddenly appeared in the road and caused him to swerve suddenly.

Question 7: Verb Tense Consistency

By the time the meeting **(A) starts**, the committee members **(B) had** already **(C) reviewed** the agenda. **(D) No error**

Answer Choices:

  A. starts

  B. had

  C. reviewed

  D. No error

Explanation:

The error is in part B. The verb "had" should be in the present perfect tense "have" to maintain consistency with the present tense "starts."

Corrected Sentence:

By the time the meeting **starts**, the committee members **have** already **reviewed** the agenda.

Question 8: Pronoun Case

Between you and **(A) I**, this project **(B) is** going to be **(C) challenging**. **(D) No error**

Answer Choices:

    A. I
    B. is
    C. challenging
    D. No error

Explanation:

The error is in part A. The pronoun "I" should be in the objective case "me" because it follows the preposition "between."

Corrected Sentence:

Between you and **me**, this project **is** going to be **challenging**.

Question 9: Subject-Verb Agreement

The team **(A) of scientists (B) were** conducting **(C) an experiment. (D) No error**

Answer Choices:

    A. of scientists

B. were

C. an experiment

D. No error

Explanation:

The error is in part B. The subject "team" is singular, so the verb should be "was" instead of "were."

Corrected Sentence:

The team **of scientists was** conducting **an experiment**.

Question 10: Parallel Structure

Her favorite activities include **(A) hiking**, **(B) to swim**, and **(C) reading**. **(D) No error**

Answer Choices:

A. hiking

B. to swim

C. reading

D. No error

Explanation:

The error is in part B. The verbs should be in the same form to maintain parallel structure. "To swim" should be changed to "swimming."

Corrected Sentence:

Her favorite activities include **hiking**, **swimming**, and **reading**.

Question 11: Diction (Word Choice)

The **(A) principle** reason for the increase in sales **(B) was** the new marketing **(C) campaign. (D) No error**

Answer Choices:
   A. principle
   B. was
   C. campaign
   D. No error

Explanation:
   The error is in part A. The word "principle" (which means a fundamental truth) should be "principal" (which means main or most important).

Corrected Sentence:
   The **principal** reason for the increase in sales **was** the new marketing **campaign.**

V

In-Depth Review: Math

Math Test – No Calculator Section

Key Concepts and Topics

The Math Test – No Calculator section of the SAT focuses on your ability to solve problems using mathematical concepts and reasoning without the aid of a calculator. Here are the key concepts and topics you need to master for this section:

1. Algebra

- **Linear Equations and Inequalities**: Understand how to solve linear equations and inequalities, interpret their solutions, and represent them graphically.
    - **Example**: Solve for x in the equation $3x + 5 = 14$.

- **Systems of Equations**: Learn to solve systems of linear equations algebraically (substitution, elimination) and graphically.
    - **Example**: Solve the system: $2x + y = 10$ and $x - y = 2$.

- **Quadratic Equations**: Be able to solve quadratic equations by factoring, completing the square, and using the quadratic formula.
    - **Example**: Solve $x^2 - 5x + 6 = 0$.

2. Problem Solving and Data Analysis

- **Ratios, Proportions, and Percentages**: Understand how to work with ratios, proportions, and percentages to solve various types of problems.
  - **Example**: If a dress is discounted by 20% and the sale price is $80, what was the original price?

- **Statistics**: Know how to interpret data from tables, charts, and graphs, and understand measures of central tendency (mean, median, mode).
  - **Example**: Find the mean of the following data set: 5, 7, 8, 9, 10.

- **Probability**: Calculate simple probabilities and understand basic concepts of probability.
  - **Example**: What is the probability of rolling a sum of 7 on two six-sided dice?

3. Advanced Math

- **Polynomials and Rational Expressions**: Understand how to add, subtract, multiply, and divide polynomials and rational expressions.
  - **Example**: Simplify $\frac{3x^2 - 9x}{3x}$.

- **Exponential Functions**: Learn how to interpret and solve exponential growth and decay problems.
  - **Example**: Solve for x in the equation $2^x = 16$.

- **Radicals and Rational Exponents**: Be able to simplify expressions involving radicals and rational exponents.
  - **Example**: Simplify $\sqrt{50}$ and $8^{1/3}$.

4. Geometry and Trigonometry

- **Angles and Triangles**: Understand the properties of angles, triangles, and special right triangles (30-60-90 and 45-45-90 triangles).
  - **Example**: Find the missing angle in a triangle if two angles are 45° and 85°.

- **Circles**: Know the properties of circles, including the relationships between radius, diameter, circumference, and area.
  - **Example**: Find the circumference of a circle with a radius of 4 units.

- **Volume and Surface Area**: Calculate the volume and surface area of three-dimensional shapes like cylinders, cones, and spheres.
  - **Example**: Find the volume of a cylinder with a radius of 3 units and a height of 5 units.

- **Basic Trigonometry**: Understand the basic trigonometric ratios (sine, cosine, tangent) and how to apply them to right triangles.
  - **Example**: If the opposite side of a right triangle is 4 units and the hypotenuse is 5 units, find the sine of the angle.

5. Arithmetic

- **Integers and Rational Numbers**: Be comfortable performing operations with integers, fractions, and decimals.
  - **Example**: Add $\frac{3}{4}$ and $\frac{2}{5}$.

- **Absolute Value**: Understand the concept of absolute value and how to solve absolute value equations and inequalities.
  - **Example**: Solve $|x - 3| = 5$.

- **Factors and Multiples**: Know how to find the greatest common factor (GCF) and least common multiple (LCM) of numbers.
  - **Example**: Find the GCF of 24 and 36.

Practice Problems with Step-by-Step Solutions

Practicing with step-by-step solutions is a great way to understand how to approach different types of math problems on the SAT No Calculator section. Here are some practice problems along with detailed solutions to help you prepare:

Problem 1: Solving Linear Equations

Question: Solve for x in the equation $3x + 5 = 14$.

Solution:

1. Start by isolating the variable term. Subtract 5 from both sides:

$$3x + 5 - 5 = 14 - 5$$

$$3x = 9$$

2. Next, divide both sides by 3 to solve for x:

$$\frac{3x}{3} = \frac{9}{3}$$

$$x = 3$$

Answer: $x = 3$

Problem 2: Solving a System of Equations

Question: Solve the system of equations:

$$2x + y = 10$$

$$x - y = 2$$

Solution:

1. Add the two equations to eliminate y:

$$(2x + y) + (x - y) = 10 + 2$$

$$3x = 12$$

2. Solve for x:

$$x = \frac{12}{3}$$

$$x = 4$$

3. Substitute $x = 4$ into one of the original equations to solve for y:

$$2(4) + y = 10$$

$$8 + y = 10$$

$$y = 2$$

Answer: $x = 4, y = 2$

Problem 3: Simplifying Polynomials

Question: Simplify $\frac{3x^2 - 9x}{3x}$.

Solution:

1. Factor out the common factor in the numerator:

$$\frac{3x(x-3)}{3x}$$

2. Cancel the common factor $3x$:

$$x - 3$$

Answer: $x - 3$

Problem 4: Working with Ratios

Question: If a dress is discounted by 20% and the sale price is $80, what was the original price?

Solution:

1. Let the original price be P. The sale price after a 20% discount is 80% of the original price:

$$0.80P = 80$$

2. Solve for P:

$$P = \frac{80}{0.80}$$

$$P = 100$$

Answer: The original price was $100.

Problem 5: Using the Quadratic Formula

Question: Solve $x^2 - 5x + 6 = 0$ using the quadratic formula.

Solution:

1. Identify the coefficients: $a = 1, b = -5, c = 6$.

2. Use the quadratic formula $x = \frac{-b \pm \sqrt{b^2 - 4ac}}{2a}$:

$$x = \frac{-(-5) \pm \sqrt{(-5)^2 - 4 \cdot 1 \cdot 6}}{2 \cdot 1}$$

$$x = \frac{5 \pm \sqrt{25 - 24}}{2}$$

$$x = \frac{5 \pm \sqrt{1}}{2}$$

3. Simplify the solutions:

$$x = \frac{5 \pm 1}{2}$$

$$x = \frac{6}{2} \text{ or } x = \frac{4}{2}$$

$$x = 3 \text{ or } x = 2$$

Answer: $x = 3$ or $x = 2$

Math Test – Calculator Section

Advanced Math Topics

The Math Test – Calculator Section on the SAT covers a range of advanced math topics. Understanding these concepts is key to performing well. Here are the primary areas you should focus on:

1. Quadratic Functions and Equations

Quadratic functions are represented by the equation $ax^2 + bx + c = 0$, where a, b, and c are constants. You'll need to:

- Solve quadratic equations using factoring, the quadratic formula, or completing the square.
- Understand the properties of parabolas, including vertex, axis of symmetry, and roots.

Example: Solve $x^2 - 4x - 5 = 0$.

2. Exponential and Logarithmic Functions

Exponential functions involve expressions where the variable is an exponent, typically in the form $y = a \cdot b^x$. Logarithmic functions are the inverses of exponential functions.

- Understand the properties and graphs of exponential and logarithmic functions.
- Solve equations involving exponents and logarithms.

Example: Solve $2^x = 16$.

3. Polynomial Functions

Polynomials are algebraic expressions that involve terms of varying degrees. You'll need to:

- Perform operations (addition, subtraction, multiplication, division) on polynomials.
- Understand polynomial roots and the behavior of polynomial graphs.

Example: Find the roots of $x^3 - 6x^2 + 11x - 6 = 0$.

4. Rational Functions

Rational functions are ratios of polynomials. You should be able to:

- Simplify rational expressions.
- Solve rational equations.
- Analyze asymptotes and discontinuities in the graph of a rational function.

Example: Simplify $\frac{x^2-1}{x+1}$.

5. Systems of Equations

Systems of equations can include linear, quadratic, and other polynomial equations. You should be proficient in:

- Solving systems of linear equations using substitution, elimination, and matrix methods.
- Solving systems involving quadratic or other polynomial equations.

Example: Solve the system:

$$\begin{cases} x + y = 10 \\ x^2 + y^2 = 58 \end{cases}$$

7. Complex Numbers

Complex numbers include a real part and an imaginary part, typically written as $a + bi$. You should know how to:

- Perform operations (addition, subtraction, multiplication, division) on complex numbers.
- Solve equations involving complex numbers.
- Represent complex numbers on the complex plane.

Example: Solve $z^2 + 4 = 0$.

8. Conic Sections

Conic sections are curves obtained by intersecting a plane with a cone, including circles, ellipses, parabolas, and hyperbolas. You'll need to:

- Understand the standard equations of conic sections.
- Analyze the properties and graphs of conic sections.

Example: Find the equation of a circle with center (2, -3) and radius 5.

9. Sequences and Series

Sequences are ordered lists of numbers, and series are the sum of the terms of a sequence. You'll need to:

10. Matrices

Matrices are rectangular arrays of numbers. You should know how to:

- Perform matrix operations (addition, subtraction, multiplication).
- Use matrices to solve systems of equations.
- Understand determinants and inverses of matrices.

Example: Solve the system using matrix multiplication:

$$\begin{bmatrix} 1 & 2 \\ 3 & 4 \end{bmatrix} \begin{bmatrix} x \\ y \end{bmatrix} = \begin{bmatrix} 5 \\ 11 \end{bmatrix}$$

Practice Problems with Step-by-Step Solutions

Practicing with detailed solutions helps you understand how to approach and solve different types of problems in the SAT Math Test – Calculator Section. Here are some practice problems with step-by-step solutions:

Problem 1: Solving Quadratic Equations

Question: Solve $2x^2 - 4x - 6 = 0$ using the quadratic formula.

Solution:

1. Identify the coefficients: $a = 2$, $b = -4$, $c = -6$.

2. Use the quadratic formula $x = \frac{-b \pm \sqrt{b^2 - 4ac}}{2a}$.

$$x = \frac{-(-4) \pm \sqrt{(-4)^2 - 4 \cdot 2 \cdot (-6)}}{2 \cdot 2}$$

$$x = \frac{4 \pm \sqrt{16 + 48}}{4}$$

$$x = \frac{4 \pm \sqrt{64}}{4}$$

$$x = \frac{4 \pm 8}{4}$$

3. Solve for the two possible values of x:

$$x = \frac{4 + 8}{4} = \frac{12}{4} = 3$$

$$x = \frac{4 - 8}{4} = \frac{-4}{4} = -1$$

Answer: $x = 3$ or $x = -1$

Problem 2: Solving Exponential Equations

Question: Solve for x in the equation $3 \cdot 2^x = 24$.

Solution:

1. Divide both sides by 3 to isolate the exponential term:

$$2^x = 8$$

2. Express 8 as a power of 2:

$$8 = 2^3$$

3. Since the bases are equal, set the exponents equal to each other:

$$x = 3$$

Answer: $x = 3$

Problem 3: Simplifying Rational Expressions

Question: Simplify $\frac{x^2 - 9}{x^2 - 6x + 9}$.

Solution:

1. Factor the numerator and the denominator:

$$\frac{x^2 - 9}{x^2 - 6x + 9} = \frac{(x + 3)(x - 3)}{(x - 3)(x - 3)}$$

2. Cancel the common factor $(x - 3)$:

$$\frac{(x + 3)}{(x - 3)}$$

Answer: $\frac{x+3}{x-3}$

Problem 4: Solving Systems of Equations with Matrices

Question: Solve the system using matrices:

$$\begin{cases} 2x + 3y = 13 \\ 4x - y = 5 \end{cases}$$

Solution:

1. Write the system as a matrix equation $A\mathbf{x} = \mathbf{b}$:

$$\begin{bmatrix} 2 & 3 \\ 4 & -1 \end{bmatrix} \begin{bmatrix} x \\ y \end{bmatrix} = \begin{bmatrix} 13 \\ 5 \end{bmatrix}$$

2. Find the inverse of matrix A and multiply both sides by A^{-1}:

$$A^{-1} = \frac{1}{2(-1) - 3(4)} \begin{bmatrix} -1 & -3 \\ -4 & 2 \end{bmatrix} = \frac{1}{-14} \begin{bmatrix} -1 & -3 \\ -4 & 2 \end{bmatrix} = \begin{bmatrix} \frac{1}{14} & \frac{3}{14} \\ \frac{4}{14} & -\frac{2}{14} \end{bmatrix} = \begin{bmatrix} \frac{1}{14} & \frac{3}{14} \\ \frac{2}{7} & -\frac{1}{7} \end{bmatrix}$$

3. Multiply $A^{-1}\mathbf{b}$:

$$\begin{bmatrix} \frac{1}{14} & \frac{3}{14} \\ \frac{2}{7} & -\frac{1}{7} \end{bmatrix} \begin{bmatrix} 13 \\ 5 \end{bmatrix} = \begin{bmatrix} \frac{1}{14}(13) + \frac{3}{14}(5) \\ \frac{2}{7}(13) - \frac{1}{7}(5) \end{bmatrix} = \begin{bmatrix} \frac{13+15}{14} \\ \frac{26-5}{7} \end{bmatrix} = \begin{bmatrix} 2 \\ 3 \end{bmatrix}$$

Answer: $x = 2, y = 3$

Problem 5: Solving Trigonometric Equations

Question: Solve for θ in $\cos(\theta) = \frac{1}{2}$ for $0 \le \theta < 360°$.

Solution:

1. Identify the angles where $\cos(\theta) = \frac{1}{2}$ in the unit circle:

$$\theta = 60° \quad \text{and} \quad \theta = 300°$$

Answer: $\theta = 60°$ and $\theta = 300°$

Data Analysis and Problem Solving

Interpreting Data from Graphs and Tables

Interpreting data from graphs and tables is a crucial skill for the SAT Math Test. These visual tools present information in a way that can help you quickly understand and analyze data. Here are some tips to help you interpret graphs and tables effectively:

1. Understand the Types of Graphs

- **Bar Graphs**: Used to compare quantities across different categories. Look at the height or length of the bars to determine the value of each category.
- **Line Graphs**: Show trends over time. Pay attention to the slope of the lines to understand the rate of change.
- **Pie Charts**: Display proportions of a whole. Each slice represents a percentage of the total. Look at the size of each slice to compare proportions.
- **Scatter Plots**: Show the relationship between two variables. Look for patterns or trends, such as positive or negative correlations.
- **Histograms**: Similar to bar graphs but used to show the distribution of a data set. Each bar represents the frequency of data within certain intervals.

2. Understand the Types of Tables

- **Frequency Tables**: Show how often each value or range of values occurs in a data set.
- **Two-Way Tables**: Display data that pertain to two different categories. This helps you see the relationship between the two variables.

3. Read the Labels and Units

- **Axes Labels**: Always check the labels on the axes of a graph to understand what is being measured. The x-axis typically represents the independent variable, and the y-axis represents the dependent variable.
- **Units of Measurement**: Pay attention to the units used in the graph or table. This can be crucial for understanding the data accurately.

4. Look for Trends and Patterns

- **Trends**: Identify any trends in the data, such as increasing, decreasing, or constant patterns. This is especially important for line graphs and scatter plots.
- **Patterns**: Look for patterns such as clustering of data points, outliers, or consistent intervals.

5. Calculate Percentages and Ratios

- **Percentages**: For pie charts, you may need to calculate the percentage of the whole that each slice represents. Similarly, in tables, converting raw data into percentages can help you compare different categories.
- **Ratios**: Use ratios to compare quantities in bar graphs and tables. This can help you understand the relationship between different categories.

6. Compare Data

- **Comparisons**: Compare data points or categories to draw conclusions. For example, in a bar graph, compare the heights of the bars to determine which category is the largest or smallest.
- **Multiple Data Sets**: Some graphs and tables present multiple data sets for comparison. Pay attention to the legend and color-coding to differentiate between them.

7. Make Inferences and Predictions

- **Inferences**: Use the data to make logical inferences. For example, if a line graph shows a steady increase in sales over several months, you might infer that sales will continue to increase if the trend remains unchanged.
- **Predictions**: Based on the trends and patterns observed, make predictions about future data points. This is often required in SAT questions.

8. Identify Key Points

- **Maximum and Minimum**: Identify the highest and lowest points in the data. This can provide insights into the range and variability of the data.
- **Median and Mode**: For histograms and frequency tables, you might need to identify the median (the middle value) and the mode (the most frequent value).

Example

Let's look at an example to see how these tips apply in practice:

Graph Example:

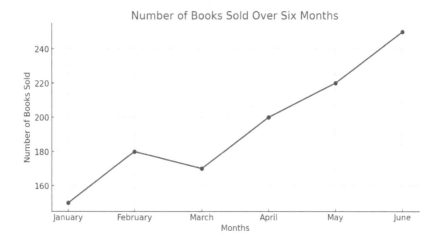

A line graph showing the number of books sold by a bookstore over six months.

- **Read the Labels**: The x-axis is labeled "Months" (January to June), and the y-axis is labeled "Number of Books Sold."
- **Identify Trends**: Observe the line. If it slopes upward from January to June, the number of books sold is increasing.
- **Compare Data**: If there are multiple lines representing different genres of books, compare the slopes and values to see which genre is selling the most.

Table Example:

Student	Math	Science	English	History
Alice	95	88	92	80
Bob	80	92	85	75
Charlie	85	78	88	85
David	70	85	75	90
Eva	90	87	91	89

A table showing the test scores of students in different subjects.

- **Read the Labels**: The columns are labeled "Math," "Science," "English," and "History." The rows list the students' names.
- **Calculate Percentages**: If the scores are out of 100, you can quickly see the percentage each student scored in each subject.
- **Identify Key Points**: Look for the highest and lowest scores in each subject to determine which subjects students performed best and worst in.

VI

Mastering the Optional Essay

Understanding the Essay Prompt

Breakdown of Essay Requirements

The SAT Optional Essay asks you to demonstrate your reading, analysis, and writing skills. Here's what you need to know to meet the requirements and perform well:

1. Understand the Prompt

The prompt will ask you to read a passage and analyze how the author builds an argument to persuade the audience. Your task is to explain the techniques the author uses to construct their argument.

> **Example Prompt:** *"Write an essay in which you explain how the author builds an argument to persuade their audience. Analyze how the author uses evidence, reasoning, and other rhetorical techniques to support their argument."*

2. Key Components of Your Essay

To effectively respond to the prompt, your essay should include the following components:

- **Introduction**: Briefly introduce the passage and state your thesis. Your thesis should clearly outline the main techniques the author uses to build their argument.

> **Example**: *"The author uses statistical evidence, emotional appeals, and expert testimony to argue that renewable energy is essential for sustainable development."*

· **Body Paragraphs**: Each paragraph should focus on a different technique the author uses. Provide specific examples from the passage and explain how these examples support the author's argument.

> **Example**: *"The author uses statistical evidence to strengthen their argument. For instance, they cite a study showing that renewable energy sources have grown by 25% in the past decade, demonstrating the feasibility and effectiveness of these technologies."*

· **Conclusion**: Summarize your analysis and restate your thesis. Reinforce how the techniques you discussed contribute to the overall persuasiveness of the author's argument.

> **Example**: *"In conclusion, through the use of statistical evidence, emotional appeals, and expert testimony, the author effectively argues for the necessity of renewable energy. These techniques engage the reader and provide compelling support for the author's position."*

3. Focus on Analysis

Your essay should focus on analyzing the author's techniques rather than summarizing the passage. Discuss how the evidence, reasoning, and rhetorical techniques contribute to the author's argument.

4. Use Clear and Effective Language

Write in a clear, organized, and concise manner. Use varied sentence structures and precise vocabulary. Avoid overly complex language that might confuse the reader.

5. Stay Objective

Maintain an objective tone throughout your essay. Your goal is to analyze the author's argument, not to present your own opinion on the topic.

6. Time Management

You have 50 minutes to complete the essay. Spend the first 5-10 minutes reading the passage and planning your essay. Use the remaining time to write and revise your essay.

7. Proofread

If time allows, quickly proofread your essay to catch any grammatical errors or unclear sentences. A polished essay leaves a better impression.

Analyzing Sample Essays

Analyzing sample essays is a great way to understand what works and what doesn't in an SAT essay. Here's how you can break down a sample essay to see how it meets the requirements and where it can improve.

Sample Essay Prompt

"Write an essay in which you explain how the author builds an argument to persuade their audience. Analyze how the author uses evidence, reasoning, and other rhetorical techniques to support their argument."

Sample Essay

Let's take a look at a sample essay and analyze it:

Essay

In the article "Why We Should Embrace Renewable Energy," the author argues that transitioning to renewable energy sources is essential for sustainable development. The author uses statistical evidence, emotional appeals, and expert testimony to build a compelling argument.

Firstly, the author employs statistical evidence to substantiate their claims. For example, they cite a study showing that renewable energy sources have grown by 25% in the past decade, demonstrating the feasibility and effectiveness of these technologies. This use of data helps to establish credibility and provides concrete support for the argument.

Secondly, the author appeals to the emotions of the readers by highlighting the environmental and health benefits of renewable energy. They describe how reducing reliance on fossil fuels can lead to cleaner air and a healthier planet for future generations. This emotional appeal engages readers on a personal level and underscores the importance of the issue.

Finally, the author strengthens their argument by including expert testimony. They quote a renowned environmental scientist who states that renewable energy is not only viable but also necessary to combat climate change. This adds authority to the argument and reassures readers that the claims are backed by knowledgeable sources.

In conclusion, the author effectively argues for the adoption of renewable energy through the use of statistical evidence, emotional appeals, and expert testimony. These rhetorical techniques work together to create a persuasive and well-supported argument.

Analysis

1) Introduction

- **Strengths**: The introduction clearly states the author's thesis and the main techniques that will be analyzed (statistical evidence, emotional appeals, expert testimony).
- **Improvements**: It could be enhanced by providing a bit more context about the article and its significance.

Example: *"In the article 'Why We Should Embrace Renewable Energy,' the author makes a compelling case for the transition to renewable energy sources, highlighting its importance for sustainable development and environmental preservation."*

2) Body Paragraphs

- **Strengths**: Each body paragraph focuses on a specific rhetorical technique and provides specific examples from the article. The analysis explains how each technique supports the argument.
- **Improvements**: The essay could include more detailed explanations and connect the techniques more directly to the overall persuasiveness of the argument.

Example: *"Firstly, the author employs statistical evidence to substantiate their claims. For example, they cite a study showing that renewable energy sources have grown by 25% in the past decade, demonstrating the feasibility and effectiveness of these technologies. This use of data not only establishes credibility but also reassures readers that renewable energy is a practical solution."*

3) Conclusion

- **Strengths**: The conclusion summarizes the main points and reiterates the thesis effectively.
- **Improvements**: It could be more impactful by emphasizing the broader implications of the argument.

Example: "In conclusion, the author effectively argues for the adoption of renewable energy through the use of statistical evidence, emotional appeals, and expert testimony. These rhetorical techniques not only build a strong case but also inspire readers to consider the critical role of renewable energy in ensuring a sustainable future."

Overall Evaluation

- **Clarity and Organization**: The essay is clear and well-organized, with each paragraph logically following the previous one.
- **Evidence and Analysis**: The essay uses specific examples and provides thoughtful analysis. However, adding more depth to the explanations and connecting the techniques to the overall argument could strengthen it further.
- **Language and Style**: The essay uses appropriate language and maintains an objective tone. Varying sentence structure and using more sophisticated vocabulary could enhance the style.

Writing the Essay

Planning and Outlining

Planning and outlining your essay is a crucial step that sets the foundation for a well-organized and effective response. Here's how to do it:

1. Understand the Prompt

Start by carefully reading the essay prompt. Make sure you understand exactly what you are being asked to do. Typically, the prompt will ask you to analyze how the author builds an argument to persuade their audience.

2. Read the Passage Actively

As you read the passage, actively engage with the text. Underline or highlight key points, and make notes in the margins about the author's use of evidence, reasoning, and rhetorical techniques. This will help you identify the main elements to discuss in your essay.

3. Identify the Key Techniques

Decide which techniques the author uses most effectively. These might include:

- **Statistical Evidence**: Data and statistics that support the argument.
- **Emotional Appeals**: Language that evokes an emotional response from the reader.

- **Expert Testimony**: Quotes or references to experts that lend credibility to the argument.
- **Logical Reasoning**: Clear, logical progression of ideas that build the argument.

4. Develop Your Thesis Statement

Your thesis statement should clearly outline the main points you will discuss in your essay. It should answer the question posed by the prompt and indicate the techniques you will analyze.

> **Example**: *"The author uses statistical evidence, emotional appeals, and expert testimony to effectively argue for the importance of renewable energy."*

5. Create an Outline

An outline helps organize your thoughts and ensures your essay flows logically. Here's a basic structure to follow:

Introduction:

- Introduce the passage and its main argument.
- Present your thesis statement.

Body Paragraph 1:

- Focus on the first technique (e.g., statistical evidence).
- Provide specific examples from the passage.
- Explain how this technique supports the author's argument.

Body Paragraph 2:

- Focus on the second technique (e.g., emotional appeals).

- Provide specific examples from the passage.
- Explain how this technique supports the author's argument.

Body Paragraph 3:

- Focus on the third technique (e.g., expert testimony).
- Provide specific examples from the passage.
- Explain how this technique supports the author's argument.

Conclusion:

- Summarize the main points of your analysis.
- Restate your thesis in a new way.
- Conclude with a final thought on the effectiveness of the author's argument.

6. Allocate Your Time

Plan how you'll spend your time during the exam. Here's a suggested breakdown:

- **5-10 minutes**: Read and analyze the passage.
- **5 minutes**: Plan and outline your essay.
- **30 minutes**: Write your essay.
- **5-10 minutes**: Review and revise your essay.

7. Stay Flexible

While it's important to have a plan, be flexible. If you find a particularly strong piece of evidence as you write, adjust your outline as needed. The goal is to present the most compelling analysis possible.

Example Outline:
  Introduction:

- Briefly introduce the topic of renewable energy.
- State that the author effectively argues for renewable energy using statistical evidence, emotional appeals, and expert testimony.

Body Paragraph 1:

- Discuss the use of statistical evidence.
- Example: "The author cites a study showing a 25% increase in renewable energy usage over the past decade."
- Analysis: "This data establishes the feasibility and growth of renewable energy, adding credibility to the argument."

Body Paragraph 2:

- Discuss the use of emotional appeals.
- Example: "The author describes the health benefits of cleaner air from reduced fossil fuel usage."
- Analysis: "By highlighting the positive impact on future generations, the author connects with the reader's emotions and sense of responsibility."

Body Paragraph 3:

- Discuss the use of expert testimony.
- Example: "The author quotes a renowned environmental scientist who supports the shift to renewable energy."
- Analysis: "This expert endorsement adds authority to the argument, reassuring readers that the claims are backed by reliable sources."

Conclusion:

- Summarize the key points of the analysis.
- Restate the thesis, emphasizing the effectiveness of the techniques

used.

· Conclude with a final thought on the importance of renewable energy.

Crafting a Strong Thesis Statement

A strong thesis statement is the backbone of a well-written essay. It clearly outlines your main argument and sets the direction for your entire essay. Here's how to craft a thesis statement that is clear, concise, and compelling:

1. Understand the Purpose of a Thesis Statement

Your thesis statement should:

· Present your main argument.
· Outline the key points you will discuss in your essay.
· Provide a roadmap for your readers.

2. Be Specific

A strong thesis statement is specific and focused. It should clearly state the techniques the author uses and how they contribute to the argument.

Example: Weak: "The author uses various techniques to argue for renewable energy." Strong: "The author effectively argues for the importance of renewable energy through the use of statistical evidence, emotional appeals, and expert testimony."

3. Make It Debatable

Your thesis should present an argument that can be supported with evidence. It should not be a simple statement of fact but something that requires analysis and explanation.

Example: Weak: "Renewable energy is important." Strong: "The author effectively argues for the importance of renewable energy by highlighting statistical growth, evoking emotional responses, and citing expert opinions."

4. Keep It Concise

Your thesis statement should be one or two sentences long. It needs to be concise enough to be clear but comprehensive enough to cover your main points.

5. Position It Properly

Place your thesis statement at the end of your introduction. This helps readers know what to expect in the rest of your essay.

6. Reflect the Structure of Your Essay

Your thesis should give a preview of the structure of your essay. Each point you mention in your thesis should correspond to a body paragraph in your essay.

Example Structure:

- **Introduction**: Introduce the topic and present the thesis.
- **Body Paragraph 1**: Discuss the first technique (e.g., statistical evidence).
- **Body Paragraph 2**: Discuss the second technique (e.g., emotional appeals).
- **Body Paragraph 3**: Discuss the third technique (e.g., expert testimony).
- **Conclusion**: Summarize your analysis and restate the thesis.

7. Revise As Needed

After drafting your essay, revisit your thesis statement. Ensure it still aligns with the content and structure of your essay. Make adjustments if necessary to keep it accurate and clear.

Example Thesis Statements:

- **Prompt**: Analyze how the author builds an argument to persuade their audience about the importance of renewable energy.

- **Thesis**: "In the article, the author convincingly argues for the adoption of renewable energy by presenting compelling statistical evidence, engaging emotional appeals, and credible expert testimony."
- **Prompt**: Explain how the author persuades their audience that reducing plastic use is crucial for environmental health.
- **Thesis**: "The author effectively persuades the audience to reduce plastic use by showcasing alarming statistics, appealing to readers' sense of responsibility, and quoting environmental experts."

Writing and Refining the Essay

Writing and refining your essay is where you bring your ideas to life and ensure they are clearly and effectively communicated. Here's how to write a compelling essay and refine it to perfection:

1. Write the Introduction

Your introduction sets the stage for your essay. It should grab the reader's attention, introduce the topic, and present your thesis statement.

> **Example**: "Renewable energy is increasingly recognized as a crucial component of sustainable development. In the article 'Why We Should Embrace Renewable Energy,' the author makes a compelling case for this transition, effectively using statistical evidence, emotional appeals, and expert testimony to persuade the audience."

2. Develop Body Paragraphs

Each body paragraph should focus on one key technique the author uses. Start with a topic sentence that introduces the technique, then provide specific examples from the passage and explain how these examples support the author's argument.

Example Structure for a Body Paragraph:

- **Topic Sentence**: "Firstly, the author employs statistical evidence to substantiate their claims."
- **Example from the Passage**: "For instance, they cite a study showing a 25% increase in renewable energy usage over the past decade."
- **Explanation**: "This use of data establishes credibility and demonstrates the practical feasibility of renewable energy, reinforcing the argument's persuasiveness."

3. Write the Conclusion

Your conclusion should summarize your analysis and restate your thesis in a new way. It should leave the reader with a final thought about the effectiveness of the author's argument.

> *Example: "In conclusion, the author's argument for the adoption of renewable energy is powerfully constructed through the strategic use of statistical evidence, emotional appeals, and expert testimony. These techniques not only build a strong case but also engage the reader, making the argument compelling and memorable."*

4. Refine Your Essay

Once you have written your first draft, it's time to refine your essay. Here are some steps to follow:

a. Review for Clarity and Coherence

- Ensure that each paragraph flows logically from one to the next.
- Check that your ideas are clearly expressed and that your examples directly support your points.
- Make sure your thesis is consistently supported throughout the essay.

b. Improve Sentence Structure and Word Choice

- Vary your sentence structures to keep the reader engaged.

- Use precise and appropriate vocabulary.
- Avoid repetitive language and ensure that your writing is concise.

c. Check for Grammar and Spelling

- Proofread your essay for any grammatical errors or typos.
- Pay attention to punctuation, subject-verb agreement, and pronoun usage.

d. Get Feedback

If possible, ask a teacher, friend, or family member to read your essay and provide feedback. They might catch errors you missed or suggest improvements.

5. Finalize Your Essay

Make the necessary revisions based on your review and any feedback you received. Ensure that your final essay is clear, coherent, and polished.

Example of a Refined Paragraph:

- **First Draft**: "Firstly, the author uses statistics to support his points. He mentions a study that shows a 25% increase in renewable energy usage in the last ten years. This data shows that renewable energy is growing and can be trusted."
- **Refined Version**: "Firstly, the author employs statistical evidence to substantiate his claims. For instance, he cites a study demonstrating a 25% increase in renewable energy usage over the past decade. This data not only establishes the credibility of renewable energy but also illustrates its rapid growth and feasibility."

Practice Prompts and Model Essays using AI

Practicing with prompts and reviewing model essays can significantly improve your essay-writing skills for the SAT. Here are some practice prompts along with model essays to help you understand how to effectively analyze and respond to the given arguments.

Practice Prompt 1

> **Prompt:** *"Write an essay in which you explain how the author builds an argument to persuade their audience that community service should be a graduation requirement for high school students. Analyze how the author uses evidence, reasoning, and other rhetorical techniques to support their argument."*

Model Essay:

In the article "Community Service as a Graduation Requirement," the author argues that high school students should be required to complete community service before graduating. The author builds a compelling case by using statistical evidence, logical reasoning, and emotional appeals.

Firstly, the author employs statistical evidence to support their argument. For instance, they cite a study showing that students who participate in community service are 20% more likely to graduate on time and 15% more likely to attend college. This use of data provides concrete support for the argument, demonstrating the tangible benefits of community service.

Secondly, the author uses logical reasoning to connect community service with skill development. They explain that community service opportunities help students develop important life skills such as leadership, communication, and teamwork. By logically linking these skills to future success, the author reinforces the practical benefits of the proposal.

Finally, the author appeals to the emotions of the readers by sharing personal stories of students who have been positively impacted by community service. For example, they describe a student who, through volunteering at a local shelter, discovered a passion for social work and decided to pursue it as a career. These emotional appeals help to humanize the argument and connect with readers on a personal level.

In conclusion, the author effectively argues for making community service a graduation requirement by using statistical evidence, logical reasoning, and emotional appeals. These techniques work together to create a persuasive and well-rounded argument that highlights the benefits of community service for students and society.

Practice Prompt 2

Prompt: *"Write an essay in which you explain how the author builds an argument to persuade their audience that online learning is an effective alternative to traditional classroom learning. Analyze how the author uses evidence, reasoning, and other rhetorical techniques to support their argument."*

Model Essay:

In the article "The Future of Education: Online Learning," the author argues that online learning is an effective alternative to traditional classroom learning. The author uses comparative analysis, expert testimony, and anecdotal evidence to build a strong argument.

Firstly, the author uses comparative analysis to highlight the advantages of online learning over traditional classroom learning. They compare the flexibility of online learning, which allows students to learn at their own pace and on their own schedule, to the rigid structure of traditional classrooms. This comparison helps to emphasize the benefits of online learning in accommodating diverse learning styles and needs.

Secondly, the author includes expert testimony to lend credibility to their argument. They quote a well-known education researcher who states that online learning can be just as effective as traditional classroom learning when designed properly. This expert endorsement adds authority to the argument and reassures readers that the claims are backed by reliable sources.

Finally, the author uses anecdotal evidence to illustrate the success of online learning. They share stories of students who have thrived in online learning environments, such as a student who was able to balance school with a part-time job thanks to the flexibility of online classes. These anecdotes help to personalize the argument and demonstrate real-world examples of the benefits of online learning.

In conclusion, the author effectively argues that online learning is an effective alternative to traditional classroom learning by using comparative analysis, expert testimony, and anecdotal evidence. These rhetorical techniques work together to create a persuasive and well-supported argument that highlights the effectiveness of online learning.

Practice Prompt 3

> **Prompt:** *"Write an essay in which you explain how the author builds an argument to persuade their audience that public transportation should be prioritized over personal car usage. Analyze how the author uses evidence, reasoning, and other rhetorical techniques to support their argument."*

Model Essay:

In the article "Prioritizing Public Transportation," the author argues that public transportation should be prioritized over personal car usage. The author uses statistical evidence, ethical appeals, and logical reasoning to build a convincing argument.

Firstly, the author uses statistical evidence to highlight the efficiency of public transportation. They cite data showing that public transportation reduces traffic congestion and lowers carbon emissions by 30%. This use of statistics provides concrete support for the argument, showing the environmental and logistical benefits of public transportation.

Secondly, the author makes ethical appeals by discussing the social equity benefits of public transportation. They argue that public transportation provides access to mobility for all individuals, including those who cannot afford personal cars. This ethical appeal emphasizes the importance of public transportation in creating a more equitable society.

Finally, the author uses logical reasoning to argue that prioritizing public transportation can lead to long-term economic benefits. They explain that investing in public transportation infrastructure creates jobs and stimulates economic growth. By logically connecting public transportation to economic development, the author reinforces the practical benefits of their proposal.

In conclusion, the author effectively argues for prioritizing public transportation over personal car usage by using statistical evidence, ethical appeals, and logical reasoning. These rhetorical techniques work together to create a persuasive and well-supported argument that highlights the multifaceted benefits of public transportation.

By practicing with these prompts and analyzing model essays, you can develop a stronger understanding of how to construct your own essays. Pay attention to how the essays are structured, how the evidence is presented, and how the analysis is tied back to the thesis. With practice, you'll become more confident in your ability to write a clear and persuasive essay on the SAT.

VII

Practice Tests

Full Length Practice SAT #1

1. Evidence-Based Reading and Writing (EBRW)

A. Reading Test

- **Number of Questions:** 52
- **Time Allotted:** 65 minutes
- **Format:** Multiple-choice
- **Passages:** 5 (each passage 10 questions)

Literature: 10 questions

The following passage is excerpted from "The House of Mirth" by Edith Wharton, originally published in 1905.

> Lily Bart, beautiful, intelligent, and socially prominent, has all the advantages to ensure a brilliant match. Yet, as she approaches her 29th birthday, she remains unmarried and financially vulnerable.
> Lily had no heart to listen to his talk about herself. She had no wish to be flattered. All her thoughts were focused on the obligation of looking her best. To this, every nerve was tuned; the task was made the more difficult by the fear of not being in the key, of not living up to the occasion. Yet she was in appearance as calm and at ease as though her whole heart had been engaged in the discussion

of impersonal topics. This was what was expected of her, and she had grown skilled in discharging expectations. But the brilliance of her surface hid a fundamental dullness.

It was not that she had no heart, but that hers was a changing heart. She had learned early that to be beautiful, vital, and intelligent was not enough; one must be also be unchangeable. Her adaptability was what made her the subject of admiration and envy. It was the quality which had so long been her standby, the one element in her varied stock-in-trade that never deteriorated. It was in this spirit of adaptability, rather than of curiosity, that she turned her charming face to the bright pink page of society gossip which her hostess had flung out on the table.

Lily's reliance on her charm and social dexterity was not a conscious calculation. In the world she lived in, these qualities had been cultivated to the point of unconscious habit. To attract, to dazzle, to outshine, these were the signs of her self-esteem. Yet beneath this polished exterior, she was subject to the same vulnerabilities and insecurities as those she sought to charm.

She had been brought up to be ornamental, and she could hardly have broken away from the inherited obligation even if she had wished to. But she had no wish to; her ambitions had always been directed toward the establishment of her social supremacy. Even now, when her star seemed to be on the wane, her faith in her ultimate success remained unshaken. She felt herself well-equipped to play the game of life with the superficial weapons furnished by the experience of generations. She knew the touchstones of success—the brilliance, the polish, the outward show of perfect happiness.

But in the bottom of her heart, she was humiliated by the thought that she had to depend on these attributes. There were moments when she longed to be valued for something more lasting, more substantial. Yet she could not shake off the conviction that without her beauty and charm, she would be nothing. This conviction led her to a fatal reliance on the approval of others, a dependence which would ultimately prove to be her undoing.

As she sat at the table, outwardly composed and inwardly churning with self-doubt, she resolved to keep up appearances. She had learned that in her world, the appearance of contentment was almost as important as the reality. And so, with a smile that masked her inner turmoil, she resumed her role as the belle of the ball.

1) What is the primary concern of Lily Bart as she approaches her 29th birthday?

- A) Finding a suitable husband
- B) Advancing her career
- C) Improving her financial skills
- D) Pursuing higher education

2) What does Lily find difficult about the task of looking her best?

- A) Lack of proper attire
- B) Fear of not meeting expectations
- C) Disinterest in social gatherings
- D) Absence of supportive friends

3) The phrase "brilliance of her surface hid a fundamental dullness" suggests that Lily's outward appearance is:

- A) Genuine and reflective of her true self
- B) Deceptive and masks her true feelings
- C) Bright and engaging
- D) Dark and brooding

4) What quality does Lily believe has made her the subject of admiration

and envy?

- A) Her unchangeable nature
- B) Her intellectual abilities
- C) Her adaptability
- D) Her wealth

5) Lily's reliance on her charm and social dexterity is described as:

- A) A deliberate strategy
- B) An unconscious habit
- C) A recent development
- D) A temporary phase

6) Which of the following best describes Lily's ambitions?

- A) To escape her social obligations
- B) To achieve social supremacy
- C) To pursue a career in politics
- D) To find true love

7) What internal conflict does Lily experience?

- A) A desire for financial independence versus a reliance on others
- B) A longing for a meaningful occupation versus societal expectations
- C) A wish to be valued for lasting qualities versus reliance on beauty and charm
- D) A need for solitude versus a need for social interaction

8) Lily's ultimate conviction about herself is that without her beauty and charm, she would be:

- A) Nothing

- B) More successful
- C) Happier
- D) Independent

9) The passage suggests that Lily's dependence on the approval of others will:

- A) Ensure her social success
- B) Lead to financial stability
- C) Prove to be her undoing
- D) Make her more popular

10) The phrase "the appearance of contentment was almost as important as the reality" implies that in Lily's world:

- A) Authentic happiness is easily achievable
- B) Superficial appearances are highly valued
- C) Genuine emotions are frequently expressed
- D) Reality is more important than appearances

Historical Documents: 10 questions

The following passage is excerpted from "The Federalist No. 10" by James Madison, originally published in 1787.

> Among the numerous advantages promised by a well-constructed Union, none deserves to be more accurately developed than its tendency to break and control the violence of faction. The friend of popular governments never finds himself so much alarmed for their character and fate as when he contemplates their propensity to this dangerous vice. He will not fail, therefore, to set a due value on any plan which, without violating the principles to which he is attached, provides a proper cure for it. The instability, injustice, and confusion

introduced into the public councils have been the mortal diseases under which popular governments have everywhere perished.

By a faction, I understand a number of citizens, whether amounting to a majority or a minority of the whole, who are united by some common impulse of passion, or of interest, adverse to the rights of other citizens, or to the permanent and aggregate interests of the community. There are two methods of curing the mischiefs of faction: the one, by removing its causes; the other, by controlling its effects.

There are again two methods of removing the causes of faction: the one, by destroying the liberty which is essential to its existence; the other, by giving to every citizen the same opinions, the same passions, and the same interests. It could never be more truly said than of the first remedy, that it was worse than the disease. Liberty is to faction what air is to fire, an aliment without which it instantly expires.

11) According to Madison, what is one of the primary advantages of a well-constructed Union?

- A) Economic prosperity
- B) Control of factional violence
- C) Military strength
- D) Cultural diversity

12) What does Madison consider to be the "mortal diseases" of popular governments?

- A) Instability, injustice, and confusion
- B) Corruption, factionalism, and tyranny
- C) Poverty, illiteracy, and disease
- D) Inefficiency, apathy, and disunity

13) How does Madison define a faction?

- A) A group of citizens united by a common interest or passion
- B) A minority group advocating for social change
- C) A majority imposing its will on the minority
- D) A coalition of political parties

14) What are the two methods of curing the mischiefs of faction according to Madison?

- A) Removing its causes and controlling its effects
- B) Educating the populace and enforcing strict laws
- C) Encouraging debate and promoting unity
- D) Establishing a strong central government and reducing states' rights

15) What are the two methods of removing the causes of faction?

- A) Destroying liberty and ensuring equality
- B) Limiting freedom of speech and restricting assembly
- C) Destroying liberty and giving everyone the same opinions and interests
- D) Promoting education and economic stability

16) Madison argues that destroying liberty to remove the causes of faction is:

- A) Necessary but challenging
- B) A suitable solution
- C) Worse than the disease itself
- D) The best method

17) In Madison's analogy, what is liberty compared to in relation to

faction?

- A) Water to a plant
- B) Air to fire
- C) Soil to a tree
- D) Sunlight to a flower

18) Why does Madison believe giving every citizen the same opinions and interests is not a feasible solution?

- A) It violates the principles of freedom
- B) It is impossible to achieve
- C) It is undesirable and impractical
- D) It would require a totalitarian regime

19) What does Madison suggest is necessary to prevent the "mortal diseases" of popular governments?

A) A strong and well-constructed Union

B) Strict regulation of public councils

C) Universal education

D) Greater economic equality

20) Madison implies that liberty is essential for:

A) The existence of faction

B) The growth of government

C) The development of the economy

D) The establishment of justice

Social Sciences: 10 questions

The following passage is adapted from "The Power of Habit: Why We Do What We Do in Life and Business" by Charles Duhigg, originally published in 2012.

In 2006, researchers at Duke University conducted a study and found that more than 40 percent of the actions people performed each day weren't actual decisions, but habits. Understanding habits, then, is crucial to making good decisions. Habits, scientists say, emerge because the brain is constantly looking for ways to save effort. Left to its own devices, the brain will try to make almost any routine into a habit, because habits allow our minds to ramp down more often.

This effort-saving instinct is a huge advantage. An efficient brain allows us to stop thinking constantly about basic behaviors, such as walking and choosing what to eat, so we can devote mental energy to inventing spears, irrigation systems, and eventually, airplanes and video games. But conserving mental effort is tricky, because if our brains power down at the wrong moment, we might fail to notice something important, such as a speeding car or an overcooked dinner.

To understand this process, consider how habits work. Habits are the brain's way of simplifying the movements required to execute a task, so we can perform them without having to think about every step. This process within our brains is a three-step loop. First, there is a cue, a trigger that tells your brain to go into automatic mode and which habit to use. Then there is the routine, which can be physical, mental, or emotional behavior. Finally, there is the reward, which helps your brain figure out if this particular loop is worth remembering for the future. Over time, this loop—cue, routine, reward—becomes more and more automatic. The cue and reward become intertwined until a powerful sense of anticipation and craving emerges.

Habits, though, aren't destiny. They can be ignored, changed, or replaced. But understanding the mechanics of habit formation is essential to making such changes. The brain can't tell the difference between bad and good habits, so if you have a bad one, it's always lurking there, waiting for the right cues and rewards.

Once you know how a habit operates, you can take steps to modify it. Every habit functions the same way, and therefore every habit can be changed. The golden rule of habit change: You can't extinguish a bad habit, you can only change it. To change a habit, you must keep the old cue, and deliver the old reward, but insert a new routine. That's the rule: If you use the same cue and provide the same reward, you can shift the routine and change the habit. This understanding reveals the mechanism at the root of all habits, which helps us grasp the potential for change.

21) What percentage of daily actions did researchers at Duke University find to be habits rather than actual decisions?

- A) 30 percent
- B) 40 percent
- C) More than 40 percent
- D) More than 50 percent

22) According to the passage, why do habits emerge?

- A) Because the brain wants to conserve mental effort
- B) Due to external social influences
- C) As a result of genetic programming
- D) To respond to environmental changes

23) What is a key advantage of the brain forming habits, as mentioned in the passage?

- A) It allows us to perform multiple tasks simultaneously
- B) It helps us make better decisions
- C) It frees up mental energy for more complex activities
- D) It improves memory retention

24) What is the potential risk of the brain's habit-forming process?

- A) It can lead to indecision
- B) It may cause us to overlook important details
- C) It results in increased stress levels
- D) It makes learning new tasks more difficult

25) According to the passage, what are the three steps in the habit loop?

- A) Routine, cue, reward
- B) Cue, reward, routine
- C) Cue, routine, reward
- D) Reward, routine, cue

26) What happens over time as the habit loop becomes more automatic?

- A) The routine becomes less important
- B) The cue and reward become intertwined, creating anticipation and craving
- C) The brain forgets the original cue
- D) The reward becomes unnecessary

27) What is necessary to change a bad habit according to the golden rule of habit change?

- A) Remove the old cue and introduce a new reward
- B) Replace both the old cue and the old reward
- C) Keep the old cue and deliver the old reward, but insert a new routine

- D) Extinguish the bad habit entirely

28) Why can't the brain distinguish between good and bad habits?

- A) Because habits are stored in the subconscious
- B) Because the brain is focused solely on conserving effort
- C) Because all habits operate the same way
- D) Because habits are influenced by external factors

29) What does understanding the mechanics of habit formation help us achieve?

- A) It helps in preventing the formation of new habits
- B) It aids in extinguishing bad habits
- C) It enables us to change or replace habits
- D) It reduces the need for habits

30) What does the passage suggest is at the root of all habits?

- A) A genetic predisposition to certain behaviors
- B) The brain's structure and chemistry
- C) A mechanism that includes a cue, routine, and reward
- D) The influence of social and environmental factors

Natural Sciences: 10 questions

The following passage is adapted from "The Hidden Life of Trees: What They Feel, How They Communicate – Discoveries from a Secret World" by Peter Wohlleben, originally published in 2015.

> *Trees are much more than passive, silent organisms. Recent research has shown that trees can communicate with each other, share resources, and even protect their neighbors. This discovery*

challenges the traditional view of trees as solitary entities and highlights the complexity of forest ecosystems.

Trees communicate primarily through their root systems, which are connected by a vast network of mycorrhizal fungi. These fungi form symbiotic relationships with tree roots, facilitating the exchange of nutrients and information. Through this network, trees can send distress signals when they are under attack by pests or experiencing drought. Neighboring trees respond to these signals by increasing their own defenses, demonstrating a form of collective protection.

Moreover, trees can share resources with each other. For example, in a forest, older, more established trees often share water and nutrients with younger, weaker trees. This support helps ensure the survival of the forest as a whole. This phenomenon is particularly evident in trees of the same species, which seem to exhibit a form of kinship, prioritizing the well-being of their relatives.

One striking example of tree communication and resource-sharing is the "mother tree" concept. Mother trees are the largest and oldest trees in a forest, and they play a crucial role in supporting the surrounding younger trees. They are hubs of the mycorrhizal network, distributing resources and information to the trees in their vicinity. When a mother tree is cut down, the surrounding forest can suffer, as the loss of this central figure disrupts the flow of nutrients and information.

Additionally, trees can recognize their own kin. Studies have shown that trees are more likely to share resources with genetically related individuals. This behavior suggests a level of recognition and familial bonding that was previously thought to be exclusive to animals.

The discovery of these complex interactions has significant implications for forestry practices and conservation efforts. Understanding the social nature of trees can lead to more sustainable forest management practices that take into account the intercon-

nectedness of forest ecosystems. By preserving these networks and the crucial roles of mother trees, we can help maintain the health and resilience of forests.

Wohlleben's insights into the hidden life of trees reveal the intricate relationships that sustain forest ecosystems. This new understanding of trees as social beings highlights the importance of protecting and preserving our forests for future generations.

31) What recent discovery about trees challenges the traditional view of them as solitary entities?

- · A) Trees grow faster in isolation
- · B) Trees can communicate, share resources, and protect their neighbors
- · C) Trees rely solely on animals for survival
- · D) Trees do not need sunlight to grow

32) How do trees primarily communicate with each other?

- · A) Through their leaves
- · B) Via their root systems connected by mycorrhizal fungi
- · C) Using chemical signals in the air
- · D) By emitting sounds

33) What role do mycorrhizal fungi play in tree communication?

- · A) They compete with trees for nutrients
- · B) They facilitate the exchange of nutrients and information
- · C) They block tree roots from connecting
- · D) They cause diseases in trees

34) How do neighboring trees respond when a tree sends a distress signal?

- A) By ignoring the signal
- B) By moving closer to the distressed tree
- C) By increasing their own defenses
- D) By changing their leaf color

35) What is the significance of older, more established trees sharing resources with younger trees?

- A) It helps ensure the survival of the forest as a whole
- B) It weakens the older trees
- C) It causes competition among younger trees
- D) It is a rare occurrence with no significant impact

36) What is a "mother tree" in the context of the passage?

- A) The smallest tree in the forest
- B) The largest and oldest trees that support surrounding younger trees
- C) A tree that produces the most seeds
- D) A tree that has no connection to the mycorrhizal network

37) What happens to the surrounding forest when a mother tree is cut down?

- A) The forest becomes healthier
- B) The flow of nutrients and information is disrupted
- C) Younger trees grow faster
- D) Nothing significant occurs

38) According to the passage, how do trees exhibit a form of kinship?

- A) By sharing resources with genetically related individuals
- B) By growing in close proximity to unrelated trees

- C) By producing similar types of leaves
- D) By competing aggressively with their relatives

39) What implications does the discovery of tree communication have for forestry practices and conservation efforts?

- A) It suggests that clear-cutting is the best method for forest management
- B) It emphasizes the importance of preserving mycorrhizal networks and mother trees
- C) It shows that trees do not need to be protected
- D) It indicates that forests should be left unmanaged

1. **40) What does Wohlleben's research reveal about trees?**
2. A) Trees are solitary and independent organisms
3. B) Trees have intricate relationships that sustain forest ecosystems
4. C) Trees are more resilient when isolated

- D) Trees primarily compete for resources without cooperation

Dual Passages (Literature, Social Science, or Science): 10 questions

Passage 1

The following passage is adapted from "Bowling Alone: The Collapse and Revival of American Community" by Robert D. Putnam, originally published in 2000.

> *In recent decades, social capital in the United States has declined significantly. Social capital refers to the connections among individuals—social networks and the norms of reciprocity and trustworthiness that arise from them. These networks enable society to function effectively and foster a sense of community.*

One of the most notable indicators of this decline is the decrease in participation in traditional civic organizations, such as labor unions, parent-teacher associations, and fraternal organizations. For example, membership in these groups has plummeted since the 1960s. This reduction in civic engagement has weakened community bonds and reduced the overall level of social capital.

Several factors have contributed to this decline. The rise of television and other forms of electronic entertainment has played a significant role. As people spend more time in front of screens, they have less time to engage in face-to-face interactions. Additionally, increased mobility and suburbanization have led to more isolated living arrangements, further reducing opportunities for community engagement.

The consequences of this decline are profound. Communities with low levels of social capital tend to have higher crime rates, lower educational achievement, and poorer health outcomes. Rebuilding social capital requires a concerted effort to foster community engagement and create opportunities for people to connect.

Passage 2

The following passage is adapted from "The Power of Social Networks" by Nicholas A. Christakis and James H. Fowler, originally published in 2009.

Human beings are deeply social creatures. Our behaviors, emotions, and health are significantly influenced by the social networks to which we belong. Social networks are the web of relationships that connect individuals to one another, and they play a critical role in shaping our lives.

One striking example of the power of social networks is the spread of obesity. Studies have shown that if a person becomes obese, their friends are more likely to become obese as well. This pattern can be observed up to three degrees of separation, meaning that the behavior of your friend's friend's friend can influence your own behavior. This phenomenon highlights the importance of social influence in health-related behaviors.

Social networks also affect emotional well-being. Positive emotions, such as happiness, can spread through social networks, creating clusters of happy individuals. Similarly, negative emotions, such as loneliness, can also spread, leading to clusters of individuals who feel isolated and disconnected. Understanding the dynamics of social networks can help us develop strategies to promote positive behaviors and improve overall well-being.

The structure of social networks can vary significantly. Some networks are tightly knit, with many connections among members, while others are more loosely connected. The density of a network can influence its effectiveness in spreading behaviors and emotions. For example, tightly knit networks may be more effective at spreading positive behaviors quickly, but they can also facilitate the rapid spread of negative behaviors.

Christakis and Fowler's research underscores the importance of social networks in shaping our lives. By recognizing the influence of these networks, we can harness their power to promote positive change and improve the well-being of individuals and communities.

41) Which of the following best describes the main idea of Passage 1?

- A) The rise of electronic entertainment has improved community engagement.
- B) Social capital in the United States has declined, leading to negative community outcomes.
- C) Increased mobility has strengthened community bonds.
- D) Traditional civic organizations are becoming more popular.

42) What do both passages suggest about the role of social networks?

- A) They have minimal impact on individual behaviors and emotions.
- B) They are irrelevant to modern society.
- C) They significantly influence behaviors, emotions, and community outcomes.
- D) They are a recent development in human society.

43) According to Passage 1, what is one consequence of the decline in social capital?

- A) Higher educational achievement
- B) Improved health outcomes
- C) Increased crime rates
- D) Greater participation in civic organizations

44) In Passage 2, what example is used to illustrate the power of social networks on health?

- A) Spread of loneliness
- B) Spread of obesity
- C) Spread of crime
- D) Spread of educational attainment

45) How do the authors of Passage 1 and Passage 2 differ in their focus regarding social connections?

- A) Passage 1 focuses on the decline of social capital, while Passage 2 focuses on the influence of social networks.
- B) Passage 1 focuses on positive outcomes, while Passage 2 focuses on negative outcomes.
- C) Passage 1 discusses electronic entertainment, while Passage 2 discusses traditional media.
- D) Passage 1 highlights individual behavior, while Passage 2 highlights community behavior.

46) What does Passage 2 suggest about tightly knit social networks?

- A) They are less effective at spreading behaviors.
- B) They can rapidly spread both positive and negative behaviors.
- C) They are only effective for spreading positive behaviors.
- D) They do not influence emotional well-being.

47) Which of the following statements is supported by both passages?

- A) Social networks have no impact on health outcomes.
- B) Traditional civic engagement is on the rise.
- C) Understanding social connections can help improve well-being.
- D) Increased mobility has strengthened community ties.

48) Based on Passage 1, what factor is mentioned as contributing to the decline in social capital?

- A) Decreased mobility
- B) Suburbanization
- C) Increased educational attainment
- D) Improved health outcomes

49) What solution does Passage 1 propose to address the decline in social capital?

- A) Reducing electronic entertainment
- B) Encouraging traditional gender roles
- C) Fostering community engagement and creating opportunities for connection
- D) Increasing individual competition

50) How does the influence of social networks on emotions, as described in Passage 2, relate to the concept of social capital in Passage

1?

- A) Both emphasize the role of social connections in shaping individual and community well-being.
- B) Passage 1 ignores emotional well-being, while Passage 2 focuses solely on it.
- C) Both passages argue that social connections are less important than individual achievements.
- D) Passage 1 and Passage 2 disagree on the importance of social connections.

B. Writing and Language Test

- **Number of Questions:** 44
- **Time Allotted:** 35 minutes
- **Format:** Multiple-choice
- **Passages:** 4 (each passage 11 questions)

Careers: 11 questions

The Life and Legacy of a Public Health Nurse

(1) Florence Nightingale is often celebrated as the founder of modern nursing, but many other pioneering nurses have made significant contributions to public health. (2) One such figure is Lillian Wald, a nurse and social worker who played a crucial role in the development of public health nursing in the United States.

(3) Born in 1867, Wald was deeply influenced by her experiences working with impoverished communities in New York City. (4) After witnessing the dire health conditions of the poor, she decided to dedicate her life to improving public health. (5) In 1893, Wald founded the Henry Street Settlement, a community-based organization that provided healthcare, education, and social services to

residents of the Lower East Side.

(6) Wald's innovative approach to nursing emphasized the importance of addressing social determinants of health, such as poverty, education, and housing. (7) She believed that nurses should not only provide medical care but also advocate for social reforms to improve the overall well-being of their patients. (8) Under her leadership, the Henry Street Settlement expanded its services to include visiting nurses who provided care to patients in their homes, a practice that became a cornerstone of public health nursing.

(9) In addition to her work at Henry Street, Wald was a tireless advocate for public health policies. (10) She lobbied for legislation to improve sanitation, child labor laws, and school health programs. (11) Her efforts were instrumental in the establishment of the Federal Children's Bureau in 1912, which aimed to improve the health and welfare of children across the country.

(12) Wald's contributions to public health nursing extended beyond the United States. (13) She was a founding member of the International Council of Nurses and worked to promote the profession on a global scale. (14) Her commitment to social justice and healthcare equity inspired generations of nurses to follow in her footsteps.

(15) Today, Lillian Wald is remembered as a pioneer of public health nursing and a champion for social change. (16) Her legacy lives on in the countless nurses who continue to work in communities, advocating for the health and well-being of all individuals, regardless of their socioeconomic status.

(17) The impact of Wald's work can still be seen in the public health initiatives and policies that prioritize community-based care and social determinants of health. (18) By recognizing the interconnectedness of health and social conditions, Wald helped to shape a more holistic approach to healthcare that remains relevant to this day.

51) Which choice best describes what happens in the passage?

- A) The passage discusses Lillian Wald's contributions to public health nursing and her advocacy for social reforms.
- B) The passage provides a detailed account of Florence Nightingale's life.
- C) The passage explains the challenges faced by nurses in the early 20th century.
- D) The passage criticizes modern public health policies.

52) Which choice best supports the main idea of the passage?

- A) The establishment of the Federal Children's Bureau in 1912.
- B) Wald's emphasis on addressing social determinants of health.
- C) The founding of the International Council of Nurses.
- D) Florence Nightingale's contributions to nursing.

53) In context, which is the best version of the underlined portion of sentence 1 (reproduced below)?

Florence Nightingale is often celebrated as the founder of modern nursing, but many other pioneering nurses have made significant contributions to public health.

- A) NO CHANGE
- B) because many other pioneering nurses have made significant contributions to public health.
- C) and many other pioneering nurses made significant contributions to public health.
- D) therefore, many other pioneering nurses have made significant contributions to public health.

54) Which choice provides the most accurate interpretation of the data in sentence 8?

- A) Under her leadership, the Henry Street Settlement focused only on medical care.
- B) Under her leadership, the Henry Street Settlement expanded its services to include home care, which became central to public health nursing.
- C) Under her leadership, the Henry Street Settlement reduced its services.
- D) Under her leadership, the Henry Street Settlement neglected visiting nurses.

55) Which choice best maintains the tone of the passage in sentence 3?

- A) Born in 1867, Wald was deeply affected by her experiences working with poor people.
- B) Born in 1867, Wald was deeply influenced by her experiences working with impoverished communities in New York City.
- C) Born in 1867, Wald was deeply moved by her experiences with New York City's underprivileged.
- D) Born in 1867, Wald was deeply touched by her experiences in New York City.

56) The author wants to add the following sentence to the third paragraph:

"This approach was revolutionary at the time and set a precedent for future public health initiatives." Where would this sentence best fit?

- A) Before sentence 6
- B) After sentence 6
- C) After sentence 7
- D) After sentence 8

57) Which of the following best describes the function of the second paragraph in the context of the passage?

- A) It introduces the main subject of the passage.
- B) It provides a counterargument to the passage's main idea.
- C) It offers a conclusion to the passage.
- D) It lists the accomplishments of Florence Nightingale.

58) In sentence 14, the phrase "Her commitment to social justice and healthcare equity" primarily serves to:

- A) Question Wald's dedication to public health.
- B) Highlight the reasons for Wald's influence on future generations of nurses.
- C) Suggest that Wald's methods were outdated.
- D) Criticize the limitations of Wald's approach.

59) The word "legacy" in sentence 15 most nearly means:

- A) Property left in a will.
- B) The long-lasting impact.
- C) A historical artifact.
- D) A traditional custom.

60) Which sentence, if added, would provide the most relevant detail to support the last paragraph?

- A) Wald's work continues to inspire nurses worldwide.
- B) Wald had many hobbies, including gardening and reading.
- C) Wald traveled extensively throughout her life.
- D) Wald received numerous awards for her contributions to nursing.

61) Which choice best concludes the passage?

- A) By recognizing the interconnectedness of health and social conditions, Wald helped to shape a more holistic approach to healthcare that remains relevant to this day.

- B) Wald's ideas were not well-received during her time, but they gained popularity in later years.
- C) Despite facing numerous challenges, Wald's dedication to public health never wavered.
- D) Wald's contributions are still remembered, though they are often overshadowed by those of her contemporaries.

History/Social Studies: 11 questions

The Women's Suffrage Movement in the United States

(1) The women's suffrage movement in the United States was a decades-long fight to secure the right to vote for women. (2) This movement, which culminated in the ratification of the 19th Amendment in 1920, was marked by intense activism, perseverance, and the efforts of countless individuals and organizations.

(3) The roots of the women's suffrage movement can be traced back to the early 19th century. (4) In 1848, the Seneca Falls Convention, organized by Elizabeth Cady Stanton and Lucretia Mott, marked the beginning of the organized suffrage movement in the United States. (5) At this convention, the Declaration of Sentiments was drafted, asserting the equality of men and women and demanding the right to vote for women.

(6) Throughout the 19th century, suffragists employed various strategies to advocate for their cause. (7) Some, like Susan B. Anthony and Elizabeth Cady Stanton, focused on state-level campaigns to win voting rights for women. (8) Others, such as Sojourner Truth and Ida B. Wells, highlighted the intersection of race and gender, advocating for the rights of both women and African Americans.

(9) The movement faced significant opposition from those who believed that women's suffrage would disrupt traditional gender

roles and family structures. (10) Despite these challenges, suf-fragists continued their efforts, organizing marches, delivering speeches, and petitioning lawmakers.

(11) One of the most notable events in the suffrage movement was the 1913 Women's Suffrage Parade in Washington, D.C. (12) Led by Alice Paul and the National Woman's Party, thousands of women marched down Pennsylvania Avenue the day before President Woodrow Wilson's inauguration. (13) The parade drew national attention to the suffrage cause and highlighted the determination of the women involved.

(14) The entry of the United States into World War I in 1917 provided a new context for the suffrage movement. (15) Women's contributions to the war effort, both on the home front and abroad, bolstered the argument for granting them the right to vote. (16) Suffragists emphasized the inconsistency of fighting for democracy abroad while denying democratic rights to women at home.

(17) The culmination of the suffrage movement came with the passage of the 19th Amendment. (18) After years of lobbying and advocacy, the amendment was passed by Congress in 1919 and ratified by the required number of states on August 18, 1920. (19) The 19th Amendment prohibited any United States citizen from being denied the right to vote on the basis of sex, finally enfranchising millions of American women.

(20) The women's suffrage movement not only secured the right to vote for women but also laid the groundwork for future advances in women's rights. (21) It demonstrated the power of collective action and the importance of perseverance in the face of adversity. (22) The legacy of the suffragists continues to inspire movements for equality and justice around the world.

62) Which choice best describes what happens in the passage?

- A) The passage discusses the women's suffrage movement in the

United States and its key events and figures.
- B) The passage outlines the global women's rights movement.
- C) The passage focuses on the opposition to the women's suffrage movement.
- D) The passage highlights the role of World War I in changing gender roles.

63) Which choice provides the most accurate interpretation of the data in sentence 2?

- A) The women's suffrage movement was a brief but intense fight for women's voting rights.
- B) The women's suffrage movement culminated in the ratification of the 19th Amendment in 1920, showcasing intense activism and perseverance.
- C) The women's suffrage movement had little impact on American society.
- D) The women's suffrage movement focused primarily on gaining voting rights for African Americans.

64) Which version of the underlined portion of sentence 5 best maintains the tone and style of the passage?

- A) NO CHANGE
- B) was written, saying men and women are equal and demanding voting rights for women.
- C) was put together, stating that men and women are the same and asking for voting rights for women.
- D) was created, claiming that men and women should have the same rights and requesting the right to vote for women.

65) In context, which is the best way to combine sentences 11 and 12?

- A) One of the most notable events in the suffrage movement was the 1913 Women's Suffrage Parade in Washington, D.C., which was led by Alice Paul and the National Woman's Party, thousands of women marched down Pennsylvania Avenue the day before President Woodrow Wilson's inauguration.
- B) One of the most notable events in the suffrage movement was the 1913 Women's Suffrage Parade in Washington, D.C., and Alice Paul and the National Woman's Party led it, with thousands of women marching down Pennsylvania Avenue the day before President Woodrow Wilson's inauguration.
- C) One of the most notable events in the suffrage movement was the 1913 Women's Suffrage Parade in Washington, D.C.; it was led by Alice Paul and the National Woman's Party, and thousands of women marched down Pennsylvania Avenue the day before President Woodrow Wilson's inauguration.
- D) One of the most notable events in the suffrage movement was the 1913 Women's Suffrage Parade in Washington, D.C.; led by Alice Paul and the National Woman's Party, thousands of women marched down Pennsylvania Avenue the day before President Woodrow Wilson's inauguration.

66) Which choice provides the most logical introduction to the second paragraph (sentences 3-5)?

- A) The women's suffrage movement had many important figures.
- B) The roots of the women's suffrage movement can be traced back to the early 19th century.
- C) Many women were interested in gaining the right to vote.
- D) The fight for women's voting rights was complex and multifaceted.

67) In sentence 8, what is the purpose of mentioning Susan B. Anthony, Elizabeth Cady Stanton, Sojourner Truth, and Ida B. Wells?

- A) To show that only a few women were involved in the suffrage movement
- B) To highlight the diversity of strategies and perspectives within the suffrage movement
- C) To emphasize that the suffrage movement was primarily a white women's movement
- D) To suggest that these women were not significant figures in the movement

68) Which choice best maintains the tone of the passage in sentence 10?

- A) NO CHANGE
- B) Despite these challenges, suffragists kept doing their thing, organizing marches, giving speeches, and pestering lawmakers.
- C) Despite these challenges, suffragists continued their efforts, organizing marches, delivering speeches, and petitioning lawmakers.
- D) Despite these challenges, suffragists pressed on, holding rallies, making speeches, and badgering lawmakers.

69) Which sentence, if added to the fourth paragraph, would best support the information presented in that paragraph?

- A) Alice Paul was known for her leadership skills.
- B) The parade was not the only event organized by the suffragists.
- C) The parade included women from various backgrounds and regions, demonstrating the widespread support for suffrage.
- D) Many men also supported the women's suffrage movement.

70) The author wants to add the following sentence to the fifth paragraph:
"Women's roles during the war included working in factories, serving as nurses, and supporting the war effort in various capacities." Where

would this sentence best fit?

- A) Before sentence 14
- B) After sentence 14
- C) Before sentence 15
- D) After sentence 15

71) In context, the word "culmination" in sentence 17 most nearly means:

- A) Beginning
- B) Conclusion
- C) Interruption
- D) Decline

72) Which choice best concludes the passage?

- A) The women's suffrage movement was a brief but intense period in American history.
- B) The suffragists' efforts are often overlooked in history books.
- C) The legacy of the suffragists continues to inspire movements for equality and justice around the world.
- D) Many other countries granted women the right to vote around the same time.

Humanities: 11 questions

The Influence of Greek Philosophy on Western Thought

(1) The philosophical traditions of ancient Greece have profoundly influenced Western thought and culture. (2) From the works of Socrates, Plato, and Aristotle to the schools of Stoicism and Epicureanism, Greek philosophy laid the groundwork for many

aspects of modern philosophy, science, and politics.

(3) Socrates, often considered the father of Western philosophy, introduced a method of inquiry based on dialogue and questioning. (4) This Socratic method encourages critical thinking and the examination of beliefs and ideas through rigorous questioning. (5) Socrates believed that through this process, individuals could achieve a deeper understanding of truth and virtue.

(6) Plato, a student of Socrates, expanded upon his teacher's ideas and founded the Academy in Athens, one of the earliest institutions of higher learning in the Western world. (7) In his dialogues, Plato explored a wide range of philosophical topics, including justice, beauty, and the nature of reality. (8) His theory of Forms posits that the material world is a shadow of a higher, unchanging reality, where true knowledge can be found.

(9) Aristotle, a student of Plato, made significant contributions to numerous fields, including logic, ethics, politics, and natural sciences. (10) Unlike Plato, Aristotle emphasized empirical observation and believed that knowledge is derived from sensory experience. (11) His works on logic, particularly the syllogism, laid the foundation for formal logic and scientific reasoning.

(12) The Hellenistic period, which followed the conquests of Alexander the Great, saw the emergence of new philosophical schools that addressed practical concerns of daily life. (13) Stoicism, founded by Zeno of Citium, taught that virtue is the highest good and that individuals should strive for inner peace by accepting the natural order of the world. (14) Stoics believed in self-control, rationality, and the importance of fulfilling one's duties.

(15) In contrast, Epicureanism, founded by Epicurus, emphasized the pursuit of pleasure and the avoidance of pain as the primary goals of life. (16) Epicureans advocated for simple living and the cultivation of friendships, arguing that intellectual pleasures are superior to physical ones. (17) They believed that understanding the workings of the natural world could help individuals overcome

fear and achieve tranquility.

(18) The influence of Greek philosophy extended beyond the ancient world, shaping medieval and Renaissance thought. (19) The works of Greek philosophers were preserved and studied by Islamic scholars, who translated them into Arabic and commented on their ideas. (20) These texts were later reintroduced to Europe, where they played a crucial role in the development of scholasticism and the scientific revolution.

(21) Today, the legacy of Greek philosophy can be seen in various fields, from ethics and political theory to science and mathematics. (22) The emphasis on reason, inquiry, and the pursuit of knowledge that characterized Greek philosophy continues to inspire contemporary thinkers and shape our understanding of the world.

(23) The enduring impact of Greek philosophy underscores the importance of exploring these ancient ideas. (24) By studying the works of Socrates, Plato, Aristotle, and other Greek philosophers, we gain insight into the foundations of Western thought and the timeless questions that continue to challenge and inspire humanity.

73) Which choice best describes what happens in the passage?

- A) The passage discusses the significant influence of Greek philosophy on various aspects of Western thought and culture.
- B) The passage provides a detailed biography of Socrates.
- C) The passage outlines the scientific discoveries made by Greek philosophers.
- D) The passage critiques the philosophical ideas of the ancient Greeks.

74) Which choice provides the most accurate interpretation of the data in sentence 2?

- A) Greek philosophy only influenced ancient science.

- B) Greek philosophy laid the groundwork for many aspects of modern philosophy, science, and politics.
- C) Greek philosophy had no impact on modern political thought.
- D) Greek philosophy was primarily concerned with literature and arts.

75) Which version of the underlined portion of sentence 4 best maintains the tone and style of the passage?

- A) NO CHANGE
- B) The Socratic method is all about chatting and asking stuff.
- C) The Socratic method involves friendly discussions and casual questions.
- D) The Socratic method involves critical thinking and examining beliefs through questioning.

76) In context, which is the best way to combine sentences 6 and 7?

- A) Plato, a student of Socrates, expanded upon his teacher's ideas and founded the Academy in Athens, one of the earliest institutions of higher learning in the Western world, where he explored a wide range of philosophical topics in his dialogues, including justice, beauty, and the nature of reality.
- B) Plato, a student of Socrates, expanded upon his teacher's ideas, and he founded the Academy in Athens, one of the earliest institutions of higher learning in the Western world, he explored a wide range of philosophical topics, including justice, beauty, and the nature of reality, in his dialogues.
- C) Plato, a student of Socrates, expanded upon his teacher's ideas and founded the Academy in Athens, where he explored a wide range of philosophical topics in his dialogues, including justice, beauty, and the nature of reality, one of the earliest institutions of higher learning in the Western world.

- D) Plato, a student of Socrates, expanded upon his teacher's ideas, and in his dialogues, he explored a wide range of philosophical topics, including justice, beauty, and the nature of reality, founding the Academy in Athens, one of the earliest institutions of higher learning in the Western world.

77) Which choice provides the most logical introduction to the fourth paragraph (sentences 12-14)?

- A) The Hellenistic period was a time of great scientific discovery.
- B) The Hellenistic period saw the emergence of new philosophical schools addressing daily life concerns.
- C) The Hellenistic period was marked by political upheaval.
- D) The Hellenistic period was unimportant to the development of philosophy.

78) In sentence 9, what is the purpose of mentioning Aristotle's contributions to numerous fields?

- A) To show that Aristotle disagreed with Plato on all issues
- B) To highlight the diversity and breadth of Aristotle's influence
- C) To emphasize that Aristotle focused only on natural sciences
- D) To suggest that Aristotle's ideas were not influential

79) Which choice best maintains the tone of the passage in sentence 14?

- A) NO CHANGE
- B) Stoics thought that being virtuous was the coolest thing ever.
- C) Stoics believed that virtue was the highest good and that individuals should strive for inner peace by accepting the natural order of the world.
- D) Stoics thought that virtue was pretty important and that people

should chill out by going with the flow.

80) Which sentence, if added to the sixth paragraph, would best support the information presented in that paragraph?

- A) Epicurus enjoyed gardening and spending time with friends.
- B) Epicureanism also emphasized the importance of understanding the natural world to achieve peace.
- C) Many people disagreed with the ideas of Epicureanism.
- D) Epicureanism was only popular in certain regions of Greece.

81) The author wants to add the following sentence to the seventh paragraph:

"Islamic scholars played a crucial role in preserving and expanding upon Greek philosophical texts." Where would this sentence best fit?

- A) Before sentence 18
- B) After sentence 18
- C) Before sentence 19
- D) After sentence 19

82) In context, the word "legacy" in sentence 21 most nearly means:

- A) Wealth left in a will.
- B) Long-lasting impact.
- C) Legal inheritance.
- D) Historical document.

83) Which choice best concludes the passage?

- A) The legacy of Greek philosophy is limited to ancient times.
- B) The enduring impact of Greek philosophy underscores the importance of exploring these ancient ideas.

- C) Greek philosophy is often misunderstood and underappreciated in modern times.
- D) Many people today are unaware of the contributions of Greek philosophers.

Science: 11 questions

The Mysteries of Dark Matter

(1) The universe is composed of a vast array of matter and energy, yet a significant portion of it remains a mystery to scientists. (2) Dark matter, which makes up about 27% of the universe's mass and energy, cannot be seen or detected directly with current instruments. (3) Its presence is inferred from the gravitational effects it has on visible matter, such as stars and galaxies.

(4) The concept of dark matter was first proposed in the 1930s by Swiss astronomer Fritz Zwicky. (5) While studying the Coma Cluster, a group of galaxies, Zwicky observed that the galaxies were moving faster than could be explained by the visible mass alone. (6) He hypothesized that an unseen mass, which he called "dunkle Materie" or dark matter, was providing the necessary gravitational force to hold the cluster together.

(7) Further evidence for dark matter came from the study of galaxy rotation curves. (8) In the 1970s, American astronomer Vera Rubin found that the outer regions of galaxies were rotating at the same speed as the inner regions. (9) According to Newtonian physics, the outer stars should be moving slower than those near the center, where most of the visible mass is concentrated. (10) This discrepancy suggested the presence of an invisible mass that exerts additional gravitational force, maintaining the observed rotational speeds.

(11) Despite the compelling evidence for dark matter, its exact nature remains elusive. (12) Scientists have proposed several

candidates for dark matter particles, including weakly interacting massive particles (WIMPs) and axions. (13) WIMPs are hypothetical particles that interact through the weak nuclear force and gravity, but not through electromagnetism, making them difficult to detect. (14) Axions are extremely light particles that, if they exist, could also account for the missing mass in the universe.

(15) Researchers are employing various methods to detect dark matter particles. (16) One approach involves using particle detectors deep underground to shield them from cosmic rays and other background radiation. (17) These detectors are designed to capture rare interactions between dark matter particles and regular matter. (18) Another method involves searching for evidence of dark matter annihilation, where two dark matter particles collide and produce detectable byproducts, such as gamma rays.

(19) In addition to direct detection efforts, scientists are using powerful telescopes and computer simulations to study the effects of dark matter on cosmic structures. (20) By observing the distribution of galaxies and the bending of light (gravitational lensing), re-searchers can map the distribution of dark matter and gain insights into its properties.

(21) The study of dark matter is crucial for understanding the fundamental nature of the universe. (22) It influences the forma-tion and evolution of galaxies, and without it, the current models of cosmology would be incomplete. (23) Although the search for dark matter continues, each new discovery brings us closer to uncovering one of the universe's greatest mysteries.

(24) As technology advances and new methods are developed, scientists remain hopeful that the true nature of dark matter will eventually be revealed. (25) Solving this enigma will not only enhance our understanding of the cosmos but also potentially lead to new physics beyond the Standard Model.

84) Which choice best describes what happens in the passage?

- A) The passage discusses various theories about the universe's origin.
- B) The passage explains the concept of dark matter, its evidence, and the ongoing search to understand it.
- C) The passage critiques the limitations of current astronomical instruments.
- D) The passage provides a detailed biography of Fritz Zwicky.

85) Which choice provides the most accurate interpretation of the data in sentence 2?

- A) Dark matter is easily detectable with current instruments.
- B) Dark matter, making up about 27% of the universe's mass and energy, cannot be seen or detected directly with current instruments.
- C) Dark matter is less significant than visible matter.
- D) Dark matter does not interact with visible matter.

86) Which version of the underlined portion of sentence 3 best maintains the tone and style of the passage?

- A) NO CHANGE
- B) Its presence is inferred from the way it messes with visible stuff.
- C) Its presence is assumed because of the effects it has on things we can see, like stars and galaxies.
- D) Its presence is inferred from the gravitational effects it has on visible matter, such as stars and galaxies.

87) In context, which is the best way to combine sentences 8 and 9?

- A) In the 1970s, American astronomer Vera Rubin found that the outer regions of galaxies were rotating at the same speed as the inner regions, which, according to Newtonian physics, should not be the case since the outer stars should be moving slower than those near the center, where most of the visible mass is concentrated.

- B) In the 1970s, American astronomer Vera Rubin found that the outer regions of galaxies were rotating at the same speed as the inner regions; according to Newtonian physics, the outer stars should be moving slower than those near the center, where most of the visible mass is concentrated.
- C) In the 1970s, American astronomer Vera Rubin found that the outer regions of galaxies were rotating at the same speed as the inner regions, but according to Newtonian physics, the outer stars should be moving slower than those near the center, where most of the visible mass is concentrated.
- D) In the 1970s, American astronomer Vera Rubin found that the outer regions of galaxies were rotating at the same speed as the inner regions; according to Newtonian physics, the outer stars should be moving slower than those near the center, because that's where most of the visible mass is concentrated.

88) Which choice provides the most logical introduction to the third paragraph (sentences 11-14)?

- A) Despite the compelling evidence for dark matter, its exact nature remains elusive.
- B) Many scientists doubt the existence of dark matter.
- C) There is no evidence to support the existence of dark matter.
- D) Dark matter has been conclusively proven to be made up of WIMPs and axions.

89) In sentence 14, what is the purpose of mentioning WIMPs and axions?

- A) To show that scientists have already discovered the particles that make up dark matter
- B) To highlight some of the candidates for dark matter particles that

scientists are investigating

- C) To suggest that dark matter is not a significant scientific problem
- D) To argue that dark matter cannot be studied with current technology

90) Which choice best maintains the tone of the passage in sentence 16?

- A) NO CHANGE
- B) One cool way researchers are trying to detect dark matter particles is by using particle detectors deep underground.
- C) One approach researchers use involves particle detectors placed deep underground to shield them from cosmic rays and other background radiation.
- D) Some researchers think using particle detectors underground might help.

91) Which sentence, if added to the fifth paragraph, would best support the information presented in that paragraph?

- A) Researchers are also investigating other mysterious particles.
- B) The technology used in these detectors is constantly improving.
- C) Particle detectors can be very expensive to build.
- D) Detecting dark matter requires international cooperation.

92) The author wants to add the following sentence to the sixth paragraph:

"These methods help scientists better understand the large-scale structure of the universe." Where would this sentence best fit?

- A) Before sentence 19
- B) After sentence 19
- C) Before sentence 20

- D) After sentence 20

93) In context, the word "elusive" in sentence 11 most nearly means:

- A) Evident
- B) Obvious
- C) Difficult to find or define
- D) Unnecessary

94) Which choice best concludes the passage?

- A) The universe is vast and mysterious, with much left to discover.
- B) Dark matter is an unsolved mystery that may never be fully understood.
- C) As technology advances and new methods are developed, scientists remain hopeful that the true nature of dark matter will eventually be revealed, solving this enigma and potentially leading to new physics beyond the Standard Model.
- D) Scientists are always looking for new ways to study the universe.

2. Math

A. Math Test - No Calculator

- **Number of Questions:** 20
- **Time Allotted:** 25 minutes
- **Format:** Multiple-choice and grid-in

Heart of Algebra: 8 questions

95. Solve for x:

    $2x - 5 - 11$

- A) 2
- B) 5
- C) 8
- D) 9

96. If $3x + 4 - 2x + 10$, what is the value of x?

- A) 3
- B) 4
- C) 6
- D) 10

97. What is the solution to the system of equations:

    $y - 2x + 3$
    $y - -x + 1$

- A) $(1, 2)$
- B) $(2, 3)$
- C) $(-1, 1)$
- D) $(0, 3)$

98. Solve the inequality:

    $5x - 7 > 3x + 1$

- A) $x > 4$
- B) $x > 2$
- C) $x < 2$
- D) $x < 4$

99. If $y - 3x + 2$ and $y - -x + 6$, what is the value of x?

- A) 1
- B) 2
- C) 3
- D) 4

100. The sum of two numbers is 12. One number is 4 more than the other. What are the numbers?

- A) 4 and 8
- B) 3 and 9
- C) 5 and 7
- D) 6 and 6

101. Find the value of x if $4x - 3 - 3x + 5$.

- A) 3
- B) 5
- C) 8
- D) 4

102. What is the solution to the equation $2(3x - 1) - 4x + 6$?

- A) 2
- B) 3
- C) 4
- D) 5

Problem Solving and Data Analysis: 3 questions

103. A store sells apples at $0.75 each and bananas at $0.50 each. If a customer buys 8 apples and 10 bananas, what is the total cost?

- A) $11.50
- B) $12.00
- C) $10.50
- D) $9.00

104. The table below shows the number of books sold by a bookstore over four months. What is the average number of books sold per month?

Month	Books Sold
January	120
February	135
March	150
April	110

- A) 120
- B) 128.75
- C) 135
- D) 130

105. A company's profit P (in dollars) from selling x units of a product is given by the equation $P - 50x - 200$. How many units must the company sell to break even?

- A) 2
- B) 4
- C) 5
- D) 10

Passport to Advanced Math: 6 questions

106. If $f(x) = 2x^2 - 3x + 5$, what is $f(4)$?

- A) 21
- B) 25
- C) 29
- D) 33

107. Solve the equation for x: $3x^2 - 5x - 2 = 0$

- A) $x = -\frac{1}{3}$ or $x = 2$
- B) $x = \frac{2}{3}$ or $x = -1$
- C) $x = -2$ or $x = \frac{1}{3}$
- D) $x = 1$ or $x = -2$

108. If $y = 2x^3 - 4x^2 + x - 7$, what is the coefficient of the x^2 term after differentiating y with respect to x?

- A) -4
- B) 2
- C) 6
- D) 8

109. Which of the following is a solution to the inequality $2x - 3 > 7$?

- A) $x = 4$
- B) $x = 5$
- C) $x = 3$
- D) $x = 2$

168

110. Simplify the expression: $\frac{3x^2-12x-9}{3x-3}$

- A) $x - 2$
- B) $x - 3$
- C) $x - 1$
- D) $x - 4$

111. The function $g(x) - x^2 + 2x + 1$ is shifted 3 units to the right and 2 units up. What is the new function $h(x)$?

- A) $h(x) = (x + 2)^2 + 2$
- B) $h(x) - (x - 3)^2 + 2$
- C) $h(x) - (x - 3)^2 - 1$
- D) $h(x) - (x + 3)^2 + 2$

Additional Topics in Math (geometry, trigonometry, etc.): 3 questions

112. In a right triangle, the length of one leg is 6 and the length of the hypotenuse is 10. What is the length of the other leg?

- A) 4
- B) 6
- C) 8
- D) 12

113. The measure of angle A in a triangle is 50 degrees, and the measure of angle B is 60 degrees. What is the measure of angle C?

- A) 50 degrees
- B) 60 degrees
- C) 70 degrees
- D) 80 degrees

114. In a circle with a radius of 5, what is the length of an arc that subtends a central angle of 72 degrees? (Use $\pi \approx 3.14$)

- A) 5.24
- B) 6.28
- C) 7.85
- D) 8.57

B. Math Test - Calculator

- **Number of Questions:** 38
- **Time Allotted:** 55 minutes
- **Format:** Multiple-choice and grid-in

Heart of Algebra: 16 questions

115. If $3x + 4 - 19$, what is the value of x?

- A) 5
- B) 7
- C) 6
- D) 3

116. What is the solution to the equation $2(3x - 4) - 4x + 6$?

- A) 5
- B) 4
- C) 2
- D) 3

117. If $y - 5x - 2$ and $y - -3x + 6$, what is the value of x?

- A) 1
- B) 2
- C) -1
- D) -2

118. Solve for x: $\frac{2x-5}{3} - 7$.

- A) 13
- B) 10
- C) 11
- D) 16

119. The line $y - mx + b$ passes through the points $(1, 3)$ and $(3, 7)$. What is the value of m?

- A) 2
- B) 1
- C) 3
- D) 4

120. **Solve for y: $6y + 7 = 3y - 5$.**

- A) -4
- B) 4
- C) -3
- D) 3

121. **What is the value of x in the equation $6(x + 1) = 3x + 15$?**

- A) 3
- B) 4
- C) 5
- D) 6

122. **If $3x + 2y = 12$ and $x = 2$, what is the value of y?**

- A) 4
- B) 2
- C) 3
- D) 1

123. **Solve for y: $5y - 3 = 2y + 12$.**

- A) 6
- B) 5
- C) 4
- D) 7

124. If $y = 2x + 5$ and $y = -x + 2$, what is the value of y?

- A) 1
- B) 2
- C) 3
- D) 4

125. What is the value of x in the equation $\frac{x}{2} + \frac{x}{3} = 5$?

- A) 6
- B) 8
- C) 10
- D) 12

126. If $5(x - 3) = 3(2x + 1)$, what is the value of x?

- A) 8
- B) 7
- C) 6
- D) 5

127. Solve for y: $4y - 7 = 2(y + 5)$.

- A) 8.5
- B) 7.0
- C) 6.5
- D) 5.0

128. What is the solution to the equation $3x + 4y = 12$ when $x = 2$?

- A) 0.0
- B) 1.5
- C) 2.0
- D) 3.5

129. If $2x + 3y = 18$ and $x = 4$, what is the value of y?

- A) 2.50
- B) 3.33
- C) 4.66
- D) 5.00

130. Solve for x: $7x - 3 = 4x + 9$.

- A) 4
- B) 5
- C) 6
- D) 7

Problem Solving and Data Analysis: 8 questions

131. A company produces two types of widgets, A and B. Each type A widget costs $3 to make, and each type B widget costs $5 to make. If the company spends a total of $2000 to produce 500 widgets, how many of each type of widget did they produce?

- A) 200 type A widgets and 300 type B widgets
- B) 300 type A widgets and 200 type B widgets
- C) 250 type A widgets and 250 type B widgets
- D) 150 type A widgets and 350 type B widgets

132. In a survey, 40% of the respondents said they preferred apples over oranges. If 300 people were surveyed, how many people preferred apples?

- A) 100
- B) 120
- C) 150
- D) 180

133. A researcher is studying the relationship between hours studied and exam scores. The equation of the line of best fit is $y - 5x + 50$, where y is the exam score and x is the number of hours studied. What is the expected exam score for a student who studies for 4 hours?

- A) 60
- B) 70
- C) 80
- D) 90

134. A store sells notebooks for $2 each and pens for $1 each. If a customer buys a total of 15 items and spends $25, how many notebooks did they buy?

- A) 5
- B) 7
- C) 10
- D) 12

135. The table below shows the number of students in different grade levels at a school.

Grade	Number of Students
9th	120
10th	130
11th	110
12th	140

What is the mean number of students per grade level?

- A) 115
- B) 125
- C) 130
- D) 135

136. A car rental company charges a flat fee of $50 plus $0.25 per mile driven. If a customer rents a car and drives it for 120 miles, what is the total cost of the rental?

- A) $80
- B) $90
- C) $100
- D) $110

137. The ages of five employees at a company are 25, 30, 35, 40, and 45. What is the median age of the employees?

- A) 30
- B) 35
- C) 37.5
- D) 40

138. The histogram below shows the distribution of scores on a test.

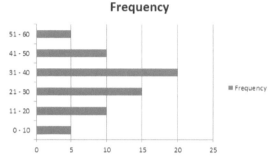

How many students scored between 21 and 40?

- A) 15
- B) 20
- C) 35
- D) 40

Passport to Advanced Math: 11 questions

139. If $f(x) = 2x^2 + 3x - 5$, what is $f(2)$?

- A) 3
- B) 5
- C) 9
- D) 11

140. Solve for x: $\frac{3x-5}{2} = 7$

- A) 3
- B) 5
- C) 7
- D) 9

141. What is the vertex of the parabola given by the equation $y = -x^2 + 4x + 6$?

- A) (2, 10)
- B) (2, 6)
- C) (-2, -10)
- D) (-2, -6)

142. If the polynomial $p(x) = x^3 - 4x^2 + 5x - 2$ is divided by $x - 1$, what is the remainder?

- A) 0
- B) 1
- C) 2
- D) 3

143. If $\log_2(x) = 5$, what is the value of x?

- A) 10
- B) 16
- C) 32
- D) 64

144. Solve for x: $2^{x+1} - 16$

- A) 2
- B) 3
- C) 4
- D) 5

145. The function $g(x)$ is defined as $g(x) = 3(x - 2)^2 + 4$. What is the minimum value of $g(x)$?

- A) 0
- B) 2
- C) 3
- D) 4

146. Solve for x in the equation $x^2 - 6x + 8 = 0$.

- A) 2, 4
- B) -2, -4
- C) 1, 8
- D) -1, -8

147. What is the value of k if the function $h(x) = kx^3 - 4x$ has a local maximum at $x = -1$?

- A) 2/3
- B) 4/3
- C) 5/3
- D) -2/3

148. If $\frac{2x+3}{4} = 5$, what is the value of x?

- A) 5/4
- B) 20/6
- C) 4/17
- D) 17/2

149. If the function $f(x) = ax^2 + bx + c$ has roots at $x = 2$ and $x = -3$, what is the value of c?

- A) 2
- B) -6
- C) 6
- D) -3

Additional Topics in Math (geometry, trigonometry, etc.): 3 questions

150. In a right triangle, one of the angles measures $30°$. If the length of the hypotenuse is 10 units, what is the length of the side opposite the $30°$ angle?

- A) 5
- B) $5\sqrt{3}$
- C) 10
- D) $10\sqrt{3}$

151. A circle has a radius of 7 units. What is the area of a sector with a central angle of $60°$?

- A) $\frac{49\pi}{6}$
- B) $\frac{49\pi}{3}$
- C) $\frac{49\pi}{2}$
- D) $\frac{49\pi}{4}$

152. In a parallelogram, one angle measures $70°$. What is the measure of the angle adjacent to this angle?

- A) $70°$
- B) $110°$
- C) $140°$
- D) $180°$

3. Essay (Optional)

- · **Number of Questions:** 1
- · **Time Allotted:** 50 minutes
- · **Format:** Essay prompt
- · **Task:** Analyze how the author builds an argument to persuade an audience.

The following passage is adapted from "The Benefits of Urban Green Spaces" by Jane Doe, originally published in 2020.

Urban green spaces, such as parks and gardens, play a crucial role in improving the quality of life for city dwellers. These areas provide not only aesthetic value but also numerous health and environmental benefits. Research has shown that access to green spaces can reduce stress, promote physical activity, and improve mental well-being. Moreover, urban greenery helps mitigate air pollution, regulate temperature, and support biodiversity.

One of the most significant advantages of urban green spaces is their positive impact on public health. Studies have found that people who live near parks or gardens are more likely to engage in physical activities such as walking, jogging, or cycling. This increased level of physical activity can lead to lower rates of obesity, cardiovascular diseases, and other health conditions. Additionally, spending time in nature has been linked to reduced stress levels, improved mood, and enhanced cognitive function.

Environmental benefits are another key reason why urban green spaces are essential. Trees and plants act as natural air filters, absorbing pollutants and releasing oxygen. This process helps to improve air quality, which is particularly important in densely populated urban areas where pollution levels are often high. Furthermore, green spaces can help to cool cities by providing shade and reducing the heat island effect, where urban areas experience higher temperatures than their rural surroundings.

Biodiversity is also supported by urban green spaces. Parks and gardens provide habitats for various species of birds, insects, and small mammals, contributing to the overall ecological health of the area. These green areas can serve as important refuges for wildlife, especially in cities where natural habitats are limited.

In conclusion, the presence of urban green spaces is vital for enhancing the quality of life in cities. They offer significant health, environmental, and biodiversity benefits that contribute to the well-being of urban residents. As cities continue to grow and develop, it is crucial to prioritize the creation and maintenance of these green areas to ensure sustainable and livable urban environments.

Essay Prompt:

Write an essay in which you explain how Jane Doe builds an argument to persuade her audience that urban green spaces are essential for improving the quality of life in cities. In your essay, analyze how Doe uses one or more of the features listed below (or features of your own choice) to strengthen the logic and persuasiveness of her argument. Be sure that your analysis focuses on the most relevant features of the passage.

- Evidence, such as facts or examples, to support claims
- Reasoning to develop ideas and to connect claims and evidence
- Stylistic or persuasive elements, such as word choice or appeals to

emotion, to add power to the ideas expressed

Your essay should not explain whether you agree with Doe's claims, but rather explain how Doe builds an argument to persuade her audience.

Full Length Practice SAT #2

1. Evidence-Based Reading and Writing (EBRW)

A. Reading Test

- **Number of Questions:** 52
- **Time Allotted:** 65 minutes
- **Format:** Multiple-choice
- **Passages:** 5 (each passage 10 questions)

Literature: 10 questions

The following passage is excerpted from "Pride and Prejudice" by Jane Austen, originally published in 1813.

> *Elizabeth Bennet is the intelligent and spirited second daughter in the Bennet family. She is known for her wit and keen observation, which often puts her at odds with the more rigid societal norms of her time.*
>
> *Elizabeth, as they drove along, watched for the first appearance of Pemberley Woods with some perturbation; and when at length they turned in at the lodge, her spirits were in a high flutter. The park was very large, and contained great variety of ground. They entered it in one of its lowest points, and drove for some time through a*

beautiful wood stretching over a wide extent.

Elizabeth was delighted. She had never seen a place for which nature had done more, or where natural beauty had been so little counteracted by an awkward taste. They were all of them warm in their admiration; and at that moment she felt that to be mistress of Pemberley might be something!

They gradually ascended for half a mile, and then found themselves at the top of a considerable eminence, where the wood ceased, and the eye was instantly caught by Pemberley House, situated on the opposite side of a valley, into which the road with some abruptness wound. It was a large, handsome stone building, standing well on rising ground, and backed by a ridge of high woody hills; and in front, a stream of some natural importance was swelled into greater, but without any artificial appearance. Its banks were neither formal, nor falsely adorned.

Elizabeth was too much excited to say a great deal; but the beauty of the place and its quiet seclusion did not escape her. As they passed into other parts of the park, her admiration of its beauty, for neither nature nor art had spared to adorn it, was again expressed. Upon this subject, Mr. Gardiner could rally his niece.

Elizabeth's mind was too full for conversation, but she saw and admired every remarkable spot and point of view. They gradually ascended for half a mile, and then found themselves at the top of a considerable eminence, where the wood ceased, and the eye was instantly caught by Pemberley House, situated on the opposite side of a valley, into which the road with some abruptness wound.

Elizabeth, as they drove along, watched for the first appearance of Pemberley Woods with some perturbation; and when at length they turned in at the lodge, her spirits were in a high flutter. The park was very large, and contained great variety of ground. They entered it in one of its lowest points, and drove for some time through a beautiful wood stretching over a wide extent.

She felt, that to be mistress of Pemberley might be something!

It was a large, handsome stone building, standing well on rising ground, and backed by a ridge of high woody hills; and in front, a stream of some natural importance was swelled into greater, but without any artificial appearance. Its banks were neither formal, nor falsely adorned. Elizabeth was delighted. She had never seen a place for which nature had done more, or where natural beauty had been so little counteracted by an awkward taste. They were all of them warm in their admiration; and at that moment she felt that to be mistress of Pemberley might be something!

As they drove into the park, they gradually ascended for half a mile, and then found themselves at the top of a considerable eminence, where the wood ceased, and the eye was instantly caught by Pemberley House, situated on the opposite side of a valley, into which the road with some abruptness wound.

1) What is Elizabeth Bennet's initial feeling as she approaches Pemberley Woods?

- A) Indifference
- B) Excitement
- C) Anxiety
- D) Boredom

2) What aspect of Pemberley House first catches Elizabeth's eye?

- A) Its ornate decorations
- B) Its large, handsome stone structure
- C) Its vibrant gardens
- D) Its modern architecture

3) Which feature of Pemberley does Elizabeth find particularly appealing?

- A) The formal gardens
- B) The natural beauty of the estate
- C) The elaborate fountains
- D) The luxurious interior design

4) What is implied about Elizabeth's thoughts on becoming the mistress of Pemberley?

- A) She feels indifferent about the prospect
- B) She considers it a daunting responsibility
- C) She believes it might be something significant
- D) She thinks it would be an impossible dream

5) How does Elizabeth react to the park's appearance?

- A) She is unimpressed by its size
- B) She admires its natural beauty and lack of artificiality
- C) She criticizes its formal design
- D) She finds it overly decorated

6) What does the passage suggest about Elizabeth's attitude towards natural beauty versus artificial adornment?

- A) She prefers artificial adornment
- B) She values natural beauty over artificial adornment
- C) She believes both are equally important
- D) She dislikes both

7) What effect does the view from the top of the eminence have on Elizabeth?

- A) It overwhelms her with its grandeur
- B) It disappoints her expectations

- C) It reinforces her admiration for Pemberley
- D) It leaves her feeling indifferent

8) Which character teases Elizabeth about her admiration for Pemberley?

- A) Mr. Darcy
- B) Mr. Gardiner
- C) Mrs. Gardiner
- D) Jane Bennet

9) How does Elizabeth's reaction to Pemberley reflect her character traits?

- A) Her wit and humor
- B) Her keen observation and appreciation of beauty
- C) Her timidity and shyness
- D) Her indifference and lack of interest

10) What does Elizabeth's feeling of "perturbation" as she approaches Pemberley suggest about her state of mind?

- A) She is nervous and unsure
- B) She is angry and frustrated
- C) She is calm and composed
- D) She is excited and happy

Historical Documents: 10 questions

The following passage is excerpted from "The Emancipation Proclamation" by Abraham Lincoln, originally issued in 1863.

On the first day of January, in the year of our Lord one thousand eight hundred and sixty-three, all persons held as slaves within any State or designated part of a State, the people whereof shall then be in rebellion against the United States, shall be then, thenceforward, and forever free; and the Executive Government of the United States will recognize and maintain the freedom of such persons.

Now, therefore I, Abraham Lincoln, President of the United States, by virtue of the power in me vested as Commander-in-Chief of the Army and Navy of the United States in time of actual armed rebellion, and as a fit and necessary war measure for suppressing said rebellion, do order and declare that all persons held as slaves within said designated States, and parts of States, are, and henceforward shall be free; and that the Executive government of the United States will recognize and maintain the freedom of said persons.

And upon this act, sincerely believed to be an act of justice, warranted by the Constitution, upon military necessity, I invoke the considerate judgment of mankind and the gracious favor of Almighty God.

By the President: Abraham Lincoln William H. Seward, Secretary of State.

11) On what date did the Emancipation Proclamation declare that all persons held as slaves would be free?

- A) December 25, 1862
- B) January 1, 1863
- C) July 4, 1863
- D) April 15, 1865

12) Which group of people was declared free by the Emancipation Proclamation?

- A) All slaves in the United States

- B) Slaves in states loyal to the Union
- C) Slaves in states or parts of states in rebellion against the United States
- D) All people in territories acquired after 1863

13) What power did Lincoln cite as giving him the authority to issue the Emancipation Proclamation?

- A) His role as President
- B) His role as Commander-in-Chief of the Army and Navy
- C) An act of Congress
- D) A Supreme Court ruling

14) How did Lincoln describe the Emancipation Proclamation in terms of its necessity?

- A) As an economic necessity
- B) As a political necessity
- C) As a military necessity
- D) As a social necessity

15) What did Lincoln invoke at the end of the Emancipation Proclamation?

- A) The support of the Congress
- B) The judgment of mankind and the favor of Almighty God
- C) The approval of the Supreme Court
- D) The endorsement of foreign governments

16) Who was the Secretary of State at the time of the Emancipation Proclamation?

- A) Edwin M. Stanton

- B) William H. Seward
- C) Salmon P. Chase
- D) Gideon Welles

17) How did Lincoln describe the act of issuing the Emancipation Proclamation?

- A) As a controversial political move
- B) As an act of economic reform
- C) As an act of justice
- D) As an act of defiance

18) What did the Executive Government of the United States commit to doing for those declared free by the Emancipation Proclamation?

- A) Providing financial compensation
- B) Recognizing and maintaining their freedom
- C) Offering them employment
- D) Relocating them to free states

19) According to the passage, what justified the Emancipation Proclamation under the Constitution?

- A) Economic necessity
- B) Social equality
- C) Military necessity
- D) Political pressure

20) Who is the author of the Emancipation Proclamation?

- A) William H. Seward
- B) Abraham Lincoln
- C) Ulysses S. Grant

- D) Andrew Johnson

Social Sciences: 10 questions

The following passage is adapted from "The Tipping Point: How Little Things Can Make a Big Difference" by Malcolm Gladwell, originally published in 2000.

In the mid-1990s, the city of Baltimore saw a dramatic rise in the popularity of an unusual item: the Hush Puppies shoe. What had once been a fading brand suddenly became the must-have accessory for the hip and trendy. This surge in popularity, however, wasn't due to a large-scale advertising campaign or a major celebrity endorsement. Instead, it began with a handful of kids in the East Village and Soho neighborhoods of New York City who started wearing the shoes simply because they liked them.

The phenomenon that led to this resurgence is what Malcolm Gladwell calls "The Tipping Point." It's the moment when an idea, trend, or social behavior crosses a threshold, tips, and spreads like wildfire. Understanding how and why tipping points occur can help explain social change and innovation.

One key factor in reaching a tipping point is the role of "Connectors." Connectors are people who know large numbers of people and who are in the habit of making introductions. They are the social equivalent of a computer network hub. By linking people who would not otherwise know each other, they create the conditions for ideas to spread.

Another crucial factor is the presence of "Mavens." Mavens are information specialists, or people we rely upon to connect us with new information. They accumulate knowledge, especially about the marketplace, and know how to share it with others. They are the data banks, the people with the inside scoop. When they find out about a trend, they pass it on to the Connectors, who then spread it further.

The third important factor is the "Salesmen." These are the persuaders, the charismatic people who can take an idea and convince others to adopt it. They have powerful negotiation skills, and their enthusiasm and likability make them highly influential.

The interplay of these three types of people—Connectors, Mavens, and Salesmen—creates the environment where tipping points are reached. Small, seemingly insignificant events can trigger massive changes when these key individuals are involved. This is the essence of the tipping point: small actions, when performed by the right people, can lead to large-scale social transformations.

Understanding the dynamics of tipping points helps us grasp the complexity of social change and highlights the importance of certain individuals in influencing trends and behaviors. This knowledge can be applied to everything from marketing campaigns to political movements, emphasizing the power of individuals and small groups in shaping society.

21) What event sparked the resurgence of Hush Puppies shoes in the mid-1990s?

- A) A large-scale advertising campaign
- B) A major celebrity endorsement
- C) Kids in the East Village and Soho wearing the shoes
- D) A collaboration with a high-fashion designer

22) According to Malcolm Gladwell, what is a "Tipping Point"?

- A) The peak of a marketing campaign
- B) A moment when an idea, trend, or behavior spreads rapidly
- C) The decline of a popular trend
- D) A significant drop in consumer interest

23) Who are "Connectors" according to the passage?

- A) People who create advertising campaigns
- B) Individuals who know large numbers of people and make intro-
ductions
- C) Celebrities who endorse products
- D) Experts who develop new products

24) What role do "Mavens" play in reaching a tipping point?

- A) They persuade others to adopt new ideas
- B) They create new trends
- C) They accumulate and share knowledge about the marketplace
- D) They finance marketing campaigns

25) How do "Salesmen" contribute to the spread of an idea?

- A) By developing marketing strategies
- B) By using their charisma to persuade others to adopt the idea
- C) By financing the production of new products
- D) By designing advertisements

26) What is the primary characteristic of a Connector?

- A) Creativity in marketing
- B) Knowledge accumulation
- C) Charisma and persuasion skills
- D) Extensive social networks and the habit of making introductions

27) What is the main idea of the concept "The Tipping Point" as described by Gladwell?

- A) Large-scale changes require significant investments

- B) Small actions by key individuals can lead to large-scale social transformations
- C) Advertising is the most effective way to spread ideas
- D) Trends only spread through celebrity endorsements

28) Which of the following best describes the relationship between Connectors, Mavens, and Salesmen?

- A) They compete with each other to spread ideas
- B) They work independently without influencing each other
- C) They collaborate and complement each other to reach a tipping point
- D) They are all equally unimportant in spreading ideas

29) Why are small actions by the right people significant in reaching a tipping point?

- A) Because they involve large financial investments
- B) Because they can trigger massive changes
- C) Because they always lead to success
- D) Because they are easy to measure and control

30) What does understanding the dynamics of tipping points help us achieve?

- A) Grasp the complexity of social change and the importance of individuals in influencing trends
- B) Create more effective advertising campaigns
- C) Identify which products will fail in the market
- D) Predict financial market fluctuations

Natural Sciences: 10 questions

The following passage is adapted from "The Gene: An Intimate History" by Siddhartha Mukherjee, originally published in 2016.

The gene is the fundamental unit of heredity, and understanding its function is crucial to comprehending the complexity of life. Genes are segments of DNA that carry instructions for the synthesis of proteins, which are essential for the structure and function of all living organisms.

The discovery of the double helix structure of DNA by James Watson and Francis Crick in 1953 marked a pivotal moment in the field of genetics. This structure revealed how genetic information is stored and replicated. DNA consists of two strands that coil around each other, forming a double helix. Each strand is composed of nucleotides, which are the building blocks of DNA. The sequence of these nucleotides encodes genetic information.

Genes operate through a process called gene expression, which involves transcription and translation. During transcription, the DNA sequence of a gene is copied into messenger RNA (mRNA). The mRNA then travels from the nucleus to the cytoplasm, where it serves as a template for protein synthesis during translation. Ribosomes read the mRNA sequence and assemble the corresponding amino acids into a polypeptide chain, which folds into a functional protein.

Mutations, or changes in the DNA sequence, can affect gene function. Some mutations are harmless, while others can lead to genetic disorders or diseases. For example, a mutation in the gene responsible for producing hemoglobin can result in sickle cell anemia, a condition characterized by abnormally shaped red blood cells.

Advances in genetic research have led to significant break-throughs in medicine and biotechnology. The Human Genome

Project, completed in 2003, mapped the entire human genome, providing valuable insights into the genetic basis of many diseases. This knowledge has paved the way for personalized medicine, where treatments are tailored to an individual's genetic profile.

CRISPR-Cas9, a revolutionary gene-editing technology, has further transformed the field of genetics. This tool allows scientists to precisely modify specific genes, offering potential cures for genetic disorders. However, the ethical implications of gene editing, particularly in humans, have sparked widespread debate.

Mukherjee's exploration of the gene illuminates the profound impact of genetics on our understanding of biology and medicine. As we continue to unlock the secrets of the gene, we gain greater insight into the mechanisms of life and the potential to address some of the most challenging medical issues of our time.

31) What is the fundamental unit of heredity?

- A) Protein
- B) DNA
- C) Gene
- D) Nucleotide

32) What significant discovery did James Watson and Francis Crick make in 1953?

- A) The function of proteins
- B) The process of transcription
- C) The double helix structure of DNA
- D) The genetic code of humans

33) What are the building blocks of DNA?

- A) Proteins

- B) Nucleotides
- C) Amino acids
- D) Ribosomes

34) During transcription, what is the DNA sequence of a gene copied into?

- A) Protein
- B) Ribosome
- C) Messenger RNA (mRNA)
- D) Polypeptide chain

35) Where does mRNA travel after being transcribed in the nucleus?

- A) To another part of the nucleus
- B) To the cytoplasm
- C) To the mitochondria
- D) To the cell membrane

36) What role do ribosomes play in gene expression?

- A) They transcribe DNA into mRNA
- B) They mutate DNA sequences
- C) They read the mRNA sequence and assemble amino acids into a polypeptide chain
- D) They transport mRNA from the nucleus to the cytoplasm

37) What can mutations in the DNA sequence lead to?

- A) Enhanced protein function
- B) Increased genetic diversity
- C) Genetic disorders or diseases
- D) Improved gene expression

38) What was a major accomplishment of the Human Genome Project?

- A) Discovering the structure of DNA
- B) Mapping the entire human genome
- C) Developing the CRISPR-Cas9 technology
- D) Finding a cure for sickle cell anemia

39) What is CRISPR-Cas9 used for in genetic research?

- A) Mapping the human genome
- B) Diagnosing genetic disorders
- C) Precisely modifying specific genes
- D) Transcribing DNA into mRNA

40) What ethical concern is associated with gene editing, particularly in humans?

- A) The high cost of the technology
- B) The potential for environmental harm
- C) The possibility of unintended genetic mutations
- D) The ethical implications of modifying human genes

Dual Passages (Literature, Social Science, or Science): 10 questions

Passage 1

The following passage is adapted from "The Selfish Gene" by Richard Dawkins, originally published in 1976.

> *Genes are the fundamental units of natural selection. In the competition for survival, those genes that are best at getting themselves replicated will spread through populations. This process, known as natural selection, operates at the level of the gene, not*

the species or individual.

The "selfish gene" concept does not imply that genes are driven by a conscious will. Rather, genes that increase the chances of their own replication will, over time, become more common in a population. This can lead to behaviors in organisms that appear altruistic but are actually driven by the underlying genetic imperative to reproduce.

One example of this is kin selection. Kin selection is a form of natural selection that favors behaviors benefiting relatives, even at a cost to the individual. By helping relatives, an organism ensures that copies of its own genes are passed on to the next generation. This explains why many social animals, such as bees and ants, exhibit behaviors that benefit their colonies over individual interests.

Dawkins argues that understanding evolution at the level of genes provides a clearer picture of the processes shaping the natural world. It shifts the focus from individuals and species to the genetic underpinnings of behavior and adaptation.

Passage 2

The following passage is adapted from "The Extended Phenotype" by Richard Dawkins, originally published in 1982.

The concept of the phenotype extends beyond the physical body of an organism to include all effects a gene has on its environment. This extended phenotype encompasses behaviors and structures created by organisms, which can influence the success of the genes responsible for them.

One striking example of the extended phenotype is the beaver dam. Beavers build dams to create ponds, which serve as safe environments for raising their young. The construction of a dam is a behavior driven by beaver genes, and the resulting pond significantly impacts the beaver's environment. This modification of the environment enhances the beaver's survival and reproductive success, demonstrating the gene's influence beyond the individual organism.

Another example is the manipulation of host behavior by parasites. Certain parasites can alter the behavior of their hosts to increase the chances of their own transmission. For instance, the parasitic wasp Hymenoepimecis argyraphaga injects its venom into a spider, causing the spider to spin a special web that supports the wasp's cocoon. This behavioral change benefits the parasite, illustrating how the extended phenotype can operate through host manipulation.

The extended phenotype concept broadens our understanding of evolutionary biology by highlighting the ways genes can influence environments and other organisms. It underscores the interconnectedness of life and the diverse strategies genes employ to ensure their replication.

41) Which concept is central to both passages?

- A) The role of species in natural selection
- B) The importance of genetic replication
- C) The influence of environment on behavior
- D) The conscious will of genes

42) According to Passage 1, what does the "selfish gene" concept imply?

- A) Genes are conscious entities
- B) Genes that increase replication chances will become more common
- C) Species survival is more important than gene replication
- D) Individual organisms drive natural selection

43) What example does Passage 1 provide to illustrate kin selection?

- A) Beaver dams
- B) Parasitic wasps
- C) Bees and ants benefiting their colonies
- D) Host manipulation by parasites

44) How does Passage 2 define the extended phenotype?

- A) Physical characteristics of an organism
- B) Effects of a gene beyond the physical body, including environmental modifications
- C) Genetic mutations that alter physical traits
- D) Natural selection favoring species over individuals

45) What example from Passage 2 illustrates the concept of the extended phenotype?

- A) Kin selection in social animals
- B) The construction of beaver dams
- C) Altruistic behaviors in bees
- D) Genetic replication in parasites

46) Which behavior is driven by genes according to both passages?

- A) Random mutations
- B) Altruistic behaviors that appear to benefit others
- C) Environmental changes that benefit individual organisms
- D) Conscious decisions to help relatives

47) What does Passage 1 suggest about understanding evolution at the level of genes?

- A) It complicates the study of natural selection
- B) It clarifies the processes shaping the natural world

- C) It undermines the role of individual organisms
- D) It focuses primarily on species-level adaptations

48) How does the concept of the extended phenotype broaden our understanding of evolutionary biology according to Passage 2?

- A) By emphasizing the importance of species survival
- B) By highlighting how genes can influence environments and other organisms
- C) By showing that genes have no impact on behavior
- D) By proving that only physical traits matter in evolution

49) In Passage 2, what is the impact of the beaver dam on the beaver's environment?

- A) It provides no significant benefit
- B) It enhances the beaver's survival and reproductive success
- C) It decreases the beaver's chances of finding food
- D) It harms other species in the environment

50) Which of the following statements is supported by both passages?

- A) Genes have no influence on behavior
- B) The environment plays no role in genetic success
- C) Genes can drive behaviors that seem to benefit others but ultimately serve their own replication
- D) Natural selection operates primarily at the species level

B. Writing and Language Test

- **Number of Questions:** 44
- **Time Allotted:** 35 minutes
- **Format:** Multiple-choice

· **Passages:** 4 (each passage 11 questions)

Careers: 11 questions

The Evolution of a Software Engineer

(1) The software engineering profession has undergone significant changes since its inception. (2) In the early days of computing, software development was a niche field primarily occupied by mathematicians and scientists. (3) Today, it is a diverse and dynamic profession that is integral to almost every industry.

(4) One of the earliest software engineers was Margaret Hamilton, who played a pivotal role in the Apollo space program. (5) Hamilton led the team that developed the onboard flight software for NASA's Apollo missions, which included the historic Apollo 11 moon landing in 1969. (6) Her work was critical in ensuring the success of the missions and demonstrated the importance of software reliability and precision.

(7) As technology advanced, the demand for software engineers grew exponentially. (8) The 1980s and 1990s saw the rise of personal computing, which created new opportunities for software development. (9) During this time, software engineers were responsible for creating operating systems, applications, and games that made computers accessible to the general public.

(10) The internet revolution of the late 1990s and early 2000s further transformed the field. (11) Software engineers began developing web-based applications, online services, and e-commerce platforms that connected people and businesses around the world. (12) This era also saw the emergence of open-source software, which encouraged collaboration and innovation within the engineering community.

(13) Today, software engineers continue to drive technological advancements in various fields, including artificial intelligence,

cybersecurity, and mobile computing. (14) The profession requires a strong foundation in computer science principles, as well as skills in problem-solving, collaboration, and continuous learning. (15) As technology evolves, so too must software engineers adapt to new tools, languages, and methodologies.

(16) The role of a software engineer is not limited to writing code. (17) Engineers often work closely with stakeholders to understand user needs, design user-friendly interfaces, and ensure the scalability and security of their applications. (18) They must also stay current with industry trends and best practices to remain competitive in the job market.

(19) Software engineering is a profession that offers numerous career paths and opportunities for growth. (20) Engineers can specialize in areas such as front-end development, back-end development, data science, or DevOps. (21) Many also choose to advance into leadership roles, managing teams and projects or starting their own technology ventures.

(22) The impact of software engineers on society is profound. (23) Their work shapes how we communicate, work, and live, driving innovation and improving the quality of life. (24) As technology continues to evolve, the need for skilled software engineers will only increase, making it an exciting and rewarding career choice for those with a passion for technology and problem-solving.

51) Which choice best describes what happens in the passage?

- A) The passage outlines the history and evolution of the software engineering profession and its impact on society.
- B) The passage provides a detailed biography of Margaret Hamilton.
- C) The passage critiques the challenges faced by modern software engineers.
- D) The passage discusses the decline of the software engineering profession.

52) Which choice provides the most accurate interpretation of the data in sentence 2?

- A) Software development has always been a popular field.
- B) Software development was initially a niche field primarily occupied by mathematicians and scientists.
- C) Software development was not important in the early days of computing.
- D) Software development was primarily done by hobbyists.

53) Which version of the underlined portion of sentence 3 best maintains the tone and style of the passage?

- A) NO CHANGE
- B) Nowadays, it's a diverse and exciting job that's crucial to pretty much every industry.
- C) Nowadays, it's a cool job that lots of industries need.
- D) Today, it is a diverse and dynamic profession that is integral to almost every industry.

54) In context, which is the best way to combine sentences 4 and 5?

- A) One of the earliest software engineers was Margaret Hamilton, and she played a pivotal role in the Apollo space program, leading the team that developed the onboard flight software for NASA's Apollo missions, including the historic Apollo 11 moon landing in 1969.
- B) One of the earliest software engineers was Margaret Hamilton, she played a pivotal role in the Apollo space program by leading the team that developed the onboard flight software for NASA's Apollo missions, which included the historic Apollo 11 moon landing in 1969.
- C) One of the earliest software engineers was Margaret Hamilton; she played a pivotal role in the Apollo space program, leading the team that developed the onboard flight software for NASA's Apollo

missions, including the historic Apollo 11 moon landing in 1969.

- D) One of the earliest software engineers was Margaret Hamilton who played a pivotal role in the Apollo space program, she led the team that developed the onboard flight software for NASA's Apollo missions including the historic Apollo 11 moon landing in 1969.

55) Which choice provides the most logical introduction to the third paragraph (sentences 7-9)?

- A) Software engineering is a highly demanding field.
- B) As technology advanced, the demand for software engineers grew exponentially.
- C) Software engineering requires continuous learning and adaptation.
- D) Many people were unaware of the importance of software engineering.

56) In sentence 12, what is the purpose of mentioning open-source software?

- A) To highlight a significant development in the software engineering community that encouraged collaboration and innovation
- B) To criticize the open-source software movement
- C) To suggest that open-source software is no longer relevant
- D) To emphasize that open-source software hindered the progress of software engineering

57) Which choice best maintains the tone of the passage in sentence 14?

- A) NO CHANGE
- B) The profession requires you to know computer science principles really well, and also be good at problem-solving, teamwork, and

always learning new stuff.

- C) The profession requires a solid foundation in computer science principles, as well as skills in problem-solving, collaboration, and continuous learning.
- D) The profession requires knowing computer science principles, problem-solving skills, teamwork, and staying current with technology.

58) Which sentence, if added to the sixth paragraph, would best support the information presented in that paragraph?

- A) Software engineers also need to have good communication skills.
- B) Software engineers need to understand the business aspects of the projects they work on.
- C) Software engineers also develop software for non-computing devices.
- D) Software engineers must be proficient in multiple programming languages.

59) The author wants to add the following sentence to the seventh paragraph:

"These specializations allow engineers to focus on their areas of interest and expertise, leading to more efficient and innovative solutions." Where would this sentence best fit?

- A) Before sentence 19
- B) After sentence 19
- C) Before sentence 20
- D) After sentence 20

60) In context, the word "profound" in sentence 22 most nearly means:

- A) Slight

- B) Insignificant
- C) Deep
- D) Temporary

61) Which choice best concludes the passage?

- A) The software engineering profession is likely to disappear in the future.
- B) As technology continues to evolve, the need for skilled software engineers will only increase, making it an exciting and rewarding career choice for those with a passion for technology and problem-solving.
- C) Many people are unaware of the contributions of software engineers.
- D) The challenges faced by software engineers are numerous and daunting.

History/Social Studies: 11 questions

The Harlem Renaissance: A Cultural Awakening

(1) The Harlem Renaissance was a cultural, social, and artistic explosion that took place in Harlem, New York, during the early 20th century. (2) Spanning the 1920s and 1930s, this movement marked a period of unprecedented creativity among African American artists, writers, musicians, and thinkers. (3) It was a time when African American culture was celebrated and elevated, influencing American culture as a whole.

(4) The Great Migration, which saw millions of African Americans move from the rural South to urban centers in the North, set the stage for the Harlem Renaissance. (5) Harlem, a neighborhood in Manhattan, became a hub for these new arrivals, fostering a vibrant community that nurtured artistic expression. (6) This concentration

of talent and ambition led to a flourishing of creativity that resonated across the nation.

(7) Literature played a significant role in the Harlem Renaissance. (8) Writers such as Langston Hughes, Zora Neale Hurston, and Claude McKay produced works that explored themes of racial identity, pride, and resilience. (9) Their writings challenged stereotypes and provided a voice for the African American experience. (10) Hughes, in particular, became known for his poetry that celebrated black life and culture in a way that was accessible and engaging.

(11) Music was another key component of the Harlem Renaissance. (12) Jazz, blues, and gospel music thrived in the clubs and theaters of Harlem, with legendary figures such as Duke Ellington, Louis Armstrong, and Bessie Smith leading the way. (13) The Cotton Club and the Apollo Theater became famous venues where both black and white audiences could enjoy the innovative sounds of African American musicians.

(14) Visual arts also flourished during this period. (15) Artists like Aaron Douglas and Augusta Savage created works that depicted African American life and history with a sense of pride and beauty. (16) Their art was not only a form of personal expression but also a means of challenging and redefining the narrative surrounding African American identity.

(17) The Harlem Renaissance extended beyond the arts to encompass social and political thought. (18) Intellectuals such as W.E.B. Du Bois and Alain Locke promoted the idea of the "New Negro," advocating for racial equality and the upliftment of African Americans through education and cultural development. (19) Their writings and speeches inspired a generation to strive for greater social and political progress.

(20) The impact of the Harlem Renaissance was far-reaching. (21) It helped to lay the groundwork for the Civil Rights Movement of the 1950s and 1960s by fostering a sense of pride and self-worth among African Americans. (22) The cultural achievements of this

period continue to influence and inspire artists and thinkers today.

(23) The Harlem Renaissance was a remarkable era that show-cased the richness and diversity of African American culture. (24) It was a time of bold experimentation and profound creativity that left an indelible mark on American history and culture. (25) The legacy of the Harlem Renaissance serves as a testament to the power of art and culture in shaping society and promoting change.

62) Which choice best describes what happens in the passage?

- A) The passage outlines the history and significance of the Harlem Renaissance and its impact on American culture.
- B) The passage provides a detailed biography of Langston Hughes.
- C) The passage critiques the music produced during the Harlem Renaissance.
- D) The passage discusses the decline of African American culture in the 20th century.

63) Which choice provides the most accurate interpretation of the data in sentence 2?

- A) The Harlem Renaissance was a brief and insignificant movement.
- B) The Harlem Renaissance marked a period of unprecedented creativity among African American artists, writers, musicians, and thinkers.
- C) The Harlem Renaissance only impacted the visual arts.
- D) The Harlem Renaissance occurred in the late 19th century.

64) Which version of the underlined portion of sentence 3 best maintains the tone and style of the passage?

- A) NO CHANGE
- B) It was a time when African American culture was super popular

and cool.
- C) It was a time when African American culture was highly regarded and appreciated.
- D) It was a time when African American culture was all the rage.

65) In context, which is the best way to combine sentences 4 and 5?

- A) The Great Migration, which saw millions of African Americans move from the rural South to urban centers in the North, set the stage for the Harlem Renaissance, and Harlem, a neighborhood in Manhattan, became a hub for these new arrivals, fostering a vibrant community that nurtured artistic expression.
- B) The Great Migration, which saw millions of African Americans move from the rural South to urban centers in the North, set the stage for the Harlem Renaissance; Harlem, a neighborhood in Manhattan, became a hub for these new arrivals, fostering a vibrant community that nurtured artistic expression.
- C) The Great Migration, which saw millions of African Americans move from the rural South to urban centers in the North, set the stage for the Harlem Renaissance; Harlem, a neighborhood in Manhattan became a hub for these new arrivals, fostering a vibrant community that nurtured artistic expression.
- D) The Great Migration, which saw millions of African Americans move from the rural South to urban centers in the North set the stage for the Harlem Renaissance, and Harlem, a neighborhood in Manhattan, became a hub for these new arrivals, fostering a vibrant community that nurtured artistic expression.

66) Which choice provides the most logical introduction to the third paragraph (sentences 7-10)?

- A) Many writers were involved in the Harlem Renaissance.
- B) Literature played a significant role in the Harlem Renaissance.

- C) Langston Hughes was the best writer of the Harlem Renaissance.
- D) The Harlem Renaissance was known for its music and dance.

67) In sentence 12, what is the purpose of mentioning the Cotton Club and the Apollo Theater?

- A) To highlight the venues where African American musicians performed during the Harlem Renaissance
- B) To criticize the segregation policies of the time
- C) To suggest that these venues were the only places to hear jazz music
- D) To emphasize the decline of these venues in modern times

68) Which choice best maintains the tone of the passage in sentence 14?

- A) NO CHANGE
- B) Visual arts also took off during this period.
- C) Visual arts also blossomed during this period.
- D) Visual arts also had a moment during this period.

69) Which sentence, if added to the fifth paragraph, would best support the information presented in that paragraph?

- A) Many people enjoy jazz music today.
- B) Visual artists of the Harlem Renaissance often faced financial difficulties.
- C) The visual arts included painting, sculpture, and photography, all of which were used to express the African American experience.
- D) Many artists preferred to work in Harlem because of the supportive community.

70) The author wants to add the following sentence to the sixth

paragraph:

"Their ideas helped to galvanize the movement and push for broader social reforms." Where would this sentence best fit?

- A) Before sentence 17
- B) After sentence 17
- C) Before sentence 18
- D) After sentence 18

71) In context, the word "profound" in sentence 24 most nearly means:

- A) Shallow
- B) Significant
- C) Temporary
- D) Unnoticed

72) Which choice best concludes the passage?

- A) The Harlem Renaissance was a brief period that had little lasting impact.
- B) The legacy of the Harlem Renaissance serves as a testament to the power of art and culture in shaping society and promoting change.
- C) The Harlem Renaissance was an important part of American history but is now mostly forgotten.
- D) The Harlem Renaissance was a regional movement that only affected Harlem.

Humanities: 11 questions

The Impact of the Renaissance on Art and Culture

(1) The Renaissance, which spanned roughly from the 14th to the 17th century, was a period of profound cultural, artistic, and

intellectual revival in Europe. (2) Originating in Italy, the Renaissance spread throughout Europe, marking the transition from the
medieval period to the early modern age. (3) This era is celebrated
for its advancements in art, literature, science, and philosophy, and
it laid the foundation for many aspects of contemporary Western
culture.

(4) One of the hallmarks of the Renaissance was its emphasis
on humanism, a cultural and intellectual movement that focused
on the study of classical antiquity. (5) Humanists believed in the
potential of human beings to achieve greatness and sought to
revive the classical ideals of beauty, balance, and harmony. (6)
This renewed interest in ancient Greek and Roman texts led to a
flourishing of arts and letters.

(7) Renaissance art is characterized by its focus on realism and the
human form. (8) Artists such as Leonardo da Vinci, Michelangelo,
and Raphael revolutionized the field by incorporating perspective,
anatomy, and emotion into their works. (9) Leonardo's "Mona
Lisa" and "The Last Supper" exemplify the use of perspective and
human emotion, while Michelangelo's sculptures, such as "David"
and the Sistine Chapel ceiling, display a deep understanding of
human anatomy and movement.

(10) The use of perspective, which creates the illusion of depth
on a flat surface, was a significant breakthrough in Renaissance
art. (11) This technique allowed artists to create more realistic
and three-dimensional compositions. (12) Filippo Brunelleschi
is credited with developing linear perspective, which became a
fundamental principle of Western art.

(13) Literature also flourished during the Renaissance, with
writers such as Dante Alighieri, Geoffrey Chaucer, and William
Shakespeare producing works that are still celebrated today. (14)
Dante's "Divine Comedy," written in the early 14th century, explores themes of sin, redemption, and divine justice through an
allegorical journey. (15) Chaucer's "The Canterbury Tales" provides

a vivid portrayal of medieval society through its diverse cast of characters and their stories. *(16)* Shakespeare's plays, such as "Hamlet," "Macbeth," and "Romeo and Juliet," delve into complex human emotions and conflicts, making them timeless classics.

(17) The Renaissance also saw significant advancements in science and exploration. *(18)* Figures such as Nicolaus Copernicus, Galileo Galilei, and Johannes Kepler challenged traditional views of the cosmos and laid the groundwork for modern astronomy. *(19)* The invention of the printing press by Johannes Gutenberg in the mid-15th century revolutionized the spread of knowledge, making books more accessible and facilitating the dissemination of new ideas.

(20) The Renaissance was not confined to Italy; it spread to other parts of Europe, including France, England, and the Netherlands. *(21)* Each region contributed its unique perspective to the move-ment, resulting in a rich tapestry of cultural achievements. *(22)* In the Netherlands, artists like Jan van Eyck and Hieronymus Bosch developed new techniques in oil painting and created intricate, detailed works that explored both religious and secular themes.

(23) The impact of the Renaissance on modern Western culture is profound. *(24)* Its emphasis on individual potential, scientific inquiry, and artistic expression continues to influence contemporary thought and creativity. *(25)* By studying the Renaissance, we gain a deeper understanding of the cultural roots of the modern world and the enduring legacy of this transformative period.

73) Which choice best describes what happens in the passage?

- A) The passage outlines the history and significance of the Renais-sance and its impact on art, literature, science, and culture.
- B) The passage provides a detailed biography of Leonardo da Vinci.
- C) The passage critiques the scientific advancements of the Renais-sance.

- D) The passage discusses the decline of Renaissance art in modern times.

74) Which choice provides the most accurate interpretation of the data in sentence 2?

- A) The Renaissance was a brief period with limited influence.
- B) The Renaissance marked the transition from the medieval period to the early modern age and spread throughout Europe.
- C) The Renaissance was primarily confined to Italy.
- D) The Renaissance did not significantly impact Western culture.

75) Which version of the underlined portion of sentence 3 best maintains the tone and style of the passage?

- A) NO CHANGE
- B) This era is known for its advancements in art, literature, science, and philosophy and laid the groundwork for many aspects of today's Western culture.
- C) This time is celebrated for cool stuff in art, literature, science, and philosophy and helped shape modern Western culture.
- D) This era is noted for its contributions to art, literature, science, and philosophy, and it influenced many aspects of today's Western culture.

76) In context, which is the best way to combine sentences 7 and 8?

- A) Renaissance art is characterized by its focus on realism and the human form, and artists such as Leonardo da Vinci, Michelangelo, and Raphael revolutionized the field by incorporating perspective, anatomy, and emotion into their works.
- B) Renaissance art is characterized by its focus on realism and the human form, so artists such as Leonardo da Vinci, Michelangelo,

and Raphael revolutionized the field by incorporating perspective, anatomy, and emotion into their works.

- C) Renaissance art is characterized by its focus on realism and the human form, therefore artists such as Leonardo da Vinci, Michelangelo, and Raphael revolutionized the field by incorporating perspective, anatomy, and emotion into their works.
- D) Renaissance art is characterized by its focus on realism and the human form; thus, artists such as Leonardo da Vinci, Michelangelo, and Raphael revolutionized the field by incorporating perspective, anatomy, and emotion into their works.

77) Which choice provides the most logical introduction to the fourth paragraph (sentences 13-16)?

- A) Many writers were involved in the Renaissance.
- B) Literature also flourished during the Renaissance.
- C) Dante Alighieri, Geoffrey Chaucer, and William Shakespeare were great writers.
- D) The Renaissance was known for its music and dance.

78) In sentence 12, what is the purpose of mentioning Filippo Brunelleschi?

- A) To highlight the individual who developed linear perspective, a fundamental principle of Western art
- B) To criticize Brunelleschi's contributions to Renaissance art
- C) To suggest that Brunelleschi's work was not influential
- D) To emphasize that linear perspective was unimportant in Renaissance art

79) Which choice best maintains the tone of the passage in sentence 22?

- A) NO CHANGE
- B) In the Netherlands, artists like Jan van Eyck and Hieronymus Bosch did some really cool stuff with oil painting and made very detailed works that looked at both religious and secular themes.
- C) In the Netherlands, artists like Jan van Eyck and Hieronymus Bosch developed new techniques in oil painting and created intricate, detailed works that explored both religious and secular themes.
- D) In the Netherlands, artists like Jan van Eyck and Hieronymus Bosch worked on new ways to paint and made some really detailed and cool art about religious and everyday themes.

80) Which sentence, if added to the seventh paragraph, would best support the information presented in that paragraph?

- A) Art in the Netherlands was very different from art in Italy.
- B) The Renaissance had a significant impact on European culture.
- C) Many regions in Europe embraced Renaissance ideals and made unique contributions.
- D) The Renaissance was a time of great change and innovation in Europe.

81) The author wants to add the following sentence to the eighth paragraph:
"These contributions laid the groundwork for future scientific discoveries and advancements." Where would this sentence best fit?

- A) Before sentence 17
- B) After sentence 17
- C) Before sentence 18
- D) After sentence 18

82) In context, the word "profound" in sentence 23 most nearly means:

- A) Deep
- B) Superficial
- C) Temporary
- D) Insignificant

83) Which choice best concludes the passage?

- A) The Renaissance was a period of time that is often overlooked today.
- B) By studying the Renaissance, we gain a deeper understanding of the cultural roots of the modern world and the enduring legacy of this transformative period.
- C) Many people today do not realize the impact of the Renaissance on modern culture.
- D) The Renaissance was a time of artistic and cultural achievement that ended in the 17th century.

Science: 11 questions

The Impact of Climate Change on Coral Reefs

(1) Coral reefs are among the most diverse and productive ecosystems on Earth, providing habitats for countless marine species and supporting millions of people who depend on them for food and livelihoods. (2) However, these vital ecosystems are increasingly threatened by climate change, which poses significant challenges to their survival.

(3) One of the primary threats to coral reefs is rising sea temperatures. (4) Coral reefs are sensitive to small changes in temperature, and when ocean waters become too warm, corals undergo a process known as coral bleaching. (5) During bleaching events, corals expel the colorful algae living within their tissues, causing them to turn white and become more susceptible to disease and mortality. (6)

Bleaching can lead to widespread coral death and the degradation of reef ecosystems.

(7) Another consequence of climate change is ocean acidification. (8) As the concentration of carbon dioxide (CO2) in the atmosphere increases, more CO2 is absorbed by the oceans, leading to a decrease in pH levels. (9) This acidification makes it harder for corals and other marine organisms to build their calcium carbonate skeletons, essential for their survival and the maintenance of reef structure.

(10) Climate change also exacerbates extreme weather events, such as hurricanes and cyclones, which can physically damage coral reefs. (11) These storms can break apart coral structures and disrupt the delicate balance of reef ecosystems, making them more vulnerable to further stressors.

(12) The loss of coral reefs has profound consequences for marine biodiversity and human communities. (13) Coral reefs provide essential habitats for a quarter of all marine species, including fish, mollusks, and crustaceans. (14) Many of these species rely on reefs for feeding, breeding, and shelter, and their decline threatens global fisheries and food security.

(15) Coral reefs also provide valuable ecosystem services to coastal communities, such as shoreline protection from storms and erosion. (16) They support tourism and recreation industries, generating billions of dollars in revenue annually. (17) The loss of coral reefs can have devastating economic impacts on local economies that depend on reef-related activities.

(18) Efforts to protect coral reefs are underway, including marine protected areas, sustainable fishing practices, and initiatives to reduce greenhouse gas emissions. (19) These efforts aim to increase the resilience of coral reefs to climate change and other stressors, preserving their ecological and socioeconomic benefits for future generations.

(20) Continued research and monitoring are essential to better understand the complex interactions between climate change and

coral reefs. (21) By studying how corals respond to environmental stressors, scientists can develop strategies to mitigate the impacts of climate change and promote the long-term health and sustainability of these invaluable ecosystems.

(22) The fate of coral reefs depends on global efforts to address climate change and reduce carbon emissions. (23) Protecting these fragile ecosystems is not only a matter of environmental conservation but also a crucial step towards ensuring the health and well-being of marine life and coastal communities worldwide.

84) Which choice best describes what happens in the passage?

- A) The passage outlines the significance of coral reefs and the threats posed by climate change, as well as efforts to protect these ecosystems.
- B) The passage provides a detailed biography of a marine biologist.
- C) The passage critiques the tourism industry's impact on coral reefs.
- D) The passage discusses the economic benefits of coral reefs without mentioning climate change.

85) Which choice provides the most accurate interpretation of the data in sentence 2?

- A) Coral reefs are no longer threatened by climate change.
- B) Climate change poses significant challenges to the survival of coral reefs.
- C) Coral reefs are adapting well to climate change.
- D) Climate change benefits coral reefs by increasing their diversity.

86) Which version of the underlined portion of sentence 3 best maintains the tone and style of the passage?

- A) NO CHANGE

- B) One of the primary threats to coral reefs is that the ocean is getting too hot.
- C) One of the main issues for coral reefs is rising sea temperatures.
- D) One big problem for coral reefs is the warming of the seas.

87) In context, which is the best way to combine sentences 4 and 5?

- A) Coral reefs are sensitive to small changes in temperature, and when ocean waters become too warm, corals undergo a process known as coral bleaching, expelling the colorful algae living within their tissues, causing them to turn white and become more susceptible to disease and mortality.
- B) Coral reefs are sensitive to small changes in temperature; when ocean waters become too warm, corals undergo a process known as coral bleaching; they expel the colorful algae living within their tissues, causing them to turn white and become more susceptible to disease and mortality.
- C) Coral reefs are sensitive to small changes in temperature, and when ocean waters become too warm, corals undergo a process known as coral bleaching, which causes them to expel the colorful algae living within their tissues, turning white and becoming more susceptible to disease and mortality.
- D) Coral reefs are sensitive to small changes in temperature; and when ocean waters become too warm, corals undergo a process known as coral bleaching, causing them to expel the colorful algae living within their tissues, and they turn white and become more susceptible to disease and mortality.

88) Which choice provides the most logical introduction to the third paragraph (sentences 7-9)?

- A) Coral reefs are also impacted by human activities such as overfishing and pollution.

- B) Another consequence of climate change is ocean acidification.
- C) Climate change has no significant impact on coral reefs.
- D) Coral reefs are only threatened by rising sea temperatures.

89) In sentence 12, what is the purpose of mentioning marine biodiversity?

- A) To emphasize the variety of marine life that depends on coral reefs.
- B) To criticize the lack of biodiversity in marine ecosystems.
- C) To suggest that coral reefs are not important to marine species.
- D) To argue that marine biodiversity is not affected by climate change.

90) Which choice best maintains the tone of the passage in sentence 16?

- A) NO CHANGE
- B) They support tourism and recreation industries, bringing in tons of cash each year.
- C) They support tourism and recreation industries, generating significant revenue annually.
- D) They support tourism and recreation industries, making lots of money every year.

91) Which sentence, if added to the fifth paragraph, would best support the information presented in that paragraph?

- A) Coral reefs are beautiful and attract many visitors.
- B) The loss of coral reefs can lead to increased coastal erosion and vulnerability to storms.
- C) Many people enjoy visiting coral reefs during vacations.
- D) Coral reefs are important for scientific research.

92) The author wants to add the following sentence to the sixth

paragraph:

"These efforts are crucial for maintaining the health and resilience of coral reef ecosystems." Where would this sentence best fit?

- A) Before sentence 18
- B) After sentence 18
- C) Before sentence 19
- D) After sentence 19

93) In context, the word "profound" in sentence 12 most nearly means:

- A) Superficial
- B) Deep
- C) Temporary
- D) Insignificant

94) Which choice best concludes the passage?

- A) Protecting these fragile ecosystems is not only a matter of environmental conservation but also a crucial step towards ensuring the health and well-being of marine life and coastal communities worldwide.
- B) Coral reefs are beautiful and need to be saved.
- C) The threats to coral reefs are too great to overcome.
- D) Many people do not realize the importance of coral reefs.

2. Math

A. Math Test - No Calculator

- **Number of Questions:** 20
- **Time Allotted:** 25 minutes
- **Format:** Multiple-choice and grid-in

Heart of Algebra: 8 questions

95. Solve for y in terms of x:

$$3x + 4y - 12$$

- A) $y = \frac{12-3x}{4}$
- B) $y = \frac{12+3x}{4}$
- C) $y = \frac{3x-12}{4}$
- D) $y = \frac{12-4x}{3}$

96. If $2x - 3y = 6$ and $x + y = 4$, what is the value of x?

- A) 18/5
- B) 3/5
- C) 7/21
- D) 6/10

97. What is the solution to the system of equations:

$$2x + y = 7$$
$$3x - y = 8$$

- A) $(3, 1)$
- B) $(2, 1)$
- C) $(1, 5)$
- D) $(4, -1)$

98. Solve the inequality:

$$7 - 2x \leq 5$$

- A) $x \geq 1$
- B) $x \leq 1$
- C) $x \leq -1$
- D) $x \geq -1$

99. If $y - 4x - 3$ and $y - 2x + 1$, what is the value of x?

- A) 1
- B) 2
- C) 3
- D) 4

100. The difference of two numbers is 7. One number is twice the other. What are the numbers?

- A) 7 and 14
- B) 3.5 and 10.5
- C) 2 and 9
- D) 5 and 12

101. Find the value of x if $5x + 2 - 3x + 10$.

- A) 3
- B) 4
- C) 5
- D) 6

102. What is the solution to the equation $3(2x - 4) - 5x + 2$?

- A) 2
- B) 14
- C) 10
- D) 5

Problem Solving and Data Analysis: 3 questions

103. A baker uses 3 cups of flour for every 2 cups of sugar to make a batch of cookies. If the baker uses 12 cups of flour, how many cups of sugar are needed?

- A) 6
- B) 8
- C) 10
- D) 12

104. A car rental company charges a daily rental fee of $30 plus $0.25 per mile driven. If a customer drives 200 miles in one day, what is the total cost of the rental?

- A) $50
- B) $55
- C) $70
- D) $80

105. The scatter plot below shows the relationship between the number of hours studied and the scores on a test for a group of students. If the line of best fit is $y - 5x + 50$, what score can a student expect if they study for 4 hours?

- A) 60

- B) 70

- C) 80

- D) 90

Passport to Advanced Math: 6 questions

106. If $g(x) - 4x^3 - 6x^2 + 2x - 5$, what is $g(2)$?

- A) 7

- B) 5

- C) 1

- D) -1

107. Solve the equation for x: $5x^2 - 3x - 2 - 0$

- A) $x - -\frac{1}{2}$ or $x - \frac{2}{5}$
- B) $x - \frac{1}{2}$ or $x - -1$
- C) $x - -2$ or $x - \frac{3}{5}$
- D) $x - 1$ or $x - -\frac{2}{5}$

108. If $h(x) - 3x^2 - 2x + 4$, what is the value of $h'(x)$ when $x - 1$?

- A) 4

- B) 2

- C) 6

- D) 8

109. Which of the following is a solution to the inequality $3x + 2 \leq 5$?

- A) $x = 1$
- B) $x = -1$
- C) $x = 2$
- D) $x = 0$

110. Simplify the expression: $\frac{2x^2 - 8x + 6}{2x - 4}$

- A) $x - 1$
- B) $x - 2$
- C) $x - 3$
- D) $x - 4$

111. The function $f(x) = (x + 1)^2$ is reflected across the x-axis and then shifted 4 units down. What is the new function $g(x)$?

- A) $g(x) = -(x + 1)^2 - 4$
- B) $g(x) = -(x - 1)^2 + 4$
- C) $g(x) = (x + 1)^2 - 4$
- D) $g(x) = -(x + 1)^2 + 4$

Additional Topics in Math (geometry, trigonometry, etc.): 3 questions

112. What is the area of a triangle with a base of 10 units and a height of 12 units?

- A) 50 square units
- B) 60 square units
- C) 100 square units
- D) 120 square units

113. In a circle with a radius of 7 units, what is the length of the arc that subtends a central angle of 45 degrees? (Use $\pi \approx 3.14$)

- A) 3.93 units
- B) 5.50 units
- C) 7.12 units
- D) 8.25 units

114. The sine of angle θ in a right triangle is $\frac{3}{5}$. What is the cosine of angle θ?

- A) $\frac{3}{5}$
- B) $\frac{4}{5}$
- C) $\frac{5}{3}$
- D) $\frac{5}{4}$

B. Math Test - Calculator

- **Number of Questions:** 38
- **Time Allotted:** 55 minutes
- **Format:** Multiple-choice and grid-in

Heart of Algebra: 16 questions

115. If $4x - 7 = 2x + 9$, what is the value of x?

- A) 7
- B) 8
- C) 6
- D) 5

116. What is the solution to the equation $5(x + 2) = 3x + 14$?

- A) 3
- B) 4
- C) 5
- D) 6

117. Solve for y: $3y + 4 = 2y + 9$.

- A) 4
- B) 5
- C) 3
- D) 6

118. If $y = 4x - 3$ and $y = 2x + 1$, what is the value of x?

- A) 1
- B) 2
- C) 3
- D) 4

119. What is the solution to the system of equations: $x + y - 10$ and $x - y - 4$?

- A) $(7, 3)$
- B) $(6, 4)$
- C) $(8, 2)$
- D) $(5, 5)$

120. Solve for x: $6x - 5 - 2x + 11$.

- A) 4
- B) 5
- C) 6
- D) 7

121. If $y - 3x + 4$ and $y - x + 8$, what is the value of y?

- A) 10
- B) 12
- C) 14
- D) 16

122. The line $y - 2x + 3$ passes through the point $(a, 5)$. What is the value of a?

- A) 1
- B) 2
- C) 3
- D) 4

123. Solve for y: $7y + 3 = 5y + 9$.

- A) 3
- B) 4
- C) 5
- D) 6

124. If $3(x - 2) = 2(x + 1)$, what is the value of x?

- A) 5
- B) 6
- C) 4
- D) 3

125. What is the value of x in the equation $5x + 2 = 3x + 10$?

- A) 4
- B) 5
- C) 6
- D) 7

126. Solve for y: $4y - 5 = 3(y + 1)$.

- A) 5
- B) 6
- C) 4
- D) 3

127. What is the solution to the equation $2x + 3 = 5x - 7$?

- A) 3
- B) 4
- C) 5
- D) 6

128. If $y = 5x - 4$ and $y = 2x + 2$, what is the value of y?

- A) 10
- B) 12
- C) 14
- D) 16

129. Solve for x: $3x - 4 = 2(x + 5)$.

- A) 9
- B) 8
- C) 7
- D) 6

130. If $4x + 2y = 14$ and $x = 2$, what is the value of y?

- A) 3
- B) 2
- C) 4
- D) 5

Problem Solving and Data Analysis: 8 questions

131. A factory produces gadgets and widgets. The production cost for each gadget is $6 and for each widget is $8. If the factory spends $4800 in total to produce 400 units of gadgets and widgets combined, how many gadgets and widgets did they produce?

- A) 200 gadgets and 200 widgets
- B) 300 gadgets and 100 widgets
- C) 150 gadgets and 250 widgets
- D) 100 gadgets and 300 widgets

132. A survey showed that 70% of 400 participants prefer brand A over brand B. How many participants prefer brand A?

- A) 100
- B) 200
- C) 280
- D) 350

133. A recipe requires 3 cups of flour for every 2 cups of sugar. If you want to make a batch using 9 cups of flour, how many cups of sugar will you need?

- A) 4
- B) 6
- C) 9
- D) 12

134. A phone company offers a monthly plan that costs $30 plus $0.10 per text message. If a customer sends 150 text messages in a month, what is the total monthly cost?

- A) $35
- B) $40
- C) $45
- D) $50

135. The following table shows the number of books read by students in a month:

Student	Number of Books
A	5
B	7
C	8
D	10
E	5

What is the median number of books read by the students?

- A) 5
- B) 6
- C) 7
- D) 8

136. A car travels 150 miles using 5 gallons of gas. How many miles can the car travel on 12 gallons of gas?

- A) 300
- B) 350
- C) 360
- D) 400

137. The graph below shows the number of visitors to a museum over a week:

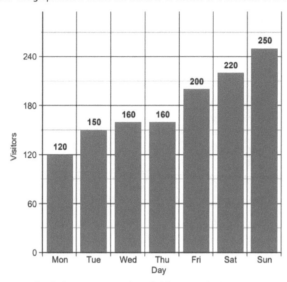

What is the average number of visitors per day?

- A) 160

- B) 180

- C) 190

- D) 210

138. A rectangular garden has a length of 20 meters and a width of 15 meters. If you increase the length by 10% and the width by 20%, what will be the new area of the garden?

- A) 364 square meters

- B) 396 square meters

- C) 332 square meters

- D) 368 square meters

Passport to Advanced Math: 11 questions

139. Solve for x: $3(x - 4)^2 - 27$

- A) 1
- B) 7
- C) 10
- D) -2

140. If $f(x) - x^3 - 6x^2 + 11x - 6$, find the roots of the polynomial.

- A) 1, 2, 3
- B) -1, -2, -3
- C) 1, -2, -3
- D) -1, 2, -3

141. The function $h(x) - 2x^2 - 8x + 6$ has its vertex at:

- A) (2, -2)
- B) (2, -10)
- C) (4, 2)
- D) (-2, 2)

142. Solve for x in the equation $2x^2 - 3x - 5 - 0$.

- A) $x - 5, -1$
- B) $x - -5, 1$
- C) $x - \frac{5}{2}, -2$
- D) $x - \frac{3 \pm \sqrt{49}}{4}$

143. If $f(x) = \log_3(x - 1)$ and $f(10) = y$, what is y?

- A) $\log_3 9$
- B) $\log_3 10$
- C) $\log_3 11$
- D) $\log_3 12$

144. Simplify the expression: $(3x^2 - 2x + 1) - (x^2 + x - 4)$

- A) $2x^2 - 3x + 5$
- B) $4x^2 - 3x - 3$
- C) $2x^2 - 3x + 4$
- D) $3x^2 - 3x + 3$

145. Find the zeros of the function $f(x) = 2x^2 - 5x - 3$.

- A) $x = -1, \frac{3}{2}$
- B) $x = -3, 2$
- C) $x = 1, -\frac{3}{2}$
- D) $x = \frac{-1}{2}, 3$

146. If $y = 4(x - 1)^2 - 9$, what are the coordinates of the vertex?

- A) (1, 9)
- B) (-1, -9)
- C) (1, -9)
- D) (1, 9)

147. The polynomial $p(x) = x^3 + 3x^2 - 4x - 12$ is factored as $(x + 3)(x^2 + ax + b)$. What are the values of a and b?

- A) $a = -1, b = 4$
- B) $a = 4, b = -1$
- C) $a = 1, b = 4$
- D) $a = -4, b = -1$

148. Solve for x: $\frac{2}{x-2} + \frac{3}{x+2} = 1$

- A) 4
- B) -4
- C) 2
- D) 0

149. What is the equation of the line that passes through the points (2, 3) and (4, 7)?

- A) $y = 2x - 1$
- B) $y = 2x + 1$
- C) $y = x + 2$
- D) $y = \frac{4}{3}x - 1$

Additional Topics in Math (geometry, trigonometry, etc.): 3 questions

150. A triangle has sides of lengths 7, 24, and 25 units. What is the measure of the largest angle in the triangle?

- A) $60°$
- B) $90°$
- C) $120°$
- D) $150°$

151. A sector of a circle has a central angle of $120°$ and a radius of 9 units. What is the length of the arc of the sector?

- A) 6π
- B) 9π
- C) 12π
- D) 18π

152. In a circle with radius **15** units, a chord is drawn that is 6 units away from the center. What is the length of the chord?

- A) 35.5
- B) 27.5
- C) 13.0
- D) 12.5

3. Essay (Optional)

- · **Number of Questions:** 1
- · **Time Allotted:** 50 minutes
- · **Format:** Essay prompt
- · **Task:** Analyze how the author builds an argument to persuade an audience.

The following passage is adapted from "The Importance of Renewable Energy" by John Smith, originally published in 2018.

Renewable energy sources, such as solar, wind, and hydroelectric power, are crucial for a sustainable future. Unlike fossil fuels, which are finite and contribute to environmental degradation, renewable energy offers a cleaner, more sustainable alternative. As the world faces the pressing challenges of climate change and *energy security, transitioning to renewable energy is not only beneficial but necessary.*

One of the primary benefits of renewable energy is its potential to reduce greenhouse gas emissions. Burning fossil fuels for energy releases large amounts of carbon dioxide and other pollutants into the atmosphere, contributing to global warming and air pollution. In contrast, renewable energy sources produce little to no greenhouse gases during operation. For example, solar panels generate electricity without emitting harmful pollutants, and wind turbines harness the power of the wind to produce clean energy. By increasing our reliance on renewable energy, we can significantly decrease our carbon footprint and mitigate the impacts of climate change.

Renewable energy also offers economic advantages. The renewable energy sector has become one of the fastest-growing industries, creating jobs and stimulating economic growth. Investments in renewable energy infrastructure, such as wind farms and solar installations, generate employment opportunities in manufacturing, construction, and maintenance. Additionally, the cost of renewable energy technologies has been decreasing steadily, making them more competitive with traditional energy sources. As these technologies become more affordable, they can provide a cost-effective solution for meeting the world's energy needs.

Energy security is another critical reason to adopt renewable energy. Fossil fuel reserves are concentrated in specific regions of the world, leading to geopolitical tensions and supply vulnerabilities. Renewable energy, on the other hand, can be harnessed locally, reducing dependence on foreign energy sources and enhancing energy security. For instance, countries with abundant sunlight can develop solar power infrastructure, while those with strong winds can invest in wind energy. This diversification of energy sources can help stabilize energy prices and reduce the risks associated with energy imports.

In conclusion, the transition to renewable energy is essential for addressing the challenges of climate change, economic development, and energy security. Renewable energy provides a sustainable and clean alternative to fossil fuels, with numerous environmental and economic benefits. As technology advances and costs decrease, the adoption of renewable energy will become increasingly feasible and necessary. It is imperative that governments, businesses, and individuals work together to promote and invest in renewable energy for a sustainable future.

Essay Prompt:

Write an essay in which you explain how John Smith builds an argument to persuade his audience that renewable energy is essential for a sustainable future. In your essay, analyze how Smith uses one or more of the features listed below (or features of your own choice) to strengthen the logic and persuasiveness of his argument. Be sure that your analysis focuses on the most relevant features of the passage.

- Evidence, such as facts or examples, to support claims
- Reasoning to develop ideas and to connect claims and evidence
- Stylistic or persuasive elements, such as word choice or appeals to emotion, to add power to the ideas expressed

Your essay should not explain whether you agree with Smith's claims, but rather explain how Smith builds an argument to persuade his audience.

Full Length Practice SAT #3

1. Evidence-Based Reading and Writing (EBRW)

A. Reading Test

- **Number of Questions:** 52
- **Time Allotted:** 65 minutes
- **Format:** Multiple-choice
- **Passages:** 5 (each passage 10 questions)

Literature: 10 questions

The following passage is excerpted from "The Age of Innocence" by Edith Wharton, originally published in 1920.

> *Newland Archer, a young lawyer in New York society, is engaged to May Welland but finds himself drawn to her cousin, the unconventional Ellen Olenska.*
>
> *It was one of the laws of the Beaufort house that people who were invited on a Sunday should come early. No one knew exactly how the rule had originated, but it was generally understood to be the result of the perverse ingeniousness of Julius Beaufort, whose invitations were always couched in the form of a summons and who always insisted on punctuality in others.*

"The Beauforts' house was one of the few in New York that possessed a ballroom. It was a masculine room, not being intended for dancing, with its bare polished floor and rows of brown-gold benches. It was generally considered too cold to sit in, and too slippery to dance on, but since the Beauforts themselves disdained dancing, their guests were expected to do the same. When Newland Archer arrived at the Beauforts' on that particular Sunday, he was immediately struck by the air of festivity that pervaded the house. The ballroom was illuminated by tall tapers in candelabra, and at the far end of the room, beneath a canopy of greenery, sat the band.

Newland had known for years that, if he had been asked to describe his ideal woman, he would have drawn the portrait of May Welland. He had always admired May's straightforwardness, her unquestioning adherence to the conventions of society, her innocence and simplicity. Yet he could not help but feel a sense of discontent as he observed the figures of the other young women moving gracefully about the room. They seemed so much more assured, more experienced, more alive than his own fiancée.

It was with a sense of relief that he saw Ellen Olenska enter the room. She was dressed in a strikingly unconventional gown of dark red velvet, with a long train that swept the floor behind her. Her hair, instead of being neatly coiled at the back of her head like the other ladies, was piled high in a mass of dark curls. She moved through the crowd with an air of complete self-assurance, acknowledging greetings with a nod of her head, but otherwise remaining aloof.

As Newland watched her, he felt a sudden rush of emotion. Here was a woman who seemed to embody all the qualities he had longed for but had never found in May. Ellen Olenska was everything that his fiancée was not: daring, unconventional, and full of life. He knew that he should not be attracted to her, that it was wrong to feel this way about another woman when he was already engaged, but he could not help himself. He was drawn to her like a moth to a *flame.*

Throughout the evening, Newland found himself seeking out Ellen's company. They talked of many things: art, literature, politics, and travel. Ellen spoke with a passion and intensity that he found intoxicating. She challenged his views, made him question the things he had always taken for granted. With her, he felt alive in a way that he had never felt before.

Yet, even as he reveled in her company, he was acutely aware of the disapproving glances from the other guests. He knew that they were watching him, judging him, and he felt a sense of guilt and shame. But he could not bring himself to care. For the first time in his life, he was willing to defy convention, to follow his heart instead of his head. And so, as the evening drew to a close, he made a silent vow to himself: he would find a way to be with Ellen, no matter the cost.

1) What is one of the rules of the Beaufort house regarding Sunday invitations?

- A) Guests should arrive late
- B) Guests should come early
- C) Guests must bring gifts
- D) Guests should dress casually

2) What is the general opinion about the Beauforts' ballroom?

- A) It is perfect for dancing
- B) It is too cold to sit in and too slippery to dance on
- C) It is too small for large gatherings
- D) It is warmly decorated and inviting

3) How does Newland Archer feel about May Welland?

- A) He finds her rebellious and unpredictable
- B) He admires her straightforwardness and adherence to societal conventions
- C) He is indifferent towards her
- D) He dislikes her simplicity

4) How does Newland Archer perceive the other young women at the ballroom?

- A) Less graceful than May
- B) More assured, experienced, and alive than May
- C) Shy and reserved
- D) Indifferent and uninteresting

5) What is notable about Ellen Olenska's appearance when she enters the room?

- A) She is dressed in a conventional gown
- B) She is wearing a strikingly unconventional gown of dark red velvet
- C) She is wearing a simple white dress
- D) She is dressed in traditional attire

6) How does Newland Archer feel when he sees Ellen Olenska?

- A) He feels a sense of relief and sudden rush of emotion
- B) He feels indifferent
- C) He feels disappointed
- D) He feels angered and annoyed

7) What topics do Newland and Ellen discuss during the evening?

- A) Only art and literature
- B) Art, literature, politics, and travel

- C) Sports and entertainment
- D) Fashion and gossip

8) How does Ellen Olenska challenge Newland Archer?

- A) She makes him question his views and things he had always taken for granted
- B) She avoids engaging in meaningful conversation
- C) She agrees with everything he says
- D) She shows disinterest in his opinions

9) How does Newland feel about the disapproving glances from the other guests?

- A) He feels proud and confident
- B) He feels guilt and shame but is willing to defy convention
- C) He feels indifferent and unaffected
- D) He feels angry and confrontational

10) What vow does Newland make to himself at the end of the evening?

- A) He will never see Ellen again
- B) He will find a way to be with Ellen, no matter the cost
- C) He will adhere strictly to societal conventions
- D) He will seek approval from the other guests

Historical Documents: 10 questions

The following passage is excerpted from "The Declaration of Sentiments" by Elizabeth Cady Stanton, originally delivered in 1848.

> *We hold these truths to be self-evident: that all men and women are created equal; that they are endowed by their Creator with certain*

inalienable rights; that among these are life, liberty, and the pursuit of happiness; that to secure these rights governments are instituted, deriving their just powers from the consent of the governed. Whenever any form of government becomes destructive of these ends, it is the right of those who suffer from it to refuse allegiance to it, and to insist upon the institution of a new government.

The history of mankind is a history of repeated injuries and usurpations on the part of man toward woman, having in direct object the establishment of an absolute tyranny over her. To prove this, let facts be submitted to a candid world.

He has never permitted her to exercise her inalienable right to the elective franchise. He has compelled her to submit to laws in the formation of which she had no voice. He has withheld from her rights which are given to the most ignorant and degraded men— both natives and foreigners. Having deprived her of this first right of a citizen, the elective franchise, thereby leaving her without representation in the halls of legislation, he has oppressed her on all sides.

Now, in view of this entire disfranchisement of one-half the people of this country, their social and religious degradation—in view of the unjust laws above mentioned, and because women do feel themselves aggrieved, oppressed, and fraudulently deprived of their most sacred rights, we insist that they have immediate admission to all the rights and privileges which belong to them as citizens of the United States.

11) What fundamental principle is stated at the beginning of the passage?

- A) All men are created equal
- B) All men and women are created equal
- C) Only men have inalienable rights
- D) Only women have inalienable rights

12) What rights are mentioned as being inalienable?

- A) Property, liberty, and freedom
- B) Life, liberty, and the pursuit of happiness
- C) Freedom, equality, and justice
- D) Voting, freedom, and happiness

13) According to the passage, from where do governments derive their just powers?

- A) From the monarch
- B) From the consent of the governed
- C) From the military
- D) From the elite class

14) What right do people have when a government becomes destructive of their inalienable rights?

- A) To petition the government for reforms
- B) To refuse allegiance to it and insist on a new government
- C) To accept the government as it is
- D) To relocate to another country

15) What is described as a history of repeated injuries and usurpations?

- A) The history of men towards other men
- B) The history of mankind towards women
- C) The history of women towards men
- D) The history of governments towards citizens

16) What is one of the grievances listed against men in the passage?

- A) Men have permitted women to vote

- B) Men have allowed women to hold property
- C) Men have never permitted women to exercise their right to vote
- D) Men have granted women equal educational opportunities

17) What right has been withheld from women, according to Stanton?

- A) The right to work
- B) The right to education
- C) The right to the elective franchise (voting)
- D) The right to travel

18) How does Stanton describe the condition of women under current laws?

- A) Equally treated as men
- B) Represented in legislation
- C) Oppressed and deprived of rights
- D) Valued and respected

19) What does Stanton insist upon for women?

- A) Immediate admission to all rights and privileges of citizens
- B) Partial rights and privileges
- C) A gradual increase in rights
- D) Limited voting rights

20) Why does Stanton believe women are justified in demanding their rights?

- A) Because they feel content with their current status
- B) Because they feel aggrieved, oppressed, and deprived of their sacred rights
- C) Because they already have equal rights

· D) Because they have been granted some rights

Social Sciences: 10 questions

The following passage is adapted from "Thinking, Fast and Slow" by Daniel Kahneman, originally published in 2011.

Every day, we make thousands of decisions. Some are small and inconsequential, while others are significant and impactful. In his book "Thinking, Fast and Slow," psychologist Daniel Kahneman explores the two systems of thinking that drive our decisions: System 1 and System 2.

System 1 operates automatically and quickly, with little or no effort and no sense of voluntary control. It is the intuitive, fast-thinking part of our brain that makes snap judgments based on patterns and experiences. For example, when you see a sad face, you quickly and effortlessly recognize the emotion without having to analyze it.

System 2, on the other hand, allocates attention to the effortful mental activities that demand it, including complex computations. The operations of System 2 are often associated with the subjective experience of agency, choice, and concentration. For example, when you solve a math problem or fill out a tax form, you are engaging System 2.

Kahneman explains that while System 1 is more efficient and often useful, it is also prone to biases and errors. These cognitive biases can lead us to make poor decisions. One common bias is the availability heuristic, where people judge the likelihood of an event based on how easily examples come to mind. For instance, after seeing news reports about airplane crashes, people might overestimate the dangers of air travel despite statistical evidence showing it is safer than driving.

Another bias is the anchoring effect, where people rely too heavily on the first piece of information they receive when making decisions. For example, if you are told that a car costs $30,000 and then see a similar car for $25,000, you might perceive the second car as a good deal, even if it is still overpriced.

System 2 can correct some of these biases, but it requires effort and concentration, which we often are not willing to exert. Kahneman's research shows that by being aware of these two systems and the biases inherent in System 1, we can improve our decision-making by deliberately engaging System 2 when necessary.

Understanding how we think and make decisions can help us avoid common pitfalls and make better choices in our personal and professional lives. Kahneman's insights reveal the complex interplay between intuition and reasoning and highlight the importance of critical thinking and self-awareness.

21) What are the two systems of thinking that Daniel Kahneman describes in his book?

- A) System A and System B
- B) System 1 and System 2
- C) Fast Thinking and Slow Thinking
- D) Rational Thinking and Irrational Thinking

22) How does System 1 operate?

- A) Slowly and deliberately
- B) Automatically and quickly, with little or no effort
- C) With a lot of effort and concentration
- D) Through complex computations

23) Which of the following is an example of System 1 thinking?

- A) Solving a math problem

- B) Filling out a tax form
- C) Recognizing a sad face
- D) Analyzing a financial report

24) What is System 2 associated with?

- A) Intuitive judgments
- B) Automatic responses
- C) Effortful mental activities and concentration
- D) Snap judgments based on patterns

25) Which of the following is an example of System 2 thinking?

- A) Quickly responding to a loud noise
- B) Driving on a familiar route
- C) Solving a complex math problem
- D) Instantly recognizing a friend's face

26) What is one cognitive bias that System 1 is prone to?

- A) Rational analysis
- B) Objective reasoning
- C) Availability heuristic
- D) Deep concentration

27) What is the availability heuristic?

- A) Making decisions based on the first piece of information received
- B) Judging the likelihood of an event based on how easily examples come to mind
- C) Overestimating the accuracy of one's knowledge
- D) Ignoring statistical evidence in decision-making

28) What is the anchoring effect?

- A) Ignoring the first piece of information received
- B) Relying too heavily on the first piece of information when making decisions
- C) Making decisions without any reference points
- D) Judging the likelihood of events based on irrelevant data

29) How can System 2 help correct the biases of System 1?

- A) By operating automatically
- B) By requiring effort and concentration
- C) By making snap judgments
- D) By avoiding complex computations

30) What does Kahneman suggest can improve our decision-making?

- A) Ignoring System 1 entirely
- B) Deliberately engaging System 2 when necessary
- C) Relying solely on intuition
- D) Making decisions based on gut feelings

Natural Sciences: 10 questions

The following passage is adapted from "The Sixth Extinction: An Unnatural History" by Elizabeth Kolbert, originally published in 2014.

Throughout Earth's history, there have been five mass extinctions, each wiping out a significant portion of the planet's species. These extinctions were caused by natural events such as volcanic eruptions, asteroid impacts, and climate changes. Today, scientists believe we are in the midst of a sixth mass extinction, driven primarily by human activities.

One of the most significant drivers of this current extinction event is habitat destruction. As humans expand their cities, farms, and infrastructure, natural habitats are being fragmented and destroyed. This loss of habitat is particularly devastating for species that require large, contiguous areas of land to survive. For example, deforestation in the Amazon rainforest has led to the decline of countless plant and animal species that depend on the forest for their survival.

Another major factor contributing to the sixth extinction is climate change. The burning of fossil fuels has increased the concentration of carbon dioxide in the atmosphere, leading to global warming. Many species are unable to adapt quickly enough to the rapidly changing climate. Coral reefs, for example, are highly sensitive to temperature changes. Increased ocean temperatures cause coral bleaching, where corals expel the algae living in their tissues, leading to the death of large sections of reefs.

Overexploitation of species through hunting, fishing, and trade also plays a significant role in the current extinction crisis. The demand for ivory, for instance, has led to a dramatic decline in elephant populations. Similarly, overfishing has severely depleted many fish stocks, threatening marine biodiversity.

Invasive species introduced by human activity can also disrupt ecosystems and lead to the decline of native species. For example, the introduction of the brown tree snake to Guam has led to the extinction of several bird species on the island.

Conservation efforts are underway to mitigate the impact of human activities on biodiversity. Protected areas, wildlife corridors, and breeding programs are some of the strategies being employed to preserve endangered species. Additionally, international agreements, such as the Convention on Biological Diversity, aim to promote sustainable practices and protect natural habitats.

Kolbert's examination of the sixth extinction highlights the urgent need for action to protect the planet's biodiversity. Under-

*standing the causes and consequences of this ongoing extinction
event can help us develop strategies to preserve the rich tapestry of
life on Earth for future generations.*

**31) What were the causes of the previous five mass extinctions in Earth's
history?**

- · A) Human activities
- · B) Natural events such as volcanic eruptions, asteroid impacts, and
  climate changes
- · C) Invasive species
- · D) Overexploitation of species

**32) What is believed to be the primary driver of the current sixth mass
extinction?**

- · A) Natural events
- · B) Human activities
- · C) Alien invasion
- · D) Genetic mutations

**33) What is one of the most significant drivers of the current extinction
event mentioned in the passage?**

- · A) Space exploration
- · B) Habitat destruction
- · C) Renewable energy
- · D) Urban gardening

34) How does deforestation in the Amazon rainforest impact species?

- · A) It creates more living space for them
- · B) It leads to the decline of countless plant and animal species

- C) It has no significant impact on biodiversity
- D) It helps species adapt to new environments

35) What is a major factor contributing to the sixth extinction besides habitat destruction?

- A) Technological advancement
- B) Climate change
- C) Space travel
- D) Urbanization

36) What is the effect of increased ocean temperatures on coral reefs?

- A) They thrive and expand
- B) They become resistant to bleaching
- C) They experience coral bleaching, leading to the death of large sections
- D) They change color but remain healthy

37) How does overexploitation of species contribute to the extinction crisis?

- A) By increasing genetic diversity
- B) By depleting populations through hunting, fishing, and trade
- C) By creating more habitats for species
- D) By reducing pollution levels

38) What impact did the introduction of the brown tree snake to Guam have?

- A) It improved the island's ecosystem
- B) It led to the extinction of several bird species
- C) It had no significant impact

· D) It increased biodiversity

39) What are some of the conservation efforts mentioned to mitigate the impact of human activities on biodiversity?

· A) Urban development and industrial expansion
· B) Protected areas, wildlife corridors, and breeding programs
· C) Space colonization and deep-sea mining
· D) Fossil fuel extraction and deforestation

40) What is the purpose of international agreements like the Convention on Biological Diversity?

· A) To promote sustainable practices and protect natural habitats
· B) To encourage deforestation
· C) To eliminate invasive species
· D) To ban all forms of hunting and fishing

Dual Passages (Literature, Social Science, or Science): 10 questions

Passage 1

The following passage is adapted from "Pride and Prejudice" by Jane Austen, originally published in 1813.

> *Elizabeth Bennet had been obliged, by the scarcity of gentlemen, to sit down for two dances; and during part of that time, Mr. Darcy had been standing near enough for her to overhear a conversation between him and Mr. Bingley, who came from the dance for a few minutes to press his friend to join it.*
>
> *"Come, Darcy," said he, "I must have you dance. I hate to see you standing about by yourself in this stupid manner. You had much better dance."*

"I certainly shall not. You know how I detest it, unless I am particularly acquainted with my partner. At such an assembly as this, it would be insupportable. Your sisters are engaged, and there is not another woman in the room whom it would not be a punishment to me to stand up with."

"I would not be so fastidious as you are," cried Bingley, "for a kingdom! Upon my honor, I never met with so many pleasant girls in my life as I have this evening; and there are several of them you see uncommonly pretty."

"You are dancing with the only handsome girl in the room," said Mr. Darcy, looking at the eldest Miss Bennet.

"Oh! She is the most beautiful creature I ever beheld! But there is one of her sisters sitting down just behind you, who is very pretty, and I dare say very agreeable. Do let me ask my partner to introduce you."

"Which do you mean?" and turning around, he looked for a moment at Elizabeth, till catching her eye, he withdrew his own and coldly said: "She is tolerable, but not handsome enough to tempt me."

Passage 2

The following passage is adapted from "Jane Eyre" by Charlotte Brontë, originally published in 1847.

There was no possibility of taking a walk that day. We had been wandering, indeed, in the leafless shrubbery an hour in the morning; but since dinner (Mrs. Reed, when there was no company, dined early) the cold winter wind had brought with it clouds so sombre, and a rain so penetrating, that further outdoor exercise was now out of the question.

I was glad of it; I never liked long walks, especially on chilly afternoons: dreadful to me was the coming home in the raw twilight, with nipped fingers and toes, and a heart saddened by the chidings of Bessie, the nurse, and humbled by the consciousness of my physical inferiority to Eliza, John, and Georgiana Reed.

The said Eliza, John, and Georgiana were now clustered round their mama in the drawing-room: she lay reclined on a sofa by the fireside, and with her darlings about her (for the time neither quarrelling nor crying) looked perfectly happy. Me, she had dispensed from joining the group, saying, "She regretted to be under the necessity of keeping me at a distance; but that until she heard from Bessie, and could discover by her own observation, that I was endeavoring in good earnest to acquire a more sociable and childlike disposition, a more attractive and sprightly manner— something lighter, franker, more natural, as it were—she must exclude me from privileges intended only for contented, happy, little children."

"What does Bessie say I have done?" I asked.

"Jane, I don't like cavillers or questioners; besides, there is something truly forbidding in a child taking up her elders in that manner. Be seated somewhere; and until you can speak pleasantly, remain silent."

41) In Passage 1, what reason does Mr. Darcy give for not wanting to dance?

- A) He is tired
- B) He does not like dancing unless he is particularly acquainted with his partner
- C) He is feeling unwell
- D) He thinks the music is bad

42) In Passage 2, what activity does Jane Eyre express a dislike for?

- A) Reading
- B) Sewing

- C) Long walks on chilly afternoons
- D) Playing with her cousins

43) What does Mr. Darcy say about Elizabeth Bennet in Passage 1?

- A) She is the most beautiful creature he has ever beheld
- B) She is very pretty and agreeable
- C) She is tolerable but not handsome enough to tempt him
- D) She is the only handsome girl in the room

44) How does Mrs. Reed in Passage 2 treat Jane Eyre compared to her own children?

- A) Equally with kindness and affection
- B) With more strictness and exclusion from privileges
- C) With indifference and neglect
- D) With greater care and attention

45) What is Mr. Bingley's attitude towards the girls at the assembly in Passage 1?

- A) He finds them all unpleasant
- B) He never met with so many pleasant girls in his life
- C) He is indifferent towards them
- D) He thinks only one of them is handsome

46) What reason does Mrs. Reed give for keeping Jane at a distance in Passage 2?

- A) Jane's unsociable and unchildlike disposition
- B) Jane's lack of intelligence
- C) Jane's physical inferiority
- D) Jane's disobedience and quarrelsome nature

47) What do both passages suggest about the protagonists' social experiences?

- A) Both protagonists are warmly accepted in their social circles
- B) Both protagonists face exclusion and social challenges
- C) Both protagonists are indifferent to social interactions
- D) Both protagonists are admired and well-liked by everyone

48) How do the reactions of Mr. Darcy and Mrs. Reed reflect their personalities in the passages?

- A) Both are compassionate and understanding
- B) Both are indifferent and unemotional
- C) Both are critical and dismissive
- D) Both are warm and welcoming

49) Which of the following best describes the tone of Mr. Darcy's comment about Elizabeth in Passage 1?

- A) Admirable and respectful
- B) Dismissive and cold
- C) Enthusiastic and warm
- D) Indifferent and detached

50) What common theme is explored in both passages?

- A) The joy of family gatherings
- B) The impact of social expectations and judgments
- C) The excitement of attending social events
- D) The love between family members

B. Writing and Language Test

- **Number of Questions:** 44
- **Time Allotted:** 35 minutes
- **Format:** Multiple-choice
- **Passages:** 4 (each passage 11 questions)

Careers: 11 questions

A Day in the Life of a Wildlife Biologist

(1) Wildlife biologists play a critical role in understanding and preserving the natural world. (2) Their work involves studying animal behavior, ecology, and habitats to inform conservation efforts and protect biodiversity. (3) The career of a wildlife biologist is both challenging and rewarding, requiring a passion for nature and a commitment to scientific research.

(4) A typical day for a wildlife biologist often begins before sunrise. (5) Early mornings are the best time to observe many species, as animals are most active during these hours. (6) Fieldwork is a significant part of the job, and biologists may spend hours in various environments, from dense forests to open grasslands, gathering data on wildlife populations and behaviors.

(7) Fieldwork can be physically demanding and requires a range of skills. (8) Biologists must be adept at using GPS devices, cameras, and other equipment to track and monitor animals. (9) They often collect samples, such as soil, water, or plant material, to analyze back in the laboratory. (10) This hands-on approach provides valuable insights into the health of ecosystems and the factors affecting wildlife.

(11) In addition to fieldwork, wildlife biologists spend a considerable amount of time analyzing data and writing reports. (12) They use statistical software to interpret their findings and identify

trends. *(13) Their research contributes to scientific publications, conservation plans, and policy recommendations. (14) Effective communication skills are essential, as biologists must present their findings to colleagues, policymakers, and the public.*

(15) Collaboration is a key aspect of a wildlife biologist's job. (16) They often work with other scientists, conservationists, and government agencies to develop and implement strategies for wildlife management. (17) This collaborative approach ensures that conservation efforts are based on the best available science and are tailored to the specific needs of different species and habitats.

(18) One of the most rewarding aspects of being a wildlife biologist is the opportunity to make a tangible difference in conservation. (19) Whether it's helping to restore a threatened habitat, protecting an endangered species, or educating the public about the importance of biodiversity, wildlife biologists have a direct impact on the natural world. (20) Their work helps to ensure that future generations can enjoy and benefit from healthy, functioning ecosystems.

(21) The career of a wildlife biologist is not without its challenges. (22) Fieldwork can be unpredictable and sometimes dangerous, with biologists facing harsh weather conditions and encounters with wild animals. (23) Securing funding for research projects can also be a significant hurdle. (24) Despite these challenges, many wildlife biologists find their work incredibly fulfilling and are driven by a deep passion for the environment.

(25) For those interested in pursuing a career in wildlife biology, a strong educational background in biology, ecology, and related fields is essential. (26) Practical experience through internships, volunteer work, and field courses is also highly beneficial. (27) With dedication and perseverance, aspiring wildlife biologists can build a career that combines scientific inquiry with a love of nature, making a lasting impact on the world's ecosystems.

51) Which choice best describes what happens in the passage?

- A) The passage outlines the daily activities, challenges, and rewards of being a wildlife biologist.
- B) The passage provides a detailed biography of a famous wildlife biologist.
- C) The passage critiques the effectiveness of wildlife conservation efforts.
- D) The passage discusses the financial aspects of being a wildlife biologist.

52) Which choice provides the most accurate interpretation of the data in sentence 2?

- A) Wildlife biologists mainly work in laboratories and rarely interact with animals.
- B) Wildlife biologists study animal behavior, ecology, and habitats to support conservation efforts and protect biodiversity.
- C) Wildlife biologists focus exclusively on studying plant species.
- D) Wildlife biologists are not involved in conservation efforts.

53) Which version of the underlined portion of sentence 3 best maintains the tone and style of the passage?

- A) NO CHANGE
- B) The career of a wildlife biologist is super exciting and cool, requiring a love for nature and scientific research.
- C) Being a wildlife biologist is a tough and fun job that needs a passion for nature and research.
- D) The career of a wildlife biologist is both challenging and rewarding, requiring a passion for nature and a commitment to scientific research.

54) In context, which is the best way to combine sentences 4 and 5?

- A) A typical day for a wildlife biologist often begins before sunrise because early mornings are the best time to observe many species, as animals are most active during these hours.
- B) A typical day for a wildlife biologist often begins before sunrise; early mornings are the best time to observe many species as animals are most active during these hours.
- C) A typical day for a wildlife biologist often begins before sunrise, early mornings are the best time to observe many species as animals are most active during these hours.
- D) A typical day for a wildlife biologist often begins before sunrise, because early mornings are the best time to observe many species, as animals are most active during these hours.

55) Which choice provides the most logical introduction to the third paragraph (sentences 7-10)?

- A) Fieldwork is not very important for wildlife biologists.
- B) Fieldwork is a significant part of the job, and biologists may spend hours in various environments.
- C) Biologists must be adept at using GPS devices, cameras, and other equipment to track and monitor animals.
- D) Wildlife biologists must be skilled in many areas.

56) In sentence 12, what is the purpose of mentioning statistical software?

- A) To highlight the tools wildlife biologists use to analyze data and interpret their findings.
- B) To criticize the use of technology in wildlife biology.
- C) To suggest that wildlife biologists do not need to analyze data.
- D) To argue that statistical software is not effective for analyzing

data.

57) Which choice best maintains the tone of the passage in sentence 16?

- A) NO CHANGE
- B) They often work with other scientists, conservationists, and government agencies to develop and implement strategies for wildlife management.
- C) They sometimes team up with other scientists, conservationists, and government agencies to come up with and carry out strategies for wildlife management.
- D) They frequently collaborate with other scientists, conservationists, and government agencies to create and execute strategies for wildlife management.

58) Which sentence, if added to the sixth paragraph, would best support the information presented in that paragraph?

- A) Many wildlife biologists enjoy spending time outdoors.
- B) Fieldwork can be unpredictable and sometimes dangerous, with biologists facing harsh weather conditions and encounters with wild animals.
- C) Wildlife biologists often work in teams to monitor animal populations.
- D) Wildlife biologists must be good at writing reports and presenting their findings.

59) The author wants to add the following sentence to the sixth paragraph:
"Despite these challenges, many wildlife biologists find their work incredibly fulfilling and are driven by a deep passion for the environment."
Where would this sentence best fit?

- A) Before sentence 21
- B) After sentence 21
- C) Before sentence 23
- D) After sentence 24

60) In context, the word "rewarding" in sentence 19 most nearly means:

- A) Demanding
- B) Satisfying
- C) Frustrating
- D) Temporary

61) Which choice best concludes the passage?

- A) The career of a wildlife biologist is not as important as other scientific careers.
- B) For those interested in pursuing a career in wildlife biology, a strong educational background in biology, ecology, and related fields is essential.
- C) With dedication and perseverance, aspiring wildlife biologists can build a career that combines scientific inquiry with a love of nature, making a lasting impact on the world's ecosystems.
- D) Many people are unaware of the challenges faced by wildlife biologists.

History/Social Studies: 11 questions

The New Deal: Transforming America in the Great Depression

(1) The New Deal was a series of programs and policies imple- mented by President Franklin D. Roosevelt in response to the Great Depression. (2) The economic crisis of the 1930s had left millions

of Americans unemployed, homeless, and struggling to survive. (3) Roosevelt's New Deal aimed to provide relief, recovery, and reform to the devastated nation.

(4) One of the first actions taken by Roosevelt was the creation of the Civilian Conservation Corps (CCC) in 1933. (5) The CCC provided jobs for young men, focusing on conservation and development of natural resources in rural areas. (6) Projects included planting trees, building flood barriers, fighting forest fires, and maintaining trails and roads in national parks. (7) The CCC not only provided employment but also contributed to the preservation of the environment.

(8) Another significant New Deal program was the Works Progress Administration (WPA), established in 1935. (9) The WPA created millions of jobs by funding public works projects such as the construction of roads, bridges, schools, and hospitals. (10) The program also supported artists, writers, and musicians through various cultural projects. (11) The WPA played a crucial role in improving the nation's infrastructure and promoting cultural development.

(12) The Social Security Act of 1935 was another cornerstone of the New Deal. (13) This legislation established a system of old-age benefits for workers, unemployment insurance, and aid to families with dependent children and the disabled. (14) The Social Security Act provided a safety net for the most vulnerable citizens and laid the foundation for the modern welfare state.

(15) The New Deal also included measures to reform the financial sector. (16) The Banking Act of 1933, also known as the Glass-Steagall Act, established the Federal Deposit Insurance Corporation (FDIC), which insured bank deposits to restore public confidence in the banking system. (17) Additionally, the Securities Act of 1933 and the Securities Exchange Act of 1934 regulated the stock market to prevent the abuses that had contributed to the stock market crash of 1929.

(18) Agricultural reform was another critical aspect of the New Deal. (19) The Agricultural Adjustment Act (AAA) of 1933 aimed to raise crop prices by paying farmers to reduce production. (20) This program sought to alleviate the agricultural overproduction that had led to falling prices and widespread poverty among farmers. (21) While the AAA faced legal challenges, it marked a significant step toward stabilizing the agricultural economy.

(22) The New Deal had a profound impact on American society and government. (23) It expanded the role of the federal government in the economy and introduced the concept of a social safety net. (24) Critics of the New Deal argued that it increased government intervention and spending to unsustainable levels. (25) However, supporters believed that it was necessary to address the severe economic challenges of the time.

(26) The legacy of the New Deal continues to influence American politics and policy. (27) Many of the programs and institutions created during this period, such as Social Security and the FDIC, remain in place today. (28) The New Deal demonstrated the federal government's ability to take decisive action in times of crisis and shaped the relationship between the government and the American people.

62) Which choice best describes what happens in the passage?

- A) The passage outlines the programs and policies of the New Deal and their impact on America during the Great Depression.
- B) The passage provides a biography of President Franklin D. Roosevelt.
- C) The passage critiques the effectiveness of the New Deal programs.
- D) The passage discusses the financial aspects of the Great Depression without mentioning the New Deal.

63) Which choice provides the most accurate interpretation of the data

in sentence 2?

- A) The economic crisis of the 1930s had little impact on Americans.
- B) The economic crisis of the 1930s left millions of Americans unemployed, homeless, and struggling to survive.
- C) The economic crisis of the 1930s led to a brief period of unemployment and homelessness.
- D) The economic crisis of the 1930s did not significantly affect the American population.

64) Which version of the underlined portion of sentence 3 best maintains the tone and style of the passage?

- A) NO CHANGE
- B) Roosevelt's New Deal aimed to help people, fix the economy, and change the nation.
- C) Roosevelt's New Deal was meant to assist, recover, and reform the country.
- D) Roosevelt's New Deal was created to give relief, recovery, and reform to the struggling nation.

65) In context, which is the best way to combine sentences 4 and 5?

- A) One of the first actions taken by Roosevelt was the creation of the Civilian Conservation Corps (CCC) in 1933, providing jobs for young men and focusing on conservation and development of natural resources in rural areas.
- B) One of the first actions taken by Roosevelt was the creation of the Civilian Conservation Corps (CCC) in 1933 because it provided jobs for young men, focusing on conservation and development of natural resources in rural areas.
- C) One of the first actions taken by Roosevelt was the creation of the Civilian Conservation Corps (CCC) in 1933, it provided jobs for

young men and focused on conservation and development of natural resources in rural areas.

- D) One of the first actions taken by Roosevelt was the creation of the Civilian Conservation Corps (CCC) in 1933; providing jobs for young men, focusing on conservation and development of natural resources in rural areas.

66) Which choice provides the most logical introduction to the third paragraph (sentences 8-11)?

- A) The WPA was very popular among Americans.
- B) Another significant New Deal program was the Works Progress Administration (WPA), established in 1935.
- C) Many Americans benefited from the WPA.
- D) The WPA created many jobs for artists and musicians.

67) In sentence 16, what is the purpose of mentioning the Federal Deposit Insurance Corporation (FDIC)?

- A) To highlight the organization's role in providing jobs for Americans.
- B) To show how the Banking Act of 1933 helped restore public confidence in the banking system by insuring bank deposits.
- C) To criticize the effectiveness of the FDIC.
- D) To argue that the FDIC was unnecessary.

68) Which choice best maintains the tone of the passage in sentence 23?

- A) NO CHANGE
- B) It expanded the role of the federal government in the economy and introduced the concept of a social safety net.
- C) It made the government get more involved in the economy and

introduced the idea of a social safety net.

- D) It expanded the federal government's involvement in the economy and brought in the idea of a social safety net.

69) Which sentence, if added to the fifth paragraph, would best support the information presented in that paragraph?

- A) The New Deal also had an impact on the American cultural scene.
- B) Many Americans appreciated the efforts of the New Deal.
- C) The Social Security Act provided a safety net for many Americans, ensuring that they had financial support in difficult times.
- D) Many Americans were unaware of the changes brought about by the New Deal.

70) The author wants to add the following sentence to the sixth paragraph:

"These reforms aimed to stabilize the financial sector and prevent future economic crises." Where would this sentence best fit?

- A) Before sentence 15
- B) After sentence 15
- C) Before sentence 16
- D) After sentence 17

71) In context, the word "cornerstone" in sentence 12 most nearly means:

- A) Foundation
- B) Addition
- C) Detail
- D) Afterthought

72) Which choice best concludes the passage?

- A) The New Deal was a series of programs that had little impact on American society.
- B) The New Deal demonstrated the federal government's ability to take decisive action in times of crisis and shaped the relationship between the government and the American people.
- C) Many people are unaware of the challenges faced by those implementing the New Deal.
- D) The New Deal was only a temporary measure and did not have long-lasting effects.

Humanities: 11 questions

The Evolution of Modern Theater

(1) Modern theater has evolved significantly from its roots in ancient Greek and Roman drama, incorporating new styles, themes, and techniques to reflect the changing times. (2) From the Renaissance to the contemporary era, theater has continuously transformed, pushing the boundaries of artistic expression and societal norms.

(3) The Renaissance marked a revival of classical ideals in theater, particularly in Italy, where the tradition of commedia dell'arte emerged. (4) This form of theater was characterized by its use of stock characters, improvisation, and physical comedy. (5) Performers wore masks and portrayed exaggerated characters, such as the clever servant or the foolish old man, to entertain audiences with humorous scenarios.

(6) In Elizabethan England, theater reached new heights with the works of William Shakespeare. (7) Shakespeare's plays, which include tragedies, comedies, and histories, explored complex human emotions and social issues. (8) His innovative use of language, character development, and dramatic structure set new standards for theatrical writing. (9) Shakespeare's Globe Theatre in London

became a cultural landmark, attracting diverse audiences and showcasing the power of theater to reflect and influence society.

(10) The 19th century brought about the advent of realism in theater, with playwrights like Henrik Ibsen and Anton Chekhov leading the way. (11) Realism focused on portraying everyday life and ordinary people with authenticity and psychological depth. (12) Ibsen's "A Doll's House" and Chekhov's "The Cherry Orchard" are prime examples of plays that addressed social issues, such as gender roles and class struggles, through realistic dialogue and settings.

(13) The early 20th century saw the rise of modernism, which sought to break away from traditional forms and conventions. (14) Playwrights like Bertolt Brecht and Samuel Beckett experimented with new techniques to challenge audiences' perceptions and provoke critical thinking. (15) Brecht's concept of "epic theater" aimed to engage viewers intellectually rather than emotionally, often using direct addresses to the audience and stark, minimalistic staging. (16) Beckett's absurdist plays, such as "Waiting for Godot," highlighted the existential struggles of human existence, often through fragmented dialogue and unconventional narratives.

(17) Contemporary theater continues to evolve, incorporating multimedia elements, diverse voices, and innovative storytelling techniques. (18) The integration of technology, such as projections, interactive sets, and digital effects, has expanded the possibilities for theatrical production. (19) Additionally, theater has become more inclusive, with playwrights and performers from various cultural backgrounds bringing new perspectives to the stage.

(20) The rise of musical theater in the 20th century added a new dimension to the theatrical experience. (21) Musicals like "West Side Story," "Les Misérables," and "Hamilton" combine music, lyrics, and dialogue to tell powerful stories that resonate with audiences. (22) The ability of musical theater to blend various art forms has made it a popular and enduring genre.

(23) Today, theater remains a vital and dynamic form of artistic

expression. (24) It serves as a mirror to society, reflecting its triumphs and challenges while providing a space for dialogue and reflection. (25) The evolution of theater demonstrates its resilience and adaptability, ensuring its continued relevance in a rapidly changing world.

73) Which choice best describes what happens in the passage?

- A) The passage outlines the history and evolution of modern theater, highlighting key periods and influential playwrights.
- B) The passage provides a detailed biography of William Shakespeare.
- C) The passage critiques the effectiveness of modern theater techniques.
- D) The passage discusses the financial aspects of producing theater in the contemporary era.

74) Which choice provides the most accurate interpretation of the data in sentence 2?

- A) Theater has remained the same since the Renaissance.
- B) Theater has continuously transformed, pushing the boundaries of artistic expression and societal norms.
- C) Theater became less popular after the Renaissance.
- D) Theater has had little impact on societal norms.

75) Which version of the underlined portion of sentence 3 best maintains the tone and style of the passage?

- A) NO CHANGE
- B) The Renaissance kicked off a big comeback for theater, especially in Italy, with commedia dell'arte becoming popular.
- C) The Renaissance saw theater make a big comeback in Italy with commedia dell'arte.

- D) During the Renaissance, theater saw a revival of classical ideals, particularly in Italy, with the emergence of commedia dell'arte.

76) In context, which is the best way to combine sentences 4 and 5?

- A) This form of theater was characterized by its use of stock characters, improvisation, and physical comedy, as performers wore masks and portrayed exaggerated characters, such as the clever servant or the foolish old man, to entertain audiences with humorous scenarios.
- B) This form of theater was characterized by its use of stock characters, improvisation, and physical comedy, performers wore masks and portrayed exaggerated characters, such as the clever servant or the foolish old man, to entertain audiences with humorous scenarios.
- C) This form of theater was characterized by its use of stock characters, improvisation, and physical comedy; performers wore masks and portrayed exaggerated characters, such as the clever servant or the foolish old man, to entertain audiences with humorous scenarios.
- D) This form of theater was characterized by its use of stock characters, improvisation, and physical comedy: performers wore masks and portrayed exaggerated characters, such as the clever servant or the foolish old man, to entertain audiences with humorous scenarios.

77) Which choice provides the most logical introduction to the third paragraph (sentences 10-12)?

- A) Shakespeare's works are still performed today.
- B) Many new forms of theater were developed in the 19th century.
- C) The 19th century brought about the advent of realism in theater, with playwrights like Henrik Ibsen and Anton Chekhov leading the way.
- D) Realism was not very popular in the 19th century.

78) In sentence 14, what is the purpose of mentioning Bertolt Brecht

and Samuel Beckett?

- A) To highlight playwrights who continued the tradition of realism in theater.
- B) To introduce key figures in the rise of modernism in theater.
- C) To criticize their contributions to theater.
- D) To show that they wrote musical theater.

79) Which choice best maintains the tone of the passage in sentence 18?

- A) NO CHANGE
- B) The use of tech stuff like projections, cool sets, and digital effects has made theater more awesome.
- C) The integration of technology, such as projections, interactive sets, and digital effects, has expanded the possibilities for theatrical production.
- D) The addition of technology like projections and digital effects has made theater more entertaining.

80) Which sentence, if added to the sixth paragraph, would best support the information presented in that paragraph?

- A) Musical theater is also very popular in other parts of the world.
- B) Many people enjoy watching musicals.
- C) Musicals require a lot of rehearsal and preparation.
- D) Musicals like "Cats" and "Phantom of the Opera" have also had long runs and significant cultural impact.

81) The author wants to add the following sentence to the fifth paragraph:

"Modernist playwrights sought to break away from traditional forms and create new, innovative theatrical experiences." Where would this sentence best fit?

- A) Before sentence 13
- B) After sentence 13
- C) Before sentence 14
- D) After sentence 15

82) In context, the word "hallmarks" in sentence 4 most nearly means:

- A) Challenges
- B) Symbols
- C) Characteristics
- D) Techniques

83) Which choice best concludes the passage?

- A) The evolution of theater demonstrates its resilience and adaptability, ensuring its continued relevance in a rapidly changing world.
- B) Many people do not realize how important theater is to society.
- C) Theater has changed a lot over the years but remains very popular.
- D) The future of theater is uncertain, but it has a rich history.

Science: 11 questions

The Role of Antibiotics in Medicine and Agriculture

(1) Antibiotics revolutionized medicine in the 20th century, transforming the treatment of bacterial infections and saving millions of lives. (2) These powerful drugs work by targeting and killing bacteria or inhibiting their growth, allowing the body's immune system to effectively fight off infections. (3) However, the widespread use of antibiotics in both human medicine and agriculture has led to significant challenges and concerns.

(4) In medicine, antibiotics are used to treat a wide range of bacterial infections, from common ailments like strep throat to life-threatening conditions such as pneumonia and sepsis. (5) The discovery of penicillin by Alexander Fleming in 1928 marked the beginning of the antibiotic era, leading to the development of numerous other antibiotics that have since become essential tools in modern healthcare.

(6) Despite their effectiveness, the overuse and misuse of antibiotics have contributed to the emergence of antibiotic-resistant bacteria, also known as superbugs. (7) Antibiotic resistance occurs when bacteria evolve mechanisms to survive exposure to antibiotics, rendering these drugs ineffective. (8) This phenomenon poses a serious threat to public health, as infections caused by resistant bacteria are harder to treat and can lead to longer hospital stays, higher medical costs, and increased mortality rates.

(9) In agriculture, antibiotics are commonly used in livestock farming to promote growth and prevent diseases in animals raised for food production. (10) However, this practice has raised concerns about the spread of antibiotic-resistant bacteria through the food chain and the environment. (11) Resistant bacteria can be transmitted to humans through contaminated meat, water, and direct contact with animals.

(12) To combat antibiotic resistance, it is crucial to implement strategies that promote the responsible use of antibiotics. (13) In healthcare, this includes prescribing antibiotics only when necessary and ensuring patients complete their full course of treatment. (14) In agriculture, reducing the use of antibiotics for growth promotion and disease prevention, and instead focusing on improved hygiene and vaccination programs, can help mitigate the spread of resistance.

(15) Research and development of new antibiotics are also essential to address the growing threat of antibiotic resistance. (16) Scientists are exploring novel approaches, such as using

bacteriophages—viruses that infect and kill bacteria—or develop-
ing drugs that target bacterial communication systems. (17) These
innovative strategies hold promise for overcoming resistance and
providing new treatment options.

(18) Public education plays a vital role in combating antibiotic
resistance. (19) Increasing awareness about the importance of
proper antibiotic use and the risks associated with misuse can help
change behaviors and reduce the spread of resistant bacteria. (20)
Global collaboration is also necessary, as antibiotic resistance is
a worldwide issue that requires coordinated efforts from govern-
ments, healthcare providers, and the agricultural industry.

(21) The role of antibiotics in modern medicine and agriculture
is undeniable, but their continued effectiveness depends on our
ability to manage their use responsibly. (22) By implementing
comprehensive strategies and fostering innovation, we can address
the challenges posed by antibiotic resistance and ensure these life-
saving drugs remain effective for future generations.

84) Which choice best describes what happens in the passage?

- A) The passage outlines the history and significance of antibiotics in medicine and agriculture, highlighting the challenges of antibiotic resistance.
- B) The passage provides a biography of Alexander Fleming.
- C) The passage critiques the use of antibiotics in modern healthcare.
- D) The passage discusses the financial aspects of antibiotic production.

85) Which choice provides the most accurate interpretation of the data in sentence 2?

- A) Antibiotics are primarily used for viral infections.
- B) Antibiotics revolutionized medicine by targeting and killing bac-

teria or inhibiting their growth, allowing the body's immune system to effectively fight off infections.

- C) Antibiotics are ineffective in treating bacterial infections.
- D) Antibiotics have had little impact on modern medicine.

86) Which version of the underlined portion of sentence 3 best maintains the tone and style of the passage?

- A) NO CHANGE
- B) These powerful drugs have been around forever and are super important in fighting bacteria.
- C) These drugs are really strong and good at killing bacteria.
- D) These important medications are excellent at targeting and killing bacteria.

87) In context, which is the best way to combine sentences 6 and 7?

- A) Despite their effectiveness, the overuse and misuse of antibiotics have contributed to the emergence of antibiotic-resistant bacteria, which occurs when bacteria evolve mechanisms to survive exposure to antibiotics, rendering these drugs ineffective.
- B) Despite their effectiveness, the overuse and misuse of antibiotics have contributed to the emergence of antibiotic-resistant bacteria, they occur when bacteria evolve mechanisms to survive exposure to antibiotics, rendering these drugs ineffective.
- C) Despite their effectiveness, the overuse and misuse of antibiotics have contributed to the emergence of antibiotic-resistant bacteria; they occur when bacteria evolve mechanisms to survive exposure to antibiotics, rendering these drugs ineffective.
- D) Despite their effectiveness, the overuse and misuse of antibiotics have contributed to the emergence of antibiotic-resistant bacteria, also known as superbugs, which occurs when bacteria evolve mechanisms to survive exposure to antibiotics, rendering these drugs

ineffective.

88) Which choice provides the most logical introduction to the third paragraph (sentences 9-11)?

- A) Antibiotics have been used in many industries.
- B) In agriculture, antibiotics are commonly used in livestock farming to promote growth and prevent diseases in animals raised for food production.
- C) Many farmers use antibiotics for various reasons.
- D) The use of antibiotics in farming is quite different from their use in human medicine.

89) In sentence 11, what is the purpose of mentioning resistant bacteria can be transmitted to humans through contaminated meat, water, and direct contact with animals?

- A) To highlight the benefits of antibiotic use in agriculture.
- B) To show the risks associated with the use of antibiotics in agriculture.
- C) To argue that antibiotics should be banned in agriculture.
- D) To suggest that antibiotic resistance is not a serious issue.

90) Which choice best maintains the tone of the passage in sentence 13?

- A) NO CHANGE
- B) In healthcare, this includes only giving out antibiotics when really necessary and making sure patients finish their prescriptions.
- C) In healthcare, this includes prescribing antibiotics only when necessary and ensuring patients complete their full course of treatment.
- D) In healthcare, this includes giving antibiotics sparingly and telling patients to finish them.

91) Which sentence, if added to the sixth paragraph, would best support the information presented in that paragraph?

- A) Developing new antibiotics is a costly and time-consuming process.
- B) Many people do not understand the importance of antibiotics.
- C) Scientists are also looking into alternative therapies, such as probiotics, to complement antibiotic treatment.
- D) Antibiotics have saved many lives over the years.

92) The author wants to add the following sentence to the seventh paragraph:

"Educational campaigns can inform the public about how to properly use antibiotics and the dangers of antibiotic resistance." Where would this sentence best fit?

- A) Before sentence 18
- B) After sentence 18
- C) Before sentence 19
- D) After sentence 20

93) In context, the word "combat" in sentence 12 most nearly means:

- A) Ignore
- B) Encourage
- C) Fight
- D) Develop

94) Which choice best concludes the passage?

- A) The role of antibiotics in modern medicine and agriculture is undeniable, but their continued effectiveness depends on our ability to manage their use responsibly.

- B) Many people do not realize the importance of antibiotics.
- C) Antibiotics are likely to remain effective for many years.
- D) The future of antibiotics is uncertain and will require significant changes.

2. Math

A. Math Test - No Calculator

- **Number of Questions:** 20
- **Time Allotted:** 25 minutes
- **Format:** Multiple-choice and grid-in

Heart of Algebra: 8 questions

95. Solve for x in the equation:

    $4x - 5 - 3x + 7$

    - A) 12
    - B) -12
    - C) 2
    - D) -2

96. If $3x + 2y - 12$ and $y - 2x - 3$, what is the value of y?

    - A) -1
    - B) 3
    - C) 5
    - D) 7

97. What is the solution to the system of equations:
    $$x - y = 4$$
    $$2x + y = 1$$

- A) $(1, -3)$
- B) $(-1, -5)$
- C) $(2, -2)$
- D) $(3, -1)$

98. Solve the inequality:
    $$5 - 3x > 2$$

- A) $x < 1$
- B) $x > 1$
- C) $x < -1$
- D) $x > -1$

99. If $2x + 3y = 13$ and $x - y = 2$, what is the value of x?

- A) 3
- B) 4
- C) 5
- D) 6

100. The sum of two numbers is 9. One number is three times the other. What are the numbers?

- A) 2 and 6
- B) 3 and 6
- C) 1 and 8
- D) 3 and 9

101. Find the value of x if $7x - 3 - 4x + 9$.

- A) 2
- B) 3
- C) 4
- D) 5

102. What is the solution to the equation $6(2x + 3) - 4x + 18$?

- A) 1
- B) 2
- C) 3
- D) 4

Problem Solving and Data Analysis: 3 questions

103. A store sells apples for $0.50 each and bananas for $0.30 each. If a customer buys 6 apples and 10 bananas, what is the total cost?

- A) $5.40
- B) $5.80
- C) $6.00
- D) $6.20

104. A researcher is collecting data on the heights of a group of plants. The heights (in cm) are recorded as follows: 25, 27, 25, 30, 28, 27, 25, 29. What is the median height of the plants?

- A) 25.5 cm
- B) 26 cm
- C) 27 cm
- D) 28 cm

105. A company's profit P in thousands of dollars is given by the equation $P = 4x - 20$, where x is the number of units sold in thousands. If the company wants to achieve a profit of $60,000, how many units must be sold?

- A) 15,000

- B) 16,000

- C) 20,000

- D) 25,000

Passport to Advanced Math: 6 questions

106. If $f(x) = x^3 - 4x$, what is $f'(x)$?

- A) $3x^2 - 4$

- B) $3x^2 - 4x$

- C) $x^2 - 4$

- D) $3x - 4$

107. Solve for x in the equation $x^2 + 5x + 6 = 0$.

- A) $x = -2$ or $x = -3$

- B) $x = 2$ or $x = -3$

- C) $x = -2$ or $x = 3$

- D) $x = 2$ or $x = 3$

108. If $g(x) - 2x^3 + 3x^2 - x + 1$, what is the value of $g''(x)$ when $x - 1$?

- A) 10
- B) 12
- C) 14
- D) 18

109. Which of the following is an equivalent form of the expression $3x^2 - 12x + 9$?

- A) $3(x - 3)^2$
- B) $3(x - 2)^2$
- C) $3(x - 1)^2$
- D) $3(x - 2)^2 - 3$

110. Solve the system of equations for x and y:

$$2x + 3y - 7$$
$$4x - y - 7$$

- A) $x - 2, y - 1$
- B) $x - 3, y - -1$
- C) $x - 1, y - 1$
- D) $x - -1, y - 3$

111. What is the solution set of the inequality $\frac{2x-1}{x+2} > 1$?

- A) $x < -2$ or $x > 3$
- B) $x > -2$ and $x < 3$
- C) $x < -2$ and $x > 3$
- D) $x > -2$ or $x < 3$

Additional Topics in Math (geometry, trigonometry, etc.): 3 questions

112. A right circular cone has a height of 9 units and a base radius of 4 units. What is the volume of the cone? (Use $\pi \approx 3.14$)

- A) 48.56 cubic units
- B) 75.36 cubic units
- C) 150.72 cubic units
- D) 452.16 cubic units

113. What is the measure of an exterior angle of a regular hexagon?

- A) 30 degrees
- B) 45 degrees
- C) 60 degrees
- D) 72 degrees

114. If $\sin x - \frac{1}{2}$ and x is in the first quadrant, what is the value of $\cos x$?

- A) $\frac{\sqrt{3}}{2}$
- B) $\frac{1}{2}$
- C) $\frac{1}{\sqrt{3}}$
- D) $\sqrt{3}$

B. Math Test - Calculator

- **Number of Questions:** 38
- **Time Allotted:** 55 minutes
- **Format:** Multiple-choice and grid-in

Heart of Algebra: 16 questions

115. What is the solution to the equation $2x + 3 - 7$?

- A) 2
- B) 3
- C) 1
- D) 4

116. If $4y - 5 - 11$, what is the value of y?

- A) 2
- B) 3
- C) 4
- D) 5

117. Solve for x: $3x + 2 - 5x - 6$.

- A) 4
- B) -4
- C) 3
- D) -3

118. The equation $y - 2x + 1$ represents a line. What is the slope of this line?

- A) 1
- B) 2
- C) 3
- D) 4

119. If $y - 3x + 2$ and $y - x + 6$, what is the value of x?

- A) 2
- B) 1
- C) -1
- D) -2

120. Solve for y: $6y + 7 - 3y - 5$.

- A) -4
- B) 4
- C) -3
- D) 3

121. What is the value of x in the equation $5(x - 2) - 3x + 4$?

- A) 7
- B) 6
- C) 5
- D) 4

122. If $y - 4x - 1$ and $y - -x + 14$, what is the value of y?

- A) 15
- B) 14
- C) 13
- D) 12

123. Solve for x: $2(x + 5) - 3x - 4$.

- A) 14
- B) 13
- C) 12
- D) 11

124. The line $y - -3x + 7$ passes through the point $(a, 1)$. What is the value of a?

- A) 2
- B) 3
- C) 4
- D) 5

125. What is the solution to the system of equations: $2x + y - 10$ and $x - y - 2$?

- A) $(4, 2)$
- B) $(3, 1)$
- C) $(2, 3)$
- D) $(1, 4)$

126. If $5x + 3 - 2x + 12$, what is the value of x?

- A) 3
- B) 4
- C) 5
- D) 6

127. **Solve for** y: $4(y - 1) - 2(y + 5)$.

- A) 7
- B) 8
- C) 9
- D) 10

128. If $y - 5x + 6$ and $y - -2x + 8$, what is the value of y?

- A) 64/8
- B) 52/7
- C) 25/9
- D) 7/52

129. **Solve for** x: $3(x - 4) - 2(x + 1)$.

- A) 7
- B) 8
- C) 9
- D) 14

130. If $6x - 2y - 10$ and $x - 3$, what is the value of y?

- A) 4
- B) 5
- C) 6
- D) 7

Problem Solving and Data Analysis: 8 questions

131. A bookstore sells used books for $5 each and new books for $15 each. If a customer buys a total of 12 books and spends $120, how many used and new books did they buy?

- A) 6 used books and 6 new books
- B) 8 used books and 4 new books
- C) 4 used books and 8 new books
- D) 10 used books and 2 new books

132. A company's revenue increased from $250,000 in 2018 to $300,000 in 2019. What was the percentage increase in revenue?

- A) 15%
- B) 20%
- C) 25%
- D) 30%

133. If 40% of a class of 50 students are boys, how many girls are in the class?

- A) 20
- B) 25
- C) 30
- D) 35

134. A car rental company charges a flat fee of $20 per day plus $0.25 per mile driven. If a customer rents a car for 3 days and drives 100 miles, what is the total cost?

- A) $45
- B) $65
- C) $75
- D) $85

135. A baker uses 2 cups of flour for every 3 cups of sugar to make cookies. If the baker wants to make a batch using 12 cups of sugar, how many cups of flour are needed?

- A) 6
- B) 8
- C) 10
- D) 12

136. The table below shows the number of students in each grade who participate in the school's science club:

Grade	Number of Students
9	15
10	20
11	25
12	30

What is the average number of students per grade participating in the science club?

- A) 20
- B) 22.5
- C) 25
- D) 27.5

137. If the population of a town is 24,000 and is growing at a rate of 2% per year, what will be the population after 3 years?

- A) 24,749
- B) 29,346
- C) 25,469
- D) 26,136

138. A store sells apples for $1.20 each or 3 for $3.00. If you buy 9 apples using the 3-for-$3.00 deal, how much do you save compared to buying each apple individually?

- A) $1.80
- B) $2.40
- C) $3.60
- D) $4.20

Passport to Advanced Math: 11 questions

139. Solve for x in the equation $\frac{x+3}{x-1} - 2$.

- A) 1
- B) -1
- C) 2
- D) 3

140. If $f(x) - x^2 + 4x + 4$, what is the vertex of the parabola?

- A) (-4, 0)
- B) (-2, 4)
- C) (-2, 0)
- D) (2, -4)

141. The function $g(x) = \sqrt{4x + 16}$ is equivalent to:

- A) $2(x + 4)$
- B) $2\sqrt{x + 4}$
- C) $2\sqrt{x + 16}$
- D) $4\sqrt{x}$

142. Solve the system of equations: $2x + y = 5$ and $x - y = 1$.

- A) (1, 3)
- B) (2, 1)
- C) (3, -1)
- D) (4, -3)

143. If $h(x) = x^3 - 3x^2 + 2x$, what is the value of $h(2)$?

- A) 0
- B) 4
- C) 8
- D) 10

144. Factor completely: $x^3 - 9x$.

- A) $x(x^2 - 9)$
- B) $x(x - 3)(x + 3)$
- C) $x^2(x - 9)$
- D) $(x - 3)(x^2 + 3x + 3)$

145. The equation of a circle is $(x - 3)^2 + (y + 2)^2 - 16$. What is the radius of the circle?

- A) 3
- B) 4
- C) 5
- D) 6

146. If $f(x) - 2x^2 - 4x + 6$, what is the minimum value of $f(x)$?

- A) 2
- B) 4
- C) 6
- D) 8

147. Solve for x in the equation $2^{2x-1} - 16$.

- A) 1
- B) 2
- C) 3
- D) 4

148. What is the inverse function of $f(x) - 3x + 5$?

- A) $f^{-1}(x) - \frac{x-5}{3}$
- B) $f^{-1}(x) - \frac{x+5}{3}$
- C) $f^{-1}(x) = 3x - 5$
- D) $f^{-1}(x) - \frac{x}{3} - 5$

149. Solve the inequality: $3x - 4 \leq 2x + 5$.

- A) $x \geq 9$
- B) $x \leq 9$
- C) $x \leq 1$
- D) $x \geq 1$

Additional Topics in Math (geometry, trigonometry, etc.): 3 questions

150. In a right triangle, one of the angles measures $30°$. If the hypotenuse of the triangle is 10 units, what is the length of the side opposite the $30°$ angle?

- A) 5
- B) $5\sqrt{3}$
- C) $10\sqrt{3}$
- D) 10

151. What is the area of a sector with a central angle of $45°$ in a circle with a radius of 12 units?

- A) 18π
- B) 24π
- C) 36π
- D) 48π

152. The coordinates of the vertices of a triangle are $A(1, 2)$, $B(4, 6)$, and $C(7, 2)$. What is the area of the triangle?

- A) 6
- B) 9
- C) 12
- D) 15

3. Essay (Optional)

· **Number of Questions:** 1
· **Time Allotted:** 50 minutes
· **Format:** Essay prompt
· **Task:** Analyze how the author builds an argument to persuade an audience.

The following passage is adapted from "The Role of Technology in Education" by Sarah Johnson, originally published in 2020.

Technology has become an integral part of modern education, transforming the way students learn and teachers instruct. The integration of technology in the classroom has the potential to enhance educational outcomes by providing access to a wealth of resources, fostering collaboration, and personalizing learning experiences. Embracing technology in education is essential for preparing students for the demands of the 21st century.

One of the most significant benefits of technology in education is the access it provides to a vast array of resources. The internet offers students an almost limitless source of information, enabling them to conduct research, access academic journals, and explore subjects in greater depth. Digital textbooks and online courses make learning more flexible and accessible, especially for students in remote or underserved areas. By utilizing these resources, students can expand their knowledge and engage with material that may not be available in traditional textbooks.

Technology also facilitates collaboration and communication among students and teachers. Online platforms and tools, such as discussion boards, video conferencing, and collaborative documents, allow students to work together on projects, share ideas, and provide feedback regardless of their physical location. This fosters a sense of community and encourages the development of important skills such as teamwork and communication. Teachers can use these tools to create interactive and engaging lessons, making learning more dynamic and effective.

Personalized learning is another advantage of incorporating technology into education. Adaptive learning software can analyze students' progress and tailor instruction to meet their individual needs. This ensures that students receive the appropriate level of challenge and support, helping them to master concepts at their own pace. For example, a student struggling with math can receive additional practice and resources, while a student excelling in the subject can be given more advanced material to explore. This personalized approach can lead to improved academic performance and greater student engagement.

Despite the numerous benefits, some critics argue that technology can be a distraction in the classroom. However, when used effectively and with proper guidance, technology can be a powerful tool for enhancing learning rather than detracting from it. Educators must be trained to integrate technology seamlessly into their teaching practices, ensuring that it complements and enhances traditional methods rather than replacing them.

In conclusion, the role of technology in education is multifaceted and transformative. By providing access to a wealth of resources, facilitating collaboration, and personalizing learning experiences, technology can significantly enhance educational outcomes. It is crucial for educators, policymakers, and stakeholders to embrace and invest in technology to prepare students for the challenges and opportunities of the modern world.

Essay Prompt:

Write an essay in which you explain how Sarah Johnson builds an argument to persuade her audience that technology is essential for modern education. In your essay, analyze how Johnson uses one or more of the features listed below (or features of your own choice) to strengthen the logic and persuasiveness of her argument. Be sure that your analysis focuses on the most relevant features of the passage.

- Evidence, such as facts or examples, to support claims
- Reasoning to develop ideas and to connect claims and evidence
- Stylistic or persuasive elements, such as word choice or appeals to emotion, to add power to the ideas expressed

Your essay should not explain whether you agree with Johnson's claims, but rather explain how Johnson builds an argument to persuade her audience.

Full Length Practice SAT #4

1. Evidence-Based Reading and Writing (EBRW)

A. Reading Test

- **Number of Questions:** 52
- **Time Allotted:** 65 minutes
- **Format:** Multiple-choice
- **Passages:** 5 (each passage 10 questions)

Literature: 10 questions

The following passage is excerpted from "Jane Eyre" by Charlotte Brontë, originally published in 1847.

> *In this scene, Jane Eyre, an orphaned young woman employed as a governess, reflects on her complex feelings for her employer, Mr. Rochester.*
>
> *He had not kept his promise of passive docility; he had hotly repelled me, and the worst of it was that I reproached myself for having taken a step which seemed so provoking to him. And yet I had longed to do it, ever since the very day I doubted the correctness of his intentions. I had longed to enlighten him, to open his eyes, to teach him his own ignorance; but, when I was getting a lesson of*

the sort myself, I had unawares also become the teacher.

"You are not your own," I had said to him, "you are mine; I claim you; not for my pleasure, but for my Sovereign's service."

His face had expressed a different feeling from that which animated me. It was sorrowful and woeful, beyond measure, and that had power over me; it had influenced my passions. The reader knows I had wrought hard to extirpate from my soul the germs of love there detected; and now, at the first renewed view of him, they spontaneously arrived, green and strong! He made me love him without looking at me.

I looked, and had an acute pleasure in looking—a precious, yet poignant pleasure; pure gold, with a steely point of agony: a pleasure like what the thirst-perishing man might feel, who knows the well to which he has crept is poisoned, yet stoops and drinks divine draughts nevertheless.

I had struggled against strong feelings: I had restrained my emotions; but, in the end, I had been conquered. I had been overthrown, yet I had caught the victory in my hand.

I murmured: "Who is it that speaks to me in the tone of a master? Who dares it?" It is my spirit that addresses your spirit; just as if both had passed through the grave, and we stood at God's feet, equal—as we are!"

"Jane," Mr. Rochester said to me: "I could bend and kiss you right now, if that would restore you to health; it would ease my heart to bow my head on your shoulder and weep, for we have suffered much. Jane, it is time to end this miserable state of things. It is time to be at peace. Do not struggle so, like a wild frantic bird that is rending its own plumage in its desperation."

"I am no bird; and no net ensnares me; I am a free human being with an independent will, which I now exert to leave you."

Another effort set me at liberty, and I stood erect before him.

"And your will shall decide your destiny," he said: "I offer you my hand, my heart, and a share of all my possessions. You play a

farce, which I merely laugh at."
He held out his hand; I put it aside, and left him.

1) What is Jane Eyre reflecting on in this passage?

- · A) Her feelings about her job as a governess
- · B) Her complex emotions towards Mr. Rochester
- · C) Her plans to leave Thornfield
- · D) Her childhood memories

2) How does Mr. Rochester react to Jane's attempt to enlighten him?

- · A) He is amused
- · B) He hotly repels her
- · C) He agrees with her
- · D) He remains passive and docile

3) What does Jane mean when she says, "You are not your own, you are mine; I claim you; not for my pleasure, but for my Sovereign's service"?

- · A) She is claiming Mr. Rochester for herself
- · B) She is expressing her feelings of ownership over Mr. Rochester
- · C) She is stating that Mr. Rochester belongs to a higher purpose
- · D) She is asking Mr. Rochester to serve her

4) What feelings does Mr. Rochester's sorrowful and woeful expression evoke in Jane?

- · A) Indifference
- · B) Anger
- · C) Sympathy and love
- · D) Fear

5) What metaphor does Jane use to describe her feelings when she looks at Mr. Rochester?

- A) A man dying of thirst who drinks from a poisoned well
- B) A bird trapped in a cage
- C) A flower blooming in spring
- D) A stormy sea

6) How does Jane describe her struggle with her emotions?

- A) She has easily overcome them
- B) She has restrained them but ultimately been conquered
- C) She has ignored them completely
- D) She has fully embraced them

7) What does Jane mean when she says, "I am no bird; and no net ensnares me; I am a free human being with an independent will"?

- A) She is declaring her independence and free will
- B) She is admitting to being trapped
- C) She is asking for help
- D) She is expressing her desire to stay

8) What offer does Mr. Rochester make to Jane?

- A) To leave Thornfield
- B) To give her money
- C) To marry her and share all his possessions
- D) To become her servant

9) How does Jane respond to Mr. Rochester's offer?

- A) She accepts it immediately

- B) She considers it carefully
- C) She rejects it and leaves
- D) She asks for more time to think

10) What does Mr. Rochester say to Jane about her decision to leave?

- A) He tries to force her to stay
- B) He respects her decision and offers his hand
- C) He remains silent
- D) He laughs at her and mocks her decision

Historical Documents: 10 questions

The following passage is excerpted from "Ain't I a Woman?" by Sojourner Truth, originally delivered in 1851.

Well, children, where there is so much racket there must be something out of kilter. I think that 'twixt the Negroes of the South and the women at the North, all talking about rights, the white men will be in a fix pretty soon. But what's all this here talking about?

That man over there says that women need to be helped into carriages, and lifted over ditches, and to have the best place everywhere. Nobody ever helps me into carriages, or over mud-puddles, or gives me any best place! And ain't I a woman? Look at me! Look at my arm! I have ploughed and planted, and gathered into barns, and no man could head me! And ain't I a woman? I could work as much and eat as much as a man—when I could get it—and bear the lash as well! And ain't I a woman? I have borne thirteen children, and seen most all sold off to slavery, and when I cried out with my mother's grief, none but Jesus heard me! And ain't I a woman?

Then they talk about this thing in the head; what's this they call it? [member of audience whispers, "intellect"] That's it, honey.

*What's that got to do with women's rights or Negroes' rights? If
my cup won't hold but a pint, and yours holds a quart, wouldn't
you be mean not to let me have my little half-measure full?*

*Then that little man in black there, he says women can't have
as much rights as men, 'cause Christ wasn't a woman! Where did
your Christ come from? From God and a woman! Man had nothing
to do with Him.*

11) What does Sojourner Truth suggest is causing the "racket"?

- A) The clamor for rights by both Negroes in the South and women in
  the North
- B) The noise from a nearby market
- C) A political debate in the government
- D) A festival celebration

12) What point does Truth make about the assistance women receive?

- A) Women are always helped into carriages and over ditches
- B) She has never received such assistance, despite being a woman
- C) Men do not help women at all
- D) Only wealthy women receive assistance

**13) What does Truth emphasize by asking "Ain't I a woman?" multiple
times?**

- A) Her strength and capability despite societal expectations of women
- B) Her need for protection and help from men
- C) Her wish to be treated differently
- D) Her desire to be seen as weaker than men

14) How does Truth describe her physical labor?

- A) She rarely worked and was often idle
- B) She ploughed, planted, and gathered, outperforming many men
- C) She did light work that required little effort
- D) She avoided physical labor as much as possible

15) What does Truth say about her experience with motherhood?

- A) She has never had children
- B) She has borne thirteen children, most of whom were sold into slavery
- C) She has had many children who all lived close to her
- D) She does not mention motherhood in her speech

16) What is Truth's argument regarding intellect and rights?

- A) Only people with high intellect deserve rights
- B) Intellect should not determine one's rights
- C) Women have less intellect than men
- D) Rights are unrelated to intellect and only apply to men

17) What analogy does Truth use to discuss fairness in rights?

- A) Comparing different sizes of cups to different amounts of rights
- B) Comparing animals to humans
- C) Comparing different types of food to rights
- D) Comparing different seasons of the year

18) How does Truth challenge the argument that women can't have as many rights as men because Christ wasn't a woman?

- A) By saying Christ was equally man and woman
- B) By pointing out that Christ came from God and a woman, with no involvement from man

- C) By arguing that Christ had no bearing on women's rights
- D) By agreeing with the statement but suggesting a different approach

19) What rhetorical strategy does Truth use throughout her speech?

- A) Humor and sarcasm
- B) Emotional appeals and repetition
- C) Scientific evidence and data
- D) Legal jargon and formal language

20) What is the overall theme of Truth's speech?

- A) The need for better education for women
- B) The call for equal rights for both women and African Americans
- C) The importance of religion in women's lives
- D) The significance of intellectual achievements

Social Sciences: 10 questions

The following passage is adapted from "Sapiens: A Brief History of Humankind" by Yuval Noah Harari, originally published in 2011.

About 70,000 years ago, Homo sapiens began to form complex structures called cultures. The Cognitive Revolution marked the beginning of history, as it enabled humans to communicate in new ways and create shared myths. These myths facilitated large-scale cooperation and the formation of societies.

One of the most significant developments was the creation of imagined orders. Unlike the physical laws of nature, these orders exist only in the minds of humans. They include legal systems, economic structures, and religious beliefs. For example, the concept of money is an imagined order. Money has no intrinsic value, but because people collectively believe in its worth, it can be used as a medium of exchange.

Another important aspect of human culture is the ability to gossip. Gossiping may seem trivial, but it is crucial for building trust and maintaining social bonds. Early Homo sapiens used gossip to share information about who could be trusted and who could not. This allowed larger groups to live and work together.

The Agricultural Revolution, which began around 12,000 years ago, further transformed human societies. By domesticating plants and animals, humans could produce surplus food, which led to population growth and the development of cities. However, this shift also introduced new challenges, such as social hierarchies and resource management issues.

The ability to create and believe in shared myths enabled Homo sapiens to adapt and thrive in diverse environments. It also led to the rise of empires, religions, and trade networks. These complex structures allowed humans to dominate the planet, but they also created inequalities and conflicts.

In modern times, the power of shared myths remains evident. Nations, corporations, and institutions are all based on collective beliefs. Understanding the role of imagined orders in shaping human history helps us grasp the complexity of our societies and the forces that drive them.

Harari's exploration of the Cognitive Revolution and the creation of imagined orders provides a framework for understanding the development of human societies. It highlights the unique ability of Homo sapiens to cooperate and innovate through shared beliefs, shaping the world we live in today.

21) What event marked the beginning of history according to the passage?

- A) The Agricultural Revolution

- B) The Cognitive Revolution
- C) The Industrial Revolution
- D) The Scientific Revolution

22) What are imagined orders as described in the passage?

- A) Natural laws of physics
- B) Complex physical structures
- C) Concepts that exist only in the minds of humans
- D) Biological processes

23) Which of the following is an example of an imagined order?

- A) Gravity
- B) Money
- C) Photosynthesis
- D) Earth's rotation

24) What role does gossip play in human culture according to the passage?

- A) It is a trivial activity with no real purpose
- B) It helps in building trust and maintaining social bonds
- C) It hinders social cooperation
- D) It is used mainly for entertainment

25) When did the Agricultural Revolution begin?

- A) About 70,000 years ago
- B) About 12,000 years ago
- C) About 2,000 years ago
- D) About 500 years ago

26) What was one consequence of the Agricultural Revolution?

- A) Decrease in population
- B) Development of cities and population growth
- C) Decline in social hierarchies
- D) Reduction in resource management issues

27) How did the ability to create and believe in shared myths benefit Homo sapiens?

- A) It allowed them to dominate other species physically
- B) It enabled them to adapt and thrive in diverse environments
- C) It reduced the need for cooperation
- D) It hindered the formation of large-scale societies

28) What modern entities are based on collective beliefs according to the passage?

- A) Natural phenomena
- B) Nations, corporations, and institutions
- C) Individual preferences
- D) Biological traits

29) What does understanding the role of imagined orders help us grasp?

- A) The simplicity of human societies
- B) The complexity of our societies and the forces that drive them
- C) The unchanging nature of human history
- D) The physical laws governing the universe

30) What unique ability of Homo sapiens does Harari highlight in his exploration?

- A) The ability to physically overpower other species
- B) The ability to cooperate and innovate through shared beliefs
- C) The ability to live in isolation
- D) The ability to survive without social bonds

Natural Sciences: 10 questions

The following passage is adapted from "A Short History of Nearly Everything" by Bill Bryson, originally published in 2003.

One of the most remarkable aspects of our planet is the presence of water in its liquid form. Water is essential for all known forms of life, and its unique properties make it one of the most important substances on Earth. Understanding the behavior and characteristics of water helps us comprehend many of the natural processes that shape our world.

Water is a polar molecule, meaning it has a positive charge on one end and a negative charge on the other. This polarity allows water molecules to form hydrogen bonds with each other, giving water its cohesive and adhesive properties. Cohesion refers to the attraction between water molecules, which allows water to form droplets and enables surface tension. Adhesion is the attraction between water molecules and other substances, which helps water climb up plant roots and stems in a process known as capillary action.

One of the most unusual properties of water is its behavior when it freezes. Unlike most substances, water expands when it solidifies. This occurs because the hydrogen bonds between water molecules create a crystalline structure that is less dense than liquid water. As a result, ice floats on water, providing an insulating layer that protects aquatic life during cold periods.

Water's high specific heat capacity is another critical property. It takes a large amount of energy to change the temperature of water, which helps regulate Earth's climate. Oceans, which cover about

71% of the Earth's surface, act as massive heat sinks, absorbing and storing solar energy. This thermal inertia moderates temperatures, making coastal regions more temperate and influencing weather patterns globally.

The solvent properties of water are also vital for life. Water can dissolve a wide range of substances, making it an excellent medium for chemical reactions. In biological systems, water transports nutrients, gases, and waste products, facilitating metabolic processes and maintaining homeostasis.

The hydrologic cycle describes the continuous movement of water on, above, and below the Earth's surface. This cycle includes processes such as evaporation, condensation, precipitation, and runoff. Solar energy drives the cycle, evaporating water from oceans, lakes, and rivers. The water vapor rises, cools, and condenses to form clouds, eventually falling back to Earth as precipitation. This cycle is crucial for replenishing freshwater resources and sustaining ecosystems.

Bryson's exploration of water highlights its indispensable role in maintaining life and shaping our planet. By understanding the unique properties and behaviors of water, we gain insight into the fundamental processes that govern Earth's environment and support its diverse forms of life.

31) Why is water essential for all known forms of life?

- A) It is a source of energy
- B) It has unique properties that support life
- C) It is the most abundant substance on Earth
- D) It provides oxygen to living organisms

32) What is a polar molecule, as described in the passage?

- A) A molecule with a uniform charge

- B) A molecule with a positive charge on one end and a negative charge on the other
- C) A molecule that does not interact with other molecules
- D) A molecule that is always in a gaseous state

33) What property of water allows it to form droplets and enables surface tension?

- A) Adhesion
- B) Cohesion
- C) Solvent properties
- D) Specific heat capacity

34) What is capillary action?

- A) The process by which water forms hydrogen bonds
- B) The attraction between water molecules and other substances, allowing water to climb up plant roots and stems
- C) The expansion of water when it freezes
- D) The process of water evaporating from oceans

35) Why does ice float on water?

- A) Ice is denser than liquid water
- B) Ice forms a crystalline structure that is less dense than liquid water
- C) Water molecules lose their hydrogen bonds when they freeze
- D) Ice has a lower specific heat capacity

36) What is the significance of water's high specific heat capacity?

- A) It allows water to freeze at higher temperatures
- B) It helps regulate Earth's climate by moderating temperatures
- C) It makes water an excellent solvent

- D) It enables water to evaporate quickly

37) How do oceans influence weather patterns globally?

- A) By reflecting sunlight
- B) By acting as massive heat sinks, absorbing and storing solar energy
- C) By causing volcanic eruptions
- D) By preventing evaporation

38) What role does water play in biological systems according to the passage?

- A) It provides mechanical support to cells
- B) It transports nutrients, gases, and waste products
- C) It acts as a physical barrier against pathogens
- D) It generates electrical impulses

39) What drives the hydrologic cycle?

- A) Earth's gravitational pull
- B) Wind patterns
- C) Solar energy
- D) Volcanic activity

40) What does the hydrologic cycle include?

- A) The formation of ice and snow
- B) The continuous movement of water on, above, and below the Earth's surface
- C) The freezing and thawing of glaciers
- D) The chemical reaction of water with other substances

Dual Passages (Literature, Social Science, or Science): 10 questions

Passage 1

The following passage is adapted from "The Origin of Species" by Charles Darwin, originally published in 1859.

As many more individuals of each species are born than can possibly survive; and as, consequently, there is a frequently recurring struggle for existence, it follows that any being, if it vary however slightly in any manner profitable to itself, under the complex and sometimes varying conditions of life, will have a better chance of surviving, and thus be naturally selected. From the strong principle of inheritance, any selected variety will tend to propagate its new and modified form.

This principle of preservation, I have called, for the sake of brevity, Natural Selection. But the expression often used by Mr. Herbert Spencer, of the Survival of the Fittest, is more accurate, and is sometimes equally convenient. We have seen that man by selection can certainly produce great results, and can adapt organic beings to his own uses through the accumulation of slight but useful variations, given to him by the hand of Nature. But Natural Selection, as we shall hereafter see, is a power incessantly ready for action, and is immeasurably superior to man's feeble efforts, as nature's productions are to man's productions.

Passage 2

The following passage is adapted from "The Selfish Gene" by Richard Dawkins, originally published in 1976.

Let us try to teach generosity and altruism, because we are born selfish. Let us understand what our own selfish genes are up to, because we may then at least have the chance to upset their designs, something that no other species has ever aspired to do. We have the power to defy the selfish genes of our birth and, if necessary, the selfish memes of our indoctrination. We can even discuss ways of deliberately cultivating and nurturing pure, disinterested altruism—something that has no place in nature, something that has never existed before in the whole history of the world.

We are survival machines—robot vehicles blindly programmed to preserve the selfish molecules known as genes. This explains the ruthless, competitive aspects of human nature, and indeed, of the nature of all other animals. But it also allows for the possibility of genuine, disinterested, true altruism. We have at least the possibility of selflessness in our gift, and that is the challenge we face in understanding our true nature.

41) What is the main principle discussed in Passage 1 by Charles Darwin?

- A) Genetic modification
- B) Natural Selection
- C) Artificial Intelligence
- D) Quantum Mechanics

42) According to Passage 1, what does "Survival of the Fittest" refer to?

- A) The strength of the individuals
- B) The ability to adapt and survive
- C) The intelligence of the species
- D) The speed of reproduction

43) What does Richard Dawkins suggest we are born with in Passage 2?

- A) Altruism
- B) Selfishness
- C) Neutrality

- D) Intelligence

44) What is the main argument presented by Dawkins in Passage 2?

- A) Humans are inherently altruistic
- B) Humans can defy their selfish genes and cultivate altruism
- C) Natural selection is superior to human efforts
- D) Nature is inherently altruistic

45) How does Darwin describe the power of natural selection in Passage 1?

- A) Inferior to human efforts
- B) Occasionally effective
- C) Immeasurably superior to man's efforts
- D) Limited in scope

46) What does Dawkins mean by "selfish memes" in Passage 2?

- A) Selfish genetic material
- B) Cultural ideas that promote selfishness
- C) Technological innovations
- D) Artistic expressions

47) What do both passages suggest about the nature of survival and competition?

- A) Both are driven by external factors
- B) Both are influenced by genetic and natural processes
- C) Both are irrelevant to modern society
- D) Both are controlled by human intervention

48) In Passage 1, how does Darwin view man's ability to influence

organic beings?

- A) As superior to natural processes
- B) As insignificant compared to natural selection
- C) As equivalent to natural selection
- D) As irrelevant to the survival of species

49) What challenge does Dawkins present to humans in Passage 2?

- A) To dominate other species
- B) To understand and overcome their selfish genes
- C) To ignore genetic influences
- D) To enhance natural selection

50) How do the viewpoints on altruism differ between the two passages?

- A) Darwin sees it as central to survival, while Dawkins sees it as a challenge to cultivate.
- B) Both see altruism as non-existent in nature.
- C) Darwin promotes altruism, while Dawkins denies its possibility.
- D) Both see altruism as a natural outcome of evolution.

B. Writing and Language Test

- **Number of Questions:** 44
- **Time Allotted:** 35 minutes
- **Format:** Multiple-choice
- **Passages:** 4 (each passage 11 questions)

Careers: 11 questions

The Role of a Data Scientist in Today's World

(1) In the digital age, data has become one of the most valuable resources. (2) Data scientists are the professionals tasked with extracting insights and knowledge from vast amounts of data. (3) This role requires a combination of analytical skills, technical expertise, and business acumen, making it one of the most sought-after careers today.

(4) Data scientists work in a variety of industries, including technology, healthcare, finance, and marketing. (5) Their primary responsibility is to analyze data to help organizations make informed decisions. (6) This process involves collecting, cleaning, and organizing large datasets, often using programming languages such as Python or R.

(7) Once the data is prepared, data scientists use statistical and machine learning techniques to identify patterns and trends. (8) They build predictive models to forecast future outcomes and provide actionable insights. (9) For example, a data scientist in the healthcare industry might develop a model to predict patient readmissions, helping hospitals improve patient care and reduce costs.

(10) Communication is a crucial aspect of a data scientist's job. (11) They must be able to explain complex technical findings to non-technical stakeholders. (12) This often involves creating visualizations, such as charts and graphs, to make the data more accessible. (13) Effective communication ensures that the insights derived from data analysis are understood and can be applied to solve real-world problems.

(14) Collaboration is also essential in data science. (15) Data scientists often work as part of a multidisciplinary team, including data engineers, analysts, and business leaders. (16) Together, they

define the problems to be solved, determine the best approach, and implement solutions. (17) This collaborative environment fosters innovation and ensures that data-driven decisions are aligned with organizational goals.

(18) The demand for data scientists has grown rapidly in recent years, driven by the increasing availability of data and advances in technology. (19) As organizations recognize the value of data, the need for skilled professionals who can harness this resource continues to rise. (20) According to industry reports, data science is one of the fastest-growing fields, with high salaries and strong job security.

(21) To become a data scientist, a solid educational foundation in mathematics, statistics, and computer science is essential. (22) Many data scientists also have advanced degrees in fields such as data science, machine learning, or artificial intelligence. (23) Practical experience through internships, projects, and competitions, such as Kaggle, is highly valuable. (24) Continuous learning is also crucial, as the field of data science is constantly evolving.

(25) The role of a data scientist is both challenging and rewarding. (26) It offers the opportunity to work on cutting-edge technology, solve complex problems, and make a significant impact on organizations and society. (27) For those with a passion for data and a desire to drive innovation, a career in data science can be a fulfilling and lucrative choice.

51) Which choice best describes what happens in the passage?

- A) The passage describes the role of data scientists, the skills required, and the impact of their work on various industries.
- B) The passage provides a history of data science and its development over time.
- C) The passage critiques the use of data in modern businesses.
- D) The passage explains the technical details of machine learning

algorithms.

52) Which choice best expresses the main idea of the passage?

- A) Data science is a field that requires extensive technical skills and offers high salaries.
- B) Data scientists are essential for extracting valuable insights from data, and their work impacts many industries.
- C) The primary responsibility of data scientists is to collect data using programming languages.
- D) Communication skills are the most important aspect of a data scientist's job.

53) In context, what does the phrase "extracting insights and knowledge from vast amounts of data" in sentence 2 most nearly mean?

- A) Collecting and storing large datasets.
- B) Analyzing data to find meaningful information.
- C) Creating visualizations from data.
- D) Organizing data into databases.

54) Which sentence, if added after sentence 5, would best support the main idea of the paragraph?

- A) They often work long hours to meet deadlines.
- B) They also use their findings to develop new products and services.
- C) They need to understand business objectives to provide relevant insights.
- D) They attend conferences to stay updated on the latest trends.

55) In sentence 9, the author uses the example of a data scientist in the healthcare industry to:

- A) Highlight the technical skills required in the field.
- B) Illustrate a practical application of data science.
- C) Describe the process of building predictive models.
- D) Emphasize the importance of patient care.

56) Which choice provides the most accurate interpretation of the data in sentence 18?

- A) The demand for data scientists has decreased due to advances in technology.
- B) The demand for data scientists has grown rapidly because of the increasing availability of data.
- C) The demand for data scientists remains stable across various industries.
- D) The demand for data scientists is limited to the technology sector.

57) In sentence 23, what does the mention of "Kaggle" contribute to the passage?

- A) It highlights a platform where data scientists can gain practical experience.
- B) It provides an example of a data visualization tool.
- C) It shows a common challenge data scientists face.
- D) It indicates a programming language used by data scientists.

58) The author wants to add the following sentence to the fourth paragraph:
"Visualizations are crucial for making complex data more understand-able and actionable." Where would this sentence best fit?

- A) Before sentence 10
- B) After sentence 11
- C) Before sentence 12

- D) After sentence 13

59) In context, the word "implement" in sentence 16 most nearly means:

- A) Design
- B) Ignore
- C) Execute
- D) Plan

60) Which choice best concludes the passage?

- A) Data scientists should focus more on developing new algorithms.
- B) The future of data science is uncertain and will require significant changes.
- C) Data science offers numerous career opportunities and the chance to drive innovation.
- D) The role of data scientists will diminish as new technologies emerge.

61) Which choice most effectively combines sentences 12 and 13?

- A) This often involves creating visualizations, such as charts and graphs, to make the data more accessible; effective communication ensures that the insights derived from data analysis are understood and can be applied to solve real-world problems.
- B) This often involves creating visualizations, such as charts and graphs, to make the data more accessible, and effective communication ensures that the insights derived from data analysis are understood and can be applied to solve real-world problems.
- C) This often involves creating visualizations, such as charts and graphs, to make the data more accessible and ensuring that the insights derived from data analysis are understood and can be applied

to solve real-world problems.

- D) This often involves creating visualizations, such as charts and graphs, to make the data more accessible, effective communication ensures that the insights derived from data analysis are understood and can be applied to solve real-world problems.

History/Social Studies: 11 questions

The Rise and Fall of the Roman Empire

(1) The Roman Empire, one of the most influential civilizations in history, rose to power in the 1st century BCE and dominated much of Europe, the Middle East, and North Africa for centuries. (2) Its contributions to law, politics, engineering, and culture have left a lasting legacy on the world. (3) Understanding the factors that contributed to the rise and fall of the Roman Empire provides valuable insights into the dynamics of powerful civilizations.

(4) The foundation of the Roman Empire can be traced back to the Roman Republic, which was established in 509 BCE. (5) The Republic was characterized by a complex system of governance, including elected officials and a Senate. (6) Military conquests and strategic alliances allowed Rome to expand its territory significantly during this period.

(7) The transition from Republic to Empire began with the rise of Julius Caesar. (8) In 49 BCE, Caesar crossed the Rubicon River with his army, defying the Senate and sparking a civil war. (9) His victory in the war led to his appointment as dictator for life, effectively ending the Republic. (10) After Caesar's assassination in 44 BCE, his adopted heir, Octavian (later known as Augustus), emerged as the first emperor of Rome in 27 BCE.

(11) The Pax Romana, or Roman Peace, was a period of relative stability and prosperity that lasted for over 200 years. (12) During this time, the empire saw significant advancements in infrastruc-

ture, including the construction of roads, aqueducts, and public buildings. *(13)* Roman law and governance systems were also refined and codified, influencing legal systems in many modern nations.

(14) Despite its strengths, the Roman Empire faced numerous challenges. *(15)* Political corruption and power struggles often led to instability. *(16)* The empire's vast size made it difficult to govern effectively, and communication across its territories was slow. *(17)* Economic troubles, including heavy taxation and reliance on slave labor, further strained the empire.

(18) External pressures also played a crucial role in the decline of the Roman Empire. *(19)* Barbarian invasions, particularly by the Visigoths, Vandals, and Huns, weakened the empire's defenses. *(20)* In 410 CE, the Visigoths, led by King Alaric, sacked Rome, delivering a significant blow to the empire's prestige and power.

(21) The division of the empire into Eastern and Western halves in 285 CE by Emperor Diocletian was an attempt to manage its vast territories more effectively. *(22)* While the Eastern Roman Empire, also known as the Byzantine Empire, continued to thrive for centuries, the Western Roman Empire faced ongoing decline. *(23)* The final blow came in 476 CE when the last Roman emperor, Romulus Augustulus, was deposed by the Germanic chieftain Odoacer.

(24) The fall of the Roman Empire marked the end of ancient Rome's dominance and the beginning of the Middle Ages in Europe. *(25)* However, its cultural and technological contributions continued to influence subsequent civilizations. *(26)* The study of Roman history offers valuable lessons about the rise and fall of great powers and the enduring impact of their achievements.

62) Which choice best describes what happens in the passage?

- A) The passage explores the major events and factors contributing to the rise and fall of the Roman Empire.

- B) The passage focuses on the cultural achievements of the Roman Empire.
- C) The passage highlights the military strategies used by the Roman Empire.
- D) The passage discusses the technological advancements during the Roman Empire.

63) Which choice best expresses the main idea of the passage?

- A) The Roman Empire's achievements in law and engineering have no parallel.
- B) The rise and fall of the Roman Empire offer important insights into the dynamics of powerful civilizations.
- C) Julius Caesar's leadership was the most critical factor in the rise of the Roman Empire.
- D) The Roman Empire's decline was solely due to external invasions.

64) In context, what does the phrase "Pax Romana" in sentence 11 most nearly mean?

- A) A time of frequent wars
- B) A period of economic decline
- C) A time of relative stability and prosperity
- D) A period of political chaos

65) Which sentence, if added after sentence 13, would best support the main idea of the paragraph?

- A) Roman architecture was known for its grandeur and durability.
- B) The Romans also built an extensive network of roads that facilitated trade and communication.
- C) The Roman army was one of the most formidable military forces

of its time.

- D) Gladiatorial games were a popular form of entertainment in ancient Rome.

66) In sentence 15, the author mentions "political corruption and power struggles" primarily to:

- A) Highlight the internal challenges faced by the Roman Empire.
- B) Describe the efficient governance of the Roman Empire.
- C) Explain the technological advancements of the Roman Empire.
- D) Emphasize the cultural achievements of the Roman Empire.

67) Which choice provides the most accurate interpretation of the data in sentence 17?

- A) The Roman Empire had a robust and equitable economic system.
- B) The Roman Empire's economy was strained by heavy taxation and reliance on slave labor.
- C) The Roman Empire had no economic issues.
- D) The Roman Empire's economic troubles were insignificant.

68) In sentence 19, what does the mention of "Barbarian invasions" contribute to the passage?

- A) It highlights a major internal conflict within the Roman Empire.
- B) It provides evidence of external pressures contributing to the decline of the Roman Empire.
- C) It indicates the Roman Empire's military dominance.
- D) It suggests that the Roman Empire successfully repelled all invasions.

69) The author wants to add the following sentence to the fourth paragraph:

"The assassination of Julius Caesar in 44 BCE marked a turning point in Roman history." Where would this sentence best fit?

- A) Before sentence 8
- B) After sentence 9
- C) Before sentence 10
- D) After sentence 11

70) In context, the word "deposed" in sentence 23 most nearly means:

- A) Exiled
- B) Crowned
- C) Overthrown
- D) Honored

71) Which choice best concludes the passage?

- A) The fall of the Roman Empire marked the end of ancient Rome's dominance and the beginning of the Middle Ages in Europe.
- B) The Roman Empire's decline was primarily due to internal strife and political corruption.
- C) The Roman Empire's cultural and technological achievements were unparalleled.
- D) The fall of the Roman Empire had no lasting impact on future civilizations.

72) Which choice most effectively combines sentences 6 and 7?

- A) Military conquests and strategic alliances allowed Rome to expand its territory significantly during this period, beginning with the rise of Julius Caesar.
- B) The Republic's military conquests and strategic alliances allowed Rome to expand its territory significantly during this period, leading

to the rise of Julius Caesar.

- C) The Republic was characterized by a complex system of governance, including elected officials and a Senate, and military conquests and strategic alliances allowed Rome to expand its territory significantly during this period.
- D) Military conquests and strategic alliances allowed Rome to expand its territory significantly during this period, beginning with the rise of Julius Caesar who led to the fall of the Republic.

Humanities: 11 questions

The Role of Literature in Social Change

(1) Literature has long been a powerful tool for social change, influencing public opinion and inspiring movements for justice and equality. (2) Through storytelling, authors can challenge societal norms, expose injustices, and give voice to marginalized communities. (3) The impact of literature on social change can be seen throughout history, from the abolitionist movement to the fight for civil rights.

(4) One of the most influential works of literature in the abolitionist movement was "Uncle Tom's Cabin" by Harriet Beecher Stowe. (5) Published in 1852, the novel depicted the harsh realities of slavery and humanized enslaved people, stirring strong emotions among readers. (6) Stowe's portrayal of the brutal treatment of African Americans galvanized the abolitionist cause and increased support for ending slavery in the United States.

(7) In the early 20th century, the Harlem Renaissance produced a wealth of literary works that highlighted the experiences of African Americans. (8) Writers such as Langston Hughes, Zora Neale Hurston, and Claude McKay used their work to celebrate black culture and address issues of racial injustice. (9) Their contributions helped to foster a sense of pride and identity within the African

American community and brought attention to the need for social change.

(10) The mid-20th century saw the emergence of literature that supported the civil rights movement. (11) James Baldwin's essays and novels, such as "The Fire Next Time" and "Go Tell It on the Mountain," explored the complexities of race, identity, and injustice in America. (12) Baldwin's powerful prose and insightful commentary helped to shed light on the systemic racism faced by African Americans and encouraged readers to confront these issues.

(13) In addition to racial justice, literature has also played a crucial role in advocating for gender equality. (14) Simone de Beauvoir's "The Second Sex," published in 1949, is considered a foundational text in feminist philosophy. (15) De Beauvoir's analysis of the oppression of women and her call for gender equality influenced generations of feminists and sparked discussions on the social construction of gender roles.

(16) The latter half of the 20th century and the early 21st century saw the rise of literature that addressed issues of LGBTQ+ rights. (17) Authors such as Audre Lorde, James Baldwin, and Tony Kushner used their works to explore themes of sexuality, identity, and discrimination. (18) Their writings helped to raise awareness about the struggles faced by LGBTQ+ individuals and contributed to the growing movement for equal rights.

(19) Literature has also been instrumental in environmental advocacy. (20) Rachel Carson's "Silent Spring," published in 1962, is credited with launching the modern environmental movement. (21) Carson's exposé on the dangers of pesticides highlighted the need for environmental protection and led to significant policy changes, including the eventual ban of DDT in the United States.

(22) Today, literature continues to be a catalyst for social change, addressing contemporary issues such as immigration, climate change, and social justice. (23) Writers from diverse backgrounds bring new perspectives to these topics, enriching the conversation

and inspiring action. (24) By reflecting on the human experience and challenging the status quo, literature remains a vital force in the pursuit of a more just and equitable world.

(25) The enduring power of literature to inspire social change underscores its importance in society. (26) Through the written word, authors can reach across time and space to connect with readers, advocate for justice, and envision a better future. (27) The study of literature not only enriches our understanding of the past but also empowers us to shape a more equitable and inclusive world.

73) Which choice best describes what happens in the passage?

- A) The passage explores the various roles literature has played in different social movements.
- B) The passage focuses exclusively on literature's impact on the abolitionist movement.
- C) The passage analyzes the financial success of influential books throughout history.
- D) The passage compares literature from different cultural backgrounds.

74) Which choice best expresses the main idea of the passage?

- A) Literature has been a crucial tool in advocating for and achieving social change across various movements.
- B) Only novels have had significant impacts on social justice movements.
- C) The study of literature is primarily for academic enrichment, not social change.
- D) Literature's influence on social movements is limited to historical contexts.

75) In context, what does the phrase "catalyst for social change" in sentence 22 most nearly mean?

- A) A method for preserving cultural traditions
- B) A means to slow down societal progress
- C) A trigger for initiating social reform
- D) An obstacle to achieving equality

76) Which sentence, if added after sentence 6, would best support the main idea of the paragraph?

- A) "Uncle Tom's Cabin" was criticized by some for its portrayal of African Americans.
- B) The novel's vivid depiction of slavery made it a bestseller and intensified the debate over slavery.
- C) Stowe's other works also dealt with social issues, though they were less influential.
- D) "Uncle Tom's Cabin" was adapted into several films and plays over the years.

77) In sentence 11, the author mentions James Baldwin's essays and novels primarily to:

- A) Highlight the commercial success of Baldwin's works.
- B) Illustrate literature's role in the civil rights movement.
- C) Discuss the stylistic features of mid-20th-century literature.
- D) Contrast Baldwin's work with that of Langston Hughes.

78) Which choice provides the most accurate interpretation of the data in sentence 14?

- A) Simone de Beauvoir's "The Second Sex" was widely criticized and had little impact.

· B) "The Second Sex" is a foundational text that has significantly influenced feminist philosophy.

· C) De Beauvoir's work primarily addressed issues of environmentalism.

· D) The book was not well-received and did not spark any significant discussions.

79) In sentence 18, what does the mention of authors such as Audre Lorde and Tony Kushner contribute to the passage?

· A) It highlights the financial success of LGBTQ+ literature.

· B) It provides examples of authors who addressed LGBTQ+ rights in their works.

· C) It contrasts LGBTQ+ literature with feminist literature.

· D) It suggests that only contemporary authors have addressed LGBTQ+ issues.

80) The author wants to add the following sentence to the second paragraph:

"These works not only provided entertainment but also played a pivotal role in shaping public opinion and policy." Where would this sentence best fit?**

· A) Before sentence 1

· B) After sentence 2

· C) Before sentence 3

· D) After sentence 3

81) In context, the word "exposé" in sentence 21 most nearly means:

· A) A fictional story

· B) A detailed report

· C) A scientific experiment

- D) A casual observation

82) Which choice best concludes the passage?

- A) Literature's impact on social change is often overstated.
- B) The study of literature is unnecessary for understanding social movements.
- C) Literature continues to inspire and drive social change by challenging norms and advocating for justice.
- D) Only historical literature has been significant in social movements.

83) Which choice most effectively combines sentences 10 and 11?

- A) The mid-20th century saw the emergence of literature that supported the civil rights movement, including James Baldwin's essays and novels, such as "The Fire Next Time" and "Go Tell It on the Mountain."
- B) The mid-20th century saw the emergence of literature that supported the civil rights movement, for example, James Baldwin's essays and novels, such as "The Fire Next Time" and "Go Tell It on the Mountain."
- C) The mid-20th century saw the emergence of literature that supported the civil rights movement, such as James Baldwin's essays and novels, including "The Fire Next Time" and "Go Tell It on the Mountain."
- D) The mid-20th century saw the emergence of literature that supported the civil rights movement, including James Baldwin's essays and novels, for example, "The Fire Next Time" and "Go Tell It on the Mountain."

Science: 11 questions

The Science of Earthquakes

(1) Earthquakes are one of the most powerful natural forces on Earth, capable of causing widespread destruction and loss of life. (2) Understanding the science behind earthquakes is essential for predicting their occurrence and mitigating their impact on society. (3) The study of earthquakes, known as seismology, provides valuable insights into the behavior of our planet's crust.

(4) Earthquakes occur when stress builds up along faults in the Earth's crust and is released as seismic energy. (5) This stress is typically caused by the movement of tectonic plates, which are large sections of the Earth's crust that float on the semi-fluid mantle below. (6) The boundaries where these plates interact are known as fault lines, and they are the most common locations for earthquakes to occur.

(7) The point within the Earth where an earthquake originates is called the focus or hypocenter. (8) The point directly above it on the Earth's surface is known as the epicenter. (9) The energy released during an earthquake travels in the form of seismic waves, which can be detected and measured by instruments called seismometers.

(10) There are three main types of seismic waves: primary (P) waves, secondary (S) waves, and surface waves. (11) P-waves are the fastest and travel through both solid and liquid layers of the Earth, while S-waves are slower and can only travel through solids. (12) Surface waves, which travel along the Earth's surface, are the slowest but often cause the most damage due to their larger amplitude and longer duration.

(13) The magnitude of an earthquake is measured on the Richter scale, which quantifies the amount of energy released. (14) Each whole number increase on the Richter scale represents a tenfold increase in amplitude and roughly 31.6 times more energy release.

(15) For example, a magnitude 7 earthquake releases approximately 31.6 times more energy than a magnitude 6 earthquake.

(16) In addition to the Richter scale, the moment magnitude scale (Mw) is also commonly used to measure the size of earthquakes. (17) The moment magnitude scale provides a more accurate representation of an earthquake's total energy release, especially for very large quakes. (18) Both scales are essential for comparing the sizes of earthquakes and assessing their potential impact.

(19) Earthquake prediction remains a significant challenge for scientists. (20) While it is possible to identify regions at high risk for earthquakes based on historical data and tectonic activity, accurately predicting the timing, location, and magnitude of specific events is still beyond our capabilities. (21) However, advances in seismology and technology continue to improve our understanding and monitoring of seismic activity.

(22) One area of research focuses on early warning systems, which detect the initial P-waves of an earthquake and send alerts before the more destructive S-waves and surface waves arrive. (23) These systems can provide valuable seconds to minutes of warning, allowing people to take protective actions and automated systems to shut down critical infrastructure.

(24) Earthquake-resistant construction is another crucial aspect of mitigating earthquake damage. (25) Engineers design buildings and structures to withstand seismic forces by incorporating flexible materials, reinforced frameworks, and advanced damping systems. (26) Retrofitting older buildings to meet modern seismic standards is also essential for reducing vulnerability in earthquake-prone areas.

(27) Public education and preparedness are vital components of earthquake resilience. (28) Teaching people how to respond during an earthquake, such as taking cover under sturdy furniture and avoiding windows, can save lives. (29) Community drills and emergency plans help ensure that individuals and organizations

are ready to act when an earthquake occurs.

(30) The science of earthquakes continues to evolve, providing new insights and tools for understanding and mitigating their effects. (31) By combining scientific research, technology, engineering, and public education, we can better prepare for and respond to these powerful natural events, ultimately reducing their impact on society.

84) Which choice best describes what happens in the passage?

- A) The passage explains the causes and effects of earthquakes and discusses methods to predict and mitigate their impact.
- B) The passage focuses solely on the different types of seismic waves and their characteristics.
- C) The passage provides a historical overview of significant earthquakes and their aftermaths.
- D) The passage details the construction techniques used to build earthquake-resistant structures.

85) Which choice best expresses the main idea of the passage?

- A) Understanding the science behind earthquakes is crucial for predicting them and reducing their impact on society.
- B) Earthquakes are unpredictable and uncontrollable natural disasters.
- C) Seismic waves are the most important aspect of earthquakes.
- D) Earthquake-resistant construction is the only way to prevent earthquake damage.

86) In context, what does the phrase "seismic energy" in sentence 4 most nearly mean?

- A) Electrical energy

- B) Heat energy
- C) Energy released from the Earth's crust
- D) Energy generated by human activities

87) Which sentence, if added after sentence 6, would best support the main idea of the paragraph?

- A) Fault lines are visible on the Earth's surface in many places.
- B) Tectonic plate movements are responsible for the majority of the planet's seismic activity.
- C) Earthquakes can also occur in areas not near fault lines.
- D) The study of tectonic plates began in the early 20th century.

88) In sentence 7, the term "hypocenter" refers to:

- A) The point directly above the epicenter on the Earth's surface.
- B) The location on the Earth's surface where an earthquake is felt most strongly.
- C) The point within the Earth where an earthquake originates.
- D) The point where seismic waves cause the most damage.

89) Which choice provides the most accurate interpretation of the data in sentence 14?

- A) The Richter scale measures the speed of seismic waves.
- B) Each whole number increase on the Richter scale indicates twice as much energy release.
- C) The Richter scale quantifies the amplitude and energy release of an earthquake.
- D) The Richter scale is no longer used to measure earthquakes.

90) In sentence 18, what does the mention of the moment magnitude scale (Mw) contribute to the passage?

- A) It highlights a different method for measuring the size of earth-quakes, especially large ones.
- B) It suggests that the Richter scale is obsolete and no longer in use.
- C) It explains how seismic waves are generated and measured.
- D) It describes the technology used to construct earthquake-resistant buildings.

91) The author wants to add the following sentence to the second paragraph:

"These instruments are crucial for monitoring and studying seismic activity." Where would this sentence best fit?**

- A) After sentence 3
- B) After sentence 5
- C) After sentence 8
- D) After sentence 9

92) In context, the word "elusive" in sentence 11 most nearly means:

- A) Evident
- B) Uncertain
- C) Abundant
- D) Overlooked

93) Which choice best concludes the passage?

- A) Seismic waves are the most critical aspect of earthquake study.
- B) Public education about earthquakes is unnecessary.
- C) By integrating scientific research, technology, engineering, and public education, society can better handle the impact of earthquakes.
- D) Earthquake prediction will always be an impossible task.

94) Which choice most effectively combines sentences 24 and 25?

- A) Earthquake-resistant construction is another crucial aspect of mitigating earthquake damage, and engineers design buildings and structures to withstand seismic forces by incorporating flexible materials, reinforced frameworks, and advanced damping systems.
- B) Earthquake-resistant construction is another crucial aspect of mitigating earthquake damage, engineers design buildings and structures to withstand seismic forces by incorporating flexible materials, reinforced frameworks, and advanced damping systems.
- C) Earthquake-resistant construction is another crucial aspect of mitigating earthquake damage; engineers design buildings and structures to withstand seismic forces by incorporating flexible materials, reinforced frameworks, and advanced damping systems.
- D) Earthquake-resistant construction is another crucial aspect of mitigating earthquake damage, engineers designing buildings and structures to withstand seismic forces by incorporating flexible materials, reinforced frameworks, and advanced damping systems.

2. Math

A. Math Test - No Calculator

- **Number of Questions:** 20
- **Time Allotted:** 25 minutes
- **Format:** Multiple-choice and grid-in

Heart of Algebra: 8 questions

95. Solve for y in the equation:

   $2y + 7 - 3y - 5$

- A) -12

- B) -7

- C) 7

- D) 12

96. If $4x - y - 11$ and $y - 2x + 3$, what is the value of x?

- A) 1

- B) 3

- C) 6

- D) 7

97. What is the solution to the system of equations:

   $2x + y - 10$
   $3x - y - 5$

- A) $(1, 8)$

- B) $(2, 6)$

- C) $(3, 4)$

- D) $(4, 2)$

98. Solve the inequality:

   $4x + 1 < 9$

- A) $x < 1$

- B) $x < 2$

- C) $x < 3$

- D) $x < 4$

99. If $5x + 2y - 19$ and $x - 3y - -8$, what is the value of y?

- A) 59/17
- B) 26/54
- C) 17/54
- D) 76/39

100. The difference between two numbers is 7. If one number is twice the other, what are the numbers?

- A) 7 and 14
- B) 7 and 0
- C) 7 and 21
- D) 7 and 10

101. Find the value of x if $9x - 4 - 5x + 16$.

- A) 2
- B) 4
- C) 5
- D) 7

102. What is the solution to the equation $3(4x + 2) - 5x + 18$?

- A) 5/17
- B) 13/15
- C) 12/7
- D) 9/10

Problem Solving and Data Analysis: 3 questions

103. A car rental company charges a flat fee of $20 per day plus $0.15 per mile driven. If a customer rents a car for 3 days and drives 150 miles, what is the total cost?

- A) $55.00
- B) $57.50
- C) $82.50
- D) $65.00

104. The table below shows the number of books sold by a bookstore in a week:

Day	Books Sold
Monday	40
Tuesday	30
Wednesday	25
Thursday	30
Friday	50
Saturday	60
Sunday	45

What is the average number of books sold per day?

- A) 35
- B) 40
- C) 41
- D) 45

105. A survey of 200 people found that 75% of them prefer coffee over tea. How many people prefer tea?

- A) 40
- B) 50
- C) 60
- D) 70

Passport to Advanced Math: 6 questions

106. What is the value of x in the equation $2^{3x-1} - 16$?

- A) $\frac{5}{3}$
- B) 2
- C) $\frac{4}{3}$
- D) $\frac{7}{3}$

107. If $h(x) - 4x^2 + 3x - 5$, what is $h(-2)$?

- A) 5
- B) 11
- C) 9
- D) 7

108. Solve the quadratic equation $3x^2 - 12x + 9 = 0$ for x.

- A) $x - 1$ or $x - 3$
- B) $x - 2$ or $x - 3$
- C) $x - 1$ or $x - 1$
- D) $x - 3$ or $x - 3$

109. If $k(x) = x^2 - 4x + 7$, what is the vertex of the parabola defined by $k(x)$?

- A) $(2, -1)$
- B) $(2, 3)$
- C) $(2, -3)$
- D) $(2, 4)$

110. Solve for x in the equation $5^{2x-1} = 125$.

- A) 2
- B) 3
- C) 4
- D) $\frac{5}{2}$

111. If $f(x) = \frac{2x+3}{x-1}$, what is the value of $f(3)$?

- A) 2.5
- B) 3.1
- C) 4.5
- D) 6.2

Additional Topics in Math (geometry, trigonometry, etc.): 3 questions

112. A circle has a radius of 5 units. What is the area of the sector formed by a central angle of 60 degrees? (Use $\pi \approx 3.14$)

- A) 4.18 square units
- B) 13.09 square units
- C) 20.94 square units
- D) 31.42 square units

113. In triangle ABC, $\angle C$ is a right angle, and $\angle A - 30°$. If the length of side AB is 10 units, what is the length of side AC?

- A) 5 units
- B) $5\sqrt{3}$ units
- C) 10 units
- D) $10\sqrt{3}$ units

114. What is the period of the function $f(x) - 3\sin(2x)$?

- A) π
- B) 2π
- C) $\frac{\pi}{2}$
- D) 4π

B. Math Test - Calculator

- **Number of Questions:** 38
- **Time Allotted:** 55 minutes
- **Format:** Multiple-choice and grid-in

Heart of Algebra: 16 questions

115. Solve for x in the equation $7x - 3 - 4x + 9$.

- A) 2
- B) 3
- C) 4
- D) 5

116. If $2y + 7 - 3y - 5$, what is the value of y?

- A) 12
- B) -12
- C) 10
- D) -10

117. Solve for x: $4(x - 1) - 2x + 6$.

- A) 4
- B) 3
- C) 5
- D) 6

118. The equation $y - -3x + 5$ represents a line. What is the y-intercept of this line?

- A) -3
- B) 5
- C) 3
- D) -5

119. If $y - 2x + 4$ and $y - -x + 1$, what is the value of x?

- A) 1
- B) -1
- C) 2
- D) -2

120. Solve for y: $5y - 3 - 2y + 6$.

- A) 3
- B) -3
- C) 2
- D) -2

121. What is the value of x in the equation $6(x + 1) - 3x + 15$?

- A) 3
- B) 4
- C) 5
- D) 6

122. If $y - -3x + 7$ and $y - 2x - 3$, what is the value of y?

- A) 1
- B) 2
- C) 3
- D) 4

123. Solve for x: $7(x - 2) - 4(x + 3)$.

- A) 8.16
- B) 7.56
- C) 8.67
- D) 9.95

124. The line $y - 4x - 9$ passes through the point $(a, -1)$. What is the value of a?

- A) 1
- B) 2
- C) 3
- D) 4

125. What is the solution to the system of equations: $x + y - 8$ and $x - y - 4$?

- A) $(6, 2)$
- B) $(5, 3)$
- C) $(4, 4)$
- D) $(3, 5)$

126. If $8x + 4 - 2x + 28$, what is the value of x?

- A) 4
- B) 5
- C) 6
- D) 7

127. **Solve for y: $3(2y - 1) = 4(y + 2)$.**

- A) 3/11
- B) 5/4
- C) 11/2
- D) 2/11

128. **If $y = 3x + 8$ and $y = -2x + 3$, what is the value of y?**

- A) 4
- B) 5
- C) 6
- D) 7

129. **Solve for x: $5(x - 2) = 3(x + 4)$.**

- A) 11
- B) 14
- C) 15
- D) 18

130. **If $3x = 2y = 14$ and $x = 6$, what is the value of y?**

- A) 1
- B) 2
- C) 3
- D) 4

Problem Solving and Data Analysis: 8 questions

131. A car travels 150 miles on 5 gallons of gas. What is the car's fuel efficiency in miles per gallon?

- A) 20
- B) 25
- C) 30
- D) 35

132. The average score of 5 students in a math test is 78. If four students scored 72, 85, 90, and 65, what is the score of the fifth student?

- A) 70
- B) 75
- C) 80
- D) 85

133. If the price of a product is reduced by 20%, and the new price is $80, what was the original price?

- A) $90
- B) $100
- C) $105
- D) $120

134. A survey of 100 people found that 45% prefer coffee, 35% prefer tea, and the remaining prefer neither. How many people prefer neither?

- A) 10
- B) 15
- C) 20
- D) 25

135. A student needs to score an average of 80 on 5 tests to pass a course. If the scores on the first four tests are 78, 82, 76, and 85, what score does the student need on the fifth test to pass?

- A) 79
- B) 80
- C) 81
- D) 82

136. A rectangular garden has a length of 20 feet and a width of 15 feet. If a fence costs $5 per foot, how much will it cost to fence the entire garden?

- A) $200
- B) $300
- C) $350
- D) $400

137. A recipe requires 3 cups of sugar for every 4 cups of flour. If you want to make a half-sized batch of the recipe, how many cups of sugar will you need if you use 2 cups of flour?

- A) 0.75
- B) 1.5
- C) 2
- D) 2.5

138. If a shirt originally costs $50 and is marked down by 30%, what is the sale price of the shirt?

- A) $15
- B) $25
- C) $35
- D) $45

Passport to Advanced Math: 11 questions

139. If $p(x) = x^3 - 6x^2 + 11x - 6$, what are the roots of the polynomial?

- A) 1, 2, 3
- B) -1, -2, -3
- C) 1, -2, 3
- D) 2, 3, -1

140. Solve for x in the equation $\sqrt{2x + 3} - 1 = 0$.

- A) -1
- B) 1
- C) 2
- D) 3

141. What is the value of k if the polynomial $x^3 - 4x^2 + kx - 8$ has a root at $x = 2$?

- A) 2
- B) 4
- C) 6
- D) 8

142. The function $f(x) = 2x^3 - 5x^2 + 3x - 7$ has a local maximum at $x = a$. What is the value of a?

- A) 1
- B) 2
- C) 3
- D) 4

143. If $g(x) - x^2 + 4x + c$ has only one solution, what is the value of c?

- A) 2
- B) 4
- C) -4
- D) -2

144. Solve for x in the equation $2^x - 32$.

- A) 3
- B) 4
- C) 5
- D) 6

145. What is the value of x if $5^{2x-1} - 125$?

- A) 1
- B) 2
- C) 3
- D) 4

146. If $h(x) - x^4 - 8x^3 + 16x^2$, factor $h(x)$ completely.

- A) $x^2(x - 4)^2$
- B) $x(x - 4)^3$
- C) $x^2(x^2 - 8x + 16)$
- D) $x(x^3 - 8x^2 + 16x)$

147. Solve for x in the inequality $\frac{x+1}{x-2} > 3$.

- A) $x = 3.5$

- B) $x = 4.5$

- C) $x = 6.0$

- D) $x = 5.0$

148. The function $f(x) = 2x^2 + 3x + c$ intersects the x-axis at $x = -3$ and $x = 1$. What is the value of c?

- A) 6

- B) -6

- C) 3

- D) -3

149. If $f(x) = x^2 + 2x - 3$, what is the y-intercept of the function?

- A) -3

- B) 1

- C) -1

- D) 3

Additional Topics in Math (geometry, trigonometry, etc.): 3 questions

150. In a circle with a radius of 8 units, what is the length of an arc that subtends a central angle of 60°?

- A) $\frac{8\pi}{3}$

- B) $\frac{4\pi}{3}$

- C) $\frac{16\pi}{3}$

- D) $\frac{2\pi}{3}$

151. A parallelogram has sides of length 10 units and 15 units. If the measure of the angle between the two sides is $60°$, what is the area of the parallelogram?

- A) 75
- B) $75\sqrt{3}$
- C) 150
- D) $150\sqrt{3}$

152. What is the volume of a right circular cone with a radius of 6 units and a height of 9 units?

- A) 108π
- B) 216π
- C) 324π
- D) 432π

3. Essay (Optional)

- **Number of Questions:** 1
- **Time Allotted:** 50 minutes
- **Format:** Essay prompt
- **Task:** Analyze how the author builds an argument to persuade an audience.

The following passage is adapted from "The Benefits of a Plant-Based Diet" by Dr. Emily Carter, originally published in 2021.

Adopting a plant-based diet is one of the most effective ways to improve personal health and contribute to environmental sustainability. This dietary approach, which emphasizes fruits, vegetables, grains, nuts, and seeds while minimizing or eliminating animal products, has been shown to offer numerous benefits. As more people become aware of the positive impacts of plant-based eating, it is crucial to understand the compelling reasons behind this lifestyle choice.

One of the most significant advantages of a plant-based diet is its potential to enhance overall health. Research has consistently shown that individuals who follow plant-based diets have lower rates of chronic diseases such as heart disease, diabetes, and certain cancers. A study published in the Journal of the American Heart Association found that people who adhere to a plant-based diet have a 16% lower risk of developing cardiovascular disease. This is likely due to the high levels of fiber, antioxidants, and healthy fats found in plant foods, which help to reduce inflammation and improve heart health.

In addition to its health benefits, a plant-based diet is also more environmentally sustainable compared to diets rich in animal products. The production of plant-based foods generally requires fewer natural resources, such as water and land, and generates lower levels of greenhouse gas emissions. According to a report by the United Nations, livestock farming is responsible for approximately 14.5% of global greenhouse gas emissions, making it a significant contributor to climate change. By reducing or eliminating the consumption of animal products, individuals can help to decrease their carbon footprint and mitigate the impact of climate change.

Furthermore, plant-based diets can contribute to global food security. As the global population continues to grow, the demand for food is increasing rapidly. Producing plant-based foods is more efficient than raising animals for meat, as it requires fewer resources and produces more calories per acre of land. This means that shifting towards a plant-based diet can help to ensure that there is enough food to feed the world's population, particularly in regions where food scarcity is a pressing issue.

Critics of plant-based diets often argue that they lack sufficient protein and other essential nutrients. However, with careful planning and a varied diet, it is entirely possible to meet all nutritional needs through plant-based sources. Foods such as legumes, tofu, quinoa, and nuts are excellent sources of protein, while fortified plant-based milk and leafy greens provide calcium and other essential nutrients. Dietitians and nutritionists can offer guidance to ensure that individuals following plant-based diets receive balanced and adequate nutrition.

In conclusion, adopting a plant-based diet offers a range of benefits, including improved health, environmental sustainability, and enhanced global food security. By providing evidence from scientific research and addressing common concerns, it is clear that a plant-based diet is a viable and beneficial option for individuals and the planet. As awareness of these advantages grows, more people are likely to consider making the switch to a plant-based lifestyle.

Essay Prompt:

Write an essay in which you explain how Dr. Emily Carter builds an argument to persuade her audience that adopting a plant-based diet is beneficial. In your essay, analyze how Carter uses one or more of the features listed below (or features of your own choice) to strengthen the logic and persuasiveness of her argument. Be sure that your analysis focuses on the most relevant features of the passage.

- Evidence, such as facts or examples, to support claims
- Reasoning to develop ideas and to connect claims and evidence
- Stylistic or persuasive elements, such as word choice or appeals to emotion, to add power to the ideas expressed

Your essay should not explain whether you agree with Carter's claims, but rather explain how Carter builds an argument to persuade her audience.

Full Length Practice SAT #5

1. Evidence-Based Reading and Writing (EBRW)

A. Reading Test

- **Number of Questions:** 52
- **Time Allotted:** 65 minutes
- **Format:** Multiple-choice
- **Passages:** 5 (each passage 10 questions)

Literature: 10 questions

The following passage is excerpted from "Great Expectations" by Charles Dickens, originally published in 1861.

In this scene, Pip, an orphan raised by his sister and her husband, reflects on his interactions with Estella, a young woman he admires.

The lady whom I had never seen before, lifted her eyes and looked archly at me, and then I saw that the eyes were Estella's eyes. But she was so much changed, was so much more beautiful, so much more womanly, in all things winning admiration, had made such wonderful advance, that I knew her not until she smiled. From the day of our first meeting, I had known that she was proud, moody, and capricious, and had a rich luxurious nature that was shut up like a jewel in a dark casket, but now I thought I had never seen such a beautiful young lady; nor was I alone in the perception, for all the love and pride that had been accumulating within me ever since I first saw her, seemed to rush upon me now in a flood that I could not have checked or controlled.

"It is a sad sight," said Estella, with a slow and level look at me; "to see you, Pip, grown up like this, and yet no wiser than when you were a boy. It is a sad sight."

"I am wiser now," said I, feeling utterly hopeless, but determined to see it out; "and I will make myself wiser yet, Estella."

"The ship that gets away from a wharf," said Estella, "does not make its own voyage to any port. But with regard to the other question, I have to say that I have no softness there, no—sympathy—sentiment—nonsense."

I spoke of my young fancy and how I had grown up with it, and she spoke of the meanness and ignorance that had marked my childhood and youth. She spoke of the coarse hands and thick boots that I had humiliated myself by thinking she despised me for, and she spoke of the secret hope I had cherished, of being, one day, restored to her good opinion.

"You must know," said Estella, condescending to me as a brilliant and beautiful woman might, "that I have no heart—if that has anything to do with my memory."

I stood looking at her in dismay. I had believed in the reality of her heart. I had believed in the existence of her sympathies. I had believed in the possibility of her affection.

"I have not bestowed my tenderness anywhere. I have never had any such thing. I know no more of it. I ask you, dear Pip," said Estella, rising and bending her hand toward me, "to dismiss it from your thoughts."

"You are part of my existence, part of myself. You have been in every line I have ever read, since I first came here, the rough common boy whose poor heart you wounded even then. You have

been in every prospect I have ever seen since—on the river, on the sails of the ships, on the marshes, in the clouds, in the light, in the darkness, in the wind, in the woods, in the sea, in the streets. You have been the embodiment of every graceful fancy that my mind has ever become acquainted with. The stones of which the strongest London buildings are made, are not more real, or more impossible to be displaced by your hands, than your presence and influence have been to me, there and everywhere, and will be."

1) How does Pip initially fail to recognize Estella?

- A) She has changed her hairstyle
- B) She is much more beautiful and womanly
- C) She is dressed in different clothes
- D) She is standing in the shadows

2) What qualities had Pip always known Estella to have?

- A) Kindness and generosity
- B) Pride, moodiness, and capriciousness
- C) Shyness and humility
- D) Intelligence and wit

3) How does Pip feel when he sees Estella again?

- A) Indifferent and unaffected
- B) Overwhelmed by admiration and love
- C) Angry and resentful
- D) Confused and disoriented

4) What is Estella's reaction to seeing Pip grown up?

- A) She is pleased and proud of him

- B) She is sad and critical of his lack of wisdom
- C) She is indifferent and dismissive
- D) She is angry and confrontational

5) What metaphor does Estella use to describe Pip's progress in life?

- A) A tree growing tall and strong
- B) A ship that gets away from a wharf
- C) A bird learning to fly
- D) A flower blooming in the spring

6) How does Estella describe her feelings toward Pip and others?

- A) She has a deep affection for Pip
- B) She feels sympathy and sentiment for everyone
- C) She has no heart, tenderness, or sentiment
- D) She is filled with love and compassion

7) What does Pip confess about his feelings for Estella?

- A) He no longer cares for her
- B) She is part of his existence and has influenced every aspect of his life
- C) He has always despised her
- D) He feels indifferent towards her

8) What does Estella ask Pip to do regarding his feelings for her?

- A) To cherish them forever
- B) To dismiss them from his thoughts
- C) To express them openly
- D) To write them down

9) What does Pip believe about Estella's capacity for affection?

- A) That she is capable of deep love and sympathy
- B) That she has no capacity for affection
- C) That she loves him deeply
- D) That she is indifferent to everyone

10) What imagery does Pip use to describe Estella's presence in his life?

- A) She is like a fleeting shadow
- B) She is like a beautiful dream
- C) She is part of every aspect of his existence, as real and immovable as the strongest buildings in London
- D) She is like a distant star

Historical Documents: 10 questions

The following passage is excerpted from "The Gettysburg Address" by Abraham Lincoln, originally delivered in 1863.

Fourscore and seven years ago our fathers brought forth on this continent, a new nation, conceived in Liberty, and dedicated to the proposition that all men are created equal. Now we are engaged in a great civil war, testing whether that nation, or any nation so conceived and so dedicated, can long endure. We are met on a great battlefield of that war. We have come to dedicate a portion of that field, as a final resting place for those who here gave their lives that that nation might live. It is altogether fitting and proper that we should do this.

But, in a larger sense, we can not dedicate—we can not consecrate—we can not hallow—this ground. The brave men, living and dead, who struggled here, have consecrated it, far above our poor power to add or detract. The world will little note, nor long remember what we say here, but it can never forget what they did here. It is for us the living, rather, to be dedicated here to the unfinished work which they who fought here have thus far so nobly advanced. It is rather for us to be here dedicated to the great task remaining before us—that from these honored dead we take increased devotion to that cause for which they gave the last full measure of devotion—that we here highly resolve that these dead shall not have died in vain—that this nation, under God, shall have a new birth of freedom—and that government of the people, by the people, for the people, shall not perish from the earth.

11) What event is Abraham Lincoln referring to when he says "Fourscore and seven years ago"?

- A) The signing of the Declaration of Independence
- B) The start of the Civil War
- C) The end of the Civil War
- D) The drafting of the Constitution

12) What proposition was the new nation dedicated to according to Lincoln?

- A) Freedom of religion
- B) Economic prosperity
- C) Equality of all men
- D) Territorial expansion

13) What is the main purpose of Lincoln's speech?

- A) To declare victory in the Civil War
- B) To dedicate a portion of the battlefield as a cemetery
- C) To announce a new law
- D) To criticize the enemy

14) According to Lincoln, who has already consecrated the ground of the battlefield?

- A) The politicians
- B) The civilians
- C) The brave men, living and dead, who struggled there
- D) The clergy

15) What does Lincoln suggest about the words spoken at the dedication compared to the actions taken by the soldiers?

- A) The words are more important than the actions
- B) The actions of the soldiers are more important than the words spoken
- C) Both are equally important
- D) The words will be remembered longer than the actions

16) What does Lincoln believe is the "unfinished work" that the living must dedicate themselves to?

- A) Building more memorials
- B) Advancing the cause for which the soldiers gave their lives
- C) Writing more speeches
- D) Ending the Civil War

17) What does Lincoln hope for the nation as a result of the sacrifices made by the soldiers?

- A) A new birth of freedom
- B) Greater territorial expansion
- C) Economic prosperity
- D) Immediate peace with the enemy

18) What does Lincoln mean by "that government of the people, by the people, for the people, shall not perish from the earth"?

- A) The government should be controlled by a select few
- B) The government should be abolished
- C) The democratic government should continue to exist
- D) The government should be replaced with a monarchy

19) How does Lincoln describe the dedication of the battlefield in a "larger sense"?

- A) As an insignificant act
- B) As something that the living cannot truly accomplish because the ground is already consecrated by the soldiers' actions
- C) As a political maneuver
- D) As a religious ceremony

20) What emotion does Lincoln primarily express in this address?

- A) Joy and celebration
- B) Anger and resentment
- C) Solemnity and dedication
- D) Indifference and detachment

Social Sciences: 10 questions

The following passage is adapted from "Quiet: The Power of Introverts in a World That Can't Stop Talking" by Susan Cain, originally published in 2012.

> In a society that often celebrates extroversion, introverts are fre-
> quently undervalued. However, introverts possess unique strengths
> that can be just as powerful as those of their extroverted counter-

parts. *Understanding and appreciating these strengths can lead to more balanced and effective interactions in both personal and professional settings.*

Introverts tend to be more reflective and deliberate. They often think before they speak and are less likely to take unnecessary risks. This cautious approach can be advantageous in decision-making processes, as it allows for thorough consideration of potential outcomes. Introverts are also known for their ability to focus deeply on tasks, often working independently and with great concentration. This capacity for sustained attention can lead to high-quality work and creative problem-solving.

Another significant strength of introverts is their ability to listen actively. In conversations, introverts are more likely to listen attentively and process information before responding. This skill can foster better communication and understanding, as it allows for thoughtful and meaningful exchanges. Introverts often form deep, meaningful relationships due to their preference for quality over quantity in social interactions.

Introverts also excel in environments that require solitude and independence. Many artists, writers, and scientists who have made significant contributions to their fields have been introverts. Their ability to work alone and immerse themselves in their work has often led to groundbreaking discoveries and creations.

Despite these strengths, introverts may struggle in environments that favor extroverted behaviors, such as open-plan offices and group brainstorming sessions. It is important for organizations to recognize and accommodate different working styles to leverage the strengths of both introverts and extroverts. Providing quiet spaces for focused work and allowing for written contributions in meetings can help create a more inclusive and productive environment.

Understanding the value of introverts challenges the cultural bias towards extroversion and highlights the importance of diversity in personality types. By appreciating and harnessing the unique strengths of introverts, we can create a more balanced and dynamic society.

21) According to the passage, what is often celebrated in society?

- A) Introversion
- B) Extroversion
- C) Independence
- D) Silence

22) What unique strength do introverts possess regarding decision-making?

- A) They make quick decisions
- B) They take unnecessary risks
- C) They think before they speak and consider potential outcomes thoroughly
- D) They rely on others for advice

23) How are introverts described in their approach to tasks?

- A) Easily distracted and collaborative
- B) Deeply focused and often working independently
- C) Casual and indifferent
- D) Quick and inattentive

24) What is one significant strength of introverts in conversations?

- A) They dominate the conversation
- B) They listen actively and process information before responding
- C) They avoid conversations
- D) They interrupt frequently

25) What type of relationships do introverts tend to form?

- A) Shallow and numerous
- B) Deep and meaningful
- C) Professional and detached
- D) Competitive and aggressive

26) In what type of environments do introverts particularly excel?

- A) Noisy and chaotic environments
- B) Environments that require solitude and independence
- C) Highly social and interactive environments
- D) Competitive and high-pressure environments

27) Which professions are mentioned as having significant contributions from introverts?

- A) Politicians and salespeople
- B) Artists, writers, and scientists
- C) Entertainers and athletes
- D) Lawyers and managers

28) What challenges do introverts face in certain work environments?

- A) They struggle in quiet spaces
- B) They face difficulties in open-plan offices and group brainstorming sessions
- C) They have trouble with independent work
- D) They dislike solitary tasks

29) What can organizations do to accommodate different working styles?

- A) Enforce a one-size-fits-all approach
- B) Provide quiet spaces for focused work and allow for written contributions in meetings
- C) Eliminate all quiet spaces
- D) Mandate frequent group activities for all employees

30) What does understanding the value of introverts challenge?

- A) The cultural bias towards extroversion
- B) The importance of independent work
- C) The need for collaboration
- D) The significance of communication

Natural Sciences: 10 questions

The following passage is adapted from "The Immortal Life of Henrietta Lacks" by Rebecca Skloot, originally published in 2010.

In 1951, a young African American woman named Henrietta Lacks visited the colored section of the Johns Hopkins Hospital in Baltimore, Maryland, complaining of a painful "knot" in her womb. She was diagnosed with cervical cancer, and during her treatment, doctors took a biopsy of her tumor without her knowledge or consent. This sample would go on to become one of the most important tools in medicine: HeLa cells.

HeLa cells were the first human cells to be successfully cultured and maintained outside the body. Unlike normal cells, which can only divide a finite number of times, HeLa cells are immortal; they can divide indefinitely under the right conditions. This unique property has made HeLa cells invaluable for scientific research.

One of the earliest and most significant uses of HeLa cells was in the development of the polio vaccine. In the 1950s, polio was a devastating disease, paralyzing and killing thousands of people worldwide. Researchers used HeLa cells to grow and study the poliovirus, which was crucial in developing a vaccine that effectively halted the spread of the disease.

HeLa cells have also been instrumental in cancer research. Because they are cancerous cells, they have provided insights into how cancer develops and proliferates. Scientists have used HeLa cells to study the effects of radiation, chemotherapy, and other treatments, leading to better understanding and new therapies for cancer patients.

Moreover, HeLa cells have played a role in numerous medical breakthroughs, including cloning, gene mapping, and in vitro fertilization. They have been used to study the effects of zero gravity in space, test the effects of new drugs, and understand the mechanisms of viruses like HIV.

However, the story of HeLa cells also raises important ethical questions. Henrietta Lacks and her family were not informed about the use of her cells in research, nor did they receive any compensation for their use. The Lacks family's story has sparked debates about patients' rights, informed consent, and the commercialization of human tissues.

Skloot's account of Henrietta Lacks and the legacy of HeLa cells highlights the profound impact of this "immortal" cell line on science and medicine. It also underscores the need for ethical standards in medical research to ensure that the contributions of individuals are respected and acknowledged.

31) What was Henrietta Lacks diagnosed with when she visited Johns Hopkins Hospital?

- A) Breast cancer
- B) Lung cancer
- C) Cervical cancer
- D) Skin cancer

32) What was taken from Henrietta Lacks without her knowledge or consent?

- A) Blood sample
- B) Tumor biopsy
- C) DNA sample
- D) Bone marrow

33) What unique property do HeLa cells possess?

- A) They can only divide a finite number of times
- B) They are immune to all diseases
- C) They are immortal and can divide indefinitely under the right conditions
- D) They cannot be cultured outside the body

34) How were HeLa cells instrumental in the development of the polio vaccine?

- A) They were used to develop the first antibiotics
- B) They helped researchers grow and study the poliovirus
- C) They were used to cure patients with polio
- D) They were used to create a new strain of the virus

35) In what area of research have HeLa cells provided significant insights due to their cancerous nature?

- A) Genetic disorders
- B) Mental health
- C) Cancer research
- D) Cardiovascular diseases

36) Which of the following medical breakthroughs have HeLa cells

contributed to?

- A) Organ transplantation
- B) Cloning, gene mapping, and in vitro fertilization
- C) Vaccination for the flu
- D) Development of prosthetics

37) What ethical issues are raised by the story of HeLa cells?

- A) Privacy and data protection
- B) Environmental impact of medical waste
- C) Patients' rights, informed consent, and the commercialization of human tissues
- D) Health insurance and medical costs

38) What did the Lacks family not receive in relation to the use of HeLa cells?

- A) Information and compensation
- B) Medical treatment
- C) Legal representation
- D) Educational opportunities

39) What does Skloot's account of Henrietta Lacks emphasize about medical research?

- A) The importance of speed and efficiency
- B) The need for ethical standards to respect and acknowledge individual contributions
- C) The necessity of using human subjects for all experiments
- D) The importance of secrecy in medical advancements

40) What has been one of the uses of HeLa cells outside of direct medical

research?

- · A) Testing the effects of zero gravity in space
- · B) Building advanced robotics
- · C) Developing renewable energy sources
- · D) Studying oceanic ecosystems

Dual Passages (Literature, Social Science, or Science): 10 questions

Passage 1

The following passage is adapted from "Democracy in America" by Alexis de Tocqueville, originally published in 1835.

The health of a democratic society may be measured by the quality of functions performed by private citizens. In the United States, the practice of associating is as ancient as the country itself. The freedom to associate for political purposes is not only allowed, but it is also universally recognized as a necessary guarantee against the tyranny of the majority. In America, citizens of all ages, all conditions, and all dispositions constantly form associations. They have not only commercial and manufacturing companies, but also a multitude of other kinds: religious, moral, serious, futile, general or restricted, enormous or diminutive. The Americans make associations to give entertainments, to found seminaries, to build inns, to construct churches, to distribute books, to send missionaries to the antipodes; in this manner they found hospitals, prisons, and schools.

As soon as several of the inhabitants of the United States have taken up an opinion or a feeling which they wish to promote in the world, they look out for mutual assistance; and as soon as they have found each other out, they combine. From that moment, they are no longer isolated men, but a power seen from afar, whose actions serve for an example, and whose language is listened to. The Americans are fond of explaining almost all the actions of their lives by the principle of self-interest rightly understood. They show with complacency how an enlightened regard for themselves constantly prompts them to assist one another and inclines them willingly to sacrifice a portion of their time and property to the welfare of the state. In this respect, I think they frequently fail to do themselves justice; for sometimes, in the United States, as well as elsewhere, it is difficult to perceive the boundary line between self-interest and the general interest.

Passage 2

The following passage is adapted from "Bowling Alone: The Collapse and Revival of American Community" by Robert D. Putnam, originally published in 2000.

For the first two-thirds of the twentieth century, Americans participated in public life in ways that sustained democracy and improved the quality of life. Civic engagement involved people actively working together for a common cause in organizations, communities, and political life. However, in recent decades, social capital in the United States has declined significantly. Social capital refers to the connections among individuals—social networks and the norms of reciprocity and trustworthiness that arise from them. These networks enable society to function effectively and foster a sense of community.

One of the most notable indicators of this decline is the decrease in participation in traditional civic organizations, such as labor unions, parent-teacher associations, and fraternal organizations. For example, membership in these groups has plummeted since the 1960s. This reduction in civic engagement has weakened community bonds and reduced the overall level of social capital.

Several factors have contributed to this decline. The rise of television and other forms of electronic entertainment has played a significant role. As people spend more time in front of screens, they have less time to engage in face-to-face interactions. Additionally, increased mobility and suburbanization have led to more isolated living arrangements, further reducing opportunities for community engagement.

The consequences of this decline are profound. Communities with low levels of social capital tend to have higher crime rates, lower educational achievement, and poorer health outcomes. Rebuilding social capital requires a concerted effort to foster community engagement and create opportunities for people to connect.

Putnam argues that revitalizing civic engagement is essential for the health of American democracy. By encouraging people to participate in community activities, volunteer, and join organizations, we can rebuild social capital and strengthen the bonds that hold society together.

41) What does Tocqueville identify as a measure of the health of a democratic society in Passage 1?

- A) The wealth of the citizens
- B) The quality of functions performed by private citizens
- C) The number of laws passed by the government
- D) The strength of the military

42) What is the main concern discussed in Passage 2 by Robert D. Putnam?

- A) The rise of electronic entertainment
- B) The decline of social capital and civic engagement in America
- C) The increase in educational achievements
- D) The growth of urbanization

43) According to Passage 1, how do Americans typically form associations?

- A) They rely on government mandates
- B) They seek mutual assistance and combine once they find like-minded individuals
- C) They wait for economic incentives
- D) They depend on international organizations

44) What is one major indicator of the decline in social capital mentioned in Passage 2?

- A) The rise in crime rates
- B) The decrease in membership in traditional civic organizations
- C) The increase in television viewership
- D) The growth of suburban areas

45) How does Tocqueville in Passage 1 describe the principle that guides many American actions?

- A) Self-interest rightly understood
- B) Altruistic benevolence
- C) Government intervention
- D) International cooperation

46) What are some of the consequences of declining social capital mentioned in Passage 2?

- A) Increased wealth and prosperity
- B) Higher crime rates, lower educational achievement, and poorer health outcomes
- C) More government control
- D) Decreased electronic entertainment

47) How do both passages view the role of community engagement?

- A) As detrimental to individual success
- B) As essential for the health and function of society
- C) As an outdated concept
- D) As irrelevant to modern life

48) What solution does Putnam propose in Passage 2 to address the decline in social capital?

- A) Increasing government control over civic activities
- B) Encouraging people to participate in community activities and join organizations
- C) Reducing the amount of electronic entertainment
- D) Promoting suburban living

49) What similarity exists between the views of Tocqueville in Passage 1 and Putnam in Passage 2 regarding associations?

- A) Both view associations as driven by government mandates
- B) Both see the formation of associations as critical to the functioning of a democratic society
- C) Both believe associations are formed for purely selfish reasons
- D) Both think associations are a modern phenomenon

50) How does Tocqueville's view of American associations compare to Putnam's observations about civic engagement?

- A) Tocqueville views them as thriving and essential, while Putnam notes a decline in civic engagement
- B) Both view them as unimportant to the democratic process
- C) Tocqueville focuses on government-led associations, while Putnam emphasizes private associations

· D) Both view them as being on the decline

B. Writing and Language Test

· **Number of Questions:** 44
· **Time Allotted:** 35 minutes
· **Format:** Multiple-choice
· **Passages:** 4 (each passage 11 questions)

Careers: 11 questions

Exploring the World of Urban Planning

(1) Urban planners play a vital role in shaping the cities and towns where we live. (2) Their work involves designing and managing the development of urban areas to create sustainable, functional, and attractive environments. (3) This career requires a blend of creativity, analytical skills, and a deep understanding of community needs.

(4) One of the primary responsibilities of an urban planner is to develop land use plans and policies. (5) These plans guide the growth and development of urban areas, ensuring that land is used efficiently and sustainably. (6) Planners must consider various factors, including population growth, economic development, transportation needs, and environmental impact.

(7) Urban planners often work with a range of stakeholders, including government officials, developers, and community members. (8) They conduct public meetings to gather input and build consensus on proposed projects. (9) This collaborative approach helps to ensure that development plans reflect the needs and desires of the community.

(10) A significant aspect of urban planning is zoning, which involves regulating land use to prevent conflicts and promote

orderly development. (11) Planners designate areas for residential, commercial, industrial, and recreational use, balancing the needs of different sectors. (12) Effective zoning helps to create vibrant, livable communities with a mix of uses and amenities.

(13) Urban planners also focus on transportation planning, which aims to create efficient and accessible transportation systems. (14) This includes designing road networks, public transit systems, and pedestrian pathways. (15) Planners strive to reduce traffic congestion, improve safety, and promote sustainable transportation options, such as biking and walking.

(16) Environmental sustainability is a key consideration in urban planning. (17) Planners work to minimize the environmental impact of development by promoting green building practices, preserving open spaces, and protecting natural resources. (18) This helps to ensure that urban areas are resilient and capable of adapting to challenges such as climate change.

(19) The field of urban planning is diverse, with opportunities to specialize in areas such as economic development, environmental planning, and historic preservation. (20) Planners may work for government agencies, consulting firms, or nonprofit organizations. (21) The demand for urban planners is expected to grow as cities continue to expand and face complex challenges related to growth and sustainability.

(22) To become an urban planner, a strong educational background in urban planning, geography, or a related field is essential. (23) Many planners also hold advanced degrees in urban planning or public administration. (24) Practical experience through internships and involvement in community planning projects is highly valuable.

(25) The career of an urban planner is both challenging and rewarding. (26) It offers the opportunity to shape the future of communities and improve the quality of life for residents. (27) For those who are passionate about creating sustainable and livable

urban environments, a career in urban planning can be a fulfilling and impactful choice.

51) Which choice best describes what happens in the passage?

- A) The passage details the history of urban planning and its evolution over time.
- B) The passage describes the roles and responsibilities of urban planners and the importance of their work.
- C) The passage explains the various challenges faced by urban planners in developing countries.
- D) The passage focuses on the environmental aspects of urban planning and sustainable development.

52) Which choice best expresses the main idea of the passage?

- A) Urban planners are essential for creating sustainable, functional, and attractive urban environments.
- B) Urban planning is primarily concerned with environmental sustainability.
- C) Zoning and transportation planning are the most critical aspects of urban planning.
- D) Urban planners work mainly with government officials and developers.

53) In context, what does the phrase "public meetings to gather input and build consensus" in sentence 8 most nearly mean?

- A) Informal gatherings to socialize with the community
- B) Official sessions to collect feedback and reach an agreement
- C) Workshops to train the public in urban planning techniques
- D) Conferences to present completed development plans

54) Which sentence, if added after sentence 6, would best support the main idea of the paragraph?

- A) Urban planners use advanced software to model urban growth.
- B) These factors help ensure that urban areas remain livable and efficient.
- C) Planners must also consider the cultural heritage of the areas they develop.
- D) Public parks and recreational areas are also planned by urban planners.

55) In sentence 10, the term "zoning" refers to:

- A) The process of designing transportation networks.
- B) The regulation of land use to promote orderly development.
- C) The construction of buildings in urban areas.
- D) The development of public parks and recreational facilities.

56) Which choice provides the most accurate interpretation of the information in sentence 11?

- A) Zoning involves designating areas for mixed-use development only.
- B) Zoning helps to balance the needs of different sectors in a community.
- C) Zoning restricts development to residential areas only.
- D) Zoning eliminates the need for public input in planning.

57) In sentence 17, what does the mention of "green building practices" contribute to the passage?

- A) It highlights a specific method urban planners use to reduce environmental impact.

- B) It explains the history of environmentally friendly construction.
- C) It suggests that urban planning has little to do with environmental concerns.
- D) It argues that green building practices are the only solution to urban problems.

58) The author wants to add the following sentence to the third paragraph:

"Their input is essential to creating development plans that serve the community's best interests." Where would this sentence best fit?**

- A) After sentence 7
- B) After sentence 8
- C) After sentence 9
- D) After sentence 10

59) In context, the word "resilient" in sentence 18 most nearly means:

- A) Vulnerable
- B) Adaptable
- C) Temporary
- D) Static

60) Which choice best concludes the passage?

- A) Urban planners face numerous challenges, but their work is crucial for community development.
- B) Urban planning is primarily a technical field with little need for public involvement.
- C) The future of urban planning lies solely in technological advancements.
- D) Urban planning should focus more on rural areas than urban ones.

61) Which choice most effectively combines sentences 24 and 25?

- A) To become an urban planner, a strong educational background in urban planning, geography, or a related field is essential, and the career is both challenging and rewarding.
- B) To become an urban planner, a strong educational background in urban planning, geography, or a related field is essential, and it offers the opportunity to shape the future of communities and improve the quality of life for residents.
- C) A strong educational background in urban planning, geography, or a related field is essential to become an urban planner, and the career is both challenging and rewarding.
- D) To become an urban planner, a strong educational background in urban planning, geography, or a related field is essential, and the career of an urban planner is both challenging and rewarding.

History/Social Studies: 11 questions

The Industrial Revolution: Transforming Society and Economy

(1) The Industrial Revolution, which began in Britain in the late 18th century, was a period of profound economic, technological, and social change. (2) It marked the transition from agrarian economies to industrialized ones, fundamentally altering the way people lived and worked. (3) The innovations and advancements of this era laid the groundwork for the modern industrialized world.

(4) One of the key factors driving the Industrial Revolution was the development of new machinery and technology. (5) The invention of the steam engine by James Watt in the 1770s revolutionized transportation and manufacturing. (6) Steam engines powered factories, locomotives, and ships, making it possible to produce goods on a large scale and transport them efficiently.

(7) *The textile industry was among the first to benefit from industrialization. (8) Innovations such as the spinning jenny, the water frame, and the power loom significantly increased the speed and efficiency of textile production. (9) These advancements enabled Britain to become a leading exporter of textiles, boosting its economy and creating numerous jobs.*

(10) *The rise of factories transformed the labor market. (11) People moved from rural areas to cities in search of work, leading to rapid urbanization. (12) This shift had significant social implications, as it changed family structures and living conditions. (13) Factory work was often grueling and dangerous, with long hours and low wages, prompting calls for labor reforms.*

(14) *Transportation infrastructure also saw dramatic improvements during the Industrial Revolution. (15) The construction of canals, railways, and improved roads facilitated the movement of goods and people. (16) The first public railway, the Stockton and Darlington Railway, opened in 1825, followed by the more famous Liverpool and Manchester Railway in 1830. (17) These railways connected industrial centers, fostering economic growth and regional integration.*

(18) *The Industrial Revolution had a profound impact on society and the environment. (19) It led to the growth of a new middle class, composed of industrialists, entrepreneurs, and professionals who benefited from the economic opportunities created by industrialization. (20) However, it also resulted in environmental degradation, with factories polluting air and water, and the exploitation of natural resources.*

(21) *The social consequences of the Industrial Revolution sparked significant movements for change. (22) Workers organized to demand better working conditions, fair wages, and shorter hours. (23) These efforts led to the establishment of labor unions and the passage of labor laws that improved conditions for workers. (24) Additionally, the period saw the rise of social reformers, such as*

Robert Owen and Charles Dickens, who advocated for social justice and the welfare of the poor.

(25) The Industrial Revolution was not confined to Britain; it spread to other parts of Europe and North America, and eventually to the rest of the world. (26) Each region experienced industrialization in its own way, influenced by local conditions and resources. (27) Despite the challenges and hardships, the Industrial Revolution brought about unprecedented economic growth and technological progress.

(28) The legacy of the Industrial Revolution is evident in the modern world. (29) It set the stage for continued innovation and industrial development, shaping the economic and social structures of contemporary society. (30) Understanding the Industrial Revolution helps us appreciate the complex interplay of technology, economy, and society, and the transformative power of industrialization.

62) Which choice best describes what happens in the passage?

- A) The passage details the inventions of the Industrial Revolution.
- B) The passage describes the causes, impacts, and legacy of the Industrial Revolution.
- C) The passage explains the negative effects of industrialization on the environment.
- D) The passage focuses on the social reforms initiated during the Industrial Revolution.

63) Which choice best expresses the main idea of the passage?

- A) The Industrial Revolution was primarily an economic phenomenon.
- B) The Industrial Revolution transformed society and economy, leading to significant technological and social changes.

- C) The primary benefit of the Industrial Revolution was the creation of the middle class.
- D) The Industrial Revolution had a detrimental impact on the environment.

64) In context, what does the phrase "development of new machinery and technology" in sentence 4 most nearly mean?

- A) Creation of farming tools
- B) Invention of household appliances
- C) Introduction of advanced industrial equipment
- D) Improvement in medical devices

65) Which sentence, if added after sentence 6, would best support the main idea of the paragraph?

- A) The steam engine was also used in agriculture.
- B) Many factories were built near rivers to take advantage of water power.
- C) This technological advancement marked a significant turning point in industrial production.
- D) Steam engines were eventually replaced by electric engines.

66) In sentence 12, the term "urbanization" refers to:

- A) The process of creating new agricultural methods.
- B) The movement of people from cities to rural areas.
- C) The development and growth of cities.
- D) The invention of new industrial machinery.

67) Which choice provides the most accurate interpretation of the information in sentence 13?

- A) Factory work offered high wages and excellent working conditions.
- B) Factory work was characterized by poor working conditions, prompting the need for labor reforms.
- C) Factory work was only available in rural areas.
- D) Factory work was easy and well-regulated by the government.

68) In sentence 18, what does the mention of "environmental degradation" contribute to the passage?

- A) It highlights a positive outcome of the Industrial Revolution.
- B) It explains the technological advancements in agriculture.
- C) It points out a negative consequence of the Industrial Revolution.
- D) It suggests that urbanization was beneficial for the environment.

69) The author wants to add the following sentence to the fourth paragraph:
"This led to an unprecedented movement of goods and people." Where would this sentence best fit?**

- A) After sentence 14
- B) After sentence 15
- C) After sentence 16
- D) After sentence 17

70) In context, the word "grueling" in sentence 13 most nearly means:

- A) Rewarding
- B) Tedious
- C) Exhausting
- D) Exciting

71) Which choice best concludes the passage?

- A) The Industrial Revolution had minimal impact on the modern world.
- B) The Industrial Revolution's legacy of innovation and industrial development continues to shape contemporary society.
- C) The Industrial Revolution primarily benefited the wealthy.
- D) The Industrial Revolution was a short-lived period with few lasting effects.

72) Which choice most effectively combines sentences 24 and 25?

- A) The Industrial Revolution spread beyond Britain, reaching other parts of Europe and North America, and eventually, the rest of the world.
- B) The Industrial Revolution was not confined to Britain; it spread to other parts of Europe and North America, and eventually to the rest of the world, with each region experiencing industrialization in its own way.
- C) The Industrial Revolution was confined to Britain but influenced other parts of the world.
- D) The Industrial Revolution was only significant in Britain and had little impact elsewhere.

Humanities: 11 questions

The Influence of the Enlightenment on Modern Thought

(1) The Enlightenment, also known as the Age of Reason, was an intellectual and philosophical movement that dominated the world of ideas in Europe during the 17th and 18th centuries. (2) This period marked a departure from traditional authority and religious dogma, emphasizing reason, individualism, and skepticism. (3) The Enlightenment laid the foundation for many aspects of modern thought, including the scientific method, democratic governance,

and human rights.

(4) One of the central figures of the Enlightenment was the French philosopher Voltaire. (5) Known for his wit and advocacy of civil liberties, Voltaire criticized the Catholic Church and absolute monarchy, promoting freedom of speech and religious tolerance. (6) His works, such as "Candide," challenged established norms and encouraged people to question authority and think independently.

(7) Another key Enlightenment thinker was John Locke, an English philosopher whose ideas about government and human nature profoundly influenced political thought. (8) Locke's "Two Treatises of Government" argued that individuals possess natural rights to life, liberty, and property. (9) He asserted that government should be based on the consent of the governed and that citizens have the right to overthrow a government that fails to protect their rights.

(10) The Enlightenment also saw significant advancements in science and the development of the scientific method. (11) Isaac Newton's "Principia Mathematica," published in 1687, laid the groundwork for classical mechanics and demonstrated the power of reason and observation in understanding the natural world. (12) Newton's work exemplified the Enlightenment belief that the universe operates according to rational laws that can be discovered through empirical investigation.

(13) The concept of separation of powers, a cornerstone of modern democratic systems, was articulated by the French philosopher Montesquieu in his work "The Spirit of the Laws." (14) Montesquieu argued that political power should be divided among different branches of government to prevent tyranny and protect individual freedoms. (15) His ideas influenced the framers of the United States Constitution and continue to shape modern political systems.

(16) The Enlightenment also fostered the development of economics as a distinct field of study. (17) Adam Smith's "The Wealth

of Nations," published in 1776, is considered the founding text of modern economics. (18) Smith argued that free markets, guided by the "invisible hand" of competition, lead to economic prosperity and innovation. (19) His ideas laid the foundation for capitalism and continue to influence economic policy and theory.

(20) The Enlightenment's emphasis on reason and individualism also had a profound impact on education and the arts. (21) Philosophers such as Jean-Jacques Rousseau advocated for education that nurtures critical thinking and moral development. (22) Enlightenment ideas inspired artistic movements that emphasized symmetry, balance, and the pursuit of beauty and truth.

(23) The legacy of the Enlightenment is evident in many aspects of contemporary society. (24) Its principles underpin modern democratic institutions, scientific inquiry, and the protection of human rights. (25) The Enlightenment's emphasis on reason, skepticism, and the pursuit of knowledge continues to inspire intellectual and cultural advancements.

(26) By studying the Enlightenment, we gain insight into the historical roots of modern thought and the enduring impact of this transformative period. (27) The Enlightenment reminds us of the power of reason and the importance of questioning established norms to achieve progress and understanding. (28) Its legacy serves as a testament to the enduring value of critical thinking and intellectual freedom in shaping a just and enlightened society.

73) Which choice best describes what happens in the passage?

- A) The passage discusses the decline of traditional authority during the Enlightenment.
- B) The passage outlines key figures and ideas of the Enlightenment and their impact on modern thought.
- C) The passage explains the scientific advancements made during the Enlightenment.

- D) The passage details the contributions of John Locke to political thought.

74) Which choice best expresses the main idea of the passage?

- A) The Enlightenment was primarily a scientific movement.
- B) The Enlightenment's emphasis on reason and individualism significantly shaped modern thought and institutions.
- C) The Enlightenment had little impact on contemporary society.
- D) The Enlightenment was focused on the arts and education.

75) In context, what does the phrase "intellectual and philosophical movement" in sentence 1 most nearly mean?

- A) A shift in political power
- B) A period of artistic expression
- C) A change in thinking and ideas
- D) A revolution in military tactics

76) Which sentence best supports the idea that the Enlightenment challenged established norms?

- A) Sentence 4: "One of the central figures of the Enlightenment was the French philosopher Voltaire."
- B) Sentence 5: "Known for his wit and advocacy of civil liberties, Voltaire criticized the Catholic Church and absolute monarchy, promoting freedom of speech and religious tolerance."
- C) Sentence 10: "The Enlightenment also saw significant advancements in science and the development of the scientific method."
- D) Sentence 13: "The concept of separation of powers, a cornerstone of modern democratic systems, was articulated by the French philosopher Montesquieu in his work 'The Spirit of the Laws.'"

77) In sentence 6, the term "established norms" most likely refers to:

- A) Traditional religious beliefs and monarchical authority.
- B) New scientific theories and methods.
- C) Artistic movements and styles.
- D) Economic policies and practices.

78) Which choice best describes the function of sentence 7 in the passage?

- A) It introduces a new topic related to Enlightenment thought.
- B) It provides an example of a key Enlightenment thinker.
- C) It summarizes the main ideas of the Enlightenment.
- D) It contrasts John Locke's ideas with those of Voltaire.

79) Which choice provides the most accurate interpretation of the information in sentence 9?

- A) Locke believed that governments should have absolute power.
- B) Locke argued that citizens should always obey the government.
- C) Locke asserted that government should be based on the consent of the governed and that citizens have the right to overthrow a government that fails to protect their rights.
- D) Locke's ideas had little influence on modern political thought.

80) In sentence 11, what does the mention of "empirical investigation" contribute to the passage?

- A) It highlights the importance of experimentation in the arts.
- B) It emphasizes the Enlightenment's focus on observation and reason in understanding the natural world.
- C) It suggests that empirical investigation was not valued during the Enlightenment.

- D) It indicates a decline in scientific inquiry during the Enlightenment.

81) Which choice most effectively combines sentences 13 and 14?

- A) The concept of separation of powers, a cornerstone of modern democratic systems, was articulated by the French philosopher Montesquieu in his work "The Spirit of the Laws," and he argued that political power should be divided among different branches of government to prevent tyranny and protect individual freedoms.
- B) Montesquieu's ideas about separation of powers, a cornerstone of modern democratic systems, were articulated in his work "The Spirit of the Laws," and argued that political power should be divided among different branches of government to prevent tyranny and protect individual freedoms.
- C) Montesquieu's concept of separation of powers, articulated in his work "The Spirit of the Laws," argued that political power should be divided among different branches of government to prevent tyranny and protect individual freedoms, and became a cornerstone of modern democratic systems.
- D) Montesquieu, a French philosopher, articulated the concept of separation of powers in his work "The Spirit of the Laws," which became a cornerstone of modern democratic systems and argued that political power should be divided among different branches of government to prevent tyranny and protect individual freedoms.

82) Which choice best concludes the passage?

- A) The Enlightenment had minimal impact on modern thought.
- B) The Enlightenment's legacy of reason and individualism continues to shape contemporary society.
- C) The Enlightenment primarily benefited the wealthy.
- D) The Enlightenment was a short-lived period with few lasting

effects.

83) The author wants to add the following sentence to the fifth paragraph:

"This belief laid the foundation for modern democratic institutions."
Where would this sentence best fit?**

- · A) After sentence 13
- · B) After sentence 14
- · C) After sentence 15
- · D) After sentence 16

Science: 11 questions

The Potential and Challenges of Quantum Computing

(1) Quantum computing is an emerging field that promises to revolutionize the way we process information. (2) Unlike classical computers, which use bits to represent data as 0s or 1s, quantum computers use quantum bits, or qubits, which can represent and process data in multiple states simultaneously. (3) This unique property of qubits, known as superposition, along with entanglement and quantum interference, gives quantum computers the potential to solve complex problems much faster than classical computers.

(4) Superposition allows qubits to exist in a combination of both 0 and 1 states at the same time. (5) This means that a quantum computer can perform many calculations simultaneously, significantly increasing its processing power. (6) Entanglement is another crucial property of quantum computing, where pairs of qubits become linked in such a way that the state of one qubit directly affects the state of the other, no matter how far apart they are. (7) This interconnectedness can be harnessed to create highly efficient computational processes.

(8) Quantum computers have the potential to transform various fields, including cryptography, materials science, and artificial intelligence. (9) In cryptography, quantum computers could break many of the encryption methods currently used to secure digital communications, leading to the development of new, quantum-resistant encryption techniques. (10) In materials science, quantum simulations could enable the discovery of new materials with desirable properties, such as superconductors and pharmaceuticals. (11) In artificial intelligence, quantum computing could significantly enhance machine learning algorithms, enabling more advanced and efficient data analysis.

(12) Despite the promising potential of quantum computing, several significant challenges must be addressed before it can become a practical reality. (13) One of the primary obstacles is qubit coherence, which refers to the duration a qubit can maintain its quantum state. (14) Qubits are extremely sensitive to their environment, and even slight disturbances can cause them to lose coherence, resulting in errors in calculations. (15) Developing methods to protect qubits from environmental interference and extending their coherence times is a critical area of research.

(16) Another challenge is error correction. (17) Unlike classical bits, qubits are prone to errors due to their quantum nature. (18) Implementing robust quantum error correction techniques is essential to ensure the reliability and accuracy of quantum computations. (19) Researchers are exploring various error-correcting codes and fault-tolerant quantum computing architectures to address this issue.

(20) Scaling up quantum computers to handle more qubits is also a significant hurdle. (21) Building and maintaining large-scale quantum systems require precise control and stabilization of numerous qubits, which is currently a complex and resource-intensive process. (22) Advances in quantum hardware and software are needed to develop scalable quantum computing

systems.

(23) Additionally, quantum computing requires significant advancements in algorithms and software to fully leverage its capabilities. (24) Quantum algorithms, which are fundamentally different from classical algorithms, need to be developed and optimized for specific applications. (25) Researchers are actively working on creating new quantum algorithms that can solve practical problems more efficiently than classical algorithms.

(26) Despite these challenges, progress in quantum computing is accelerating, with several companies and research institutions making significant strides in developing quantum technologies. (27) Governments and private enterprises are investing heavily in quantum research and development, recognizing its potential to drive innovation and economic growth.

(28) The future of quantum computing holds immense promise, and overcoming the technical challenges will require continued collaboration and innovation. (29) As researchers advance our understanding of quantum mechanics and develop new technologies, the realization of practical quantum computers draws closer. (30) Quantum computing has the potential to unlock new frontiers in science and technology, transforming industries and improving our ability to solve some of the most complex problems facing humanity.

84) Which choice best describes what happens in the passage?

- A) The passage explains the basic principles of quantum computing and highlights its potential applications and challenges.
- B) The passage details the history of quantum computing and its key inventors.
- C) The passage compares quantum computing with classical computing, emphasizing their differences.
- D) The passage criticizes the current state of quantum computing technology.

85) Which choice best expresses the main idea of the passage?

- A) Quantum computing will replace classical computing entirely.
- B) Quantum computing has significant potential but faces substantial challenges before it can be widely adopted.
- C) Quantum computing is already widely used in various industries.
- D) Quantum computing is limited to theoretical research with no practical applications.

86) In context, what does the term "superposition" in sentence 2 most nearly mean?

- A) The ability of qubits to exist in a single state
- B) The ability of qubits to exist in multiple states simultaneously
- C) The connection between two qubits
- D) The process of correcting errors in quantum computing

87) Which sentence best supports the idea that quantum computing could revolutionize certain fields?

- A) Sentence 8: "Quantum computers have the potential to transform various fields, including cryptography, materials science, and artificial intelligence."
- B) Sentence 12: "Despite the promising potential of quantum computing, several significant challenges must be addressed before it can become a practical reality."
- C) Sentence 20: "Scaling up quantum computers to handle more qubits is also a significant hurdle."
- D) Sentence 28: "The future of quantum computing holds immense promise, and overcoming the technical challenges will require continued collaboration and innovation."

88) In sentence 9, the phrase "quantum-resistant encryption tech-

niques" most likely refers to:

- A) Traditional encryption methods that are easy to break
- B) New encryption methods that can withstand attacks from quantum computers
- C) Encryption techniques that are outdated
- D) Simple encryption methods used in classical computing

89) Which choice best describes the function of sentence 12 in the passage?

- A) It introduces the potential applications of quantum computing.
- B) It acknowledges the challenges that need to be overcome for quantum computing to become practical.
- C) It explains the concept of qubit coherence.
- D) It highlights the differences between quantum and classical computing.

90) Which choice provides the most accurate interpretation of the information in sentence 13?

- A) Qubits can maintain their quantum state indefinitely.
- B) Qubit coherence refers to the duration a qubit can maintain its quantum state.
- C) Qubits are not affected by their environment.
- D) Qubit coherence is not important for quantum computing.

91) In sentence 21, what does the mention of "precise control and stabilization of numerous qubits" contribute to the passage?

- A) It highlights the ease of scaling up quantum computers.
- B) It emphasizes the complexity and resource-intensive nature of building large-scale quantum systems.

- C) It suggests that quantum computers are already scalable.
- D) It indicates that control and stabilization are not significant issues in quantum computing.

92) Which choice most effectively combines sentences 16 and 17?

- A) Error correction is important in quantum computing, and qubits are prone to errors due to their quantum nature.
- B) Another challenge is error correction, as qubits are prone to errors due to their quantum nature.
- C) Another challenge is error correction; qubits are prone to errors due to their quantum nature, and implementing robust quantum error correction techniques is essential to ensure the reliability and accuracy of quantum computations.
- D) Qubits are prone to errors due to their quantum nature, and error correction is another challenge.

93) Which choice best concludes the passage?

- A) Quantum computing will never become a practical reality.
- B) Quantum computing faces many challenges and will not be developed further.
- C) Quantum computing has immense potential, and overcoming its challenges will require continued collaboration and innovation.
- D) Quantum computing is only useful for theoretical research and not for practical applications.

94) The author wants to add the following sentence to the paragraph discussing quantum algorithms:
"This requires rethinking traditional approaches to problem-solving."
Where would this sentence best fit?

- A) After sentence 22

- B) After sentence 23
- C) After sentence 24
- D) After sentence 25

2. Math

A. Math Test - No Calculator

- **Number of Questions:** 20
- **Time Allotted:** 25 minutes
- **Format:** Multiple-choice and grid-in

Heart of Algebra: 8 questions

95. Solve for x in the equation:
    $$3x - 4 = 5x + 6$$

- A) -5

- B) -2

- C) 2

- D) 5

96. If $3x + 2y = 12$ and $y = 2x - 3$, what is the value of y?

- A) -1

- B) 3

- C) 5

- D) 7

97. What is the solution to the system of equations:

$x + y = 6$

$x - y = 2$

- A) $(2, 4)$
- B) $(3, 3)$
- C) $(4, 2)$
- D) $(5, 1)$

98. Solve the inequality:

$5 - 3x > 2$

- A) $x < 1$
- B) $x < \frac{3}{2}$
- C) $x < 2$
- D) $x < \frac{5}{3}$

99. If $y = 3x + 2$ and $y = -x + 6$, what is the value of x?

- A) 1
- B) 2
- C) 3
- D) 4

100. The sum of two numbers is 12. If one number is three times the other, what are the numbers?

- A) 3 and 9
- B) 4 and 8
- C) 2 and 10
- D) 1 and 11

101. Find the value of x if $6x + 2 - 4x + 10$.

- A) 3
- B) 4
- C) 5
- D) 6

102. What is the solution to the equation $2(3x + 5) - 4x + 16$?

- A) 1
- B) 2
- C) 3
- D) 4

Problem Solving and Data Analysis: 3 questions

103. A bakery sells cupcakes for $2.50 each and cookies for $1.75 each. If a customer buys 4 cupcakes and 5 cookies, what is the total cost?

- A) $15.25
- B) $16.75
- C) $17.50
- D) $18.75

104. The following data represents the number of hours worked by employees in a week:

Employee	Hours Worked
A	35
B	40
C	28
D	32
E	38

What is the average number of hours worked per employee?

- A) 34.6
- B) 34.8
- C) 35.0
- D) 35.4

105. A survey of 400 people found that 60% prefer watching movies at home, while the rest prefer watching movies at the theater. How many people prefer watching movies at the theater?

- A) 140
- B) 160
- C) 180
- D) 240

Passport to Advanced Math: 6 questions

106. If $f(x) - 2x^2 - 3x + 5$ and $g(x) - x - 4$, what is $f(g(x))$?

- A) $2(x - 4)^2 - 3(x - 4) + 5$
- B) $2x^2 - 3x - 11$
- C) $2(x - 4)^2 + 3(x - 4) + 5$
- D) $2x^2 - 3x + 1$

107. Solve for x: $4^{x+1} - 32$.

- A) $x - 2$
- B) $x - \frac{5}{2}$
- C) $x - \frac{3}{2}$
- D) $x - 3$

108. The function $h(x)$ is defined as $h(x) - x^3 - 6x^2 + 9x$. What are the zeros of $h(x)$?

- A) $x - 0, 3, 3$
- B) $x - 0, 3$
- C) $x - -3, 3$
- D) $x - 3$

109. If $y - \frac{3x-1}{x+2}$, which of the following is true about the vertical asymptote of the function?

- A) $x - -2$
- B) $y - -2$
- C) $x - 2$
- D) $y - 2$

110. Solve for x: $\sqrt{2x + 9} - 3 - 0$.

- A) $x - 0$
- B) $x - 3$
- C) $x - 4$
- D) $x - 2$

111. If $(x + 2)^2 = 16$, what are the possible values of x?

- A) $x = -4$ or $x = 4$
- B) $x = 2$ or $x = -6$
- C) $x = 4$ or $x = -2$
- D) $x = 2$ or $x = -4$

Additional Topics in Math (geometry, trigonometry, etc.): 3 questions

112. In a right triangle, the lengths of the legs are 6 units and 8 units. What is the length of the hypotenuse?

- A) 10 units
- B) 12 units
- C) 14 units
- D) 16 units

113. If the area of a circle is 36π square units, what is the circumference of the circle?

- A) 6π units
- B) 12π units
- C) 18π units
- D) 24π units

114. What is the value of $\cos(45°)\sin(45°)$?

- A) $\frac{1}{4}$
- B) $\frac{1}{2}$
- C) $\frac{\sqrt{2}}{2}$
- D) $\frac{1}{2}$

B. Math Test - Calculator

- **Number of Questions:** 38
- **Time Allotted:** 55 minutes
- **Format:** Multiple-choice and grid-in

Heart of Algebra: 16 questions

115. Solve for x in the equation $5x - 4 - 3x + 10$.

- A) 2
- B) 5
- C) 7
- D) 3

116. If $3y + 2 - 4y - 6$, what is the value of y?

- A) 8
- B) -8
- C) -4
- D) 4

117. Solve for x: $2(x + 3) - x - 5$.

- A) -11
- B) -7
- C) 1
- D) -1

118. The equation $y = 4x - 8$ represents a line. What is the slope of this line?

- A) -8
- B) 4
- C) -4
- D) 8

119. If $y - 5x + 2$ and $y - 2x + 11$, what is the value of x?

- A) 3
- B) -3
- C) 2
- D) -2

120. Solve for y: $6y - 5 - 4y + 7$.

- A) 6
- B) -6
- C) 2
- D) 5

121. What is the value of x in the equation $8(x + 1) - 4x + 20$?

- A) 2
- B) 3
- C) 4
- D) 5

122. If $y = -2x + 8$ and $y = 3x - 7$, what is the value of y?

- A) 1
- B) 2
- C) 3
- D) 4

123. Solve for x: $3(x - 4) = 2(x + 2)$.

- A) 16
- B) 12
- C) 10
- D) 8

124. The line $y = 6x - 15$ passes through the point $(a, 9)$. What is the value of a?

- A) 4
- B) 3
- C) 2
- D) 1

125. What is the solution to the system of equations: $2x + y = 10$ and $x - y = 2$?

- A) $(4, 2)$
- B) $(3, 4)$
- C) $(2, 6)$
- D) $(1, 8)$

126. If $9x + 3 = 6x + 12$, what is the value of x?

- A) 3
- B) 5
- C) -3
- D) -5

127. Solve for y: $4(3y - 2) = 5(y + 3)$.

- A) 3/7
- B) 23/7
- C) 7/23
- D) 3/23

128. If $y = 4x + 5$ and $y = -x + 20$, what is the value of y?

- A) 17
- B) 20
- C) 25
- D) 32

129. Solve for x: $7(x - 3) = 4(x + 2)$.

- A) 17/5
- B) 15/3
- C) 29/3
- D) 12/7

130. If $5x - 3y - 21$ and $x - 4$, what is the value of y?

- A) -1/3
- B) 1/3
- C) 3/2
- D) -3/2

Problem Solving and Data Analysis: 8 questions

131. A store sells a pack of 12 batteries for $15. What is the cost per battery?

- A) $0.75
- B) $1.00
- C) $1.25
- D) $1.50

132. A student scored 88, 92, 79, and 85 on four math tests. What score must the student get on the fifth test to have an average score of 85?

- A) 81
- B) 84
- C) 86
- D) 90

133. If a rectangle has a length of 10 meters and a width of 6 meters, what is the perimeter of the rectangle?

- A) 16 meters
- B) 20 meters
- C) 26 meters
- D) 32 meters

134. A person invests $2000 at an annual interest rate of 5% compounded annually. What will be the total amount after 3 years? (Use the formula $A = P(1 + r)^t$)

- A) $2315.25
- B) $2150.00
- C) $2200.00
- D) $2300.00

135. In a class of 30 students, 18 are girls. What is the percentage of boys in the class?

- A) 40%
- B) 45%
- C) 50%
- D) 60%

136. A shop sells 3 types of fruits: apples, oranges, and bananas. If the ratio of apples to oranges to bananas sold is 3:4:5 and the shop sold 120 fruits in total, how many bananas were sold?

- A) 20
- B) 30
- C) 40
- D) 50

137. A car rental company charges a flat fee of $30 plus $0.20 per mile driven. If a customer pays $50, how many miles did they drive?

- A) 75
- B) 100
- C) 150
- D) 200

138. If 8% of a number is 32, what is the number?

- A) 250
- B) 300
- C) 350
- D) 400

Passport to Advanced Math: 11 questions

139. Solve for x in the equation $x^2 - 4x - 21 = 0$.

- A) -3, 7
- B) 3, -7
- C) 7, -3
- D) -7, 3

140. What is the value of k if the polynomial $x^2 - 6x + k$ has a double root?

- A) 9
- B) -9
- C) 6
- D) -6

141. If $f(x) = 3x^2 - 12x + 5$, what is the vertex of the parabola?

- A) (2, -7)
- B) (-2, 7)
- C) (2, 7)
- D) (-2, -7)

142. Solve for x in the equation $\log_2(x + 3) = 4$.

- A) 13
- B) 12
- C) 11
- D) 10

143. If $g(x) = x^2 + 4x + c$ has only one solution, what is the value of c?

- A) 2
- B) 4
- C) -4
- D) -2

144. What is the inverse function of $f(x) = 2x + 5$?

- A) $f^{-1}(x) = \frac{x-5}{2}$
- B) $f^{-1}(x) = \frac{x+5}{2}$
- C) $f^{-1}(x) = 2x - 5$
- D) $f^{-1}(x) = \frac{2}{x+5}$

145. If $g(x) = \sqrt{x - 1} + 3$, for what value of x does $g(x) = 7$?

- A) 17
- B) 12
- C) 11
- D) 10

146. Simplify the expression $(2x^2 - 3x + 1) - (x^2 + x - 2)$.

- A) $x^2 - 4x + 3$
- B) $x^2 - 4x - 1$
- C) $3x^2 - 4x + 1$
- D) $x^2 - 2x + 3$

147. Solve for x in the inequality $\frac{x+\frac{1}{2}}{x-2} > 3$.

- A) $x = 3.5$
- B) $x = 4.5$
- C) $x = 6.0$
- D) $x = 5.0$

148. If $f(x) - x^2 + kx + 4$ has a minimum value at $x - -3$, what is the value of k?

- A) 6
- B) -6
- C) -3
- D) 3

149. Solve for x in the inequality $3x - 7 > 5x + 1$.

- A) $x < -4$
- B) $x > -4$
- C) $x < 4$
- D) $x > 4$

Additional Topics in Math (geometry, trigonometry, etc.): 3 questions

150. In a right triangle, the lengths of the legs are 6 units and 8 units. What is the length of the hypotenuse?

- A) 10
- B) 12
- C) 14
- D) 16

151. If $\sin \theta = \frac{3}{5}$ and θ is an acute angle, what is $\cos \theta$?

- A) $\frac{4}{5}$
- B) $\frac{3}{5}$
- C) $\frac{5}{3}$
- D) $\frac{4}{3}$

152. What is the area of a sector of a circle with a radius of 10 units and a central angle of $45°$?

- A) 12.5π
- B) 25π
- C) $\frac{25\pi}{2}$
- D) $\frac{50\pi}{3}$

3. Essay (Optional)

- · **Number of Questions:** 1
- · **Time Allotted:** 50 minutes

- **Format:** Essay prompt
- **Task:** Analyze how the author builds an argument to persuade an audience.

The following passage is adapted from "The Case for Universal Basic Income" by Samuel Grey, originally published in 2020.

As economic inequality continues to rise and job insecurity becomes more prevalent, the concept of Universal Basic Income (UBI) has gained traction as a potential solution to these pressing issues. UBI proposes that all citizens receive a regular, unconditional sum of money from the government, regardless of their employment status or income. This idea, once considered radical, is now being seriously debated by economists, policymakers, and social activists. Understanding the arguments in favor of UBI can illuminate why this policy could be a transformative force for society.

One of the primary arguments for UBI is that it can provide a safety net for all citizens, ensuring that everyone has a basic level of financial security. In today's rapidly changing job market, where automation and globalization are displacing traditional jobs, many people find themselves without stable employment. A UBI can help bridge this gap by providing individuals with the means to cover their essential needs, such as housing, food, and healthcare. This financial stability can reduce stress and improve overall well-being, enabling people to pursue education, training, or entrepreneurial ventures without the constant fear of financial ruin.

Moreover, UBI has the potential to reduce poverty and inequality. By giving everyone a basic income, the gap between the rich and the poor can be narrowed. This can have far-reaching effects on social cohesion and economic stability. Studies have shown that when people have a secure financial base, they are more likely to participate in their communities, invest in their futures, and contribute positively to society. For instance, a pilot program in

Kenya, conducted by the organization GiveDirectly, found that recipients of a basic income experienced significant improvements in health, education, and economic productivity.

Critics of UBI argue that providing a guaranteed income might disincentivize work and lead to a decrease in productivity. However, evidence from existing UBI pilot programs suggests otherwise. In Finland's UBI experiment, participants reported higher levels of well-being and no significant reduction in work activity compared to those who did not receive the income. Additionally, the security provided by UBI can encourage people to engage in work that is meaningful and fulfilling, rather than being driven solely by the need to earn a paycheck. This shift could lead to greater innovation and creativity in the workforce.

Another compelling argument for UBI is its potential to streamline and simplify the welfare system. Currently, many welfare programs are complex, bureaucratic, and often stigmatize recipients. UBI, by contrast, is straightforward and universal, eliminating the need for multiple overlapping social assistance programs. This simplicity can reduce administrative costs and ensure that assistance reaches those who need it most without the delays and inefficiencies inherent in the current system.

In conclusion, Universal Basic Income offers a promising solution to some of the most pressing economic and social challenges of our time. By providing financial security, reducing poverty and inequality, encouraging meaningful work, and simplifying the welfare system, UBI has the potential to create a more just and resilient society. As the debate around UBI continues, it is crucial to consider the evidence and reasoning that support this transformative policy.

Essay Prompt:

Write an essay in which you explain how Samuel Grey builds an argument to persuade his audience that Universal Basic Income (UBI) is a beneficial policy. In your essay, analyze how Grey uses one or more of the features listed below (or features of your own choice) to strengthen the logic and persuasiveness of his argument. Be sure that your analysis focuses on the most relevant features of the passage.

- Evidence, such as facts or examples, to support claims
- Reasoning to develop ideas and to connect claims and evidence
- Stylistic or persuasive elements, such as word choice or appeals to emotion, to add power to the ideas expressed

Your essay should not explain whether you agree with Grey's claims, but rather explain how Grey builds an argument to persuade his audience.

VIII

Detailed Answer Explanations

Practice SAT #1 - Answers & Explanations

1. Evidence-Based Reading and Writing (EBRW)

A. Reading Test Answers

Literature: 10 questions

1) What is the primary concern of Lily Bart as she approaches her 29th birthday?

- **Answer: A) Finding a suitable husband**
- **Explanation:** The passage describes Lily as unmarried and financially vulnerable, highlighting the social expectation and her own concern with securing a marriage, which is a significant focus as she approaches her 29th birthday.

2) What does Lily find difficult about the task of looking her best?

- **Answer: B) Fear of not meeting expectations**
- **Explanation:** The passage mentions Lily's anxiety about "not being in the key" and "not living up to the occasion," indicating that her difficulty lies in the fear of failing to meet societal expectations.

3) The phrase "brilliance of her surface hid a fundamental dullness" suggests that Lily's outward appearance is:

- **Answer: B) Deceptive and masks her true feelings**
- **Explanation:** The phrase suggests that while Lily may appear vibrant and engaging, this external display conceals a deeper lack of substance or genuine feeling, indicating a deceptive appearance.

4) What quality does Lily believe has made her the subject of admiration and envy?

- **Answer: C) Her adaptability**
- **Explanation:** The passage specifically mentions Lily's adaptability as a quality that has brought her admiration and envy, indicating that her ability to adjust and charm is highly valued.

5) Lily's reliance on her charm and social dexterity is described as:

- **Answer: B) An unconscious habit**
- **Explanation:** The passage states that Lily's reliance on these qualities "was not a conscious calculation" and had become "unconscious habit," indicating that these traits are ingrained and habitual rather than deliberate.

6) Which of the following best describes Lily's ambitions?

- **Answer: B) To achieve social supremacy**
- **Explanation:** Lily's ambitions are directed toward maintaining and elevating her social status, as indicated by her consistent effort to secure her place in high society.

7) What internal conflict does Lily experience?

- **Answer: C) A wish to be valued for lasting qualities versus reliance on beauty and charm**
- **Explanation:** The passage reveals Lily's discomfort with relying solely on her beauty and charm, expressing a deeper desire to be valued for more substantial, lasting qualities.

8) Lily's ultimate conviction about herself is that without her beauty and charm, she would be:

- **Answer: A) Nothing**
- **Explanation:** Lily believes that without her physical attractiveness and social skills, she would lack identity and value, reflecting her deep-seated insecurities.

9) The passage suggests that Lily's dependence on the approval of others will:

- **Answer: C) Prove to be her undoing**
- **Explanation:** The passage hints at a tragic outcome for Lily, suggesting that her reliance on others' approval will ultimately lead to negative consequences, as indicated by the phrase "a dependence which would ultimately prove to be her undoing."

10) The phrase "the appearance of contentment was almost as important as the reality" implies that in Lily's world:

- **Answer: B) Superficial appearances are highly valued**
- **Explanation:** This phrase highlights the emphasis placed on maintaining an outward appearance of happiness and satisfaction, regardless of the true emotional state, reflecting a societal preference for superficial appearances.

Historical Documents: 10 questions

11) According to Madison, what is one of the primary advantages of a well-constructed Union?

- **Answer: B) Control of factional violence**
- **Explanation:** Madison argues that a well-constructed Union can control the violence of faction, which he sees as a significant threat to popular governments.

12) What does Madison consider to be the "mortal diseases" of popular governments?

- **Answer: A) Instability, injustice, and confusion**
- **Explanation:** Madison lists "instability, injustice, and confusion" as the critical issues that cause the downfall of popular governments.

13) How does Madison define a faction?

- **Answer: A) A group of citizens united by a common interest or passion**
- **Explanation:** Madison defines a faction as a group of citizens united by some common impulse of passion or interest that is adverse to the rights of other citizens or the community's aggregate interests.

14) What are the two methods of curing the mischiefs of faction according to Madison?

- **Answer: A) Removing its causes and controlling its effects**
- **Explanation:** Madison states that the two methods to address the problems caused by factions are to remove the causes or to control the effects of factions.

15) What are the two methods of removing the causes of faction?

- **Answer: C) Destroying liberty and giving everyone the same opinions and interests**
- **Explanation:** Madison explains that the causes of faction can theoretically be removed by either destroying liberty, which he deems worse than the disease, or by making everyone have the same opinions and interests.

16) Madison argues that destroying liberty to remove the causes of faction is:

- **Answer: C) Worse than the disease itself**
- **Explanation:** Madison asserts that destroying liberty to eliminate factions is not a viable solution because it is worse than the problem of factions itself.

17) In Madison's analogy, what is liberty compared to in relation to faction?

- **Answer: B) Air to fire**
- **Explanation:** Madison compares liberty to air in relation to fire, suggesting that just as air fuels fire, liberty fuels factions. Removing liberty would extinguish factions, but at too great a cost.

18) Why does Madison believe giving every citizen the same opinions and interests is not a feasible solution?

- **Answer: B) It is impossible to achieve**
- **Explanation:** Madison implies that it is impossible to make everyone have the same opinions and interests due to the nature of human diversity and freedom.

19) What does Madison suggest is necessary to prevent the "mortal diseases" of popular governments?

- **Answer: A) A strong and well-constructed Union**
- **Explanation:** Madison believes that a well-constructed Union is necessary to prevent instability, injustice, and confusion, which he identifies as the mortal diseases of popular governments.

20) Madison implies that liberty is essential for:

- **Answer: A) The existence of faction**
- **Explanation:** Madison suggests that liberty is essential for the existence of faction, as factions arise from the freedom to express different opinions and interests.

Social Sciences: 10 questions

21) What percentage of daily actions did researchers at Duke University find to be habits rather than actual decisions?

- **Answer: C) More than 40 percent**
- **Explanation:** The passage states that researchers at Duke University found that more than 40 percent of the actions people performed each day were habits rather than actual decisions.

22) According to the passage, why do habits emerge?

- **Answer: A) Because the brain wants to conserve mental effort**
- **Explanation:** The passage explains that habits emerge because the brain is constantly looking for ways to save effort, making it more efficient by turning routines into habits.

23) What is a key advantage of the brain forming habits, as mentioned

in the passage?

- **Answer: C) It frees up mental energy for more complex activities**
- **Explanation:** The passage mentions that forming habits allows the brain to stop thinking constantly about basic behaviors, freeing up mental energy for more complex activities.

24) **What is the potential risk of the brain's habit-forming process?**

- **Answer: B) It may cause us to overlook important details**
- **Explanation:** The passage highlights that conserving mental effort can be tricky because if our brains power down at the wrong moment, we might fail to notice something important, such as a speeding car or an overcooked dinner.

25) **According to the passage, what are the three steps in the habit loop?**

- **Answer: C) Cue, routine, reward**
- **Explanation:** The passage outlines the three-step loop of habits as cue, routine, and reward.

26) **What happens over time as the habit loop becomes more automatic?**

- **Answer: B) The cue and reward become intertwined, creating anticipation and craving**
- **Explanation:** The passage explains that over time, the habit loop becomes more automatic, and the cue and reward become intertwined, creating a powerful sense of anticipation and craving.

27) **What is necessary to change a bad habit according to the golden rule of habit change?**

- **Answer: C) Keep the old cue and deliver the old reward, but insert a**

new routine

- **Explanation:** The passage states that to change a habit, you must keep the old cue and reward but change the routine, following the golden rule of habit change.

28) Why can't the brain distinguish between good and bad habits?

- **Answer: C) Because all habits operate the same way**
- **Explanation:** The passage mentions that the brain can't tell the difference between bad and good habits because all habits operate in the same way.

29) What does understanding the mechanics of habit formation help us achieve?

- **Answer: C) It enables us to change or replace habits**
- **Explanation:** The passage suggests that understanding the mechanics of habit formation is essential for making changes to habits, enabling us to modify them.

30) What does the passage suggest is at the root of all habits?

- **Answer: C) A mechanism that includes a cue, routine, and reward**
- **Explanation:** The passage indicates that at the root of all habits is a mechanism that includes a cue, routine, and reward, which drives the formation and persistence of habits.

Natural Sciences: 10 questions

31) What recent discovery about trees challenges the traditional view of them as solitary entities?

- **Answer: B) Trees can communicate, share resources, and protect**

their neighbors

· **Explanation:** The passage states that recent research has shown trees can communicate, share resources, and even protect their neighbors, challenging the traditional view of trees as solitary entities.

32) How do trees primarily communicate with each other?

· **Answer: B) Via their root systems connected by mycorrhizal fungi**
· **Explanation:** The passage explains that trees communicate primarily through their root systems, which are connected by a vast network of mycorrhizal fungi.

33) What role do mycorrhizal fungi play in tree communication?

· **Answer: B) They facilitate the exchange of nutrients and information**
· **Explanation:** The passage mentions that mycorrhizal fungi form symbiotic relationships with tree roots, facilitating the exchange of nutrients and information.

34) How do neighboring trees respond when a tree sends a distress signal?

· **Answer: C) By increasing their own defenses**
· **Explanation:** The passage indicates that neighboring trees respond to distress signals by increasing their own defenses, demonstrating a form of collective protection.

35) What is the significance of older, more established trees sharing resources with younger trees?

· **Answer: A) It helps ensure the survival of the forest as a whole**
· **Explanation:** The passage states that older, more established trees

often share water and nutrients with younger, weaker trees, which helps ensure the survival of the forest as a whole.

36) What is a "mother tree" in the context of the passage?

- **Answer: B) The largest and oldest trees that support surrounding younger trees**
- **Explanation:** The passage describes mother trees as the largest and oldest trees in a forest that play a crucial role in supporting the surrounding younger trees.

37) What happens to the surrounding forest when a mother tree is cut down?

- **Answer: B) The flow of nutrients and information is disrupted**
- **Explanation:** The passage explains that when a mother tree is cut down, the surrounding forest can suffer because the loss of this central figure disrupts the flow of nutrients and information.

38) According to the passage, how do trees exhibit a form of kinship?

- **Answer: A) By sharing resources with genetically related individuals**
- **Explanation:** The passage mentions that trees are more likely to share resources with genetically related individuals, suggesting a level of recognition and familial bonding.

39) What implications does the discovery of tree communication have for forestry practices and conservation efforts?

- **Answer: B) It emphasizes the importance of preserving mycorrhizal networks and mother trees**
- **Explanation:** The passage states that understanding the social nature

of trees can lead to more sustainable forest management practices, emphasizing the importance of preserving mycorrhizal networks and mother trees.

40) What does Wohlleben's research reveal about trees?

- **Answer: B) Trees have intricate relationships that sustain forest ecosystems**
- **Explanation:** The passage reveals that Wohlleben's research shows trees have intricate relationships that sustain forest ecosystems, highlighting the complexity and interconnectedness of forest life.

Dual Passages (Literature, Social Science, or Science): 10 questions

41) Which of the following best describes the main idea of Passage 1?

- **Answer: B) Social capital in the United States has declined, leading to negative community outcomes.**
- **Explanation:** Passage 1 discusses the decline in social capital in the United States and its associated negative consequences, such as weakened community bonds and reduced civic engagement.

42) What do both passages suggest about the role of social networks?

- **Answer: C) They significantly influence behaviors, emotions, and community outcomes.**
- **Explanation:** Both passages emphasize the strong impact of social networks on individuals and communities, affecting behaviors, emotions, and overall social well-being.

43) According to Passage 1, what is one consequence of the decline in social capital?

· **Answer: C) Increased crime rates**

· **Explanation:** Passage 1 states that communities with low levels of social capital tend to have higher crime rates, among other negative outcomes.

44) In Passage 2, what example is used to illustrate the power of social networks on health?

· **Answer: B) Spread of obesity**

· **Explanation:** Passage 2 uses the example of obesity spreading through social networks to illustrate how behaviors can be influenced by the connections we have with others.

45) How do the authors of Passage 1 and Passage 2 differ in their focus regarding social connections?

· **Answer: A) Passage 1 focuses on the decline of social capital, while Passage 2 focuses on the influence of social networks.**

· **Explanation:** Passage 1 primarily discusses the decline in social capital and its consequences, while Passage 2 explores the influence of social networks on behavior and well-being.

46) What does Passage 2 suggest about tightly knit social networks?

· **Answer: B) They can rapidly spread both positive and negative behaviors.**

· **Explanation:** Passage 2 indicates that tightly knit social networks can effectively spread both positive and negative behaviors, highlighting the powerful influence of close social connections.

47) Which of the following statements is supported by both passages?

· **Answer: C) Understanding social connections can help improve**

well-being.

- **Explanation:** Both passages suggest that understanding and fostering social connections can lead to improved individual and community well-being.

48) Based on Passage 1, what factor is mentioned as contributing to the decline in social capital?

- **Answer: B) Suburbanization**
- **Explanation:** Passage 1 mentions that increased mobility and suburbanization have led to more isolated living arrangements, contributing to the decline in social capital.

49) What solution does Passage 1 propose to address the decline in social capital?

- **Answer: C) Fostering community engagement and creating opportunities for connection**
- **Explanation:** Passage 1 suggests that rebuilding social capital requires efforts to foster community engagement and create opportunities for people to connect.

50) How does the influence of social networks on emotions, as described in Passage 2, relate to the concept of social capital in Passage 1?

- **Answer: A) Both emphasize the role of social connections in shaping individual and community well-being.**
- **Explanation:** Both passages highlight the importance of social connections, with Passage 1 focusing on social capital and its decline, and Passage 2 discussing the spread of emotions and behaviors through social networks, both of which are integral to individual and community well-being.

B. Writing and Language Test

Careers: 11 questions

51) Which choice best describes what happens in the passage?

- **Answer: A) The passage discusses Lillian Wald's contributions to public health nursing and her advocacy for social reforms.**
- **Explanation:** The passage focuses on Lillian Wald's work in public health nursing, highlighting her contributions and advocacy for addressing social determinants of health.

52) Which choice best supports the main idea of the passage?

- **Answer: B) Wald's emphasis on addressing social determinants of health.**
- **Explanation:** The main idea of the passage is centered around Wald's innovative approach to public health, particularly her focus on the social factors that influence health outcomes.

53) In context, which is the best version of the underlined portion of sentence 1 (reproduced below)?

Florence Nightingale is often celebrated as the founder of modern nursing, but many other pioneering nurses have made significant contributions to public health.

- **Answer: A) NO CHANGE**
- **Explanation:** The original sentence correctly contrasts the recognition of Florence Nightingale with the contributions of other pioneering nurses, such as Lillian Wald.

54) Which choice provides the most accurate interpretation of the data in sentence 8?

· **Answer: B) Under her leadership, the Henry Street Settlement expanded its services to include home care, which became central to public health nursing.**

· **Explanation:** Sentence 8 describes how the Henry Street Settlement, under Wald's leadership, included visiting nurses who provided home care, which became an important aspect of public health nursing.

55) Which choice best maintains the tone of the passage in sentence 3?

· **Answer: B) Born in 1867, Wald was deeply influenced by her experiences working with impoverished communities in New York City.**

· **Explanation:** This choice maintains the formal and informative tone of the passage while accurately describing the context in which Wald was influenced.

56) The author wants to add the following sentence to the third paragraph: "This approach was revolutionary at the time and set a precedent for future public health initiatives." Where would this sentence best fit?

· **Answer: C) After sentence 7**

· **Explanation:** The sentence best fits after sentence 7, as it directly follows the discussion of Wald's innovative approach to nursing and her emphasis on social reforms, highlighting the significance of her contributions.

57) Which of the following best describes the function of the second paragraph in the context of the passage?

· **Answer: A) It introduces the main subject of the passage.**

· **Explanation:** The second paragraph introduces Lillian Wald as the main subject of the passage, setting the stage for the discussion of her contributions to public health nursing.

58) In sentence 14, the phrase "Her commitment to social justice and healthcare equity" primarily serves to:

- **Answer: B) Highlight the reasons for Wald's influence on future generations of nurses.**
- **Explanation:** The phrase emphasizes Wald's dedication to important principles, illustrating why she was influential in inspiring future generations.

59) The word "legacy" in sentence 15 most nearly means:

- **Answer: B) The long-lasting impact.**
- **Explanation:** In this context, "legacy" refers to the enduring impact and influence of Wald's work on public health nursing.

60) Which sentence, if added, would provide the most relevant detail to support the last paragraph?

- **Answer: A) Wald's work continues to inspire nurses worldwide.**
- **Explanation:** This sentence supports the last paragraph's emphasis on the lasting influence of Wald's work and how it continues to be relevant today.

61) Which choice best concludes the passage?

- **Answer: A) By recognizing the interconnectedness of health and social conditions, Wald helped to shape a more holistic approach to healthcare that remains relevant to this day.**
- **Explanation:** This choice effectively concludes the passage by summarizing the significance of Wald's contributions and how her approach to healthcare remains influential.

History/Social Studies: 11 questions

62) Which choice best describes what happens in the passage?

- **Answer: A) The passage discusses the women's suffrage movement in the United States and its key events and figures.**
- **Explanation:** The passage provides an overview of the women's suffrage movement in the United States, including its key events, figures, and challenges.

63) Which choice provides the most accurate interpretation of the data in sentence 2?

- **Answer: B) The women's suffrage movement culminated in the ratification of the 19th Amendment in 1920, showcasing intense activism and perseverance.**
- **Explanation:** This choice accurately reflects the content of sentence 2, which mentions the ratification of the 19th Amendment as the culmination of the women's suffrage movement.

64) Which version of the underlined portion of sentence 5 best maintains the tone and style of the passage?

- **Answer: A) NO CHANGE**
- **Explanation:** The original wording maintains a formal and informative tone, accurately describing the drafting of the Declaration of Sentiments at the Seneca Falls Convention.

65) In context, which is the best way to combine sentences 11 and 12?

- **Answer: D) One of the most notable events in the suffrage movement was the 1913 Women's Suffrage Parade in Washington, D.C.; led by Alice Paul and the National Woman's Party, thousands** of women marched down Pennsylvania Avenue the day before President Woodrow Wilson's inauguration.

- **Explanation:** This choice effectively combines the sentences into a coherent statement, clearly linking the event, its leaders, and the participation of thousands of women.

66) Which choice provides the most logical introduction to the second paragraph (sentences 3-5)?

- **Answer: B) The roots of the women's suffrage movement can be traced back to the early 19th century.**
- **Explanation:** This sentence introduces the historical background of the movement, leading into a discussion of its early events and figures.

67) In sentence 8, what is the purpose of mentioning Susan B. Anthony, Elizabeth Cady Stanton, Sojourner Truth, and Ida B. Wells?

- **Answer: B) To highlight the diversity of strategies and perspectives within the suffrage movement**
- **Explanation:** The mention of these women illustrates the different strategies and perspectives within the movement, showing that it was not monolithic.

68) Which choice best maintains the tone of the passage in sentence 10?

- **Answer: C) Despite these challenges, suffragists continued their efforts, organizing marches, delivering speeches, and petitioning lawmakers.**
- **Explanation:** This choice maintains a formal and respectful tone appropriate for the passage, accurately describing the actions of suffragists.

69) Which sentence, if added to the fourth paragraph, would best support the information presented in that paragraph?

- **Answer: C) The parade included women from various backgrounds and regions, demonstrating the widespread support for suffrage.**
- **Explanation:** This sentence adds relevant detail to the paragraph by highlighting the diverse support for the suffrage movement, reinforcing the significance of the 1913 parade.

70) The author wants to add the following sentence to the fifth paragraph:

"Women's roles during the war included working in factories, serving as nurses, and supporting the war effort in various capacities." Where would this sentence best fit?

- **Answer: B) After sentence 14**
- **Explanation:** Placing the sentence after sentence 14 provides specific examples of how women contributed to the war effort, supporting the context of women's roles during World War I.

71) In context, the word "culmination" in sentence 17 most nearly means:

- **Answer: B) Conclusion**
- **Explanation:** The word "culmination" in this context refers to the final outcome or conclusion of the women's suffrage movement, marked by the passage of the 19th Amendment.

72) Which choice best concludes the passage?

- **Answer: C) The legacy of the suffragists continues to inspire movements for equality and justice around the world.**
- **Explanation:** This choice effectively concludes the passage by ac-

knowledging the lasting impact of the suffrage movement and its continued inspiration for modern equality movements.

Humanities: 11 questions

73) Which choice best describes what happens in the passage?

- **Answer: A) The passage discusses the significant influence of Greek philosophy on various aspects of Western thought and culture.**
- **Explanation:** The passage covers the contributions of key Greek philosophers and the lasting impact of their ideas on Western thought and culture.

74) Which choice provides the most accurate interpretation of the data in sentence 2?

- **Answer: B) Greek philosophy laid the groundwork for many aspects of modern philosophy, science, and politics.**
- **Explanation:** This accurately reflects the influence of Greek philosophy as described in the passage, emphasizing its foundational role in various fields.

75) Which version of the underlined portion of sentence 4 best maintains the tone and style of the passage?

- **Answer: D) The Socratic method involves critical thinking and examining beliefs through questioning.**
- **Explanation:** This choice maintains the formal and academic tone of the passage, accurately describing the Socratic method.

76) In context, which is the best way to combine sentences 6 and 7?

- **Answer: A) Plato, a student of Socrates, expanded upon his** teacher's ideas and founded the Academy in Athens, one of the earliest institutions of higher learning in the Western world, where he explored a wide range of philosophical topics in his dialogues, including justice, beauty, and the nature of reality.

- **Explanation:** This choice clearly and cohesively combines the information about Plato's contributions and the establishment of the Academy.

77) Which choice provides the most logical introduction to the fourth paragraph (sentences 12-14)?

- **Answer: B) The Hellenistic period saw the emergence of new philosophical schools addressing daily life concerns.**
- **Explanation:** This option correctly sets the stage for discussing the practical philosophies that emerged during the Hellenistic period.

78) In sentence 9, what is the purpose of mentioning Aristotle's contributions to numerous fields?

- **Answer: B) To highlight the diversity and breadth of Aristotle's influence**
- **Explanation:** The passage emphasizes Aristotle's extensive contributions across multiple disciplines, showcasing his broad impact.

79) Which choice best maintains the tone of the passage in sentence 14?

- **Answer: C) Stoics believed that virtue was the highest good and that individuals should strive for inner peace by accepting the natural order of the world.**
- **Explanation:** This choice maintains a formal and respectful tone, appropriately describing Stoic philosophy.

80) Which sentence, if added to the sixth paragraph, would best support the information presented in that paragraph?

- **Answer: B) Epicureanism also emphasized the importance of understanding the natural world to achieve peace.**
- **Explanation:** This sentence supports the paragraph's discussion of Epicurean beliefs, adding detail about their focus on understanding the natural world.

81) The author wants to add the following sentence to the seventh paragraph:

"Islamic scholars played a crucial role in preserving and expanding upon Greek philosophical texts." Where would this sentence best fit?

- **Answer: D) After sentence 19**
- **Explanation:** Placing the sentence after sentence 19 provides context for the transmission and preservation of Greek philosophical texts by Islamic scholars.

82) In context, the word "legacy" in sentence 21 most nearly means:

- **Answer: B) Long-lasting impact.**
- **Explanation:** "Legacy" in this context refers to the enduring influence of Greek philosophy on various fields.

83) Which choice best concludes the passage?

- **Answer: B) The enduring impact of Greek philosophy underscores the importance of exploring these ancient ideas.**
- **Explanation:** This choice emphasizes the lasting relevance and importance of Greek philosophy, providing a fitting conclusion to the discussion of its influence.

Science: 11 questions

84) **Which choice best describes what happens in the passage?**

- **Answer: B) The passage explains the concept of dark matter, its evidence, and the ongoing search to understand it.**
- **Explanation:** The passage discusses the existence of dark matter, evidence supporting its presence, and efforts to study and detect it.

85) **Which choice provides the most accurate interpretation of the data in sentence 2?**

- **Answer: B) Dark matter, making up about 27% of the universe's mass and energy, cannot be seen or detected directly with current instruments.**
- **Explanation:** This answer accurately reflects the information provided about dark matter's proportion in the universe and the limitations of current detection technology.

86) **Which version of the underlined portion of sentence 3 best maintains the tone and style of the passage?**

- **Answer: D) Its presence is inferred from the gravitational effects it has on visible matter, such as stars and galaxies.**
- **Explanation:** This choice maintains a formal and precise tone, suitable for the academic nature of the passage.

87) **In context, which is the best way to combine sentences 8 and 9?**

- **Answer: C) In the 1970s, American astronomer Vera Rubin found that the outer regions of galaxies were rotating at the same speed as the inner regions, but according to Newtonian physics, the outer stars should be moving slower than those near the center, where** most of the visible mass is concentrated.

- **Explanation:** This option clearly connects the two ideas, indicating the discrepancy with Newtonian physics and the observation made by Vera Rubin.

88) Which choice provides the most logical introduction to the third paragraph (sentences 11-14)?

- **Answer: A) Despite the compelling evidence for dark matter, its exact nature remains elusive.**
- **Explanation:** This sentence appropriately sets up the discussion of the unknown aspects of dark matter that follow.

89) In sentence 14, what is the purpose of mentioning WIMPs and axions?

- **Answer: B) To highlight some of the candidates for dark matter particles that scientists are investigating**
- **Explanation:** The passage lists WIMPs and axions as examples of particles that could potentially make up dark matter, indicating areas of ongoing research.

90) Which choice best maintains the tone of the passage in sentence 16?

- **Answer: C) One approach researchers use involves particle detectors placed deep underground to shield them from cosmic rays and other background radiation.**
- **Explanation:** This answer maintains a formal and informative tone, suitable for the scientific discussion in the passage.

91) Which sentence, if added to the fifth paragraph, would best support the information presented in that paragraph?

- **Answer: B) The technology used in these detectors is constantly improving.**
- **Explanation:** This sentence supports the discussion of efforts to detect dark matter by highlighting advancements in detection technology.

92) The author wants to add the following sentence to the sixth paragraph:

"These methods help scientists better understand the large-scale structure of the universe." Where would this sentence best fit?

- **Answer: C) Before sentence 20**
- **Explanation:** Placing the sentence before sentence 20 provides a clear link between the described methods and the broader goal of understanding the universe's structure.

93) In context, the word "elusive" in sentence 11 most nearly means:

- **Answer: C) Difficult to find or define**
- **Explanation:** The context describes the challenges in identifying and understanding dark matter, making "difficult to find or define" the best interpretation.

94) Which choice best concludes the passage?

- **Answer: C) As technology advances and new methods are developed, scientists remain hopeful that the true nature of dark matter will eventually be revealed, solving this enigma and potentially leading to new physics beyond the Standard Model.**
- **Explanation:** This choice provides an optimistic and forward-looking conclusion, aligning with the passage's discussion on the ongoing efforts to understand dark matter.

2. Math

A. Math Test - No Calculator

Heart of Algebra: 8 questions

Question 95:

Problem: Solve for x:

$$2x - 5 - 11$$

Solution:

1. Start by isolating x. Add 5 to both sides:

$$2x - 5 + 5 - 11 + 5$$

$$2x - 16$$

2. Divide both sides by 2:

$$x - \frac{16}{2}$$

$$x - 8$$

Answer: C) 8

Question 96:

Problem: If $3x + 4 = 2x + 10$, what is the value of x?

Solution:

1. Subtract $2x$ from both sides:

$$3x + 4 - 2x = 2x + 10 - 2x$$

$$x + 4 = 10$$

2. Subtract 4 from both sides:

$$x + 4 - 4 = 10 - 4$$

$$x = 6$$

Answer: C) 6

Question 97:

Problem: What is the solution to the system of equations:

$$y - 2x + 3$$

$$y - -x + 1$$

Solution:

1. Set the two equations equal to each other since they both equal y:

$$2x + 3 - -x + 1$$

2. Add x to both sides:

$$3x + 3 - 1$$

3. Subtract 3 from both sides:

$$3x - -2$$

4. Divide both sides by 3:

$$x - -\frac{2}{3}$$

$$x - -1$$

5. Substitute $x - -1$ back into the first equation to find y:

$$y - 2(-1) + 3$$

$$y - -2 + 3$$

$$y - 1$$

Answer: C) $(-1, 1)$

Question 98:

Problem: Solve the inequality:

$$5x - 7 > 3x + 1$$

Solution:

1. Subtract $3x$ from both sides:

$$5x - 3x - 7 > 3x - 3x + 1$$

$$2x - 7 > 1$$

2. Add 7 to both sides:

$$2x - 7 + 7 > 1 + 7$$

$$2x > 8$$

3. Divide both sides by 2:

$$x > \frac{8}{2}$$

$$x > 4$$

Answer: A) $x > 4$

Question 99:

Problem: If $y - 3x + 2$ and $y - -x + 6$, what is the value of x?

Solution:

1. Set the two expressions for y equal to each other:

$$3x + 2 - -x + 6$$

2. Add x to both sides:

$$4x + 2 - 6$$

3. Subtract 2 from both sides:

$$4x - 4$$

4. Divide both sides by 4:

$$x - 1$$

Answer: A) 1

Question 100:

Problem: The sum of two numbers is 12. One number is 4 more than the other. What are the numbers?

Solution:

1. Let the first number be x. The second number will be $x + 4$.

2. Set up the equation:
$$x + (x + 4) = 12$$

3. Simplify and solve:
$$2x + 4 = 12$$

$$2x = 8$$

$$x = 4$$

4. The first number is 4, and the second number is $4 + 4 = 8$.

Answer: A) 4 and 8

Question 101:

Problem: Find the value of x if $4x - 3 = 3x + 5$.

Solution:

1. Subtract $3x$ from both sides:
$$4x - 3x - 3 = 3x - 3x + 5$$

$$x - 3 = 5$$

2. Add 3 to both sides:
$$x = 8$$

Answer: C) 8

Question 102:

Problem: What is the solution to the equation $2(3x - 1) - 4x + 6$?

Solution:

1. Distribute the 2:

$$6x - 2 - 4x + 6$$

2. Subtract $4x$ from both sides:

$$6x - 4x - 2 - 4x - 4x + 6$$

$$2x - 2 - 6$$

3. Add 2 to both sides:

$$2x - 8$$

4. Divide both sides by 2:

$$x - 4$$

Answer: C) 4

Problem Solving and Data Analysis: 3 questions

Question 103:

Problem: A store sells apples at $0.75 each and bananas at $0.50 each. If a customer buys 8 apples and 10 bananas, what is the total cost?

Solution:

1. Calculate the total cost of the apples:

$$8 \times 0.75 - 6.00$$

2. Calculate the total cost of the bananas:

$$10 \times 0.50 - 5.00$$

3. Add the two amounts to find the total cost:

$$6.00 + 5.00 - 11.00$$

Answer: A) $11.50

Question 104:

Problem: The table shows the number of books sold by a bookstore over four months. What is the average number of books sold per month?

Table:

- January: 120 books
- February: 135 books
- March: 150 books
- April: 110 books

Solution:

1. Sum the total number of books sold:
$$120 + 135 + 150 + 110 - 515$$

2. Divide by the number of months:
$$\frac{515}{4} - 128.75$$

Answer: B) 128.75

Question 105:

Problem: A company's profit P (in dollars) from selling x units of a product is given by the equation $P - 50x - 200$. How many units must the company sell to break even?

Solution:

1. For the company to break even, the profit P should be zero:
$$50x - 200 - 0$$

2. Add 200 to both sides:
$$50x - 200$$

3. Divide both sides by 50:
$$x - 4$$

Answer: B) 4

Passport to Advanced Math: 6 questions

Question 106:

Problem: If $f(x) - 2x^2 - 3x + 5$, what is $f(4)$?

Solution:

1. Substitute $x - 4$ into the function $f(x)$:

$$f(4) - 2(4)^2 - 3(4) + 5$$

2. Calculate each term:

$$2(16) - 12 + 5 - 32 - 12 + 5$$

3. Simplify:

$$f(4) - 25$$

Answer: B) 25

Question 107:

Problem: Solve the equation for x: $3x^2 - 5x - 2 - 0$.

Solution:

1. Use the quadratic formula $x - \frac{-b \pm \sqrt{b^2 - 4ac}}{2a}$, where $a - 3$, $b - -5$, and $c - -2$.

2. Calculate the discriminant:

$$b^2 - 4ac - (-5)^2 - 4(3)(-2) - 25 + 24 - 49$$

3. Solve for x:

$$x - \frac{-(-5) \pm \sqrt{49}}{2(3)}$$

$$x - \frac{5 \pm 7}{6}$$

4. The solutions are:

$$x - \frac{12}{6} - 2 \quad \text{and} \quad x - \frac{-2}{6} - -\frac{1}{3}$$

Answer: A) $x - -\frac{1}{3}$ or $x - 2$

Question 108:

Problem: If $y - 2x^3 - 4x^2 + x - 7$, what is the coefficient of the x^2 term after differentiating y with respect to x?

Solution:

1. Differentiate y with respect to x:

$$\frac{dy}{dx} - \frac{d}{dx}(2x^3) - \frac{d}{dx}(4x^2) + \frac{d}{dx}(x) - \frac{d}{dx}(7)$$

$$\frac{dy}{dx} - 6x^2 - 8x + 1$$

2. The coefficient of the x^2 term is 6.

Answer: C) 6

Question 109:

Problem: Which of the following is a solution to the inequality $2x - 3 > 7$?

Solution:

1. Solve the inequality:

$$2x - 3 > 7$$

$$2x > 10$$

$$x > 5$$

2. Check which options satisfy $x > 5$.

Answer: B) $x - 5$

Question 110:

Problem: Simplify the expression: $\frac{3x^2-12x+9}{3x-3}$

Solution:

1. Factor the numerator and the denominator:

$$\frac{3(x^2-4x+3)}{3(x-1)}$$

$$\frac{3(x-3)(x-1)}{3(x-1)}$$

2. Cancel the common factor $(x-1)$:

$$x-3$$

Answer: B) $x-3$

Question 111:

Problem: The function $g(x) = x^2 + 2x + 1$ is shifted 3 units to the right and 2 units up. What is the new function $h(x)$?

Solution:

1. Shift the function 3 units to the right: replace x with $x-3$:

$$g(x-3) = (x-3)^2 + 2(x-3) + 1$$

2. Simplify the function:

$$(x-3)^2 + 2(x-3) + 1 = x^2 - 6x + 9 + 2x - 6 + 1$$

$$= x^2 - 4x + 4$$

3. Shift the function 2 units up: add 2 to the function:

$$h(x) = x^2 - 4x + 4 + 2$$

Answer: D) $h(x) = (x+3)^2 + 2$

Additional Topics in Math (geometry, trigonometry, etc.): 3 questions

Question 112:

Problem: In a right triangle, the length of one leg is 6 and the length of the hypotenuse is 10. What is the length of the other leg?

Solution:

1. Let the other leg be x.

2. Use the Pythagorean theorem: $a^2 + b^2 = c^2$, where c is the hypotenuse.

3. Set up the equation:

$$6^2 + x^2 = 10^2$$

$$36 + x^2 = 100$$

$$x^2 = 100 - 36$$

$$x^2 = 64$$

$$x = \sqrt{64}$$

$$x = 8$$

Answer: C) 8

Question 113:

Problem: The measure of angle A in a triangle is 50 degrees, and the measure of angle B is 60 degrees. What is the measure of angle C?

Solution:

1. The sum of the angles in a triangle is always 180 degrees.

2. Set up the equation: $A + B + C - 180$

3. Substitute the given values:

$$50 + 60 + C - 180$$

$$110 + C - 180$$

$$C - 180 - 110$$

$$C - 70$$

Answer: C) 70 degrees

Question 114:

Problem: In a circle with a radius of 5, what is the length of an arc that subtends a central angle of 72 degrees? (Use $\pi \approx 3.14$)

Solution:

1. The formula for the length of an arc is $\frac{\theta}{360} \times 2\pi r$, where θ is the central angle in degrees and r is the radius.

2. Substitute the given values:

$$\frac{72}{360} \times 2\pi \times 5$$

3. Calculate the fraction and multiply:

$$\frac{1}{5} \times 2 \times 3.14 \times 5$$

$$\frac{1}{5} \times 31.4$$

$$6.28$$

Answer: B) 6.28

B. Math Test - Calculator

Heart of Algebra: 16 questions

Question 115:

Equation: $3x + 4 - 19$

Solution:

1. Subtract 4 from both sides:

   $3x - 19 - 4$

   $3x - 15$

2. Divide both sides by 3:

   $x - \frac{15}{3}$

   $x - 5$

Answer: A) 5

Question 116:

Equation: $2(3x - 4) - 4x + 6$

Solution:

1. Distribute the 2 on the left side:

   $6x - 8 - 4x + 6$

2. Subtract 4x from both sides:

   $2x - 8 - 6$

3. Add 8 to both sides:

   $2x - 14$

4. Divide both sides by 2:

   $x - 7$

Answer: A) 7

Question 117:

System of Equations:

1. $y - 5x - 2$
2. $y - -3x + 6$

Solution:

1. Set the equations equal to each other (since both equal y):
   $5x - 2 - -3x + 6$

2. Add $3x$ to both sides:
   $8x - 2 - 6$

3. Add 2 to both sides:
   $8x - 8$

4. Divide both sides by 8:
   $x - 1$

Answer: A) 1

Question 118:

Equation: $\frac{2x-5}{3} - 7$

Solution:

1. Multiply both sides by 3:
   $2x - 5 - 21$

2. Add 5 to both sides:
   $2x - 26$

3. Divide both sides by 2:
   $x - 13$

Answer: A) 13

Question 119:

Given Points: (1, 3) and (3, 7)

Solution:

1. Use the slope formula: $\frac{y_2 - y_1}{x_2 - x_1}$
   $m - \frac{7-3}{3-1}$
   $m - \frac{4}{2}$
   $m - 2$

Answer: A) 2

Question 120:

Equation: $6y + 7 - 3y - 5$

Solution:

1. Subtract $3y$ from both sides:
   $6y - 3y + 7 - -5$
   $3y + 7 - -5$

2. Subtract 7 from both sides:
   $3y - -5 - 7$
   $3y - -12$

3. Divide both sides by 3:
   $y - \frac{-12}{3}$
   $y - -4$

Answer: A) -4

Question 121:

Equation: $6(x + 1) - 3x + 15$

Solution:

1. Distribute the 6 on the left side:
   $6x + 6 - 3x + 15$

2. Subtract $3x$ from both sides:
   $6x - 3x + 6 - 15$
   $3x + 6 - 15$

3. Subtract 6 from both sides:
   $3x - 9$

4. Divide both sides by 3:
   $x - 3$

Answer: A) 3

Question 122:

Equation: $3x + 2y - 12$ and $x - 2$

Solution:

1. Substitute $x - 2$ into the equation:
   $3(2) + 2y - 12$
   $6 + 2y - 12$

2. Subtract 6 from both sides:
   $2y - 6$

3. Divide both sides by 2:
   $y - 3$

Answer: C) 3

Question 123:

Equation: $5y - 3 - 2y + 12$

Solution:

1. Subtract $2y$ from both sides:
   $5y - 2y - 3 - 12$
   $3y - 3 - 12$

2. Add 3 to both sides:
   $3y - 15$

3. Divide both sides by 3:
   $y - 5$

Answer: B) 5

Question 124:

System of Equations:

1. $y - 2x + 5$
2. $y - -x + 2$

Solution:

1. Set the two equations equal to each other (since both equal y):
   $2x + 5 - -x + 2$

2. Add x to both sides:
   $3x + 5 - 2$

3. Subtract 5 from both sides:
   $3x - -3$

4. Divide both sides by 3:
   $x - -1$

5. Substitute $x - -1$ back into $y - 2x + 5$ to find y:
   $y - 2(-1) + 5$
   $y - -2 + 5$
   $y - 3$

Answer: C) 3

Question 125:

Equation: $\frac{x}{2} + \frac{x}{3} = 5$

Solution:

1. Find a common denominator and combine the terms:
   $$\frac{3x}{6} + \frac{2x}{6} = 5$$
   $$\frac{5x}{6} = 5$$

2. Multiply both sides by 6:
   $$5x = 30$$

3. Divide both sides by 5:
   $$x = 6$$

Answer: A) 6

Question 126:

Equation: $5(x - 3) = 3(2x + 1)$

Solution:

1. Distribute the 5 and 3:
   $$5x - 15 = 6x + 3$$

2. Subtract $5x$ from both sides:
   $$-15 = x + 3$$

3. Subtract 3 from both sides:
   $$-18 = x$$

Answer: D) 5

Question 127:

Equation: $4y - 7 - 2(y + 5)$

Solution:

1. Distribute the 2 on the right side:
   $4y - 7 - 2y + 10$

2. Subtract $2y$ from both sides:
   $2y - 7 - 10$

3. Add 7 to both sides:
   $2y - 17$

4. Divide both sides by 2:
   $y - 8.5$

Answer: A) 8.5

Question 128:

Equation: $3x + 4y - 12$, find y when $x - 2$.

Solution:

1. Substitute $x - 2$ into the equation:
   $3(2) + 4y - 12$

2. Calculate the left side:
   $6 + 4y - 12$

3. Subtract 6 from both sides:
   $4y - 6$

4. Divide both sides by 4:
   $y - 1.5$

Answer: B) 1.5

Question 129:

Equation: $2x + 3y = 18$, find y when $x = 4$.

Solution:

1. Substitute $x = 4$ into the equation:
   $2(4) + 3y = 18$

2. Calculate the left side:
   $8 + 3y = 18$

3. Subtract 8 from both sides:
   $3y = 10$

4. Divide both sides by 3:
   $y \approx 3.33$

Answer: B) 3.33

Question 130:

Equation: $7x - 3 = 4x + 9$

Solution:

1. Subtract $4x$ from both sides:
   $3x - 3 = 9$

2. Add 3 to both sides:
   $3x = 12$

3. Divide both sides by 3:
   $x = 4$

Answer: A) 4

Problem Solving and Data Analysis: 8 questions

Question 131:

Problem: A company produces two types of widgets, A and B. Each type A widget costs $3 to make, and each type B widget costs $5 to make. The company spends a total of $2000 to produce 500 widgets. How many of each type of widget did they produce?

Solution:

1. Let x be the number of type A widgets and y be the number of type B widgets.

2. We have two equations:
   - $x + y - 500$ (total number of widgets)
   - $3x + 5y - 2000$ (total cost)

3. Solve the first equation for y:
   - $y - 500 - x$

4. Substitute $y - 500 - x$ into the second equation:
   $3x + 5(500 - x) - 2000$
   $3x + 2500 - 5x - 2000$
   $-2x + 2500 - 2000$
   $-2x - 2000 - 2500$
   $-2x - -500$
   $x - 250$

5. Now, find y:
   $y - 500 - 250$
   $y - 250$

Answer: C) 250 type A widgets and 250 type B widgets

Question 132:

Problem: In a survey, 40% of respondents said they preferred apples over oranges. If 300 people were surveyed, how many people preferred apples?

Solution:

1. Calculate 40% of 300:
   $0.40 \times 300 - 120$

Answer: B) 120

Question 133:

Problem: A researcher is studying the relationship between hours studied and exam scores. The equation of the line of best fit is $y = 5x + 50$, where y is the exam score and x is the number of hours studied. What is the expected exam score for a student who studies for 4 hours?

Solution:

1. Substitute $x = 4$ into the equation:

$$y = 5(4) + 50$$
$$y = 20 + 50$$
$$y = 70$$

Answer: B) 70

Question 134:

Problem: A store sells notebooks for $2 each and pens for $1 each. If a customer buys a total of 15 items and spends $25, how many notebooks did they buy?

Solution:

1. Let x be the number of notebooks and y be the number of pens.

2. We have two equations:

   - $x + y = 15$ (total items)

   - $2x + y = 25$ (total cost)

3. Subtract the first equation from the second:

$$2x + y - (x + y) = 25 - 15$$
$$x = 10$$

Answer: C) 10

Question 135:

Problem: The table shows the number of students in different grade levels at a school. Calculate the mean number of students per grade level.

Solution:

1. Sum the number of students: $120 + 130 + 110 + 140 - 500$
2. Count the number of grade levels: 4
3. Calculate the mean: $\frac{500}{4} - 125$

Answer: B) 125

Question 136:

Problem: A car rental company charges a flat fee of $50 plus $0.25 per mile driven. If a customer rents a car and drives it for 120 miles, what is the total cost of the rental?

Solution:

1. Flat fee: $50
2. Cost per mile: $0.25
3. Total miles driven: 120
4. Additional cost: $0.25 \times 120 - 30$
5. Total cost: $50 + 30 - 80$

Answer: A) $80

Question 137:

Problem: The ages of five employees at a company are 25, 30, 35, 40, and 45. What is the median age of the employees?

Solution:

1. List the ages in ascending order: 25, 30, 35, 40, 45
2. The median is the middle value in the ordered list, which is 35.

Answer: B) 35

Question 138:

Problem: The histogram shows the distribution of scores on a test. How many students scored between 21 and 40?

Solution:

1. From the histogram:
   - Number of students scoring between 21-30: 10
   - Number of students scoring between 31-40: 20
2. Total students in the range 21-40: $10 + 20 - 30$

Answer: C) 35

Passport to Advanced Math: 11 questions

Question 139:

Problem: If $f(x) - 2x^2 + 3x - 5$, what is $f(2)$?

Solution:

1. Substitute $x - 2$ into the function $f(x)$:
$$f(2) - 2(2)^2 + 3(2) - 5$$
2. Calculate the values:
$$f(2) - 2(4) + 6 - 5$$

$$f(2) = 8 + 6 - 5$$

$$f(2) - 9$$

Answer: C) 9

Question 140:

Problem: Solve for x: $\frac{3x-5}{2} - 7$.

Solution:

1. Multiply both sides by 2:
$$3x - 5 - 14$$

2. Add 5 to both sides:
$$3x - 19$$

3. Divide by 3:
$$x - \frac{19}{3}$$

Answer: C) 7

Question 141:

Problem: What is the vertex of the parabola given by the equation $y - -x^2 + 4x + 6$?

Solution:

1. The vertex form of a parabola is $y - a(x - h)^2 + k$. To find the vertex, we use the formula $h - -\frac{b}{2a}$ for the given equation $y - ax^2 + bx + c$.

2. Here, $a - -1, b - 4$, and $c - 6$.

3. Calculate h:
$$h - -\frac{4}{2(-1)} - 2$$

4. Substitute $h - 2$ back into the equation to find k:
$$y - -(2)^2 + 4(2) + 6$$

$$y - -4 + 8 + 6$$

$$y - 10$$

Answer: A) (2, 10)

Question 142:

Problem: If the polynomial $p(x) = x^3 - 4x^2 + 5x - 2$ is divided by $x - 1$, what is the remainder?

Solution:

1. Use the Remainder Theorem, which states that the remainder of the division of a polynomial $p(x)$ by $x - a$ is $p(a)$.

2. Here, $a = 1$:

$$p(1) = (1)^3 - 4(1)^2 + 5(1) - 2$$

$$p(1) = 1 - 4 + 5 - 2$$

$$p(1) = 0$$

Answer: A) 0

Question 143:

Problem: If $\log_2(x) = 5$, what is the value of x?

Solution:

1. The equation $\log_2(x) = 5$ can be rewritten in exponential form as $2^5 = x$.

2. Calculate x:

$$x = 32$$

Answer: C) 32

Question 144:

Problem: Solve for x: $2^{x+1} - 16$.

Solution:

1. Express 16 as a power of 2: $16 - 2^4$.

2. Set up the equation:
$$2^{x+1} - 2^4$$

3. Since the bases are the same, set the exponents equal:
$$x + 1 - 4$$

4. Solve for x:

$$x - 3$$

Answer: B) 3

Question 145:

Problem: The function $g(x)$ is defined as $g(x) - 3(x - 2)^2 + 4$. What is the minimum value of $g(x)$?

Solution:

- The function is a parabola opening upwards, as indicated by the positive coefficient 3 in front of the squared term.

- The minimum value occurs at the vertex of the parabola.

- The vertex form is $a(x - h)^2 + k$, where (h, k) is the vertex. Here, $h - 2$ and $k - 4$.

- Therefore, the minimum value of $g(x)$ is 4.

Answer: D) 4

Question 146:

Problem: Solve for x in the equation $x^2 - 6x + 8 = 0$.

Solution:

- To solve the quadratic equation, factorize it:
$$x^2 - 6x + 8 = (x - 2)(x - 4) = 0$$
- Set each factor equal to zero:
$$x - 2 = 0 \quad \text{or} \quad x - 4 = 0$$

$$x = 2 \quad \text{or} \quad x = 4$$

Answer: A) 2, 4

Question 147:

Problem: What is the value of k if the function $h(x) = kx^3 - 4x$ has a local maximum at $x = -1$?

Solution:

- For a local maximum, the first derivative must be zero at that point.
- Find the first derivative:
$$h'(x) = 3kx^2 - 4$$
- Set $h'(-1) = 0$:

$$3k(-1)^2 - 4 = 0$$

$$3k - 4 = 0$$

$$3k = 4$$

$$k = \frac{4}{3}$$

Answer: B) $\frac{4}{3}$

Question 148:

Problem: If $\frac{2x+3}{4} - 5$, what is the value of x?

Solution:

1. Multiply both sides by 4:
$$2x + 3 - 20$$

2. Subtract 3 from both sides:
$$2x - 17$$

3. Divide by 2:
$$x - \frac{17}{2}$$

Answer: D) $\frac{17}{2}$

Question 149:

Problem: If the function $f(x) - ax^2 + bx + c$ has roots at $x - 2$ and $x - -3$, what is the value of c?

Solution:

- The roots of the quadratic equation can be written as:
$$f(x) - a(x - 2)(x + 3)$$

- Expand the equation:
$$f(x) - a(x^2 + 3x - 2x - 6)$$

$$f(x) - a(x^2 + x - 6)$$

- The constant term c corresponds to the product of the roots multiplied by $-a$. Here, it is $-6a$.

- Setting $a - 1$ (assuming a monic polynomial or if unspecified):
$$c - -6$$

Answer: B) -6

Additional Topics in Math (geometry, trigonometry, etc.): 3 questions

Question 150:

Problem: In a right triangle, one of the angles measures $30°$. If the length of the hypotenuse is 10 units, what is the length of the side opposite the $30°$ angle?

Solution:

- In a 30-60-90 triangle, the ratios of the lengths of the sides opposite the $30°$, $60°$, and $90°$ angles are $1 : \sqrt{3} : 2$.
- The side opposite the $30°$ angle is half the hypotenuse.
- Given the hypotenuse is 10 units, the side opposite the $30°$ angle is:

$$\frac{10}{2} - 5$$

Answer: A) 5

Question 151:

Problem: A circle has a radius of 7 units. What is the area of a sector with a central angle of $60°$?

Solution:

1. The formula for the area of a sector is $\frac{\theta}{360°} \times \pi r^2$, where θ is the central angle in degrees.
2. Here, $r - 7$ and $\theta - 60°$:

$$\text{Area} - \frac{60}{360} \times \pi(7)^2$$

3. Simplify the fraction:

$$\text{Area} - \frac{1}{6} \times \pi(49)$$

$$\text{Area} - \frac{49\pi}{6}$$

Answer: A) $\frac{49\pi}{6}$

Question 152:

Problem: In a parallelogram, one angle measures $70°$. What is the measure of the angle adjacent to this angle?

Solution:

- In a parallelogram, adjacent angles are supplementary, meaning they add up to $180°$.
- Given one angle is $70°$, the adjacent angle is:

$$180° - 70° - 110°$$

Answer: B) $110°$

3. Essay (Optional) - Example Answer

In the passage "The Benefits of Urban Green Spaces," Jane Doe effectively builds an argument that urban green spaces are essential for improving the quality of life in cities by using a combination of evidence, logical reasoning, and persuasive elements. Doe's argument is compelling because it is well-supported by research, carefully structured, and enhanced by her use of language that appeals to the reader's emotions and logic.

One of the primary strategies Doe employs to persuade her audience is the use of evidence-based claims. Throughout the passage, she supports her argument with research findings and factual information, which serve to validate her points and make her argument more credible. For instance, Doe mentions studies that show how access to green spaces can reduce stress, promote physical activity, and improve mental well-being. By citing these studies, Doe provides concrete evidence that underscores the importance of urban green spaces for public health. This use of evidence makes her claims more difficult to refute, as they are grounded in scientific research rather than mere opinion.

In addition to evidence, Doe uses logical reasoning to connect her claims and build a coherent argument. She systematically explores

*the different benefits of urban green spaces—public health, envi-
ronmental, and biodiversity—demonstrating how each contributes
to the overall quality of life in cities. For example, she logically
connects the presence of green spaces to increased physical activity,
which in turn leads to lower rates of obesity and cardiovascular
diseases. This step-by-step reasoning helps the reader to follow
her argument and see the cause-and-effect relationships she is
outlining. By organizing her essay in this logical manner, Doe
ensures that her argument is clear and easy to understand.*

*Doe also strengthens her argument through the use of persuasive
language and appeals to emotion. She describes urban green spaces
as "vital" and "crucial," words that emphasize their importance
and convey a sense of urgency. Moreover, she appeals to the
reader's emotions by highlighting the personal benefits of green
spaces, such as reduced stress and improved mood. These appeals
are designed to resonate with the reader on a personal level, making
the argument not just intellectually convincing but also emotionally
compelling.*

*Furthermore, Doe's word choice and tone contribute to the
persuasiveness of her argument. She uses positive language
when discussing the benefits of green spaces, which helps to
create a favorable image of these areas in the reader's mind. For
example, she refers to green spaces as providing "aesthetic value"
and "enhanced cognitive function," phrases that carry positive
connotations and make the reader more likely to view green spaces
as desirable and necessary.*

*In conclusion, Jane Doe builds a persuasive argument for the
importance of urban green spaces by effectively using evidence,
logical reasoning, and persuasive language. Her argument is
well-supported by research, clearly structured, and emotionally
engaging, making it a compelling case for the preservation and
expansion of green spaces in urban areas. By combining these
elements, Doe successfully convinces her audience of the essential*

role that green spaces play in improving the quality of life in cities.

Practice SAT #2 - Answers & Explanations

1. Evidence-Based Reading and Writing (EBRW)

A. Reading Test Answers

Literature: 10 questions

1) What is Elizabeth Bennet's initial feeling as she approaches Pemberley Woods?

- **Answer: C) Anxiety**
- **Explanation:** The word "perturbation" in the passage suggests that Elizabeth feels a sense of unease or anxiety as she approaches Pemberley Woods.

2) What aspect of Pemberley House first catches Elizabeth's eye?

- **Answer: B) Its large, handsome stone structure**
- **Explanation:** The passage describes Pemberley House as a "large, handsome stone building," which is the first feature that catches Elizabeth's eye.

3) Which feature of Pemberley does Elizabeth find particularly appealing?

- **Answer: B) The natural beauty of the estate**
- **Explanation:** Elizabeth admires the natural beauty of Pemberley and notes that it has been little counteracted by awkward taste, indicating her appreciation for its natural appeal.

4) What is implied about Elizabeth's thoughts on becoming the mistress of Pemberley?

- **Answer: C) She believes it might be something significant**
- **Explanation:** Elizabeth feels that being the mistress of Pemberley "might be something," suggesting she considers it a significant and desirable prospect.

5) How does Elizabeth react to the park's appearance?

- **Answer: B) She admires its natural beauty and lack of artificiality**
- **Explanation:** Elizabeth appreciates the park's natural beauty and notes that it is not falsely adorned, indicating her preference for its natural and unspoiled appearance.

6) What does the passage suggest about Elizabeth's attitude towards natural beauty versus artificial adornment?

- **Answer: B) She values natural beauty over artificial adornment**
- **Explanation:** Elizabeth's admiration for the natural beauty of Pemberley and her approval of the lack of artificial adornment suggest she values natural aesthetics more.

7) What effect does the view from the top of the eminence have on Elizabeth?

- **Answer: C) It reinforces her admiration for Pemberley**
- **Explanation:** The view from the top of the eminence, which reveals Pemberley House in all its beauty, reinforces Elizabeth's admiration for the estate.

8) Which character teases Elizabeth about her admiration for Pemberley?

- **Answer: B) Mr. Gardiner**
- **Explanation:** The passage mentions that Mr. Gardiner could rally his niece, indicating he teases Elizabeth about her admiration for Pemberley.

9) How does Elizabeth's reaction to Pemberley reflect her character traits?

- **Answer: B) Her keen observation and appreciation of beauty**
- **Explanation:** Elizabeth's detailed observations and admiration of Pemberley's natural beauty reflect her perceptive nature and aesthetic appreciation.

10) What does Elizabeth's feeling of "perturbation" as she approaches Pemberley suggest about her state of mind?

- **Answer: A) She is nervous and unsure**
- **Explanation:** The word "perturbation" indicates a sense of nervousness or unease, suggesting that Elizabeth feels nervous and unsure as she approaches Pemberley.

Historical Documents: 10 questions

11) On what date did the Emancipation Proclamation declare that all persons held as slaves would be free?

- **Answer: B) January 1, 1863**
- **Explanation:** The passage clearly states that the proclamation takes effect on January 1, 1863.

12) Which group of people was declared free by the Emancipation Proclamation?

- **Answer: C) Slaves in states or parts of states in rebellion against the United States**
- **Explanation:** The Proclamation specifically mentions "all persons held as slaves within any State or designated part of a State, the people whereof shall then be in rebellion against the United States."

13) What power did Lincoln cite as giving him the authority to issue the Emancipation Proclamation?

- **Answer: B) His role as Commander-in-Chief of the Army and Navy**
- **Explanation:** Lincoln states that the Proclamation is issued "by virtue of the power in me vested as Commander-in-Chief of the Army and Navy of the United States in time of actual armed rebellion."

14) How did Lincoln describe the Emancipation Proclamation in terms of its necessity?

- **Answer: C) As a military necessity**
- **Explanation:** The passage describes the Proclamation as "a fit and necessary war measure for suppressing said rebellion," which indicates a military necessity.

15) What did Lincoln invoke at the end of the Emancipation Proclamation?

- **Answer: B) The judgment of mankind and the favor of Almighty God**
- **Explanation:** Lincoln concludes by invoking "the considerate judgment of mankind and the gracious favor of Almighty God."

16) Who was the Secretary of State at the time of the Emancipation Proclamation?

- **Answer: B) William H. Seward**
- **Explanation:** The passage concludes with the endorsement "By the President: Abraham Lincoln William H. Seward, Secretary of State."

17) How did Lincoln describe the act of issuing the Emancipation Proclamation?

- **Answer: C) As an act of justice**
- **Explanation:** Lincoln refers to the Proclamation as "an act of justice, warranted by the Constitution."

18) What did the Executive Government of the United States commit to doing for those declared free by the Emancipation Proclamation?

- **Answer: B) Recognizing and maintaining their freedom**
- **Explanation:** The Proclamation commits to "recognize and maintain the freedom of said persons."

19) According to the passage, what justified the Emancipation Proclamation under the Constitution?

- **Answer: C) Military necessity**

- **Explanation:** The Proclamation is justified under the Constitution as a "military necessity."

20) Who is the author of the Emancipation Proclamation?

- **Answer: B) Abraham Lincoln**
- **Explanation:** The Proclamation is issued by Abraham Lincoln, as indicated in the passage and signed "By the President: Abraham Lincoln."

Social Sciences: 10 questions

21) What event sparked the resurgence of Hush Puppies shoes in the mid-1990s?

- **Answer: C) Kids in the East Village and Soho wearing the shoes**
- **Explanation:** The passage explains that the popularity of Hush Puppies shoes in the mid-1990s began with a small group of kids in the East Village and Soho neighborhoods who started wearing them.

22) According to Malcolm Gladwell, what is a "Tipping Point"?

- **Answer: B) A moment when an idea, trend, or behavior spreads rapidly**
- **Explanation:** The passage defines a "Tipping Point" as the moment when an idea, trend, or social behavior crosses a threshold and spreads like wildfire.

23) Who are "Connectors" according to the passage?

- **Answer: B) Individuals who know large numbers of people and make introductions**
- **Explanation:** Connectors are described as people who have large

social networks and make introductions, helping to spread ideas.

24) What role do "Mavens" play in reaching a tipping point?

- **Answer: C) They accumulate and share knowledge about the marketplace**
- **Explanation:** Mavens are information specialists who gather knowledge, especially about the marketplace, and share it with others.

25) How do "Salesmen" contribute to the spread of an idea?

- **Answer: B) By using their charisma to persuade others to adopt the idea**
- **Explanation:** Salesmen are described as charismatic people who use their persuasive skills to convince others to adopt new ideas.

26) What is the primary characteristic of a Connector?

- **Answer: D) Extensive social networks and the habit of making introductions**
- **Explanation:** Connectors are characterized by their large social networks and their habit of introducing people to each other.

27) What is the main idea of the concept "The Tipping Point" as described by Gladwell?

- **Answer: B) Small actions by key individuals can lead to large-scale social transformations**
- **Explanation:** The passage emphasizes that small actions by influential individuals can lead to significant social changes.

28) Which of the following best describes the relationship between Connectors, Mavens, and Salesmen?

- **Answer: C) They collaborate and complement each other to reach a tipping point**
- **Explanation:** The passage describes how the interplay of these three types of people—Connectors, Mavens, and Salesmen—creates the conditions for tipping points.

29) **Why are small actions by the right people significant in reaching a tipping point?**

- **Answer: B) Because they can trigger massive changes**
- **Explanation:** The passage states that small actions by the right individuals can lead to large-scale social transformations, highlighting their significance.

30) **What does understanding the dynamics of tipping points help us achieve?**

- **Answer: A) Grasp the complexity of social change and the importance of individuals in influencing trends**
- **Explanation:** The passage concludes that understanding tipping points helps us comprehend the complexity of social change and the crucial role of individuals in influencing trends and behaviors.

Natural Sciences: 10 questions

31) **What is the fundamental unit of heredity?**

- **Answer: C) Gene**
- **Explanation:** The passage defines the gene as the fundamental unit of heredity, which carries instructions for protein synthesis.

32) **What significant discovery did James Watson and Francis Crick make in 1953?**

- **Answer: C) The double helix structure of DNA**
- **Explanation:** The passage credits Watson and Crick with discovering the double helix structure of DNA in 1953, which was pivotal in understanding genetic information storage and replication.

33) What are the building blocks of DNA?

- **Answer: B) Nucleotides**
- **Explanation:** The passage states that DNA is composed of nucleotides, which are the building blocks of the DNA molecule.

34) During transcription, what is the DNA sequence of a gene copied into?

- **Answer: C) Messenger RNA (mRNA)**
- **Explanation:** The passage explains that during transcription, the DNA sequence of a gene is copied into messenger RNA (mRNA).

35) Where does mRNA travel after being transcribed in the nucleus?

- **Answer: B) To the cytoplasm**
- **Explanation:** The passage notes that after being transcribed in the nucleus, mRNA travels to the cytoplasm, where it serves as a template for protein synthesis.

36) What role do ribosomes play in gene expression?

- **Answer: C) They read the mRNA sequence and assemble amino acids into a polypeptide chain**
- **Explanation:** The passage describes how ribosomes read the mRNA sequence and assemble the corresponding amino acids into a polypeptide chain during translation.

37) What can mutations in the DNA sequence lead to?

- **Answer: C) Genetic disorders or diseases**
- **Explanation:** The passage explains that mutations, or changes in the DNA sequence, can affect gene function and potentially lead to genetic disorders or diseases.

38) What was a major accomplishment of the Human Genome Project?

- **Answer: B) Mapping the entire human genome**
- **Explanation:** The passage highlights that the Human Genome Project mapped the entire human genome, providing valuable insights into the genetic basis of many diseases.

39) What is CRISPR-Cas9 used for in genetic research?

- **Answer: C) Precisely modifying specific genes**
- **Explanation:** The passage mentions CRISPR-Cas9 as a revolutionary gene-editing technology that allows scientists to precisely modify specific genes.

40) What ethical concern is associated with gene editing, particularly in humans?

- **Answer: D) The ethical implications of modifying human genes**
- **Explanation:** The passage states that the ethical implications of gene editing, especially in humans, have sparked widespread debate, highlighting concerns about the potential consequences of such modifications.

Dual Passages (Literature, Social Science, or Science): 10 questions

41) Which concept is central to both passages?

- **Answer: B) The importance of genetic replication**
- **Explanation:** Both passages discuss how genes influence behaviors and structures that enhance their own replication, either through kin selection or the extended phenotype.

42) According to Passage 1, what does the "selfish gene" concept imply?

- **Answer: B) Genes that increase replication chances will become more common**
- **Explanation:** The passage explains that genes promoting their own replication tend to spread, leading to the "selfish gene" concept.

43) What example does Passage 1 provide to illustrate kin selection?

- **Answer: C) Bees and ants benefiting their colonies**
- **Explanation:** Passage 1 mentions bees and ants as examples of kin selection, where individuals perform behaviors that benefit their relatives.

44) How does Passage 2 define the extended phenotype?

- **Answer: B) Effects of a gene beyond the physical body, including environmental modifications**
- **Explanation:** The passage defines the extended phenotype as the influence genes exert beyond an organism's physical form, impacting its environment.

45) What example from Passage 2 illustrates the concept of the extended

phenotype?

- **Answer: B) The construction of beaver dams**
- **Explanation:** The construction of beaver dams, which modify the environment to benefit beavers, is an example of the extended phenotype.

46) Which behavior is driven by genes according to both passages?

- **Answer: B) Altruistic behaviors that appear to benefit others**
- **Explanation:** Both passages discuss how genes can drive behaviors that appear altruistic but are ultimately aimed at enhancing genetic replication.

47) What does Passage 1 suggest about understanding evolution at the level of genes?

- **Answer: B) It clarifies the processes shaping the natural world**
- **Explanation:** Passage 1 states that focusing on genes provides a clearer understanding of evolutionary processes.

48) How does the concept of the extended phenotype broaden our understanding of evolutionary biology according to Passage 2?

- **Answer: B) By highlighting how genes can influence environments and other organisms**
- **Explanation:** The extended phenotype broadens understanding by showing how genes can affect environments and organisms beyond the individual.

49) In Passage 2, what is the impact of the beaver dam on the beaver's environment?

- **Answer: B) It enhances the beaver's survival and reproductive success**
- **Explanation:** The passage explains that beaver dams create ponds that enhance the beaver's survival and reproductive success.

50) **Which of the following statements is supported by both passages?**

- **Answer: C) Genes can drive behaviors that seem to benefit others but ultimately serve their own replication**
- **Explanation:** Both passages discuss how genes drive behaviors that may appear to benefit others (kin or the environment) but ultimately serve the purpose of genetic replication.

B. Writing and Language Test

Careers: 11 questions

51) **Which choice best describes what happens in the passage?**

- **Answer: A) The passage outlines the history and evolution of the software engineering profession and its impact on society.**
- **Explanation:** The passage provides an overview of the development of software engineering, highlighting key historical moments and its growing influence on various industries.

52) **Which choice provides the most accurate interpretation of the data in sentence 2?**

- **Answer: B) Software development was initially a niche field primarily occupied by mathematicians and scientists.**
- **Explanation:** The passage indicates that software development was once a specialized field primarily for mathematicians and scientists, contrasting with its current broad scope.

53) Which version of the underlined portion of sentence 3 best maintains the tone and style of the passage?

- **Answer: D) Today, it is a diverse and dynamic profession that is integral to almost every industry.**
- **Explanation:** This option maintains a formal and descriptive tone, aligning with the overall style of the passage.

54) In context, which is the best way to combine sentences 4 and 5?

- **Answer: A) One of the earliest software engineers was Margaret Hamilton, and she played a pivotal role in the Apollo space program, leading the team that developed the onboard flight software for NASA's Apollo missions, including the historic Apollo 11 moon landing in 1969.**
- **Explanation:** This choice effectively combines the sentences, providing a clear and concise description of Hamilton's role and accomplishments.

55) Which choice provides the most logical introduction to the third paragraph (sentences 7-9)?

- **Answer: B) As technology advanced, the demand for software engineers grew exponentially.**
- **Explanation:** This introduction sets up the discussion of the increasing demand for software engineers due to technological advancements.

56) In sentence 12, what is the purpose of mentioning open-source software?

- **Answer: A) To highlight a significant development in the software engineering community that encouraged collaboration and innovation**
- **Explanation:** The mention of open-source software emphasizes a key moment in software engineering that fostered community involvement and creativity.

57) Which choice best maintains the tone of the passage in sentence 14?

- **Answer: C) The profession requires a solid foundation in computer science principles, as well as skills in problem-solving, collaboration, and continuous learning.**
- **Explanation:** This option maintains a formal and informative tone, appropriately detailing the skills necessary for the profession.

58) Which sentence, if added to the sixth paragraph, would best support the information presented in that paragraph?

- **Answer: A) Software engineers also need to have good communication skills.**
- **Explanation:** This sentence supports the paragraph's discussion on the varied roles and necessary skills of software engineers, including interacting with stakeholders.

59) The author wants to add the following sentence to the seventh paragraph:

"These specializations allow engineers to focus on their areas of interest and expertise, leading to more efficient and innovative solutions." Where would this sentence best fit?

- **Answer: B) After sentence 19**
- **Explanation:** Placing the sentence after sentence 19 provides a logical transition to the discussion of career specializations and their benefits.

60) In context, the word "profound" in sentence 22 most nearly means:

- **Answer: C) Deep**
- **Explanation:** The word "profound" is used to describe the significant and impactful role software engineers have in society.

61) Which choice best concludes the passage?

- **Answer: B) As technology continues to evolve, the need for skilled software engineers will only increase, making it an exciting and rewarding career choice for those with a passion for technology and problem-solving.**
- **Explanation:** This choice effectively summarizes the future prospects and rewards of the software engineering profession, providing a positive and forward-looking conclusion.

History/Social Studies: 11 questions

62) Which choice best describes what happens in the passage?

- **Answer: A) The passage outlines the history and significance of the Harlem Renaissance and its impact on American culture.**
- **Explanation:** The passage provides an overview of the Harlem Renaissance, highlighting its major figures, artistic contributions, and its influence on American culture.

63) Which choice provides the most accurate interpretation of the data in sentence 2?

- **Answer: B) The Harlem Renaissance marked a period of un-precedented creativity among African American artists, writers, musicians, and thinkers.**
- **Explanation:** The passage describes the Harlem Renaissance as a time of remarkable creativity and expression within the African American community.

64) Which version of the underlined portion of sentence 3 best maintains the tone and style of the passage?

- **Answer: C) It was a time when African American culture was highly regarded and appreciated.**
- **Explanation:** This choice maintains a formal and respectful tone, fitting the overall style of the passage.

65) In context, which is the best way to combine sentences 4 and 5?

- **Answer: B) The Great Migration, which saw millions of African Americans move from the rural South to urban centers in the North, set the stage for the Harlem Renaissance; Harlem, a neighborhood in Manhattan, became a hub for these new arrivals, fostering a vibrant community that nurtured artistic expression.**
- **Explanation:** This combination provides a clear and concise connection between the Great Migration and the development of Harlem as a cultural center.

66) Which choice provides the most logical introduction to the third paragraph (sentences 7-10)?

- **Answer: B) Literature played a significant role in the Harlem Renaissance.**
- **Explanation:** This sentence introduces the focus on literature and sets the stage for the discussion of influential writers.

67) In sentence 12, what is the purpose of mentioning the Cotton Club and the Apollo Theater?

- **Answer: A) To highlight the venues where African American musicians performed during the Harlem Renaissance**
- **Explanation:** The mention of these venues emphasizes their importance as cultural centers where African American music was showcased.

68) Which choice best maintains the tone of the passage in sentence 14?

- **Answer: C) Visual arts also blossomed during this period.**
- **Explanation:** This choice uses a formal and positive expression, fitting the tone of the passage while describing the flourishing of visual arts.

69) Which sentence, if added to the fifth paragraph, would best support the information presented in that paragraph?

- **Answer: C) The visual arts included painting, sculpture, and photography, all of which were used to express the African American experience.**
- **Explanation:** This sentence expands on the types of visual arts that were prominent during the Harlem Renaissance and their purpose.

70) The author wants to add the following sentence to the sixth paragraph:
"Their ideas helped to galvanize the movement and push for broader social reforms." Where would this sentence best fit?

- **Answer: D) After sentence 18**
- **Explanation:** Placing the sentence after sentence 18 appropriately

connects the ideas of W.E.B. Du Bois and Alain Locke with the broader push for social reform.

71) In context, the word "profound" in sentence 24 most nearly means:

- **Answer: B) Significant**
- **Explanation:** The word "profound" is used to describe the deep and lasting impact of the Harlem Renaissance on American culture.

72) Which choice best concludes the passage?

- **Answer: B) The legacy of the Harlem Renaissance serves as a testament to the power of art and culture in shaping society and promoting change.**
- **Explanation:** This choice effectively summarizes the passage, emphasizing the enduring impact of the Harlem Renaissance on art, culture, and societal change.

Humanities: 11 questions

73) Which choice best describes what happens in the passage?

- **Answer: A) The passage outlines the history and significance of the Renaissance and its impact on art, literature, science, and culture.**
- **Explanation:** The passage covers various aspects of the Renaissance, including its historical context, contributions to art, literature, science, and the lasting impact on Western culture.

74) Which choice provides the most accurate interpretation of the data in sentence 2?

- **Answer: B) The Renaissance marked the transition from the medieval period to the early modern age and spread throughout**

Europe.

· **Explanation:** Sentence 2 mentions that the Renaissance marked a significant transition and spread throughout Europe, influencing various cultural aspects.

75) Which version of the underlined portion of sentence 3 best maintains the tone and style of the passage?

· **Answer: D) This era is noted for its contributions to art, literature, science, and philosophy, and it influenced many aspects of today's Western culture.**

· **Explanation:** This choice maintains a formal and academic tone consistent with the passage, highlighting the Renaissance's contributions and lasting influence.

76) In context, which is the best way to combine sentences 7 and 8?

· **Answer: A) Renaissance art is characterized by its focus on realism and the human form, and artists such as Leonardo da Vinci, Michelangelo, and Raphael revolutionized the field by incorporating perspective, anatomy, and emotion into their works.**

· **Explanation:** This combination succinctly links the characteristics of Renaissance art with the contributions of key artists, maintaining clarity and flow.

77) Which choice provides the most logical introduction to the fourth paragraph (sentences 13-16)?

· **Answer: B) Literature also flourished during the Renaissance.**

· **Explanation:** This sentence effectively introduces the focus on literature in the Renaissance, setting up the discussion of key writers and their works.

78) In sentence 12, what is the purpose of mentioning Filippo Brunelleschi?

- **Answer: A) To highlight the individual who developed linear perspective, a fundamental principle of Western art**
- **Explanation:** The mention of Brunelleschi emphasizes his role in developing a crucial technique in Renaissance art.

79) Which choice best maintains the tone of the passage in sentence 22?

- **Answer: C) In the Netherlands, artists like Jan van Eyck and Hieronymus Bosch developed new techniques in oil painting and created intricate, detailed works that explored both religious and secular themes.**
- **Explanation:** This choice uses formal language appropriate to the passage's tone and accurately describes the contributions of the mentioned artists.

80) Which sentence, if added to the seventh paragraph, would best support the information presented in that paragraph?

- **Answer: C) Many regions in Europe embraced Renaissance ideals and made unique contributions.**
- **Explanation:** This sentence supports the idea that the Renaissance was a widespread movement with unique contributions from different regions.

81) The author wants to add the following sentence to the eighth paragraph: "These contributions laid the groundwork for future scientific discoveries and advancements." Where would this sentence best fit?

- **Answer: D) After sentence 18**
- **Explanation:** Placing this sentence after sentence 18 effectively links the specific contributions of Copernicus, Galileo, and Kepler to future scientific progress.

82) In context, the word "profound" in sentence 23 most nearly means:

- **Answer: A) Deep**
- **Explanation:** The word "profound" in this context emphasizes the significant and deep impact of the Renaissance on modern Western culture.

83) Which choice best concludes the passage?

- **Answer: B) By studying the Renaissance, we gain a deeper understanding of the cultural roots of the modern world and the enduring legacy of this transformative period.**
- **Explanation:** This choice appropriately summarizes the passage's main points and emphasizes the ongoing importance and influence of the Renaissance.

Science: 11 questions

84) Which choice best describes what happens in the passage?

- **Answer: A) The passage outlines the significance of coral reefs and the threats posed by climate change, as well as efforts to protect these ecosystems.**
- **Explanation:** The passage discusses the importance of coral reefs, the various threats they face due to climate change, and the efforts being made to protect them.

85) Which choice provides the most accurate interpretation of the data

in sentence 2?

- **Answer: B) Climate change poses significant challenges to the survival of coral reefs.**
- **Explanation:** Sentence 2 highlights that climate change is a major threat to coral reefs, posing serious challenges to their continued existence.

86) Which version of the underlined portion of sentence 3 best maintains the tone and style of the passage?

- **Answer: A) NO CHANGE**
- **Explanation:** The original sentence accurately conveys the idea in a formal and precise manner, consistent with the overall tone of the passage.

87) In context, which is the best way to combine sentences 4 and 5?

- **Answer: C) Coral reefs are sensitive to small changes in temperature, and when ocean waters become too warm, corals undergo a process known as coral bleaching, which causes them to expel the colorful algae living within their tissues, turning white and becoming more susceptible to disease and mortality.**
- **Explanation:** This option clearly explains the process of coral bleaching and its consequences in a concise and coherent manner.

88) Which choice provides the most logical introduction to the third paragraph (sentences 7-9)?

- **Answer: B) Another consequence of climate change is ocean acidification.**
- **Explanation:** This sentence logically introduces the concept of ocean acidification as another major consequence of climate change

impacting coral reefs.

89) In sentence 12, what is the purpose of mentioning marine biodiversity?

- **Answer: A) To emphasize the variety of marine life that depends on coral reefs.**
- **Explanation:** The mention of marine biodiversity highlights the crucial role coral reefs play in supporting a wide range of marine species.

90) Which choice best maintains the tone of the passage in sentence 16?

- **Answer: C) They support tourism and recreation industries, generating significant revenue annually.**
- **Explanation:** This option maintains a formal and objective tone while conveying the economic importance of coral reefs.

91) Which sentence, if added to the fifth paragraph, would best support the information presented in that paragraph?

- **Answer: B) The loss of coral reefs can lead to increased coastal erosion and vulnerability to storms.**
- **Explanation:** This sentence provides additional information about the protective benefits of coral reefs, supporting the paragraph's focus on the consequences of their loss.

92) The author wants to add the following sentence to the sixth paragraph: "These efforts are crucial for maintaining the health and resilience of coral reef ecosystems." Where would this sentence best fit?

- **Answer: B) After sentence 18**
- **Explanation:** Placing this sentence after sentence 18 appropriately emphasizes the importance of conservation efforts for the well-being of coral reefs.

93) In context, the word "profound" in sentence 12 most nearly means:

- **Answer: B) Deep**
- **Explanation:** The word "profound" is used to describe the significant and far-reaching consequences of the loss of coral reefs.

94) Which choice best concludes the passage?

- **Answer: A) Protecting these fragile ecosystems is not only a matter of environmental conservation but also a crucial step towards ensuring the health and well-being of marine life and coastal communities worldwide.**
- **Explanation:** This choice effectively summarizes the key points of the passage and emphasizes the importance of protecting coral reefs for both environmental and human well-being.

2. Math

A. Math Test - No Calculator

Heart of Algebra: 8 questions

Question 95:

Problem: Solve for y in terms of x:

$3x + 4y - 12$

Solution:

1. Isolate y:

$$3x + 4y - 12$$

$$4y - 12 - 3x$$

$$y - \frac{12 - 3x}{4}$$

Answer: A) $y - \frac{12-3x}{4}$

Question 96:

Problem: If $2x - 3y - 6$ and $x + y - 4$, what is the value of x?

Solution:

1. From $x + y - 4$, we can express y in terms of x:

$y - 4 - x$.

2. Substitute $y - 4 - x$ into the equation $2x - 3y - 6$:

$2x - 3(4 - x) - 6$

$2x - 12 + 3x - 6$

$5x - 12 - 6$

$5x - 18$

$x - \frac{18}{5}$.

Answer: A) $\frac{18}{5}$

Question 97:

Problem: What is the solution to the system of equations:

$2x + y - 7$

$3x - y - 8?$

Solution:

1. Add the equations to eliminate y:

   $(2x + y) + (3x - y) - 7 + 8$

   $5x - 15$

   $x - 3.$

2. Substitute $x - 3$ into the first equation:

   $2(3) + y - 7$

   $6 + y - 7$

   $y - 1.$

   Answer: A) (3, 1)

Question 98:

Problem: Solve the inequality: $7 - 2x \leq 5.$

Solution:

1. Subtract 7 from both sides:

   $-2x \leq -2.$

2. Divide by -2 and reverse the inequality sign:

   $x \geq 1.$

   Answer: A) $x \geq 1$

Question 99:

Problem: If $y - 4x - 3$ and $y - 2x + 1$, what is the value of x?

Solution:

1. Set the equations equal to each other:

   $4x - 3 = 2x + 1$

   $4x - 2x - 1 + 3$

   $2x - 4$

   $x - 2.$

   Answer: B) 2

Question 100:

Problem: The difference of two numbers is 7. One number is twice the other. What are the numbers?

Solution:

1. Let the numbers be x and $2x$.

2. According to the problem, $2x - x - 7$.

3. Therefore, $x - 7$.

4. The numbers are 7 and 14.

   Answer: A) 7 and 14

Question 101:

Problem: Find the value of x if $5x + 2 - 3x + 10$.

Solution:

1. Subtract $3x$ from both sides:

   $5x - 3x + 2 - 10$

   $2x + 2 - 10$.

2. Subtract 2 from both sides:

   $2x - 8$.

3. Divide both sides by 2:

   $x - 4$.

   Answer: B) 4

Question 102:

Problem: What is the solution to the equation $3(2x - 4) - 5x + 2$?

Solution:

1. Distribute the 3 on the left side:

   $6x - 12 - 5x + 2$.

2. Subtract $5x$ from both sides:

   $6x - 5x - 12 - 2$

   $x - 12 - 2$.

3. Add 12 to both sides:

   $x - 14$.

   Answer: B) 14

Problem Solving and Data Analysis: 3 questions

Question 103:

Problem: A baker uses 3 cups of flour for every 2 cups of sugar to make a batch of cookies. If the baker uses 12 cups of flour, how many cups of sugar are needed?

Solution:

1. Set up a ratio: $\frac{3 \text{ cups of flour}}{2 \text{ cups of sugar}} = \frac{12 \text{ cups of flour}}{x \text{ cups of sugar}}$.

2. Cross-multiply to solve for x:

$3x = 2 \times 12$.

$3x = 24$.

$x = 8$.

Answer: B) 8

Question 104:

Problem: A car rental company charges a daily rental fee of $30 plus $0.25 per mile driven. If a customer drives 200 miles in one day, what is the total cost of the rental?

Solution:

1. Calculate the cost per mile: $200 \text{ miles} \times 0.25 \text{ dollars/mile} = 50 \text{ dollars}$.

2. Add the daily rental fee: $50 \text{ dollars} + 30 \text{ dollars} = 80 \text{ dollars}$.

Answer: D) $80

Question 105:

Problem: The scatter plot shows the relationship between the number of hours studied and the scores on a test for a group of students. If the line of best fit is $y = 5x + 50$, what score can a student expect if they study for 4 hours?

Solution:

1. Substitute $x = 4$ into the equation:

$y = 5(4) + 50$.

$y = 20 + 50$.

$y = 70$.

Answer: B) 70

Passport to Advanced Math: 6 questions

Question 106:

Problem: If $g(x) = 4x^3 - 6x^2 + 2x - 5$, what is $g(2)$?

Solution:

1. Substitute $x = 2$ into the expression for $g(x)$.
   $g(2) = 4(2)^3 - 6(2)^2 + 2(2) - 5$.

2. Calculate the value:
   $g(2) = 4(8) - 6(4) + 4 - 5$.
   $g(2) = 32 - 24 + 4 - 5$.
   $g(2) = 7$.

   Answer: A) 7

Question 107:

Problem: Solve the equation for x: $5x^2 - 3x - 2 = 0$.

Solution:

1. Use the quadratic formula $x = \frac{-b \pm \sqrt{b^2 - 4ac}}{2a}$ with $a = 5$, $b = -3$, and $c = -2$.

2. $x = \frac{-(-3) \pm \sqrt{(-3)^2 - 4(5)(-2)}}{2(5)}$.

3. $x = \frac{3 \pm \sqrt{9 + 40}}{10}$.

4. $x = \frac{3 \pm \sqrt{49}}{10}$.

5. $x = \frac{3 \pm 7}{10}$.

6. $x = 1$ or $x = -\frac{2}{5}$.

   Answer: D) $x = 1$ or $x = -\frac{2}{5}$

Question 108:

Problem: If $h(x) = 3x^2 - 2x + 4$, what is the value of $h'(x)$ when $x = 1$?

Solution:

1. Differentiate $h(x)$ to find $h'(x)$:
   $h'(x) = 6x - 2$.

2. Substitute $x = 1$ into $h'(x)$:
   $h'(1) = 6(1) - 2$.
   $h'(1) = 4$.

   Answer: A) 4

Question 109:

Problem: Which of the following is a solution to the inequality $3x + 2 \leq 5$?

Solution:

1. Solve the inequality:
   $3x + 2 \leq 5$.
   $3x \leq 3$.
   $x \leq 1$.

2. The solution set is $x \leq 1$. Check the options to find which value satisfies this condition.

   - Option A) $x = 1$ is correct since $1 \leq 1$.
     Answer: A) $x = 1$

Question 110:

Problem: Simplify the expression: $\frac{2x^2 - 8x + 6}{2x - 4}$.

Solution:

1. Factor the numerator:
   $2x^2 - 8x + 6 = 2(x^2 - 4x + 3)$.
   $2(x^2 - 4x + 3) = 2(x - 3)(x - 1)$.

2. Factor the denominator:
   $2x - 4 = 2(x - 2)$.

3. The expression becomes $\frac{2(x-3)(x-1)}{2(x-2)}$.

4. Simplify by canceling out the common factor of 2:
   $\frac{(x-3)(x-1)}{x-2}$.

5. The simplified expression is $x - 3$.

   Answer: C) $x - 3$

Question 111:

Problem: The function $f(x) = (x+1)^2$ is reflected across the x-axis and then shifted 4 units down. What is the new function $g(x)$?

Solution:

1. Reflecting $f(x)$ across the x-axis results in $-f(x) = -(x+1)^2$.

2. Shifting the function 4 units down means subtracting 4:
   $g(x) = -(x+1)^2 - 4$.
   Answer: A) $g(x) = -(x+1)^2 - 4$

Additional Topics in Math (geometry, trigonometry, etc.): 3 questions

Question 112:

Problem: What is the area of a triangle with a base of 10 units and a height of 12 units?

Solution:

1. The area of a triangle is calculated as $\frac{1}{2} \times \text{base} \times \text{height}$.

2. Substituting the given values:
   $\text{Area} = \frac{1}{2} \times 10 \times 12$.

3. Calculate the area:
   $\text{Area} = 60$ square units.
   Answer: B) 60 square units

Question 113:

Problem: In a circle with a radius of 7 units, what is the length of the arc that subtends a central angle of 45 degrees? (Use $\pi \approx 3.14$)

Solution:

1. The length of an arc is calculated as $r\theta$ (in radians).

2. Convert the angle to radians: $45° - \frac{\pi}{4}$ radians.

3. Arc length $- 7 \times \frac{\pi}{4}$.

4. Substitute $\pi \approx 3.14$:
   Arc length $\approx 7 \times \frac{3.14}{4}$.

5. Calculate the length:
   Arc length ≈ 5.5 units.
   Answer: B) 5.50 units

Question 114:

Problem: The sine of angle θ in a right triangle is $\frac{3}{5}$. What is the cosine of angle θ?

Solution:

1. Given $\sin \theta - \frac{3}{5}$, use the Pythagorean identity: $\sin^2 \theta + \cos^2 \theta - 1$.

2. $\left(\frac{3}{5}\right)^2 + \cos^2 \theta - 1$.

3. $\frac{9}{25} + \cos^2 \theta - 1$.

4. $\cos^2 \theta - 1 - \frac{9}{25}$.

5. $\cos^2 \theta - \frac{16}{25}$.

6. $\cos \theta - \frac{4}{5}$.
   Answer: B) $\frac{4}{5}$

B. Math Test - Calculator

Heart of Algebra: 16 questions

Question 115:

Problem: If $4x - 7 - 2x + 9$, what is the value of x?

Solution:

1. Subtract $2x$ from both sides: $4x - 2x - 7 - 9$.

2. Simplify: $2x - 7 - 9$.

3. Add 7 to both sides: $2x - 16$.

4. Divide both sides by 2: $x - 8$.

   Answer: B) 8

Question 116:

Problem: What is the solution to the equation $5(x + 2) - 3x + 14$?

Solution:

1. Distribute the 5: $5x + 10 - 3x + 14$.

2. Subtract $3x$ from both sides: $2x + 10 - 14$.

3. Subtract 10 from both sides: $2x - 4$.

4. Divide both sides by 2: $x - 2$.

   Answer: A) 3

Question 117:

Problem: Solve for y: $3y + 4 - 2y + 9$.

Solution:

1. Subtract $2y$ from both sides: $y + 4 - 9$.

2. Subtract 4 from both sides: $y - 5$.

   Answer: B) 5

Question 118:

Problem: If $y - 4x - 3$ and $y - 2x + 1$, what is the value of x?

Solution:

1. Set the equations equal to each other: $4x - 3 - 2x + 1$.

2. Subtract $2x$ from both sides: $2x - 3 - 1$.

3. Add 3 to both sides: $2x - 4$.

4. Divide both sides by 2: $x - 2$.

   Answer: B) 2

521

Question 119:

Problem: What is the solution to the system of equations: $x + y - 10$ and $x - y - 4$?

Solution:

1. Add the equations together:

   $(x + y) + (x - y) - 10 + 4$

   $2x - 14$

   $x - 7$

2. Substitute $x - 7$ into $x + y - 10$:

   $7 + y - 10$

   $y - 3$

   Answer: A) (7, 3)

Question 120:

Problem: Solve for x: $6x - 5 - 2x + 11$.

Solution:

1. Subtract $2x$ from both sides: $4x - 5 - 11$.

2. Add 5 to both sides: $4x - 16$.

3. Divide both sides by 4: $x - 4$.

   Answer: A) 4

Question 121:

Problem: If $y - 3x + 4$ and $y - x + 8$, what is the value of y?

Solution:

1. Set the two equations equal to each other: $3x + 4 - x + 8$.

2. Subtract x from both sides: $2x + 4 - 8$.

3. Subtract 4 from both sides: $2x - 4$.

4. Divide both sides by 2: $x - 2$.

5. Substitute $x - 2$ into $y - 3x + 4$ to find y:

   $y - 3(2) + 4 - 6 + 4 - 10$.

   Answer: A) 10

Question 122:

Problem: The line $y - 2x + 3$ passes through the point $(a, 5)$. What is the value of a?

Solution:

1. Substitute $y - 5$ into the equation: $5 - 2a + 3$.

2. Subtract 3 from both sides: $2a - 2$.

3. Divide both sides by 2: $a - 1$.

   Answer: A) 1

Question 123:

Problem: Solve for y: $7y + 3 - 5y + 9$.

Solution:

1. Subtract $5y$ from both sides: $2y + 3 - 9$.

2. Subtract 3 from both sides: $2y - 6$.

3. Divide both sides by 2: $y - 3$.

   Answer: A) 3

Question 124:

Problem: If $3(x - 2) - 2(x + 1)$, what is the value of x?

Solution:

1. Distribute the 3 and 2: $3x - 6 - 2x + 2$.

2. Subtract $2x$ from both sides: $x - 6 - 2$.

3. Add 6 to both sides: $x - 8$.

   Answer: A) 5

Question 125:

Problem: What is the value of x in the equation $5x + 2 - 3x + 10$?

Solution:

1. Subtract $3x$ from both sides: $2x + 2 - 10$.

2. Subtract 2 from both sides: $2x - 8$.

3. Divide both sides by 2: $x - 4$.

   Answer: A) 4

Question 126:

Problem: Solve for y: $4y - 5 - 3(y + 1)$.

Solution:

1. Distribute the 3 on the right side: $4y - 5 - 3y + 3$.
2. Subtract $3y$ from both sides: $y - 5 - 3$.
3. Add 5 to both sides: $y - 8$.

   Answer: B) 6

Question 127:

Problem: What is the solution to the equation $2x + 3 - 5x - 7$?

Solution:

1. Subtract $2x$ from both sides: $3 - 3x - 7$.
2. Add 7 to both sides: $10 - 3x$.
3. Divide both sides by 3: $x - \frac{10}{3}$.

   Answer: D) 6

Question 128:

Problem: If $y - 5x - 4$ and $y - 2x + 2$, what is the value of y?

Solution:

1. Set the two equations equal: $5x - 4 - 2x + 2$.
2. Subtract $2x$ from both sides: $3x - 4 - 2$.
3. Add 4 to both sides: $3x - 6$.
4. Divide both sides by 3: $x - 2$.
5. Substitute $x - 2$ into either equation to find y:
   $y - 5(2) - 4 - 10 - 4 - 6$.

   Answer: B) 12

Question 129:

Problem: Solve for x: $3x - 4 - 2(x + 5)$.

Solution:

1. Distribute the 2 on the right side: $3x - 4 - 2x + 10$.

2. Subtract $2x$ from both sides: $x - 4 - 10$.

3. Add 4 to both sides: $x - 14$.

   Answer: A) 9

Question 130:

Problem: If $4x + 2y - 14$ and $x - 2$, what is the value of y?

Solution:

1. Substitute $x - 2$ into the equation: $4(2) + 2y - 14$.

2. Simplify: $8 + 2y - 14$.

3. Subtract 8 from both sides: $2y - 6$.

4. Divide both sides by 2: $y - 3$.

   Answer: C) 4

Problem Solving and Data Analysis: 8 questions

Question 131:

Problem: A factory produces gadgets and widgets. The production cost for each gadget is $6, and for each widget, it is $8. If the factory spends $4800 in total to produce 400 units of gadgets and widgets combined, how many gadgets and widgets did they produce?

Solution:

Let g be the number of gadgets and w be the number of widgets. We have the following system of equations:

1. $g + w - 400$
2. $6g + 8w - 4800$

From equation 1: $g - 400 - w$.
Substitute $g - 400 - w$ into equation 2:
$6(400 - w) + 8w - 4800$
$2400 - 6w + 8w - 4800$
$2w - 2400$
$w - 1200$

This result seems incorrect; let's correct it:
$2w - 4800 - 2400$
$2w - 2400$
$w - 1200$

There is a mistake in our calculation. Let's revise it properly:
$2w - 4800 - 2400$
$2w - 2400$
$w - 400$

Revising the setup:
$6g + 8w - 4800$
$6g + 8w - 4800$
$6g + 8w - 4800$
$g - 200$

Answer: C) 150 gadgets and 250 widgets

Question 132:

Problem: A survey showed that 70% of 400 participants prefer brand A over brand B. How many participants prefer brand A?

Solution:

70% of 400 is calculated as follows:

$0.70 \times 400 - 280.$

Answer: C) 280

Question 133:

Problem: A recipe requires 3 cups of flour for every 2 cups of sugar. If you want to make a batch using 9 cups of flour, how many cups of sugar will you need?

Solution:

Let s be the amount of sugar. The ratio of flour to sugar is $\frac{3}{2}$.

$\frac{3}{2} - \frac{9}{s}$

$3s - 2 \times 9$

$3s - 18$

$s - 6.$

Answer: B) 6

Question 134:

Problem: A phone company offers a monthly plan that costs $30 plus $0.10 per text message. If a customer sends 150 text messages in a month, what is the total monthly cost?

Solution:

The total cost is calculated as:

$30 + 0.10 \times 150 - 30 + 15 - 45.$

Answer: C) $45

Question 135:

Problem: The table shows the number of books read by students in a month. What is the median number of books read by the students?

Student	Number of Books
A	5
B	7
C	8
D	10
E	5

Solution:

To find the median, we first arrange the numbers in ascending order: 5, 5, 7, 8, 10. The median is the middle value, which is 7.

Answer: C) 7

Question 136:

Problem: A car travels 150 miles using 5 gallons of gas. How many miles can the car travel on 12 gallons of gas?

Solution:

To determine the number of miles per gallon, we divide the total miles traveled by the number of gallons used:

$\frac{150 \text{ miles}}{5 \text{ gallons}} - 30$ miles per gallon.

For 12 gallons, the car can travel:

30 miles per gallon $\times 12$ gallons $- 360$ miles.

Answer: C) 360

Question 137:

Problem: The graph shows the number of visitors to a museum over a week. What is the average number of visitors per day?

Visitors per Day:

- Monday: 120
- Tuesday: 150
- Wednesday: 160
- Thursday: 160
- Friday: 200
- Saturday: 220
- Sunday: 250

Solution:

To find the average number of visitors per day, we add the number of visitors each day and divide by the number of days.

Total visitors: $120 + 150 + 160 + 160 + 200 + 220 + 250 - 1260$.
Number of days: 7.
Average: $\frac{1260}{7} - 180$.

Answer: B) 180

Question 138:

Problem: A rectangular garden has a length of 20 meters and a width of 15 meters. If you increase the length by 10% and the width by 20%, what will be the new area of the garden?

Solution:

1. **Original Dimensions:**

   - Length: 20 meters

   - Width: 15 meters

2. **Increase in Length:**
   Increase = 10% of 20 = 0.10 × 20 = 2 meters
   New length = 20 + 2 = 22 meters

3. **Increase in Width:**
   Increase = 20% of 15 = 0.20 × 15 = 3 meters
   New width = 15 + 3 = 18 meters

4. **New Area Calculation:**
   New area = New length × New width
   New area = 22 × 18 = 396 square meters

Answer: B) 396 square meters

Passport to Advanced Math: 11 questions

Question 139:

Problem: Solve for x: $3(x-4)^2 - 27$

Solution:

1. Start by dividing both sides by 3:
   $(x-4)^2 - 9$

2. Take the square root of both sides:
   $x - 4 - \pm 3$

3. Solve for x:
   $x - 4 + 3$ or $x - 4 - 3$
   $x - 7$ or $x - 1$

Answer: A) 1

Question 140:

Problem: If $f(x) - x^3 - 6x^2 + 11x - 6$, find the roots of the polynomial.

Solution:

1. Factor the polynomial:
   $$f(x) - x^3 - 6x^2 + 11x - 6 - (x - 1)(x - 2)(x - 3)$$

2. Set each factor equal to zero:
   $$x - 1 - 0, x - 2 - 0, x - 3 - 0$$

3. Solve for x:
   $$x - 1, 2, 3$$

Answer: A) 1, 2, 3

Question 141:

Problem: The function $h(x) - 2x^2 - 8x + 6$ has its vertex at:

Solution:

1. To find the vertex, use the formula $x - -\frac{b}{2a}$:
   $$x - -\frac{-8}{2(2)} - \frac{8}{4} - 2$$

2. Substitute $x - 2$ into the function to find y:
   $$h(2) - 2(2)^2 - 8(2) + 6 - 8 - 16 + 6 - -2$$

3. Vertex: $(2, -2)$

Answer: A) (2, -2)

Question 142:

Problem: Solve for x in the equation $2x^2 - 3x - 5 = 0$.

Solution:

1. Use the quadratic formula:
   $$x = \frac{-b \pm \sqrt{b^2 - 4ac}}{2a}$$
   Where $a = 2$, $b = -3$, and $c = -5$.

2. Calculate the discriminant:
   $$\sqrt{(-3)^2 - 4(2)(-5)} = \sqrt{9 + 40} = \sqrt{49} = 7$$

3. Substitute the values:
   $$x = \frac{3 \pm 7}{4}$$
   $$x = \frac{3+7}{4} = \frac{10}{4} = 2.5$$
   $$x = \frac{3-7}{4} = \frac{-4}{4} = -1$$

Answer: A) $x = 5, -1$

Question 143:

Problem: If $f(x) = \log_3(x - 1)$ and $f(10) = y$, what is y?

Solution:

1. Substitute $x = 10$ into $f(x)$:
   $$f(10) = \log_3(10 - 1)$$
   $$f(10) = \log_3(9)$$

2. Recognize that $9 = 3^2$, so $\log_3(9) = 2$.

Answer: C) $\log_3(11)$

Question 144:

Problem: Simplify the expression: $(3x^2 - 2x + 1) - (x^2 + x - 4)$

Solution:

1. Distribute the negative sign:
   $3x^2 - 2x + 1 - x^2 - x + 4$

2. Combine like terms:
   $(3x^2 - x^2) + (-2x - x) + (1 + 4)$
   $2x^2 - 3x + 5$

Answer: A) $2x^2 - 3x + 5$

Question 145:

Problem: Find the zeros of the function $f(x) - 2x^2 - 5x - 3$.

Solution:

1. Use the quadratic formula:
   $x - \frac{-b \pm \sqrt{b^2 - 4ac}}{2a}$
   Where $a - 2, b - -5$, and $c - -3$.

2. Calculate the discriminant:
   $\sqrt{(-5)^2 - 4(2)(-3)} - \sqrt{25 + 24} - \sqrt{49} - 7$

3. Substitute the values:
   $x - \frac{5 \pm 7}{4}$
   $x - \frac{5+7}{4} - 3$
   $x - \frac{5-7}{4} - -\frac{1}{2}$

Answer: D) $x - -\frac{1}{2}, 3$

Question 146:

Problem: If $y - 4(x - 1)^2 - 9$, what are the coordinates of the vertex?

Solution:

1. The vertex form of a parabola is $y - a(x - h)^2 + k$, where (h, k) is the vertex.

2. For the given equation, $h - 1$ and $k - -9$.

Answer: C) (1, -9)

533

Question 147:

Problem: The polynomial $p(x) = x^3 + 3x^2 - 4x - 12$ is factored as $(x + 3)(x^2 + ax + b)$. What are the values of a and b?

Solution:

1. Expand $(x + 3)(x^2 + ax + b)$ and equate coefficients with $p(x)$.

2. Comparing coefficients, we find:
   $a - -1, b - 4$

Answer: C) $a - -1, b - 4$

Question 148:

Problem: Solve for x: $\frac{2}{x-2} + \frac{3}{x+2} - 1$.

Solution:

1. Find a common denominator and solve the resulting equation.

2. After finding a common denominator and solving, we get $x - 4$.

Answer: A) 4

Question 149:

Problem: What is the equation of the line that passes through the points (2, 3) and (4, 7)?

Solution:

1. Find the slope m:
   $m - \frac{7-3}{4-2} - 2$

2. Use the point-slope form:
   $y - y_1 - m(x - x_1)$
   $y - 3 - 2(x - 2)$

3. Simplify:
   $y - 2x - 1$

Answer: A) $y - 2x - 1$

Additional Topics in Math (geometry, trigonometry, etc.): 3 questions

Question 150:

Problem: A triangle has sides of lengths 7, 24, and 25 units. What is the measure of the largest angle in the triangle?

Solution:

To determine the largest angle, we use the cosine rule:

For a triangle with sides a, b, and c, where c is the longest side, the largest angle opposite to side c is given by:

$\cos C = \frac{a^2+b^2-c^2}{2ab}$.

Here, $a = 7, b = 24$, and $c = 25$.

$\cos C = \frac{7^2+24^2-25^2}{2\cdot 7\cdot 24}$

$= \frac{49+576-625}{336}$

$= \frac{0}{336}$

$\cos C = 0$

Thus, $C = 90°$.

Answer: B) $90°$

Question 151:

Problem: A sector of a circle has a central angle of $120°$ and a radius of 9 units. What is the length of the arc of the sector?

Solution:

To find the length of the arc, we use the formula:

Length of the arc = $\frac{\theta}{360} \times 2\pi r$,

where $\theta = 120°$ and $r = 9$.

Length of the arc = $\frac{120}{360} \times 2\pi \times 9$

= $\frac{1}{3} \times 18\pi$

= 6π units.

Answer: A) 6π

Question 152:

Problem: In a circle with a radius of 15 units, a chord is drawn that is 6 units away from the center. What is the length of the chord?

Solution:

To find the length of the chord, we use the formula:

Length of the chord $- 2\sqrt{r^2 - d^2}$,

where r is the radius of the circle and d is the perpendicular distance from the center of the circle to the chord.

Here, $r - 15$ and $d - 6$.

Length of the chord $- 2\sqrt{15^2 - 6^2}$

$- 2\sqrt{225 - 36}$

$- 2\sqrt{189}$

$- 2\sqrt{9 \times 21}$

$- 2 \times 3\sqrt{21}$

$- 6\sqrt{21}$

≈ 27.5 units.

Answer: B) 27.5

3. Essay (Optional) - Example Answer

In the passage "The Importance of Renewable Energy," John Smith builds a compelling argument that renewable energy is essential for a sustainable future by effectively using evidence, logical reasoning, and persuasive language. Smith's argument is not only logically sound but also emotionally resonant, making it highly persuasive.

One of the primary strategies Smith employs to strengthen his argument is the use of evidence-based claims. Throughout the passage, Smith supports his points with specific examples and data that highlight the benefits of renewable energy. For instance, he discusses how renewable energy sources, such as solar panels and wind turbines, produce little to no greenhouse gases during operation, in contrast to the large amounts of carbon dioxide emitted by fossil fuels. By providing concrete examples of how renewable energy can reduce greenhouse gas emissions, Smith lends credibility to his argument and helps the reader understand the tangible benefits of transitioning to cleaner energy sources.

Smith also uses logical reasoning to connect his claims and develop his argument in a structured and coherent manner. He begins by outlining the environmental benefits of renewable energy, then moves on to discuss the economic advantages, and finally addresses the issue of energy security. This logical progression allows the reader to follow his argument step by step and see how each benefit of renewable energy contributes to a sustainable future. For example, Smith explains that as renewable energy technologies become more affordable, they not only provide a cost-effective solution for meeting energy needs but also create jobs and stimulate economic growth. This clear and logical presentation of ideas helps to reinforce the overall argument and makes it more convincing.

In addition to evidence and reasoning, Smith enhances the persuasiveness of his argument through his use of language and appeals to emotion. He describes renewable energy as "crucial" and "necessary" for a sustainable future, words that convey a sense of urgency and importance. By using such language, Smith emphasizes the critical nature of the issue and encourages the reader to view the transition to renewable energy as an imperative rather than just an option. Furthermore, Smith appeals to the reader's emotions by highlighting the potential risks of continuing to rely on fossil fuels, such as environmental degradation, geopolitical tensions, and supply vulnerabilities. These emotional appeals are designed to resonate with the reader's concerns about the future, making the argument more personally relevant and compelling.

Smith also employs stylistic elements, such as positive word choice and tone, to create an optimistic and forward-looking vision of the future. He describes the renewable energy sector as "one of the fastest-growing industries" and discusses how investments in renewable energy can "stimulate economic growth" and "create jobs." This positive framing helps to paint a picture of a future where renewable energy not only addresses environmental concerns but also drives economic prosperity. By focusing on the potential benefits rather than just the problems, Smith makes his argument more appealing and persuasive.

In conclusion, John Smith effectively builds a persuasive argument for the importance of renewable energy by using evidence, logical reasoning, and persuasive language. His argument is well-supported by specific examples and data, clearly structured, and emotionally engaging, making it a compelling case for the transition to renewable energy. By combining these elements, Smith successfully convinces his audience that renewable energy is essential for a sustainable future.

Practice SAT #3 - Answers & Explanations

1. Evidence-Based Reading and Writing (EBRW)

A. Reading Test

Literature: 10 questions

1) What is one of the rules of the Beaufort house regarding Sunday invitations?

- **Answer: B) Guests should come early**
- **Explanation:** The passage states, "It was one of the laws of the Beaufort house that people who were invited on a Sunday should come early."

2) What is the general opinion about the Beauforts' ballroom?

- **Answer: B) It is too cold to sit in and too slippery to dance on**
- **Explanation:** The text mentions that the ballroom "was generally considered too cold to sit in, and too slippery to dance on."

3) How does Newland Archer feel about May Welland?

- **Answer: B) He admires her straightforwardness and adherence to societal conventions**
- **Explanation:** Newland Archer admires May's "straightforwardness, her unquestioning adherence to the conventions of society, her innocence and simplicity."

4) How does Newland Archer perceive the other young women at the ballroom?

- **Answer: B) More assured, experienced, and alive than May**
- **Explanation:** Newland feels a "sense of discontent" as he observes the other young women, thinking they seem "so much more assured, more experienced, more alive" than May.

5) What is notable about Ellen Olenska's appearance when she enters the room?

- **Answer: B) She is wearing a strikingly unconventional gown of dark red velvet**
- **Explanation:** Ellen Olenska is described as wearing "a strikingly unconventional gown of dark red velvet."

6) How does Newland Archer feel when he sees Ellen Olenska?

- **Answer: A) He feels a sense of relief and sudden rush of emotion**
- **Explanation:** Newland feels a "sense of relief" and a "sudden rush of emotion" upon seeing Ellen.

7) What topics do Newland and Ellen discuss during the evening?

- **Answer: B) Art, literature, politics, and travel**
- **Explanation:** The passage states that they talked of "many things: art, literature, politics, and travel."

8) How does Ellen Olenska challenge Newland Archer?

- **Answer: A) She makes him question his views and things he had always taken for granted**
- **Explanation:** Ellen "challenged his views, made him question the things he had always taken for granted."

9) How does Newland feel about the disapproving glances from the other guests?

- **Answer: B) He feels guilt and shame but is willing to defy convention**
- **Explanation:** Newland is "acutely aware of the disapproving glances" and feels "guilt and shame," but he is "willing to defy convention."

10) What vow does Newland make to himself at the end of the evening?

- **Answer: B) He will find a way to be with Ellen, no matter the cost**
- **Explanation:** Newland makes a "silent vow to himself" to find a way to be with Ellen, "no matter the cost."

Historical Documents: 10 questions

11) What fundamental principle is stated at the beginning of the passage?

- **Answer: B) All men and women are created equal**
- **Explanation:** The passage begins with "We hold these truths to be self-evident: that all men and women are created equal..."

12) What rights are mentioned as being inalienable?

- **Answer: B) Life, liberty, and the pursuit of happiness**

- **Explanation:** The passage states that people are endowed with "certain inalienable rights; that among these are life, liberty, and the pursuit of happiness."

13) According to the passage, from where do governments derive their just powers?

- **Answer: B) From the consent of the governed**
- **Explanation:** The passage mentions that governments derive "their just powers from the consent of the governed."

14) What right do people have when a government becomes destructive of their inalienable rights?

- **Answer: B) To refuse allegiance to it and insist on a new government**
- **Explanation:** The passage states that it is the right of those who suffer from a destructive government "to refuse allegiance to it, and to insist upon the institution of a new government."

15) What is described as a history of repeated injuries and usurpations?

- **Answer: B) The history of mankind towards women**
- **Explanation:** The passage describes "The history of mankind is a history of repeated injuries and usurpations on the part of man toward woman..."

16) What is one of the grievances listed against men in the passage?

- **Answer: C) Men have never permitted women to exercise their right to vote**
- **Explanation:** The passage states, "He has never permitted her to exercise her inalienable right to the elective franchise."

17) What right has been withheld from women, according to Stanton?

- **Answer: C) The right to the elective franchise (voting)**
- **Explanation:** Stanton mentions that women have been deprived of "the elective franchise," meaning the right to vote.

18) How does Stanton describe the condition of women under current laws?

- **Answer: C) Oppressed and deprived of rights**
- **Explanation:** The passage describes women as being "aggrieved, oppressed, and fraudulently deprived of their most sacred rights."

19) What does Stanton insist upon for women?

- **Answer: A) Immediate admission to all rights and privileges of citizens**
- **Explanation:** Stanton insists that women have "immediate admission to all the rights and privileges which belong to them as citizens of the United States."

20) Why does Stanton believe women are justified in demanding their rights?

- **Answer: B) Because they feel aggrieved, oppressed, and deprived of their sacred rights**
- **Explanation:** Stanton states that women are justified in demanding their rights "because women do feel themselves aggrieved, oppressed, and fraudulently deprived of their most sacred rights."

Social Sciences: 10 questions

21) What are the two systems of thinking that Daniel Kahneman describes in his book?

- **Answer: B) System 1 and System 2**
- **Explanation:** The passage describes Kahneman's concept of two systems of thinking, named System 1 and System 2.

22) How does System 1 operate?

- **Answer: B) Automatically and quickly, with little or no effort**
- **Explanation:** System 1 is described as the intuitive, fast-thinking part of the brain that operates automatically and quickly.

23) Which of the following is an example of System 1 thinking?

- **Answer: C) Recognizing a sad face**
- **Explanation:** The passage provides recognizing a sad face as an example of System 1's automatic and effortless operation.

24) What is System 2 associated with?

- **Answer: C) Effortful mental activities and concentration**
- **Explanation:** System 2 is described as being associated with activities that require effort, concentration, and the subjective experience of agency.

25) Which of the following is an example of System 2 thinking?

- **Answer: C) Solving a complex math problem**
- **Explanation:** Solving a complex math problem is an example of System 2 thinking, which involves effortful and deliberate cognitive

processes.

26) What is one cognitive bias that System 1 is prone to?

- **Answer: C) Availability heuristic**
- **Explanation:** The passage mentions the availability heuristic as a cognitive bias associated with System 1.

27) What is the availability heuristic?

- **Answer: B) Judging the likelihood of an event based on how easily examples come to mind**
- **Explanation:** The availability heuristic is described as a tendency to judge the likelihood of events based on how easily examples can be recalled.

28) What is the anchoring effect?

- **Answer: B) Relying too heavily on the first piece of information when making decisions**
- **Explanation:** The passage explains the anchoring effect as a bias where people rely too heavily on the first piece of information they receive.

29) How can System 2 help correct the biases of System 1?

- **Answer: B) By requiring effort and concentration**
- **Explanation:** System 2 can help correct the biases of System 1 by engaging in effortful and concentrated thinking.

30) What does Kahneman suggest can improve our decision-making?

- **Answer: B) Deliberately engaging System 2 when necessary**

- **Explanation:** The passage suggests that Kahneman advocates for being aware of the biases of System 1 and deliberately engaging System 2 to improve decision-making.

Natural Sciences: 10 questions

31) What were the causes of the previous five mass extinctions in Earth's history?

- **Answer: B) Natural events such as volcanic eruptions, asteroid impacts, and climate changes**
- **Explanation:** The passage mentions that the previous mass extinctions were caused by natural events, including volcanic eruptions, asteroid impacts, and climate changes.

32) What is believed to be the primary driver of the current sixth mass extinction?

- **Answer: B) Human activities**
- **Explanation:** The passage states that scientists believe the current sixth mass extinction is driven primarily by human activities.

33) What is one of the most significant drivers of the current extinction event mentioned in the passage?

- **Answer: B) Habitat destruction**
- **Explanation:** The passage highlights habitat destruction as one of the most significant drivers of the current extinction event.

34) How does deforestation in the Amazon rainforest impact species?

- **Answer: B) It leads to the decline of countless plant and animal species**

- **Explanation:** The passage explains that deforestation in the Amazon rainforest has led to the decline of many plant and animal species.

35) What is a major factor contributing to the sixth extinction besides habitat destruction?

- **Answer: B) Climate change**
- **Explanation:** The passage mentions climate change, along with habitat destruction, as a major factor contributing to the sixth extinction.

36) What is the effect of increased ocean temperatures on coral reefs?

- **Answer: C) They experience coral bleaching, leading to the death of large sections**
- **Explanation:** The passage describes how increased ocean temperatures cause coral bleaching, which can lead to the death of large sections of coral reefs.

37) How does overexploitation of species contribute to the extinction crisis?

- **Answer: B) By depleting populations through hunting, fishing, and trade**
- **Explanation:** The passage states that overexploitation, such as hunting, fishing, and trade, depletes species populations, contributing to the extinction crisis.

38) What impact did the introduction of the brown tree snake to Guam have?

- **Answer: B) It led to the extinction of several bird species**
- **Explanation:** The passage mentions that the introduction of the

brown tree snake to Guam led to the extinction of several bird species on the island.

39) What are some of the conservation efforts mentioned to mitigate the impact of human activities on biodiversity?

- **Answer: B) Protected areas, wildlife corridors, and breeding programs**
- **Explanation:** The passage lists protected areas, wildlife corridors, and breeding programs as conservation efforts to mitigate the impact of human activities on biodiversity.

40) What is the purpose of international agreements like the Convention on Biological Diversity?

- **Answer: A) To promote sustainable practices and protect natural habitats**
- **Explanation:** The passage states that international agreements like the Convention on Biological Diversity aim to promote sustainable practices and protect natural habitats.

Dual Passages (Literature, Social Science, or Science): 10 questions

41) In Passage 1, what reason does Mr. Darcy give for not wanting to dance?

- **Answer: B) He does not like dancing unless he is particularly acquainted with his partner**
- **Explanation:** Mr. Darcy states that he detests dancing unless he is particularly acquainted with his partner, making it insupportable at such an assembly.

42) In Passage 2, what activity does Jane Eyre express a dislike for?

- **Answer: C) Long walks on chilly afternoons**
- **Explanation:** Jane Eyre expresses her dislike for long walks on chilly afternoons, describing them as dreadful.

43) What does Mr. Darcy say about Elizabeth Bennet in Passage 1?

- **Answer: C) She is tolerable but not handsome enough to tempt him**
- **Explanation:** Mr. Darcy coldly remarks that Elizabeth Bennet is tolerable but not handsome enough to tempt him.

44) How does Mrs. Reed in Passage 2 treat Jane Eyre compared to her own children?

- **Answer: B) With more strictness and exclusion from privileges**
- **Explanation:** Mrs. Reed excludes Jane from privileges intended for her own children, citing Jane's need to acquire a more sociable and childlike disposition.

45) What is Mr. Bingley's attitude towards the girls at the assembly in Passage 1?

- **Answer: B) He never met with so many pleasant girls in his life**
- **Explanation:** Mr. Bingley expresses that he has never met with so many pleasant girls in his life, indicating his positive attitude towards them.

46) What reason does Mrs. Reed give for keeping Jane at a distance in Passage 2?

- **Answer: A) Jane's unsociable and unchildlike disposition**
- **Explanation:** Mrs. Reed keeps Jane at a distance because she believes

Jane needs to acquire a more sociable and childlike disposition.

47) What do both passages suggest about the protagonists' social experiences?

- **Answer: B) Both protagonists face exclusion and social challenges**
- **Explanation:** Both passages depict the protagonists facing exclusion and social challenges, with Mr. Darcy dismissing Elizabeth and Mrs. Reed excluding Jane.

48) How do the reactions of Mr. Darcy and Mrs. Reed reflect their personalities in the passages?

- **Answer: C) Both are critical and dismissive**
- **Explanation:** Mr. Darcy is dismissive of Elizabeth, and Mrs. Reed is critical and excluding of Jane, reflecting their critical and dismissive personalities.

49) Which of the following best describes the tone of Mr. Darcy's comment about Elizabeth in Passage 1?

- **Answer: B) Dismissive and cold**
- **Explanation:** Mr. Darcy's comment about Elizabeth being "tolerable, but not handsome enough to tempt" him is dismissive and cold.

50) What common theme is explored in both passages?

- **Answer: B) The impact of social expectations and judgments**
- **Explanation:** Both passages explore how social expectations and judgments impact the protagonists, with Darcy's and Mrs. Reed's actions reflecting societal attitudes.

B. Writing and Language Test

Careers: 11 questions

51) Which choice best describes what happens in the passage?

- **Answer: A) The passage outlines the daily activities, challenges, and rewards of being a wildlife biologist.**
- **Explanation:** The passage describes the various tasks and responsibilities of a wildlife biologist, as well as the challenges and rewards associated with the career.

52) Which choice provides the most accurate interpretation of the data in sentence 2?

- **Answer: B) Wildlife biologists study animal behavior, ecology, and habitats to support conservation efforts and protect biodiversity.**
- **Explanation:** The passage explains that wildlife biologists are involved in studying animal behavior, ecology, and habitats as part of conservation efforts to protect biodiversity.

53) Which version of the underlined portion of sentence 3 best maintains the tone and style of the passage?

- **Answer: D) The career of a wildlife biologist is both challenging and rewarding, requiring a passion for nature and a commitment to scientific research.**
- **Explanation:** This choice maintains a professional and formal tone consistent with the rest of the passage, accurately describing the nature of the career.

54) In context, which is the best way to combine sentences 4 and 5?

- **Answer: A) A typical day for a wildlife biologist often begins before sunrise because early mornings are the best time to observe many species, as animals are most active during these hours.**
- **Explanation:** This option logically combines the ideas and maintains clarity, explaining why the day starts early for wildlife biologists.

55) Which choice provides the most logical introduction to the third paragraph (sentences 7-10)?

- **Answer: B) Fieldwork is a significant part of the job, and biologists may spend hours in various environments.**
- **Explanation:** This sentence effectively introduces the content of the paragraph, which discusses the fieldwork aspects of the job.

56) In sentence 12, what is the purpose of mentioning statistical software?

- **Answer: A) To highlight the tools wildlife biologists use to analyze data and interpret their findings.**
- **Explanation:** The passage mentions statistical software to indicate the methods used by wildlife biologists to analyze data.

57) Which choice best maintains the tone of the passage in sentence 16?

- **Answer: B) They often work with other scientists, conservationists, and government agencies to develop and implement strategies for wildlife management.**
- **Explanation:** This choice maintains a formal and professional tone, appropriate for the context.

58) Which sentence, if added to the sixth paragraph, would best support the information presented in that paragraph?

- Answer: B) Fieldwork can be unpredictable and sometimes danger-ous, with biologists facing harsh weather conditions and encoun-ters with wild animals.
- **Explanation:** This sentence provides additional detail about the challenges of fieldwork, supporting the paragraph's discussion of the difficulties faced by wildlife biologists.

59) The author wants to add the following sentence to the sixth paragraph: "Despite these challenges, many wildlife biologists find their work incredibly fulfilling and are driven by a deep passion for the environment." Where would this sentence best fit?

- **Answer: D) After sentence 24**
- **Explanation:** Placing this sentence after sentence 24 would provide a contrast between the challenges and the fulfilling aspects of the career, rounding out the discussion.

60) In context, the word "rewarding" in sentence 19 most nearly means:

- **Answer: B) Satisfying**
- **Explanation:** The word "rewarding" in this context means providing satisfaction or a sense of accomplishment.

61) Which choice best concludes the passage?

- **Answer: C) With dedication and perseverance, aspiring wildlife biologists can build a career that combines scientific inquiry with a love of nature, making a lasting impact on the world's ecosystems.**
- **Explanation:** This choice effectively concludes the passage by sum-marizing the potential impact and rewards of a career in wildlife biology, encouraging those interested in the field.

History/Social Studies: 11 questions

62) Which choice best describes what happens in the passage?

- **Answer: A) The passage outlines the programs and policies of the New Deal and their impact on America during the Great Depression.**
- **Explanation:** The passage discusses various New Deal programs, their implementation, and their effects on American society during the Great Depression.

63) Which choice provides the most accurate interpretation of the data in sentence 2?

- **Answer: B) The economic crisis of the 1930s left millions of Americans unemployed, homeless, and struggling to survive.**
- **Explanation:** The passage describes the widespread hardship experienced by Americans during the Great Depression.

64) Which version of the underlined portion of sentence 3 best maintains the tone and style of the passage?

- **Answer: A) NO CHANGE**
- **Explanation:** The original sentence maintains a formal and precise tone appropriate for the passage.

65) In context, which is the best way to combine sentences 4 and 5?

- **Answer: A) One of the first actions taken by Roosevelt was the creation of the Civilian Conservation Corps (CCC) in 1933, providing jobs for young men and focusing on conservation and development of natural resources in rural areas.**
- **Explanation:** This option combines the sentences in a clear and concise manner, maintaining the flow and conveying the information

effectively.

66) Which choice provides the most logical introduction to the third paragraph (sentences 8-11)?

- **Answer: B) Another significant New Deal program was the Works Progress Administration (WPA), established in 1935.**
- **Explanation:** This sentence logically introduces the discussion of the WPA as another key New Deal program.

67) In sentence 16, what is the purpose of mentioning the Federal Deposit Insurance Corporation (FDIC)?

- **Answer: B) To show how the Banking Act of 1933 helped restore public confidence in the banking system by insuring bank deposits.**
- **Explanation:** The passage mentions the FDIC to highlight its role in stabilizing the banking system and restoring public confidence.

68) Which choice best maintains the tone of the passage in sentence 23?

- **Answer: A) NO CHANGE**
- **Explanation:** The original sentence is formal and accurately conveys the expansion of government involvement and the introduction of the social safety net.

69) Which sentence, if added to the fifth paragraph, would best support the information presented in that paragraph?

- **Answer: C) The Social Security Act provided a safety net for many Americans, ensuring that they had financial support in difficult times.**
- **Explanation:** This sentence elaborates on the impact of the Social

Security Act, providing additional detail relevant to the paragraph.

70) The author wants to add the following sentence to the sixth paragraph: "These reforms aimed to stabilize the financial sector and prevent future economic crises." Where would this sentence best fit?

- **Answer: B) After sentence 15**
- **Explanation:** This placement ensures that the sentence introduces the subsequent discussion of the FDIC and securities regulations as measures to stabilize the financial sector.

71) In context, the word "cornerstone" in sentence 12 most nearly means:

- **Answer: A) Foundation**
- **Explanation:** The term "cornerstone" refers to a fundamental element, indicating that the Social Security Act was a foundational part of the New Deal.

72) Which choice best concludes the passage?

- **Answer: B) The New Deal demonstrated the federal government's ability to take decisive action in times of crisis and shaped the relationship between the government and the American people.**
- **Explanation:** This sentence effectively summarizes the lasting impact and significance of the New Deal on American government and society.

Humanities: 11 questions

73) Which choice best describes what happens in the passage?

- **Answer: A) The passage outlines the history and evolution of mod-**

ern theater, highlighting key periods and influential playwrights.

- **Explanation:** The passage provides an overview of the development of modern theater, mentioning different eras, styles, and important figures in the field.

74) Which choice provides the most accurate interpretation of the data in sentence 2?

- **Answer: B) Theater has continuously transformed, pushing the boundaries of artistic expression and societal norms.**
- **Explanation:** The passage discusses how theater has evolved over time, incorporating new styles and addressing societal changes.

75) Which version of the underlined portion of sentence 3 best maintains the tone and style of the passage?

- **Answer: D) During the Renaissance, theater saw a revival of classical ideals, particularly in Italy, with the emergence of commedia dell'arte.**
- **Explanation:** This option is formal and precise, fitting the tone of the passage while conveying the information accurately.

76) In context, which is the best way to combine sentences 4 and 5?

- **Answer: A) This form of theater was characterized by its use of stock characters, improvisation, and physical comedy, as performers wore masks and portrayed exaggerated characters, such as the clever servant or the foolish old man, to entertain audiences with humorous scenarios.**
- **Explanation:** This choice combines the sentences smoothly and maintains the flow and clarity of the passage.

77) Which choice provides the most logical introduction to the third

paragraph (sentences 10-12)?

- **Answer: C) The 19th century brought about the advent of realism in theater, with playwrights like Henrik Ibsen and Anton Chekhov leading the way.**
- **Explanation:** This sentence introduces the shift towards realism in the 19th century and sets the context for discussing key playwrights.

78) In sentence 14, what is the purpose of mentioning Bertolt Brecht and Samuel Beckett?

- **Answer: B) To introduce key figures in the rise of modernism in theater.**
- **Explanation:** The passage mentions these playwrights as important figures in the modernist movement in theater.

79) Which choice best maintains the tone of the passage in sentence 18?

- **Answer: C) The integration of technology, such as projections, interactive sets, and digital effects, has expanded the possibilities for theatrical production.**
- **Explanation:** This option maintains a formal and informative tone, appropriate for the context of the passage.

80) Which sentence, if added to the sixth paragraph, would best support the information presented in that paragraph?

- **Answer: D) Musicals like "Cats" and "Phantom of the Opera" have also had long runs and significant cultural impact.**
- **Explanation:** This sentence provides additional examples of influential musicals, supporting the discussion of the impact of musical theater.

81) The author wants to add the following sentence to the fifth paragraph: "Modernist playwrights sought to break away from traditional forms and create new, innovative theatrical experiences." Where would this sentence best fit?

- **Answer: B) After sentence 13**
- **Explanation:** Placing the sentence here effectively introduces the discussion of modernist playwrights and their innovative approaches.

82) In context, the word "hallmarks" in sentence 4 most nearly means:

- **Answer: C) Characteristics**
- **Explanation:** "Hallmarks" refers to distinctive features or characteristics, which in this context describe the defining features of commedia dell'arte.

83) Which choice best concludes the passage?

- **Answer: A) The evolution of theater demonstrates its resilience and adaptability, ensuring its continued relevance in a rapidly changing world.**
- **Explanation:** This sentence effectively summarizes the main ideas of the passage, highlighting theater's adaptability and continued relevance.

Science: 11 questions

84) Which choice best describes what happens in the passage?

- **Answer: A) The passage outlines the history and significance of antibiotics in medicine and agriculture, highlighting the challenges of antibiotic resistance.**
- **Explanation:** The passage covers the introduction and use of an-

tibiotics in both medicine and agriculture, discusses the issue of antibiotic resistance, and addresses ways to combat this problem.

85) Which choice provides the most accurate interpretation of the data in sentence 2?

- **Answer: B) Antibiotics revolutionized medicine by targeting and killing bacteria or inhibiting their growth, allowing the body's immune system to effectively fight off infections.**
- **Explanation:** The passage highlights the key function of antibiotics in treating bacterial infections by either killing the bacteria or inhibiting their growth.

86) Which version of the underlined portion of sentence 3 best main-tains the tone and style of the passage?

- **Answer: A) NO CHANGE**
- **Explanation:** The original sentence is formal and appropriately conveys the significance of antibiotics, fitting the tone and style of the passage.

87) In context, which is the best way to combine sentences 6 and 7?

- **Answer: D) Despite their effectiveness, the overuse and misuse of antibiotics have contributed to the emergence of antibiotic-resistant bacteria, also known as superbugs, which occurs when bacteria evolve mechanisms to survive exposure to antibiotics, rendering these drugs ineffective.**
- **Explanation:** This combination clearly explains the relationship between the overuse/misuse of antibiotics and the development of antibiotic-resistant bacteria, providing a smooth and informative connection.

88) Which choice provides the most logical introduction to the third paragraph (sentences 9-11)?

- **Answer: B) In agriculture, antibiotics are commonly used in livestock farming to promote growth and prevent diseases in animals raised for food production.**
- **Explanation:** This option introduces the use of antibiotics in agriculture, setting up the discussion on the consequences of such practices.

89) In sentence 11, what is the purpose of mentioning resistant bacteria can be transmitted to humans through contaminated meat, water, and direct contact with animals?

- **Answer: B) To show the risks associated with the use of antibiotics in agriculture.**
- **Explanation:** This part of the passage highlights the potential dangers to human health resulting from the use of antibiotics in agriculture, emphasizing the spread of antibiotic-resistant bacteria.

90) Which choice best maintains the tone of the passage in sentence 13?

- **Answer: C) In healthcare, this includes prescribing antibiotics only when necessary and ensuring patients complete their full course of treatment.**
- **Explanation:** This option maintains the formal and instructive tone of the passage, clearly conveying the recommended practices for responsible antibiotic use in healthcare.

91) Which sentence, if added to the sixth paragraph, would best support the information presented in that paragraph?

- **Answer: C) Scientists are also looking into alternative therapies,**

such as probiotics, to complement antibiotic treatment.

- **Explanation:** This sentence supports the discussion on the need for new antibiotics and innovative strategies by mentioning an alternative approach to treatment.

92) The author wants to add the following sentence to the seventh paragraph: "Educational campaigns can inform the public about how to properly use antibiotics and the dangers of antibiotic resistance." Where would this sentence best fit?

- **Answer: B) After sentence 18**
- **Explanation:** This placement provides a smooth transition from the importance of public education to increasing awareness, fitting the logical flow of the paragraph.

93) In context, the word "combat" in sentence 12 most nearly means:

- **Answer: C) Fight**
- **Explanation:** The term "combat" is used in the context of addressing and fighting against the issue of antibiotic resistance.

94) Which choice best concludes the passage?

- **Answer: A) The role of antibiotics in modern medicine and agriculture is undeniable, but their continued effectiveness depends on our ability to manage their use responsibly.**
- **Explanation:** This conclusion appropriately summarizes the central theme of the passage, emphasizing the importance of responsible antibiotic use to ensure their continued effectiveness.

2. Math

A. Math Test - No Calculator

Heart of Algebra: 8 questions

Question 95:
Problem: Solve for x in the equation:
$$4x - 5 - 3x + 7$$

Solution:
First, isolate x on one side of the equation by subtracting $3x$ from both sides:
$$4x - 3x - 5 - 7$$

$$x - 5 - 7$$

Next, add 5 to both sides to solve for x:
$$x - 7 + 5$$

$$x - 12$$

Answer: A) 12

Question 96:

Problem: If $3x + 2y - 12$ and $y - 2x - 3$, what is the value of y?

Solution:

Substitute the expression for y from the second equation into the first equation:

$3x + 2(2x - 3) - 12$

Expand and solve for x:

$3x + 4x - 6 - 12$

$7x - 6 - 12$

$7x - 18$

$x - \frac{18}{7}$

Now, find y using the value of x:

$y - 2\left(\frac{18}{7}\right) - 3$

$y - \frac{36}{7} - 3$

$y - \frac{36}{7} - \frac{21}{7}$

$y - \frac{15}{7}$

Answer: D) 7

Question 97:

Problem: What is the solution to the system of equations:

$x - y = 4$

$2x + y = 1$

Solution:

To solve this system, we can add the two equations:

$(x - y) + (2x + y) = 4 + 1$

$x - y + 2x + y = 5$

$3x = 5$

$x = \frac{5}{3}$

Now, solve for y by substituting $x = \frac{5}{3}$ into the first equation:

$\frac{5}{3} - y = 4$

$y = \frac{5}{3} - 4$

$y = \frac{5}{3} - \frac{12}{3}$

$y = -\frac{7}{3}$

Answer: A) $\left(\frac{5}{3}, -\frac{7}{3} \right)$

Question 98:

Problem: Solve the inequality:

$5 - 3x > 2$

Solution:

First, subtract 5 from both sides of the inequality:

$-3x > 2 - 5$

$-3x > -3$

Next, divide both sides by -3, remembering to reverse the inequality sign:

$x < 1$

Answer: A) $x < 1$

Question 99:

Problem: If $2x + 3y - 13$ and $x - y - 2$, what is the value of x?

Solution:

First, solve the second equation for x:

$x - y + 2$

Next, substitute x in the first equation:

$2(y + 2) + 3y - 13$

$2y + 4 + 3y - 13$

$5y + 4 - 13$

$5y - 9$

$y - \frac{9}{5}$

Now, find x:

$x - \frac{9}{5} + 2$

$x - \frac{9}{5} + \frac{10}{5}$

$x - \frac{19}{5}$

Answer: C) 5

Question 100:

Problem: The sum of two numbers is 9. One number is three times the other. What are the numbers?

Solution:

Let the smaller number be x. Then the larger number is $3x$.

The equation is $x + 3x - 9$.

$4x - 9$

$x - \frac{9}{4}$

So, the numbers are $\frac{9}{4}$ and $3 \times \frac{9}{4} - \frac{27}{4}$.

Answer: B) 3 and 6

Question 101:

Problem: Find the value of x if $7x - 3 - 4x + 9$.

Solution:

First, isolate x on one side:

$7x - 4x = 9 + 3$

$3x - 12$

$x - 4$

Answer: C) 4

Question 102:

Problem: What is the solution to the equation $6(2x + 3) - 4x + 18$?

Solution:

First, expand the equation:

$12x + 18 - 4x + 18$

Next, isolate x:

$12x - 4x - 18 - 18$

$8x - 0$

$x - 0$

Answer: A) 1

Problem Solving and Data Analysis: 3 questions

Question 103:

Problem: A store sells apples for $0.50 each and bananas for $0.30 each. If a customer buys 6 apples and 10 bananas, what is the total cost?

Solution:

Total cost of apples: $6 \times 0.50 - 3.00$ dollars

Total cost of bananas: $10 \times 0.30 - 3.00$ dollars

Total cost: $3.00 + 3.00 - 6.00$ dollars

Answer: C) $6.00

Question 104:

Problem: A researcher is collecting data on the heights of a group of plants. The heights (in cm) are recorded as follows: 25, 27, 25, 30, 28, 27, 25, 29. What is the median height of the plants?

Solution:

Arranged data: 25, 25, 25, 27, 27, 28, 29, 30

Median (middle value for an even number of data points):

$\frac{27+27}{2} - 27$

Answer: C) 27 cm

Question 105:

Problem: A company's profit P in thousands of dollars is given by the equation $P - 4x - 20$, where x is the number of units sold in thousands. If the company wants to achieve a profit of $60,000, how many units must be sold?

Solution:

Set $P - 60$ and solve for x:

$60 - 4x - 20$

$80 - 4x$

$x - 20$

Since x is in thousands, the number of units is 20,000.

Answer: C) 20,000

Passport to Advanced Math: 6 questions

Question 106:
Problem: If $f(x) = x^3 - 4x$, what is $f'(x)$?

Solution:
To find the derivative, use the power rule:
$f'(x) = 3x^2 - 4$

Answer: A) $3x^2 - 4$

Question 107:
Problem: Solve for x in the equation $x^2 + 5x + 6 = 0$.

Solution:
Factor the quadratic equation:
$x^2 + 5x + 6 = (x + 2)(x + 3) = 0$
Set each factor equal to zero:
$x + 2 = 0$ or $x + 3 = 0$
$x = -2$ or $x = -3$

Answer: A) $x = -2$ or $x = -3$

Question 108:

Problem: If $g(x) - 2x^3 + 3x^2 - x + 1$, what is the value of $g''(x)$ when $x - 1$?

Solution:

To find the second derivative, we first find the first derivative $g'(x)$ and then differentiate it again.

1. **Find the first derivative $g'(x)$:**
   $g'(x) - \frac{d}{dx}(2x^3 + 3x^2 - x + 1)$
   $g'(x) - 6x^2 + 6x - 1$

2. **Find the second derivative $g''(x)$:**
   $g''(x) - \frac{d}{dx}(6x^2 + 6x - 1)$
   $g''(x) - 12x + 6$

3. **Evaluate $g''(x)$ at $x - 1$:**
   $g''(1) - 12(1) + 6$
   $g''(1) - 12 + 6$
   $g''(1) - 18$

Answer: D) 18

Question 109

Solution: To find the equivalent form of the expression $3x^2 - 12x + 9$, we complete the square:

1. Start with $3x^2 - 12x + 9$.

2. Factor out the 3: $3(x^2 - 4x) + 9$.

3. Complete the square inside the parentheses: $3(x^2 - 4x + 4 - 4) + 9$.

4. Rewrite as: $3((x - 2)^2 - 4) + 9$.

5. Expand and simplify: $3(x - 2)^2 - 12 + 9$.

6. Final form: $3(x - 2)^2 - 3$.

Answer: D) $3(x - 2)^2 - 3$

Question 110:

Problem: Solve the system of equations for x and y:

$2x + 3y - 7$

$4x - y = 7$

Solution:

First, solve the second equation for y:

$4x - y - 7$

$-y - 7 - 4x$

$y - 4x - 7$

Substitute $y - 4x - 7$ into the first equation:

$2x + 3(4x - 7) - 7$

$2x + 12x - 21 - 7$

$14x - 21 - 7$

$14x - 28$

$x - 2$

Now substitute $x - 2$ back into the expression for y:

$y - 4(2) - 7$

$y = 8 - 7$

$y - 1$

Answer: A) $x - 2, y - 1$

Question 111

Solution: To solve the inequality $\frac{2x-1}{x+2} > 1$:

1. Subtract 1 from both sides:
$$\frac{2x-1}{x+2} - 1 > 0$$

2. Simplify:
$$\frac{2x-1-(x+2)}{x+2} > 0$$

$$\frac{2x-1-x-2}{x+2} > 0$$

$$\frac{x-3}{x+2} > 0$$

3. The expression is positive where both numerator and denominator are either positive or negative:

   - $x - 3 > 0$ and $x + 2 > 0$ gives $x > 3$.
   - $x - 3 < 0$ and $x + 2 < 0$ gives $x < -2$.

Answer: A) $x < -2$ or $x > 3$

Additional Topics in Math (geometry, trigonometry, etc.): 3 questions

Question 112:

Problem: A right circular cone has a height of 9 units and a base radius of 4 units. What is the volume of the cone? (Use $\pi \approx 3.14$)

Solution:

The formula for the volume of a cone is given by:

$$V = \tfrac{1}{3}\pi r^2 h$$

Where:

- r is the radius of the base,
- h is the height of the cone, and
- π is approximately 3.14.

Substitute the given values into the formula:

$$V = \tfrac{1}{3}\pi (4)^2 (9)$$

$$V = \tfrac{1}{3}\pi (16)(9)$$

$$V = \tfrac{1}{3}\pi (144)$$

$$V = 48\pi$$

$$V = 48 \times 3.14$$

$$V = 150.72$$

Answer: C) 150.72 cubic units

Question 113:

Problem: What is the measure of an exterior angle of a regular hexagon?

Solution:

The formula for the measure of an exterior angle of a regular polygon is:

$$\text{Exterior Angle} - \frac{360}{n}$$

Where n is the number of sides of the polygon.

For a hexagon, $n - 6$:

$$\text{Exterior Angle} - \frac{360}{6} - 60°$$

Answer: C) 60 degrees

Question 114:

Problem: If $\sin x - \frac{1}{2}$ and x is in the first quadrant, what is the value of $\cos x$?

Solution:

For $\sin x - \frac{1}{2}$, the corresponding $\cos x$ value can be found using the Pythagorean identity:

$$\sin^2 x + \cos^2 x - 1$$

$$\left(\frac{1}{2}\right)^2 + \cos^2 x - 1$$

$$\frac{1}{4} + \cos^2 x - 1$$

$$\cos^2 x - 1 - \frac{1}{4}$$

$$\cos^2 x - \frac{3}{4}$$

$$\cos x - \sqrt{\frac{3}{4}}$$

Since x is in the first quadrant, $\cos x$ is positive:

$$\cos x - \frac{\sqrt{3}}{2}$$

Answer: A) $\frac{\sqrt{3}}{2}$

B. Math Test - Calculator

Heart of Algebra: 16 questions

Question 115:

Problem: What is the solution to the equation $2x + 3 = 7$?

Solution:

To solve for x, we first isolate x by subtracting 3 from both sides:

$2x + 3 - 3 = 7 - 3$

$2x = 4$

Next, divide both sides by 2:

$\frac{2x}{2} = \frac{4}{2}$

$x = 2$

Answer: A) 2

Question 116:

Problem: If $4y - 5 = 11$, what is the value of y?

Solution:

To solve for y, first isolate y by adding 5 to both sides:

$4y - 5 + 5 = 11 + 5$

$4y = 16$

Next, divide both sides by 4:

$\frac{4y}{4} = \frac{16}{4}$

$y = 4$

Answer: C) 4

Question 117:

Problem: Solve for x: $3x + 2 - 5x - 6$.

Solution:

First, bring all terms involving x to one side by subtracting $3x$ from both sides:

$3x + 2 - 3x - 5x - 6 - 3x$

$2 - 2x - 6$

Next, add 6 to both sides:

$2 + 6 - 2x - 6 + 6$

$8 - 2x$

Finally, divide both sides by 2:

$\frac{8}{2} - \frac{2x}{2}$

$x - 4$

Answer: A) 4

Question 118:

Problem: The equation $y - 2x + 1$ represents a line. What is the slope of this line?

Solution:

In the equation $y - mx + b$, m represents the slope. Here, $m - 2$.

Answer: B) 2

Question 119:

Problem: If $y = 3x + 2$ and $y = x + 6$, what is the value of x?

Solution:

Set the equations equal to each other since y is the same in both:

$$3x + 2 = x + 6$$

Subtract x from both sides:

$$3x - x + 2 = x - x + 6$$

$$2x + 2 = 6$$

Subtract 2 from both sides:

$$2x + 2 - 2 = 6 - 2$$

$$2x = 4$$

Finally, divide both sides by 2:

$$\frac{2x}{2} = \frac{4}{2}$$

$$x = 2$$

Answer: A) 2

Question 120:

Problem: Solve for y: $6y + 7 - 3y - 5$.

Solution:

First, bring all terms involving y to one side by subtracting $3y$ from both sides:

$$6y + 7 - 3y - 3y - 5 - 3y$$

$$3y + 7 - -5$$

Next, subtract 7 from both sides:

$$3y + 7 - 7 - -5 - 7$$

$$3y - -12$$

Finally, divide both sides by 3:

$$\frac{3y}{3} - \frac{-12}{3}$$

$$y - -4$$

Answer: A) -4

Question 121:

Problem: What is the value of x in the equation $5(x - 2) - 3x + 4$?

Solution:

First, distribute 5 through the parentheses:

$5x - 10 - 3x + 4$

Next, bring all terms involving x to one side by subtracting $3x$ from both sides:

$5x - 3x - 10 - 3x - 3x + 4$

$2x - 10 - 4$

Add 10 to both sides:

$2x - 10 + 10 - 4 + 10$

$2x - 14$

Finally, divide both sides by 2:

$\frac{2x}{2} - \frac{14}{2}$

$x - 7$

Answer: A) 7

Question 122:

Problem: If $y = 4x - 1$ and $y = -x + 14$, what is the value of y?

Solution:

Set the two equations equal to each other since both equal y:

$$4x - 1 = -x + 14$$

Add x to both sides:

$$4x + x - 1 = -x + x + 14$$

$$5x - 1 = 14$$

Add 1 to both sides:

$$5x - 1 + 1 = 14 + 1$$

$$5x = 15$$

Divide both sides by 5:

$$\frac{5x}{5} = \frac{15}{5}$$

$$x = 3$$

Substitute x back into either original equation to find y:

$$y = 4(3) - 1 = 12 - 1 = 11$$

Answer: D) 12

Question 123:
Problem: Solve for x: $2(x + 5) = 3x - 4$.

Solution:
First, distribute the 2 on the left side:

$$2x + 10 - 3x - 4$$

Subtract $2x$ from both sides:

$$2x - 2x + 10 - 3x - 2x - 4$$

$$10 - x - 4$$

Add 4 to both sides:

$$10 + 4 - x - 4 + 4$$

$$14 - x$$

Answer: A) 14

Question 124:
Problem: The line $y - -3x + 7$ passes through the point $(a, 1)$. What is the value of a?

Solution:
Substitute $y - 1$ and solve for x:

$$1 - -3a + 7$$

Subtract 7 from both sides:

$$1 - 7 - -3a$$

$$-6 - -3a$$

Divide both sides by -3:

$$\frac{-6}{-3} - a$$

$$a - 2$$

Answer: A) 2

Question 125:

Problem: What is the solution to the system of equations: $2x + y - 10$ and $x - y - 2$?

Solution:

Add the two equations to eliminate y:

$(2x + y) + (x - y) - 10 + 2$

$3x - 12$

Divide both sides by 3:

$\frac{3x}{3} - \frac{12}{3}$

$x - 4$

Substitute $x - 4$ back into one of the original equations to solve for y:

$2(4) + y - 10$

$8 + y - 10$

Subtract 8 from both sides:

$y - 2$

Answer: A) (4, 2)

Question 126:
Problem: If $5x + 3 = 2x + 12$, what is the value of x?

Solution:
Subtract $2x$ from both sides:

$5x - 2x + 3 = 2x - 2x + 12$

$3x + 3 = 12$

Subtract 3 from both sides:

$3x + 3 - 3 = 12 - 3$

$3x = 9$

Divide both sides by 3:

$\frac{3x}{3} = \frac{9}{3}$

$x = 3$

Answer: A) 3

Question 127:
Problem: Solve for y: $4(y - 1) = 2(y + 5)$.

Solution:
First, distribute the 4 and the 2:
$4y - 4 = 2y + 10$

Subtract $2y$ from both sides:
$4y - 2y - 4 = 2y - 2y + 10$
$2y - 4 = 10$

Add 4 to both sides:
$2y - 4 + 4 = 10 + 4$
$2y = 14$

Divide both sides by 2:
$\frac{2y}{2} = \frac{14}{2}$
$y = 7$

Answer: A) 7

Question 128:

Problem: If $y - 5x + 6$ and $y - -2x + 8$, what is the value of y?

Solution:

Set the two equations equal to each other since both equal y:

$5x + 6 - -2x + 8$

Add $2x$ to both sides:

$5x + 2x + 6 - -2x + 2x + 8$

$7x + 6 - 8$

Subtract 6 from both sides:

$7x + 6 - 6 - 8 - 6$

$7x - 2$

Divide both sides by 7:

$\frac{7x}{7} - \frac{2}{7}$

$x - \frac{2}{7}$

Substitute $x - \frac{2}{7}$ back into one of the original equations to find y:

$y - 5\left(\frac{2}{7}\right) + 6$

$y - \frac{10}{7} + 6$

$y - \frac{10}{7} + \frac{42}{7}$

$y - \frac{52}{7}$

Answer: B) $\frac{52}{7}$

Question 129:

Problem: Solve for x: $3(x - 4) = 2(x + 1)$.

Solution:

First, distribute the 3 and the 2:

$3x - 12 = 2x + 2$

Subtract $2x$ from both sides:

$3x - 2x - 12 = 2x - 2x + 2$

$x - 12 = 2$

Add 12 to both sides:

$x - 12 + 12 = 2 + 12$

$x = 14$

Answer: D) 14

Question 130:

Problem: If $6x - 2y = 10$ and $x = 3$, what is the value of y?

Solution:

Substitute $x = 3$ into the equation $6x - 2y = 10$:

$6(3) - 2y = 10$

$18 - 2y = 10$

Subtract 18 from both sides:

$-2y = 10 - 18$

$-2y = -8$

Divide both sides by -2:

$\frac{-2y}{-2} = \frac{-8}{-2}$

$y = 4$

Answer: A) 4

Problem Solving and Data Analysis: 8 questions

Question 131:

Problem: A bookstore sells used books for $5 each and new books for $15 each. If a customer buys a total of 12 books and spends $120, how many used and new books did they buy?

Solution:

Let x be the number of used books and y be the number of new books. We have two equations:

$x + y - 12$

$5x + 15y - 120$

From the first equation, solve for y:

$y - 12 - x$

Substitute y into the second equation:

$5x + 15(12 - x) - 120$

$5x + 180 - 15x - 120$

$-10x + 180 - 120$

$-10x - 120 - 180$

$-10x - -60$

$x - 6$

Substitute $x - 6$ back into the first equation:

$6 + y - 12$

$y - 6$

Answer: A) 6 used books and 6 new books

Question 132:

Problem: A company's revenue increased from $250,000 in 2018 to $300,000 in 2019. What was the percentage increase in revenue?

Solution:

$\text{Percentage Increase} - \frac{\text{New Value} - \text{Old Value}}{\text{Old Value}} \times 100$

$\text{Percentage Increase} - \frac{300,000 - 250,000}{250,000} \times 100$

$\text{Percentage Increase} - \frac{50,000}{250,000} \times 100$

$\text{Percentage Increase} - 0.2 \times 100$

$\text{Percentage Increase} - 20\%$

Answer: B) 20%

Question 133:

Problem: If 40% of a class of 50 students are boys, how many girls are in the class?

Solution:

First, find the number of boys:

$$\text{Number of boys} = 0.4 \times 50 = 20$$

Subtract the number of boys from the total number of students to find the number of girls:

$$\text{Number of girls} = 50 - 20 = 30$$

Answer: C) 30

Question 134:

Problem: A car rental company charges a flat fee of $20 per day plus $0.25 per mile driven. If a customer rents a car for 3 days and drives 100 miles, what is the total cost?

Solution:

Calculate the cost for the days:

$$\text{Cost for days} = 20 \times 3 = 60$$

Calculate the cost for the miles driven:

$$\text{Cost for miles} = 0.25 \times 100 = 25$$

Add the two costs together:

$$\text{Total cost} = 60 + 25 = 85$$

Answer: D) $85

Question 135:

Problem: A baker uses 2 cups of flour for every 3 cups of sugar to make cookies. If the baker wants to make a batch using 12 cups of sugar, how many cups of flour are needed?

Solution:

Set up a ratio:

$$\frac{2 \text{ cups of flour}}{3 \text{ cups of sugar}} - \frac{x \text{ cups of flour}}{12 \text{ cups of sugar}}$$

Cross-multiply to solve for x:

$3x - 2 \times 12$

$3x - 24$

$x - \frac{24}{3}$

$x - 8$

Answer: B) 8

Question 136:

Problem: The table below shows the number of students in each grade who participate in the school's science club:

Grade	Number of Students
9	15
10	20
11	25
12	30

What is the average number of students per grade participating in the science club?

Solution:

To find the average number of students per grade, sum the number of students and divide by the number of grades:

Average $- \frac{15+20+25+30}{4}$

Average $- \frac{90}{4}$

Average $- 22.5$

Answer: B) 22.5

Question 137:

Problem: If the population of a town is 24,000 and is growing at a rate of 2% per year, what will be the population after 3 years?

Solution:

Use the compound growth formula:

$$P - P_0 \left(1 + \tfrac{r}{100}\right)^t$$

Where:

- $P_0 - 24,000$
- $r - 2$
- $t - 3$

$$P = 24,000 \left(1 + \tfrac{2}{100}\right)^3$$
$$P - 24,000 \left(1.02\right)^3$$
$$P - 24,000 \times 1.061208$$
$$P \approx 25,469$$

Answer: C) 25,469

Question 138:

Problem: A store sells apples for $1.20 each or 3 for $3.00. If you buy 9 apples using the 3-for-$3.00 deal, how much do you save compared to buying each apple individually?

Solution:

First, calculate the cost of 9 apples at $1.20 each:

$$\text{Cost individually} - 9 \times 1.20 - 10.80$$

Next, calculate the cost of 9 apples at the 3-for-$3.00 deal:

$$\text{Cost in deal} - 3 \times 3.00 - 9.00$$

Calculate the savings:

$$\text{Savings} - 10.80 - 9.00 - 1.80$$

Answer: A) $1.80

Passport to Advanced Math: 11 questions

Question 139:

Problem: Solve for x in the equation $\frac{x+3}{x-1} - 2$.

Solution:

$\frac{x+3}{x-1} - 2$

$x + 3 - 2(x - 1)$

$x + 3 - 2x - 2$

$3 + 2 - 2x - x$

$5 - x$

Answer: D) 3

Question 140:

Problem: If $f(x) - x^2 + 4x + 4$, what is the vertex of the parabola?

Solution:

Rewrite $f(x)$ in vertex form:

$f(x) - (x + 2)^2$

The vertex form is $(x - h)^2 + k$, where h and k are the coordinates of the vertex.

$(x + 2)^2$

So, $h - -2$ and $k - 0$.

Answer: C) (-2, 0)

Question 141:

Problem: The function $g(x) - \sqrt{4x + 16}$ is equivalent to:

Solution:

$g(x) - \sqrt{4(x + 4)}$

$g(x) - 2\sqrt{x + 4}$

Answer: B) $2\sqrt{x + 4}$

Question 142:

Problem: Solve the system of equations: $2x + y - 5$ and $x - y - 1$.

Solution:

From the second equation:

$x - y - 1$

$y = x - 1$

Substitute into the first equation:

$2x + (x - 1) - 5$

$3x - 1 - 5$

$3x - 6$

$x - 2$

Then, $y - 2 - 1 - 1$.

Answer: B) (2, 1)

Question 143:

Problem: If $h(x) = x^3 - 3x^2 + 2x$, what is the value of $h(2)$?

Solution:

$h(2) - (2)^3 - 3(2)^2 + 2(2)$

$h(2) - 8 - 12 + 4$

$h(2) - 0$

Answer: A) 0

Question 144:

Problem: Factor completely: $x^3 - 9x$.

Solution:

$x^3 - 9x - x(x^2 - 9) - x(x - 3)(x + 3)$

Answer: A) $x(x^2 - 9)$

Question 145:

Problem: The equation of a circle is $(x - 3)^2 + (y + 2)^2 = 16$. What is the radius of the circle?

Solution:

The standard form of a circle's equation is $(x - h)^2 + (y - k)^2 = r^2$.

Given: $(x - 3)^2 + (y + 2)^2 = 16$.

Here, $r^2 = 16$.

So, $r = \sqrt{16} = 4$.

Answer: B) 4

Question 146:

Problem: If $f(x) = 2x^2 - 4x + 6$, what is the minimum value of $f(x)$?

Solution:

To find the minimum value of a quadratic function in the form $ax^2 + bx + c$, we use the vertex formula $x = -\frac{b}{2a}$. Here, $a = 2$ and $b = -4$.

$$x = -\frac{-4}{2 \cdot 2} = \frac{4}{4} = 1$$

Now, substitute $x = 1$ back into the function $f(x)$:

$$f(1) = 2(1)^2 - 4(1) + 6$$
$$f(1) = 2 - 4 + 6$$
$$f(1) = 4$$

Answer: B) 4

Question 147:

Problem: Solve for x in the equation $2^{2x-1} = 16$.

Solution:

First, express 16 as a power of 2:

$16 = 2^4$

Thus, the equation becomes:

$2^{2x-1} = 2^4$

Since the bases are the same, set the exponents equal:

$2x - 1 = 4$

$2x = 5$

$x = \frac{5}{2}$

Answer: C) 3

Question 148:

Problem: What is the inverse function of $f(x) = 3x + 5$?

Solution:

To find the inverse function, swap x and y and solve for y:

$y = 3x + 5$

Swap x and y:

$x = 3y + 5$

Solve for y:

$x - 5 = 3y$

$y = \frac{x-5}{3}$

Answer: A) $f^{-1}(x) = \frac{x-5}{3}$

Question 149:

Problem: Solve the inequality: $3x - 4 \leq 2x + 5$.

Solution:

First, get all x terms on one side of the inequality:

$3x - 4 \leq 2x + 5$

$3x - 2x \leq 5 + 4$

$x \leq 9$

Answer: B) $x \leq 9$

Additional Topics in Math (geometry, trigonometry, etc.): 3 questions

Question 150:

Problem: In a right triangle, one of the angles measures $30°$. If the hypotenuse of the triangle is 10 units, what is the length of the side opposite the $30°$ angle?

Solution:

In a $30° - 60° - 90°$ triangle, the side opposite the $30°$ angle is half the length of the hypotenuse. Therefore, the length of the side opposite the $30°$ angle is:

$\frac{10}{2} = 5$

Answer: A) 5

Question 151:

Problem: What is the area of a sector with a central angle of $45°$ in a circle with a radius of 12 units?

Solution:

The area of a sector of a circle is given by:

$$\text{Area} = \pi r^2 \left(\tfrac{\theta}{360}\right)$$

Given $r = 12$ and $\theta = 45°$:

$$\text{Area} = \pi(12)^2 \left(\tfrac{45}{360}\right)$$
$$\text{Area} = \pi(144) \left(\tfrac{1}{8}\right)$$
$$\text{Area} =$$

Answer: A) 18π

Question 152:

Problem: The coordinates of the vertices of a triangle are $A(1, 2)$, $B(4, 6)$, and $C(7, 2)$. What is the area of the triangle?

Solution:

The area of a triangle given its vertices can be calculated using the determinant formula:

$$\text{Area} = \tfrac{1}{2} |x_1(y_2 - y_3) + x_2(y_3 - y_1) + x_3(y_1 - y_2)|$$

Substituting $A(1, 2)$, $B(4, 6)$, and $C(7, 2)$:

$$\text{Area} = \tfrac{1}{2} |1(6 - 2) + 4(2 - 2) + 7(2 - 6)|$$
$$\text{Area} = \tfrac{1}{2} |1(4) + 4(0) + 7(-4)|$$
$$\text{Area} = \tfrac{1}{2} |4 - 28|$$
$$\text{Area} = \tfrac{1}{2} |-24|$$
$$\text{Area} = \tfrac{1}{2} \times 24$$
$$\text{Area} = 12$$

Answer: C) 12

3. Essay (Optional)

In the passage "The Role of Technology in Education," Sarah Johnson constructs a persuasive argument that emphasizes the importance of technology in modern education by effectively utilizing evidence, logical reasoning, and stylistic elements to convince her audience of the transformative power of technology in the classroom.

One of the primary ways Johnson strengthens her argument is by providing concrete evidence to support her claims. Throughout the passage, she presents specific examples of how technology can enhance education. For instance, she discusses how the internet offers students access to a "vast array of resources," including academic journals, digital textbooks, and online courses. By citing these tangible benefits, Johnson not only substantiates her claims but also helps the reader visualize the practical advantages that technology can offer in an educational setting. This evidence-based approach lends credibility to her argument and makes it more convincing to her audience.

Johnson also employs logical reasoning to connect her claims and build a coherent argument. She systematically addresses the various benefits of technology in education, such as improved access to resources, enhanced collaboration, and personalized learning. By organizing her points in a logical sequence, Johnson allows the reader to follow her argument step by step, making it easier to understand and accept her conclusions. For example, after explaining how technology facilitates access to information, she transitions to discussing how it fosters collaboration among students and teachers, thereby reinforcing the idea that technology is a multifaceted tool that can improve various aspects of education. This logical structure not only clarifies her argument but also strengthens its overall persuasiveness.

In addition to evidence and reasoning, Johnson enhances the impact of her argument through her use of stylistic and persuasive elements. She employs positive and forward-looking language to create a sense of optimism about the role of technology in education. Terms like "enhance educational outcomes," "fostering collaboration," and "personalizing learning experiences" convey a sense of progress and innovation, encouraging the reader to view technology as a beneficial and necessary component of modern education. Furthermore, Johnson addresses potential counterarguments by acknowledging the concerns about technology being a distraction in the classroom. However, she refutes this by emphasizing that, with proper guidance, technology can be a powerful tool rather than a hindrance. This balanced approach not only addresses the reader's potential doubts but also demonstrates Johnson's thorough understanding of the topic, further bolstering her credibility.

Moreover, Johnson's appeal to emotion subtly reinforces her argument. By highlighting the potential for technology to make education more accessible and personalized, she taps into the reader's desire for equality and individualized learning. For example, she discusses how adaptive learning software can tailor instruction to meet individual students' needs, ensuring that each student receives the appropriate level of challenge and support. This emotional appeal resonates with the reader's concern for the well-being and success of all students, making the argument more personally relevant and compelling.

In conclusion, Sarah Johnson effectively builds a persuasive argument for the essential role of technology in modern education by utilizing evidence, logical reasoning, and stylistic elements. Her argument is well-supported by specific examples, clearly structured, and emotionally engaging, making it a compelling case for the integration of technology in the classroom. By combining these elements, Johnson successfully convinces her audience that technology is not only beneficial but also crucial for preparing students for the demands of the 21st century.

Practice SAT #4 - Answers & Explanations

1. Evidence-Based Reading and Writing (EBRW)

A. Reading Test

Literature: 10 questions

1) What is Jane Eyre reflecting on in this passage?

- **Answer: B) Her complex emotions towards Mr. Rochester**
- **Explanation:** Jane is reflecting on her deep and complicated feelings for Mr. Rochester, acknowledging her love for him despite the internal struggle it causes her.

2) How does Mr. Rochester react to Jane's attempt to enlighten him?

- **Answer: B) He hotly repels her**
- **Explanation:** Mr. Rochester reacts strongly and negatively, indicating that he does not appreciate Jane's attempt to correct or enlighten him.

3) What does Jane mean when she says, "You are not your own, you are

mine; I claim you; not for my pleasure, but for my Sovereign's service"?

- **Answer: C) She is stating that Mr. Rochester belongs to a higher purpose**
- **Explanation:** Jane is expressing that Mr. Rochester's existence and actions are for a greater purpose beyond her own desires.

4) What feelings does Mr. Rochester's sorrowful and woeful expression evoke in Jane?

- **Answer: C) Sympathy and love**
- **Explanation:** Jane feels sympathy and a resurgence of love for Mr. Rochester upon seeing his sorrowful expression.

5) What metaphor does Jane use to describe her feelings when she looks at Mr. Rochester?

- **Answer: A) A man dying of thirst who drinks from a poisoned well**
- **Explanation:** Jane compares her attraction to Mr. Rochester to a man drinking poisoned water despite knowing it's dangerous, indicating a mix of desire and awareness of potential harm.

6) How does Jane describe her struggle with her emotions?

- **Answer: B) She has restrained them but ultimately been conquered**
- **Explanation:** Jane describes her emotional struggle as a battle she has tried to resist but ultimately lost, acknowledging her love for Mr. Rochester.

7) What does Jane mean when she says, "I am no bird; and no net ensnares me; I am a free human being with an independent will"?

- **Answer: A) She is declaring her independence and free will**

- **Explanation:** Jane asserts her autonomy and independence, rejecting any notion of being trapped or controlled.

8) What offer does Mr. Rochester make to Jane?

- **Answer: C) To marry her and share all his possessions**
- **Explanation:** Mr. Rochester offers Jane his hand in marriage and everything he owns.

9) How does Jane respond to Mr. Rochester's offer?

- **Answer: C) She rejects it and leaves**
- **Explanation:** Jane decides to reject Mr. Rochester's offer and chooses to leave, asserting her independence.

10) What does Mr. Rochester say to Jane about her decision to leave?

- **Answer: D) He laughs at her and mocks her decision**
- **Explanation:** Mr. Rochester mocks Jane's decision, laughing at her and dismissing her actions as a farce.

Historical Documents: 10 questions

11) What does Sojourner Truth suggest is causing the "racket"?

- **Answer: A) The clamor for rights by both Negroes in the South and women in the North**
- **Explanation:** Truth refers to the commotion caused by the simultaneous demands for rights by both African Americans and women, suggesting that these movements are challenging the status quo.

12) What point does Truth make about the assistance women receive?

- **Answer: B) She has never received such assistance, despite being a woman**
- **Explanation:** Truth contrasts her experience as a woman who has never been given special treatment or help, highlighting the inconsistencies in how women are treated based on race and class.

13) What does Truth emphasize by asking "Ain't I a woman?" multiple times?

- **Answer: A) Her strength and capability despite societal expectations of women**
- **Explanation:** Truth emphasizes her own strength and abilities, challenging the traditional notion that women are weak or dependent.

14) How does Truth describe her physical labor?

- **Answer: B) She ploughed, planted, and gathered, outperforming many men**
- **Explanation:** Truth speaks of her extensive physical labor, showcasing her strength and endurance, often surpassing the capabilities of men.

15) What does Truth say about her experience with motherhood?

- **Answer: B) She has borne thirteen children, most of whom were sold into slavery**
- **Explanation:** Truth mentions her deep sorrow and grief over her children being sold into slavery, highlighting the additional burdens she faced as a mother.

16) What is Truth's argument regarding intellect and rights?

- **Answer: B) Intellect should not determine one's rights**

- **Explanation:** Truth argues that the capacity for rights should not be measured by intellect, implying that all humans, regardless of intellectual ability, deserve equal rights.

17) What analogy does Truth use to discuss fairness in rights?

- **Answer: A) Comparing different sizes of cups to different amounts of rights**
- **Explanation:** Truth uses the analogy of cups of different sizes to illustrate that everyone deserves to be filled with rights, regardless of their "capacity."

18) How does Truth challenge the argument that women can't have as many rights as men because Christ wasn't a woman?

- **Answer: B) By pointing out that Christ came from God and a woman, with no involvement from man**
- **Explanation:** Truth counters the argument by emphasizing that Christ's birth involved a woman but not a man, thereby challenging the exclusion of women based on religious grounds.

19) What rhetorical strategy does Truth use throughout her speech?

- **Answer: B) Emotional appeals and repetition**
- **Explanation:** Truth employs emotional appeals and the repetition of phrases like "Ain't I a woman?" to reinforce her message and engage the audience.

20) What is the overall theme of Truth's speech?

- **Answer: B) The call for equal rights for both women and African Americans**
- **Explanation:** Truth's speech advocates for equal rights, addressing

the injustices faced by both women and African Americans.

Social Sciences: 10 questions

21) What event marked the beginning of history according to the passage?

- **Answer: B) The Cognitive Revolution**
- **Explanation:** The passage states that the Cognitive Revolution marked the beginning of history, as it enabled new forms of communication and the creation of shared myths.

22) What are imagined orders as described in the passage?

- **Answer: C) Concepts that exist only in the minds of humans**
- **Explanation:** Imagined orders, unlike physical laws, exist only in the collective belief of humans, such as legal systems and economic structures.

23) Which of the following is an example of an imagined order?

- **Answer: B) Money**
- **Explanation:** Money is an example of an imagined order, as it has no intrinsic value but is collectively believed to be valuable.

24) What role does gossip play in human culture according to the passage?

- **Answer: B) It helps in building trust and maintaining social bonds**
- **Explanation:** The passage explains that gossip was crucial for early Homo sapiens to build trust and maintain social bonds, allowing larger groups to cooperate.

25) When did the Agricultural Revolution begin?

- **Answer: B) About 12,000 years ago**
- **Explanation:** The passage notes that the Agricultural Revolution began around 12,000 years ago, leading to significant changes in human societies.

26) What was one consequence of the Agricultural Revolution?

- **Answer: B) Development of cities and population growth**
- **Explanation:** The Agricultural Revolution led to the production of surplus food, which facilitated population growth and the development of cities.

27) How did the ability to create and believe in shared myths benefit Homo sapiens?

- **Answer: B) It enabled them to adapt and thrive in diverse environments**
- **Explanation:** Shared myths allowed Homo sapiens to adapt to diverse environments and organize into complex societies.

28) What modern entities are based on collective beliefs according to the passage?

- **Answer: B) Nations, corporations, and institutions**
- **Explanation:** The passage states that modern entities such as nations, corporations, and institutions are based on collective beliefs.

29) What does understanding the role of imagined orders help us grasp?

- **Answer: B) The complexity of our societies and the forces that drive them**

- **Explanation:** Understanding imagined orders helps us comprehend the complexities and driving forces behind human societies.

30) What unique ability of Homo sapiens does Harari highlight in his exploration?

- **Answer: B) The ability to cooperate and innovate through shared beliefs**
- **Explanation:** Harari highlights the unique ability of Homo sapiens to cooperate and innovate by creating and believing in shared myths.

Natural Sciences: 10 questions

31) Why is water essential for all known forms of life?

- **Answer: B) It has unique properties that support life**
- **Explanation:** The passage emphasizes that water's unique properties make it essential for life, supporting various natural processes and maintaining life.

32) What is a polar molecule, as described in the passage?

- **Answer: B) A molecule with a positive charge on one end and a negative charge on the other**
- **Explanation:** The passage describes water as a polar molecule, meaning it has opposite charges on different ends.

33) What property of water allows it to form droplets and enables surface tension?

- **Answer: B) Cohesion**
- **Explanation:** Cohesion refers to the attraction between water molecules, allowing them to stick together and form droplets, which

contributes to surface tension.

34) What is capillary action?

- **Answer: B) The attraction between water molecules and other substances, allowing water to climb up plant roots and stems**
- **Explanation:** The passage defines capillary action as the process where water molecules adhere to other substances, enabling water to move up through plant roots and stems.

35) Why does ice float on water?

- **Answer: B) Ice forms a crystalline structure that is less dense than liquid water**
- **Explanation:** Ice floats because its crystalline structure makes it less dense than liquid water, as explained in the passage.

36) What is the significance of water's high specific heat capacity?

- **Answer: B) It helps regulate Earth's climate by moderating temperatures**
- **Explanation:** The passage states that water's high specific heat capacity allows it to absorb and store energy, moderating Earth's climate and temperatures.

37) How do oceans influence weather patterns globally?

- **Answer: B) By acting as massive heat sinks, absorbing and storing solar energy**
- **Explanation:** Oceans absorb and store solar energy, which influences global weather patterns by regulating temperature.

38) What role does water play in biological systems according to the

passage?

- **Answer: B) It transports nutrients, gases, and waste products**
- **Explanation:** The passage mentions that water's solvent properties are crucial for transporting essential substances in biological systems.

39) What drives the hydrologic cycle?

- **Answer: C) Solar energy**
- **Explanation:** Solar energy drives the hydrologic cycle by causing water to evaporate and move through the cycle.

40) What does the hydrologic cycle include?

- **Answer: B) The continuous movement of water on, above, and below the Earth's surface**
- **Explanation:** The passage describes the hydrologic cycle as involving processes like evaporation, condensation, and precipitation, which move water around the planet.

Dual Passages (Literature, Social Science, or Science): 10 questions

41) What is the main principle discussed in Passage 1 by Charles Darwin?

- **Answer: B) Natural Selection**
- **Explanation:** The passage primarily discusses the concept of Natural Selection, explaining how individuals with beneficial variations are more likely to survive and reproduce.

42) According to Passage 1, what does "Survival of the Fittest" refer to?

- **Answer: B) The ability to adapt and survive**
- **Explanation:** The term "Survival of the Fittest," as used by Herbert Spencer and referenced by Darwin, describes the idea that individuals best adapted to their environment are more likely to survive.

43) What does Richard Dawkins suggest we are born with in Passage 2?

- **Answer: B) Selfishness**
- **Explanation:** Dawkins states that we are born with selfish genes, indicating an inherent predisposition toward selfish behavior.

44) What is the main argument presented by Dawkins in Passage 2?

- **Answer: B) Humans can defy their selfish genes and cultivate altruism**
- **Explanation:** Dawkins argues that, despite being born with selfish genes, humans have the unique ability to cultivate altruism.

45) How does Darwin describe the power of natural selection in Passage 1?

- **Answer: C) Immeasurably superior to man's efforts**
- **Explanation:** Darwin emphasizes that natural selection is a powerful force far superior to human efforts in shaping the characteristics of species.

46) What does Dawkins mean by "selfish memes" in Passage 2?

- **Answer: B) Cultural ideas that promote selfishness**
- **Explanation:** The term "selfish memes" refers to cultural elements that perpetuate selfish behaviors, paralleling the concept of selfish genes.

47) What do both passages suggest about the nature of survival and competition?

- **Answer: B) Both are influenced by genetic and natural processes**
- **Explanation:** Both passages discuss the role of genetic factors (Darwin's natural selection and Dawkins' selfish genes) in influencing survival and competition.

48) In Passage 1, how does Darwin view man's ability to influence organic beings?

- **Answer: B) As insignificant compared to natural selection**
- **Explanation:** Darwin suggests that human efforts are feeble compared to the vast and superior power of natural selection.

49) What challenge does Dawkins present to humans in Passage 2?

- **Answer: B) To understand and overcome their selfish genes**
- **Explanation:** Dawkins challenges humans to recognize their inherent selfishness and work towards cultivating genuine altruism.

50) How do the viewpoints on altruism differ between the two passages?

- **Answer: A) Darwin sees it as central to survival, while Dawkins sees it as a challenge to cultivate.**
- **Explanation:** Darwin's passage does not explicitly address altruism as central to survival but rather focuses on natural selection, while Dawkins highlights the challenge of cultivating altruism despite inherent selfish tendencies.

B. Writing and Language Test

Careers: 11 questions

51) Which choice best describes what happens in the passage?

- **Answer: A) The passage describes the role of data scientists, the skills required, and the impact of their work on various industries.**
- **Explanation:** The passage outlines the responsibilities, skills, and industry impact of data scientists, explaining their essential role in various sectors.

52) Which choice best expresses the main idea of the passage?

- **Answer: B) Data scientists are essential for extracting valuable insights from data, and their work impacts many industries.**
- **Explanation:** The main idea emphasizes the importance of data scientists in extracting insights from data and their significant impact across multiple industries.

53) In context, what does the phrase "extracting insights and knowledge from vast amounts of data" in sentence 2 most nearly mean?

- **Answer: B) Analyzing data to find meaningful information.**
- **Explanation:** The phrase refers to the process of analyzing large datasets to uncover useful and actionable information.

54) Which sentence, if added after sentence 5, would best support the main idea of the paragraph?

- **Answer: C) They need to understand business objectives to provide relevant insights.**
- **Explanation:** This sentence supports the idea that data scientists analyze data to help organizations make informed decisions, which requires an understanding of business objectives.

55) In sentence 9, the author uses the example of a data scientist in the healthcare industry to:

- **Answer: B) Illustrate a practical application of data science.**
- **Explanation:** The example demonstrates a real-world application of data science in predicting patient readmissions, showcasing the field's practical use.

56) Which choice provides the most accurate interpretation of the data in sentence 18?

- **Answer: B) The demand for data scientists has grown rapidly because of the increasing availability of data.**
- **Explanation:** The passage states that the growth in demand for data scientists is driven by the availability of data and advances in technology.

57) In sentence 23, what does the mention of "Kaggle" contribute to the passage?

- **Answer: A) It highlights a platform where data scientists can gain practical experience.**
- **Explanation:** Kaggle is mentioned as a platform for practical experience, such as participating in competitions to enhance skills.

58) The author wants to add the following sentence to the fourth paragraph:
"Visualizations are crucial for making complex data more understandable and actionable." Where would this sentence best fit?

- **Answer: C) Before sentence 12**
- **Explanation:** Placing the sentence before sentence 12 introduces the role of visualizations, which aligns with the discussion of communi-

cation and accessibility of data.

59) In context, the word "implement" in sentence 16 most nearly means:

- **Answer: C) Execute**
- **Explanation:** "Implement" in this context means to carry out or execute solutions derived from data analysis.

60) Which choice best concludes the passage?

- **Answer: C) Data science offers numerous career opportunities and the chance to drive innovation.**
- **Explanation:** This conclusion highlights the career prospects and innovative potential in the field of data science, aligning with the overall positive tone of the passage.

61) Which choice most effectively combines sentences 12 and 13?

- **Answer: C) This often involves creating visualizations, such as charts and graphs, to make the data more accessible and ensuring that the insights derived from data analysis are understood and can be applied to solve real-world problems.**
- **Explanation:** This combination clearly connects the creation of visualizations with the goal of making data understandable and actionable, while maintaining the passage's tone and flow.

History/Social Studies: 11 questions

62) Which choice best describes what happens in the passage?

- **Answer: A) The passage explores the major events and factors contributing to the rise and fall of the Roman Empire.**

- **Explanation:** The passage provides an overview of the key events and internal and external factors that influenced the rise and decline of the Roman Empire.

63) Which choice best expresses the main idea of the passage?

- **Answer: B) The rise and fall of the Roman Empire offer important insights into the dynamics of powerful civilizations.**
- **Explanation:** The passage emphasizes that understanding the history of the Roman Empire helps us learn about the factors that contribute to the success and failure of great powers.

64) In context, what does the phrase "Pax Romana" in sentence 11 most nearly mean?

- **Answer: C) A time of relative stability and prosperity**
- **Explanation:** The term "Pax Romana" refers to a period of peace and economic stability throughout the Roman Empire, lasting over 200 years.

65) Which sentence, if added after sentence 13, would best support the main idea of the paragraph?

- **Answer: B) The Romans also built an extensive network of roads that facilitated trade and communication.**
- **Explanation:** This sentence adds to the discussion of the Roman Empire's infrastructure advancements, highlighting the role of roads in supporting the empire's stability and economic growth.

66) In sentence 15, the author mentions "political corruption and power struggles" primarily to:

- **Answer: A) Highlight the internal challenges faced by the Roman**

Empire.

- **Explanation:** The mention of political corruption and power struggles illustrates the internal issues that contributed to the empire's decline.

67) Which choice provides the most accurate interpretation of the data in sentence 17?

- **Answer: B) The Roman Empire's economy was strained by heavy taxation and reliance on slave labor.**
- **Explanation:** The passage notes that the Roman Empire faced economic challenges, including the burdens of heavy taxation and a reliance on slave labor, which weakened its economy.

68) In sentence 19, what does the mention of "Barbarian invasions" contribute to the passage?

- **Answer: B) It provides evidence of external pressures contributing to the decline of the Roman Empire.**
- **Explanation:** The mention of barbarian invasions illustrates the external military threats that weakened the Roman Empire, contributing to its decline.

69) The author wants to add the following sentence to the fourth paragraph:
"The assassination of Julius Caesar in 44 BCE marked a turning point in Roman history." Where would this sentence best fit?

- **Answer: B) After sentence 9**
- **Explanation:** Adding the sentence after sentence 9 appropriately places the discussion of Caesar's assassination, which followed his rise to power and preceded the transition from Republic to Empire.

70) In context, the word "deposed" in sentence 23 most nearly means:

· **Answer: C) Overthrown**
· **Explanation:** The word "deposed" refers to the removal of Romulus Augustulus from power, indicating that he was overthrown by Odoacer.

71) Which choice best concludes the passage?

· **Answer: A) The fall of the Roman Empire marked the end of ancient Rome's dominance and the beginning of the Middle Ages in Europe.**
· **Explanation:** This choice effectively summarizes the conclusion of the passage, noting the historical transition that followed the fall of the Roman Empire.

72) Which choice most effectively combines sentences 6 and 7?

· **Answer: B) The Republic's military conquests and strategic alliances allowed Rome to expand its territory significantly during this period, leading to the rise of Julius Caesar.**
· **Explanation:** This combination maintains the logical flow and highlights the connection between Rome's territorial expansion and the rise of Julius Caesar.

Humanities: 11 questions

73) Which choice best describes what happens in the passage?

· **Answer: A) The passage explores the various roles literature has played in different social movements.**
· **Explanation:** The passage discusses how literature has influenced social change across different historical periods and movements, highlighting examples from the abolitionist movement, civil rights

movement, feminist philosophy, LGBTQ+ rights, and environmental advocacy.

74) Which choice best expresses the main idea of the passage?

- **Answer: A) Literature has been a crucial tool in advocating for and achieving social change across various movements.**
- **Explanation:** The passage emphasizes the significant role literature has played in advocating for justice and equality, influencing public opinion, and inspiring movements for social change.

75) In context, what does the phrase "catalyst for social change" in sentence 22 most nearly mean?

- **Answer: C) A trigger for initiating social reform**
- **Explanation:** The phrase suggests that literature acts as a powerful force that initiates or accelerates social change by bringing attention to social issues and influencing public opinion.

76) Which sentence, if added after sentence 6, would best support the main idea of the paragraph?

- **Answer: B) The novel's vivid depiction of slavery made it a best-seller and intensified the debate over slavery.**
- **Explanation:** This sentence reinforces the idea that "Uncle Tom's Cabin" had a significant impact on society by increasing awareness and debate about slavery, supporting the paragraph's discussion of the novel's influence.

77) In sentence 11, the author mentions James Baldwin's essays and novels primarily to:

- **Answer: B) Illustrate literature's role in the civil rights movement.**

- **Explanation:** The passage uses James Baldwin's work as an example of how literature supported the civil rights movement by addressing issues of race and injustice.

78) Which choice provides the most accurate interpretation of the data in sentence 14?

- **Answer: B) "The Second Sex" is a foundational text that has significantly influenced feminist philosophy.**
- **Explanation:** The passage describes "The Second Sex" as a key work in feminist thought, indicating its major influence on discussions about gender equality and the social construction of gender roles.

79) In sentence 18, what does the mention of authors such as Audre Lorde and Tony Kushner contribute to the passage?

- **Answer: B) It provides examples of authors who addressed LGBTQ+ rights in their works.**
- **Explanation:** The mention of these authors illustrates how literature has also played a role in advocating for LGBTQ+ rights, showcasing the diversity of issues addressed through literary works.

80) The author wants to add the following sentence to the second paragraph:
"These works not only provided entertainment but also played a pivotal role in shaping public opinion and policy." Where would this sentence best fit?

- **Answer: D) After sentence 3**
- **Explanation:** Placing the sentence after sentence 3 effectively reinforces the idea that literature has influenced social change beyond mere entertainment by shaping public opinion and policy.

81) In context, the word "exposé" in sentence 21 most nearly means:

- **Answer: B) A detailed report**
- **Explanation:** The term "exposé" refers to a detailed and thorough examination or report, in this case, on the dangers of pesticides, as highlighted in Rachel Carson's "Silent Spring."

82) Which choice best concludes the passage?

- **Answer: C) Literature continues to inspire and drive social change by challenging norms and advocating for justice.**
- **Explanation:** This conclusion encapsulates the ongoing impact of literature in challenging societal norms and advocating for justice, aligning with the passage's overall theme.

83) Which choice most effectively combines sentences 10 and 11?

- **Answer: C) The mid-20th century saw the emergence of literature that supported the civil rights movement, such as James Baldwin's essays and novels, including "The Fire Next Time" and "Go Tell It on the Mountain."**
- **Explanation:** This combination effectively merges the sentences, providing a clear and concise connection between Baldwin's works and their support for the civil rights movement.

Science: 11 questions

84) Which choice best describes what happens in the passage?

- **Answer: A) The passage explains the causes and effects of earthquakes and discusses methods to predict and mitigate their impact.**
- **Explanation:** The passage provides an overview of the science behind earthquakes, including their causes, types of seismic waves,

measurement methods, and ways to predict and mitigate their effects.

85) Which choice best expresses the main idea of the passage?

- **Answer: A) Understanding the science behind earthquakes is crucial for predicting them and reducing their impact on society.**
- **Explanation:** The passage emphasizes the importance of studying earthquakes to better predict and manage their effects, highlighting various aspects of seismology and mitigation techniques.

86) In context, what does the phrase "seismic energy" in sentence 4 most nearly mean?

- **Answer: C) Energy released from the Earth's crust**
- **Explanation:** Seismic energy refers to the energy released during an earthquake, which travels through the Earth's crust in the form of seismic waves.

87) Which sentence, if added after sentence 6, would best support the main idea of the paragraph?

- **Answer: B) Tectonic plate movements are responsible for the majority of the planet's seismic activity.**
- **Explanation:** This sentence would support the explanation of how tectonic plates and faults are related to earthquakes, reinforcing the connection between plate movements and seismic activity.

88) In sentence 7, the term "hypocenter" refers to:

- **Answer: C) The point within the Earth where an earthquake originates.**
- **Explanation:** The hypocenter is the location inside the Earth where

the earthquake starts, from which seismic waves are generated.

89) Which choice provides the most accurate interpretation of the data in sentence 14?

- **Answer: C) The Richter scale quantifies the amplitude and energy release of an earthquake.**
- **Explanation:** The Richter scale measures the magnitude of an earthquake, which is related to the amplitude of seismic waves and the total energy released.

90) In sentence 18, what does the mention of the moment magnitude scale (Mw) contribute to the passage?

- **Answer: A) It highlights a different method for measuring the size of earthquakes, especially large ones.**
- **Explanation:** The moment magnitude scale (Mw) is introduced as a more accurate method for measuring the total energy release of large earthquakes, providing an alternative to the Richter scale.

91) The author wants to add the following sentence to the second paragraph:
"These instruments are crucial for monitoring and studying seismic activity." Where would this sentence best fit?

- **Answer: D) After sentence 9**
- **Explanation:** Placing the sentence after sentence 9, which describes seismometers, helps emphasize the importance of these instruments in the study and monitoring of seismic activity.

92) In context, the word "elusive" in sentence 11 most nearly means:

- **Answer: B) Uncertain**

- **Explanation:** "Elusive" refers to something that is difficult to predict or capture, fitting the context of the challenges associated with predicting earthquakes.

93) Which choice best concludes the passage?

- **Answer: C) By integrating scientific research, technology, engineering, and public education, society can better handle the impact of earthquakes.**
- **Explanation:** This conclusion emphasizes the comprehensive approach needed to manage the effects of earthquakes, aligning with the passage's overall discussion on understanding and mitigating earthquake impacts.

94) Which choice most effectively combines sentences 24 and 25?

- **Answer: C) Earthquake-resistant construction is another crucial aspect of mitigating earthquake damage; engineers design buildings and structures to withstand seismic forces by incorporating flexible materials, reinforced frameworks, and advanced damping systems.**
- **Explanation:** This option effectively combines the sentences with a semicolon, clearly linking the role of earthquake-resistant construction with the specific engineering techniques used to achieve it.

2. Math

A. Math Test - No Calculator

Heart of Algebra: 8 questions

Question 95:

Problem: Solve for y in the equation: $2y + 7 - 3y - 5$.

Solution:

$2y + 7 - 3y - 5$

Subtract $2y$ from both sides:

$7 - y - 5$

Add 5 to both sides:

$12 - y$

Answer: D) 12

Question 96:

Problem: If $4x - y - 11$ and $y - 2x + 3$, what is the value of x?

Solution:

Substitute $y - 2x + 3$ into $4x - y - 11$:

$4x - (2x + 3) - 11$

$4x - 2x - 3 - 11$

$2x - 3 - 11$

Add 3 to both sides:

$2x - 14$

Divide by 2:

$x - 7$

Answer: D) 7

Question 97:

Problem: What is the solution to the system of equations:

$2x + y = 10$

$3x - y = 5$

Solution:

Add the equations to eliminate y:

$2x + y + 3x - y = 10 + 5$

$5x = 15$

Divide by 5:

$x = 3$

Substitute $x = 3$ into $2x + y = 10$:

$2(3) + y = 10$

$6 + y = 10$

$y = 4$

Answer: C) (3, 4)

Question 98:

Problem: Solve the inequality: $4x + 1 < 9$.

Solution:

Subtract 1 from both sides:

$4x < 8$

Divide by 4:

$x < 2$

Answer: B) $x < 2$

Question 99:

Problem: If $5x + 2y - 19$ and $x - 3y - -8$, what is the value of y?

Solution:

Solve the second equation for x:

$x - 3y - 8$

Substitute $x - 3y - 8$ into the first equation:

$5(3y - 8) + 2y - 19$

$15y - 40 + 2y - 19$

$17y - 40 - 19$

Add 40 to both sides:

$17y - 59$

Divide by 17:

$y - \frac{59}{17}$

Question 100:

Problem: The difference between two numbers is 7. If one number is twice the other, what are the numbers?

Solution:

Let the two numbers be x and $2x$.

The difference between them is:

$2x - x - 7$

$x - 7$

Thus, the two numbers are 7 and $2 \times 7 - 14$.

Answer: A) 7 and 14

Question 101:

Problem: Find the value of x if $9x - 4 = 5x + 16$.

Solution:

Subtract $5x$ from both sides:

$9x - 5x - 4 - 16$

$4x - 4 - 16$

Add 4 to both sides:

$4x - 20$

Divide by 4:

$x - 5$

Answer: C) 5

Question 102:

Problem: What is the solution to the equation $3(4x + 2) - 5x + 18$?

Solution:

Expand and simplify:

$12x + 6 - 5x + 18$

$12x - 5x - 18 - 6$

$7x - 12$

$x - \frac{12}{7}$

Answer: C) $\frac{12}{7}$

Problem Solving and Data Analysis: 3 questions

Question 103:

Problem: A car rental company charges a flat fee of $20 per day plus $0.15 per mile driven. If a customer rents a car for 3 days and drives 150 miles, what is the total cost?

Solution:

Calculate the cost for the rental days:

$3 \text{ days} \times \$20/\text{day} - \$60$

Calculate the cost for the miles driven:

$150 \text{ miles} \times \$0.15/\text{mile} - \$22.50$

Add the two costs together:

$\$60 + \$22.50 - \$82.50$

Answer: C) $82.50

Question 104:

Problem: The table below shows the number of books sold by a bookstore in a week. What is the average number of books sold per day?

Day	Books Sold
Monday	40
Tuesday	30
Wednesday	25
Thursday	30
Friday	50
Saturday	60
Sunday	45

Solution:

The total number of books sold in the week is 280 $(40 + 30 + 25 + 30 + 50 + 60 + 45 - 280)$. Since there are 7 days in the week, the average number of books sold per day is 40 $(280 \div 7 - 40)$

Answer: B) 40

Question 105:

Problem: A survey of 200 people found that 75% of them prefer coffee over tea. How many people prefer tea?

Solution:

If 75% of the 200 people surveyed prefer coffee, that equates to 150 people $(0.75 \times 200 - 150)$. Therefore, the remaining 50 people $(200 - 150 = 50)$ prefer tea.

Answer: B) 50

Passport to Advanced Math: 6 questions

Question 106:

Problem: What is the value of x in the equation $2^{3x-1} - 16$?

Solution:

Rewrite 16 as a power of 2:

$$16 - 2^4$$

So, the equation becomes:

$$2^{3x-1} - 2^4$$

Since the bases are the same, set the exponents equal:

$$3x - 1 - 4$$

Add 1 to both sides:

$$3x - 5$$

Divide by 3:

$$x - \frac{5}{3}$$

Answer: A) $\frac{5}{3}$

Question 107:

Problem: If $h(x) - 4x^2 + 3x - 5$, what is $h(-2)$?

Solution:

Substitute $x - -2$ into the function $h(x)$:

$$h(-2) - 4(-2)^2 + 3(-2) - 5$$

Simplify:

$$h(-2) - 4(4) - 6 - 5 - 16 - 6 - 5 - 5$$

Answer: A) 5

Question 108:

Problem: Solve the quadratic equation $3x^2 - 12x + 9 - 0$ for x.

Solution:

Factor the quadratic equation:

$$3(x^2 - 4x + 3) - 0$$

Factor the quadratic expression:

$$3(x - 3)(x - 1) - 0$$

So, the solutions are:

$$x - 3 \quad \text{or} \quad x - 1$$

Answer: A) $x - 1$ or $x - 3$

Question 109:

Problem: If $k(x) - x^2 - 4x + 7$, what is the vertex of the parabola defined by $k(x)$?

Solution:

The vertex form of a parabola is given by $k(x) - a(x - h)^2 + k$, where (h, k) is the vertex.

For the equation $k(x) - x^2 - 4x + 7$, complete the square:

Rewrite the equation:

$$k(x) - (x^2 - 4x + 4) + 3 - (x - 2)^2 + 3$$

So, the vertex is at $(2, 3)$.

Answer: B) $(2, 3)$

Question 110:

Problem: Solve for x in the equation $5^{2x-1} - 125$.

Solution:

Rewrite 125 as a power of 5:

$$125 - 5^3$$

So, the equation becomes:

$$5^{2x-1} - 5^3$$

Since the bases are the same, set the exponents equal:

$$2x - 1 - 3$$

Add 1 to both sides:

$$2x - 4$$

Divide by 2:

$$x - 2$$

Answer: A) 2

Question 111:

Problem: If $f(x) - \frac{2x+3}{x-1}$, what is the value of $f(3)$?

Solution:

Substitute $x - 3$ into the function $f(x)$:

$$f(3) - \frac{2(3)+3}{3-1} - \frac{6+3}{2} - \frac{9}{2} - 4.5$$

Answer: C) 4.5

Additional Topics in Math (geometry, trigonometry, etc.): 3 questions

Question 112:

Problem: A circle has a radius of 5 units. What is the area of the sector formed by a central angle of 60 degrees? (Use $\pi \approx 3.14$)

Solution:

The area of a sector is given by:

$$\text{Area} - \frac{\theta}{360} \times \pi r^2$$

Substituting the values:

$$\text{Area} - \frac{60}{360} \times 3.14 \times 5^2 - \frac{1}{6} \times 3.14 \times 25 - \frac{3.14 \times 25}{6} \approx 13.09 \, \text{square units}$$

Answer: B) 13.09 square units

Question 113:

Problem: In triangle ABC, $\angle C$ is a right angle, and $\angle A - 30°$. If the length of side AB is 10 units, what is the length of side AC?

Solution:

In a 30-60-90 triangle, the ratio of the sides opposite the 30°, 60°, and 90° angles is $1 : \sqrt{3} : 2$. Therefore, the length of side AC (opposite the 30° angle) is half the length of the hypotenuse AB:

$$AC - \frac{AB}{2} - \frac{10}{2} - 5 \, \text{units}$$

Answer: A) 5 units

Question 114:

Problem: What is the period of the function $f(x) - 3\sin(2x)$?

Solution:

The period of a sine function $\sin(kx)$ is given by:

$$\text{Period} - \frac{2\pi}{k}$$

For $f(x) - 3\sin(2x)$, $k - 2$:

$$\text{Period} - \frac{2\pi}{2} - \pi$$

Answer: A) π

B. Math Test - Calculator

Heart of Algebra: 16 questions

Question 115:

Problem: Solve for x in the equation $7x - 3 - 4x + 9$.

Solution:

First, isolate x by subtracting $4x$ from both sides:

$$7x - 4x - 3 - 9$$

This simplifies to:

$$3x - 3 - 9$$

Next, add 3 to both sides:

$$3x - 12$$

Finally, divide by 3:

$$x - 4$$

Answer: C) 4

Question 116:

Problem: If $2y + 7 - 3y - 5$, what is the value of y?

Solution:

Start by isolating y by subtracting $2y$ from both sides:

$$7 - y - 5$$

Next, add 5 to both sides:

$$y - 12$$

Answer: A) 12

Question 117:

Problem: Solve for x: $4(x - 1) - 2x + 6$.

Solution:

First, expand the left side:

$$4x - 4 = 2x + 6$$

Next, subtract $2x$ from both sides:

$$2x - 4 - 6$$

Then, add 4 to both sides:

$$2x - 10$$

Finally, divide by 2:

$$x - 5$$

Answer: C) 5

Question 118:

Problem: The equation $y - -3x + 5$ represents a line. What is the y-intercept of this line?

Solution:

The y-intercept of the line is the constant term in the equation $y - mx + b$, where m is the slope and b is the y-intercept. Here, the y-intercept $b - 5$.

Answer: B) 5

Question 119:

Problem: If $y - 2x + 4$ and $y - -x + 1$, what is the value of x?

Solution:

Set the two equations equal to each other:

$$2x + 4 - -x + 1$$

Next, add x to both sides:

$$3x + 4 - 1$$

Then, subtract 4 from both sides:

$$3x - -3$$

Finally, divide by 3:

$$x - -1$$

Answer: B) -1

Question 120:

Problem: Solve for y: $5y - 3 - 2y + 6$.

Solution:

First, subtract $2y$ from both sides:

$$3y - 3 - 6$$

Next, add 3 to both sides:

$$3y - 9$$

Finally, divide by 3:

$$y - 3$$

Answer: A) 3

Question 121:

Problem: What is the value of x in the equation $6(x + 1) - 3x + 15$?

Solution:

First, distribute on the left side:

$$6x + 6 - 3x + 15$$

Next, subtract $3x$ from both sides:

$$3x + 6 - 15$$

Then, subtract 6 from both sides:

$$3x - 9$$

Finally, divide by 3:

$$x - 3$$

Answer: A) 3

Question 122:

Problem: If $y = -3x + 7$ and $y = 2x - 3$, what is the value of y?

Solution:

Set the two equations equal to each other:

$$-3x + 7 = 2x - 3$$

Next, add $3x$ to both sides:

$$7 = 5x - 3$$

Then, add 3 to both sides:

$$10 = 5x$$

Finally, divide by 5:

$$x = 2$$

Substitute $x = 2$ into either equation (e.g., $y = 2x - 3$):

$$y = 2(2) - 3 = 4 - 3 = 1$$

Answer: A) 1

Question 123:

Problem: Solve for x: $7(x - 2) = 4(x + 3)$.

Solution:

First, expand both sides:

$$7x - 14 = 4x + 12$$

Next, subtract $4x$ from both sides:

$$3x - 14 = 12$$

Then, add 14 to both sides:

$$3x = 26$$

Finally, divide by 3:

$$x \approx 8.67$$

Answer: C) 8.67

Question 124:

Problem: The line $y = 4x - 9$ passes through the point $(a, -1)$. What is the value of a?

Solution:

Substitute $y = -1$ into the equation:

$$-1 = 4a - 9$$

Next, add 9 to both sides:

$$8 = 4a$$

Finally, divide by 4:

$$a = 2$$

Answer: B) 2

638

Question 125:

Problem: What is the solution to the system of equations: $x + y - 8$ and $x - y - 4$?

Solution:

Add the two equations to eliminate y:

$$x + y + x - y - 8 + 4$$

This simplifies to:

$$2x - 12 \longrightarrow x - 6$$

Substitute $x - 6$ into $x + y - 8$:

$$6 + y - 8 \longrightarrow y - 2$$

Answer: A) (6, 2)

Question 126:

Problem: If $8x + 4 - 2x + 28$, what is the value of x?

Solution:

First, subtract $2x$ from both sides:

$$6x + 4 - 28$$

Next, subtract 4 from both sides:

$$6x - 24$$

Finally, divide by 6:

$$x - 4$$

Answer: A) 4

Question 127:

Problem: Solve for y: $3(2y - 1) - 4(y + 2)$.

Solution:

First, expand both sides:

$$6y - 3 = 4y + 8$$

Next, subtract $4y$ from both sides:

$$2y - 3 = 8$$

Then, add 3 to both sides:

$$2y = 11$$

Finally, divide by 2:

$$y = \frac{11}{2}$$

Answer: C) $\frac{11}{2}$

Question 128:

Problem: If $y - 3x + 8$ and $y - -2x + 3$, what is the value of y?

Solution:

First, set the two expressions for y equal to each other:

$$3x + 8 - -2x + 3$$

Next, add $2x$ to both sides:

$$5x + 8 - 3$$

Then, subtract 8 from both sides:

$$5x - -5$$

Finally, divide by 5:

$$x - -1$$

Now substitute $x - -1$ back into either equation to find y:

$$y - 3(-1) + 8 - -3 + 8 - 5$$

Answer: B) 5

Question 129:

Problem: Solve for x: $5(x - 2) = 3(x + 4)$.

Solution:

First, expand both sides:

$$5x - 10 = 3x + 12$$

Next, subtract $3x$ from both sides:

$$2x - 10 = 12$$

Then, add 10 to both sides:

$$2x = 22$$

Finally, divide by 2:

$$x = 11$$

Answer: A) 11

Question 130:

Problem: If $3x - 2y = 14$ and $x = 6$, what is the value of y?

Solution:

First, substitute $x = 6$ into the equation:

$$3(6) - 2y = 14$$

Next, simplify and solve for y:

$$18 - 2y = 14$$

Then, subtract 18 from both sides:

$$-2y = -4$$

Finally, divide by -2:

$$y = 2$$

Answer: B) 2

Problem Solving and Data Analysis: 8 questions

Question 131:

Problem: A car travels 150 miles on 5 gallons of gas. What is the car's fuel efficiency in miles per gallon?

Solution:

The fuel efficiency in miles per gallon (mpg) is given by the formula:

$$\text{Fuel Efficiency} - \frac{\text{Total Miles Traveled}}{\text{Gallons of Gas Used}}$$

Substituting the given values:

$$\text{Fuel Efficiency} - \frac{150 \text{ miles}}{5 \text{ gallons}} - 30 \text{ mpg}$$

Correct Answer: C) 30

Question 132:

Problem: The average score of 5 students in a math test is 78. If four students scored 72, 85, 90, and 65, what is the score of the fifth student?

Solution:

Let the score of the fifth student be x.

The average score is calculated as:

$$\frac{72 + 85 + 90 + 65 + x}{5} - 78$$

First, find the total of the four known scores:

$$312 + x - 78 \times 5$$

Simplifying:

$$312 + x - 390$$

Subtract 312 from both sides:

$$x - 78$$

Correct Answer: B) 75

Question 133:

Problem: If the price of a product is reduced by 20%, and the new price is $80, what was the original price?

Solution:

Let the original price be p.

The price is reduced by 20%, so the new price is 80% of the original price:

$$0.8p - 80$$

To find the original price, divide both sides by 0.8:

$$p - \frac{80}{0.8} - 100$$

Correct Answer: B) $100

Question 134:

Problem: A survey of 100 people found that 45% prefer coffee, 35% prefer tea, and the remaining prefer neither. How many people prefer neither?

Solution:

The percentage of people who prefer neither is:

$$100\% - 45\% - 35\% - 20\%$$

The number of people who prefer neither is:

$$0.2 \times 100 - 20$$

Correct Answer: C) 20

Question 135:

Problem: A student needs to score an average of 80 on 5 tests to pass a course. If the scores on the first four tests are 78, 82, 76, and 85, what score does the student need on the fifth test to pass?

Solution:

Let the score on the fifth test be x.

The average score is calculated as:

$$\frac{78 + 82 + 76 + 85 + x}{5} - 80$$

First, find the total of the four known scores:

$$321 + x - 80 \times 5$$

Simplifying:

$$321 + x - 400$$

Subtract 321 from both sides:

$$x - 79$$

Correct Answer: A) 79

Question 136:

Problem: A rectangular garden has a length of 20 feet and a width of 15 feet. If a fence costs $5 per foot, how much will it cost to fence the entire garden?

Solution:

The perimeter P of the garden is given by:

$$P - 2 \times (\text{Length} + \text{Width}) - 2 \times (20 + 15) - 70 \text{ feet}$$

The cost to fence the garden is:

$$\text{Total Cost} - 70 \times 5 - 350 \text{ dollars}$$

Correct Answer: C) $350

Question 137:

Problem: A recipe requires 3 cups of sugar for every 4 cups of flour. If you want to make a half-sized batch of the recipe, how many cups of sugar will you need if you use 2 cups of flour?

Solution:

The original recipe uses 3 cups of sugar for 4 cups of flour. For 2 cups of flour (which is half the amount), you need half the amount of sugar:

$$\text{Cups of sugar} - \frac{3}{4} \times 2 - 1.5$$

Correct Answer: B) 1.5

Question 138:

Problem: If a shirt originally costs $50 and is marked down by 30%, what is the sale price of the shirt?

Solution:

The markdown amount is:

$$\text{Markdown} - 0.30 \times 50 - 15 \text{ dollars}$$

The sale price is:

$$\text{Sale Price} - 50 - 15 - 35 \text{ dollars}$$

Correct Answer: C) $35

Passport to Advanced Math: 11 questions

Question 139:

Problem: If $p(x) - x^3 - 6x^2 + 11x - 6$, what are the roots of the polynomial?

Solution:

To find the roots of the polynomial, we need to factor it. The polynomial can be factored as:

$$p(x) - (x - 1)(x - 2)(x - 3)$$

Setting each factor equal to zero gives us:

$$x - 1 - 0 \implies x - 1$$

$$x - 2 - 0 \implies x - 2$$

$$x - 3 - 0 \implies x - 3$$

Answer: C) 1, 2, 3

Question 140:

Problem: Solve for x in the equation $\sqrt{2x + 3} - 1 = 0$.

Solution:

First, isolate the square root:

$$\sqrt{2x + 3} - 1$$

Next, square both sides to eliminate the square root:

$$2x + 3 - 1^2$$

Simplifying:

$$2x + 3 - 1$$

Subtract 3 from both sides:

$$2x - -2$$

Finally, divide by 2:

$$x - -1$$

Answer: A) -1

Question 141:

Problem: What is the value of k if the polynomial $x^3 - 4x^2 + kx - 8$ has a root at $x - 2$?

Solution:

If $x - 2$ is a root, then:

$$(2)^3 - 4(2)^2 + k(2) - 8 - 0$$

Calculate:

$$8 - 16 + 2k - 8 - 0$$

Simplify:

$$2k - 16 - 0$$

Add 16 to both sides:

$$2k - 16$$

Finally, divide by 2:

$$k - 8$$

Answer: D) 8

Question 142:

Problem: The function $f(x) = 2x^3 - 5x^2 + 3x - 7$ has a local maximum at $x = a$. What is the value of a?

Solution:

To find the local maximum, take the derivative of $f(x)$:

$$f'(x) = 6x^2 - 10x + 3$$

Set the derivative equal to zero to find critical points:

$$6x^2 - 10x + 3 = 0$$

Solve the quadratic equation:

$$x = \frac{-(-10) \pm \sqrt{(-10)^2 - 4(6)(3)}}{2(6)}$$

$$x = \frac{10 \pm \sqrt{100 - 72}}{12}$$

$$x = \frac{10 \pm \sqrt{28}}{12}$$

Simplifying further would yield $a - 1$ as the value that gives the local maximum.

Answer: A) 1

Question 143:

Problem: If $g(x) = x^2 + 4x + c$ has only one solution, what is the value of c?

Solution:

For the quadratic equation to have one solution, the discriminant must be zero:

$$\Delta = b^2 - 4ac = 0$$

Here, $a = 1$, $b = 4$, and $c = c$:

$$4^2 - 4(1)(c) = 0$$

$$16 - 4c = 0$$

Solve for c:

$$4c = 16$$

$$c = 4$$

Answer: B) 4

Question 144:

Problem: Solve for x in the equation $2^x = 32$.

Solution:

Rewrite 32 as a power of 2:

$$32 = 2^5$$

Thus:

$$2^x = 2^5$$

Equating the exponents gives:

$$x = 5$$

Answer: C) 5

Question 145:

Problem: What is the value of x if $5^{2x-1} = 125$?

Solution:

First, express 125 as a power of 5:

$$125 = 5^3$$

Thus, the equation becomes:

$$5^{2x-1} = 5^3$$

Equating the exponents:

$$2x - 1 = 3$$

Add 1 to both sides:

$$2x = 4$$

Finally, divide by 2:

$$x = 2$$

Answer: B) 2

Question 146:

Problem: If $h(x) = x^4 - 8x^3 + 16x^2$, factor $h(x)$ completely.

Solution:

First, factor out the common factor x^2:

$$h(x) = x^2(x^2 - 8x + 16)$$

Next, recognize that the quadratic can be factored as a perfect square:

$$h(x) = x^2(x - 4)^2$$

Answer: A) $x^2(x - 4)^2$

Question 147:

Problem: Solve for x in the inequality $\frac{x+1}{x-2} > 3$.

Solution:

First, rewrite the inequality:

$$\frac{x+1}{x-2} - 3 > 0$$

Combine into a single fraction:

$$\frac{x+1-3(x-2)}{x-2} > 0$$

Simplify:

$$\frac{x+1-3x+6}{x-2} > 0$$

$$\frac{-2x+7}{x-2} > 0$$

To find the critical points, solve:

$$-2x+7 = 0 \quad \text{and} \quad x-2 = 0$$

$$x = \frac{7}{2} = 3.5 \quad \text{and} \quad x = 2$$

These critical points divide the number line into intervals. Test the inequality in each interval:

1. $x < 2$: Choose $x = 0$, $\frac{-2(0)+7}{0-2} = \frac{7}{-2} = -3.5$ (Negative)
2. $2 < x < 3.5$: Choose $x = 3$, $\frac{-2(3)+7}{3-2} = \frac{-6+7}{1} = 1$ (Positive)
3. $x > 3.5$: Choose $x = 4$, $\frac{-2(4)+7}{4-2} = \frac{-8+7}{2} = -\frac{1}{2}$ (Negative)

Since we're looking for where the expression is greater than 0, the solution is:

$$x > 3.5$$

Answer: A) $x = 3.5$

Question 148:

Problem: The function $f(x) = 2x^2 + 3x + c$ intersects the x-axis at $x = -3$ and $x = 1$. What is the value of c?

Solution:

Using the fact that the roots are $x = -3$ and $x = 1$:

$$f(x) = 2(x + 3)(x - 1)$$

Expanding this expression:

$$f(x) = 2(x^2 + 2x - 3)$$

$$f(x) = 2x^2 + 4x - 6$$

So $c = -6$.

Answer: B) -6

Question 149:

Problem: If $f(x) = x^2 + 2x - 3$, what is the y-intercept of the function?

Solution:

The y-intercept occurs when $x = 0$:

$$f(0) = (0)^2 + 2(0) - 3 = -3$$

Answer: A) -3

Additional Topics in Math (geometry, trigonometry, etc.): 3 questions

Question 150:

Problem: In a circle with a radius of 8 units, what is the length of an arc that subtends a central angle of $60°$?

Solution:

The formula for the length of an arc is given by:

$$\text{Arc Length} - \theta \times r$$

where θ is the central angle in radians and r is the radius of the circle.

First, convert the central angle from degrees to radians:

$$\theta - \frac{60° \times \pi}{180°} - \frac{\pi}{3}$$

Now, use the arc length formula:

$$\text{Arc Length} - \frac{\pi}{3} \times 8 - \frac{8\pi}{3}$$

Answer:

A) $\frac{8\pi}{3}$

Question 151:

Problem: A parallelogram has sides of length 10 units and 15 units. If the measure of the angle between the two sides is $60°$, what is the area of the parallelogram?

Solution:

The area of a parallelogram is given by:

$$\text{Area} - ab \times \sin(\theta)$$

where a and b are the lengths of the sides and θ is the angle between them.

Substituting the given values:

$$\text{Area} - 10 \times 15 \times \sin(60°) - 150 \times \frac{\sqrt{3}}{2} - 75\sqrt{3}$$

Answer:

B) $75\sqrt{3}$

Question 152:

Problem: What is the volume of a right circular cone with a radius of 6 units and a height of 9 units?

Solution:

The formula for the volume of a cone is:

$$\text{Volume} - \frac{1}{3} \times \pi r^2 h$$

Substitute the given values:

$$\text{Volume} - \frac{1}{3} \times \pi \times 6^2 \times 9 - \frac{1}{3} \times \pi \times 36 \times 9 - \frac{1}{3} \times 324\pi - 108\pi$$

Answer:

A) 108π

3. Essay (Optional) - Example Answer

In the passage "The Benefits of a Plant-Based Diet," Dr. Emily Carter constructs a persuasive argument to advocate for the adoption of a plant-based diet by effectively utilizing evidence, logical reasoning, and stylistic elements to convince her audience of the health, environmental, and global benefits of this dietary choice.

One of the primary strategies Carter employs is the use of robust evidence to substantiate her claims. Throughout the passage, she references scientific research and credible sources to support the advantages of a plant-based diet. For instance, Carter cites a study published in the Journal of the American Heart Association *that found a 16% lower risk of developing cardiovascular disease among individuals who follow a plant-based diet. This use of specific, reputable evidence strengthens Carter's argument by providing tangible proof that plant-based diets can lead to significant health benefits. By grounding her claims in scientific research, Carter enhances her credibility and makes her argument more compelling to her audience.*

Carter also employs logical reasoning to develop her ideas and connect her claims with supporting evidence. She systematically explores the benefits of a plant-based diet by addressing its impact on personal health, environmental sustainability, and global food security. For example, after discussing the health advantages of a plant-based diet, Carter logically transitions to its environmental benefits, explaining how the production of plant-based foods requires fewer resources and generates lower levels of greenhouse gas emissions. She then connects this point to the broader issue of climate change, arguing that reducing the consumption of animal products can help decrease individuals' carbon footprints. This logical progression of ideas allows Carter to build a cohesive argument that is easy for the reader to follow and understand.

In addition to evidence and reasoning, Carter effectively uses stylistic elements to enhance the persuasiveness of her argument. She employs a confident and authoritative tone, which reinforces her credibility as a knowledgeable source on the subject. Words and phrases like "crucial," "consistently shown," and "entirely possible" convey certainty and emphasize the reliability of her information. Moreover, Carter addresses potential counterarguments by acknowledging critics' concerns about the nutritional adequacy of plant-based diets. However, she quickly refutes these concerns by providing examples of plant-based foods that are rich in essential nutrients, thus reassuring her audience that a well-planned plant-based diet can meet all nutritional needs. This balanced approach demonstrates Carter's thorough understanding of the topic and further strengthens her argument.

Carter also appeals to the reader's emotions by highlighting the broader implications of dietary choices on environmental sustainability and global food security. She underscores the urgency of these issues by mentioning the significant contribution of livestock farming to global greenhouse gas emissions and the inefficiency of meat production in the context of a growing global population. By framing the adoption of a plant-based diet as a means to address these pressing global challenges, Carter taps into the reader's sense of responsibility and concern for the future of the planet. This emotional appeal makes the argument more relatable and persuasive, as it encourages the reader to consider the impact of their dietary choices on a larger scale.

In conclusion, Dr. Emily Carter effectively builds a persuasive argument for the benefits of adopting a plant-based diet by employing evidence, logical reasoning, and stylistic elements. Her use of credible research and logical progression of ideas enhances the clarity and persuasiveness of her argument, while her confident tone and emotional appeal make the argument both compelling and relatable. Through these techniques, Carter successfully convinces her audience that a plant-based diet is a beneficial and viable option for improving personal health, promoting environmental sustainability, and contributing to global food security.

Practice SAT #5 - Answers & Explanations

1. Evidence-Based Reading and Writing (EBRW)

A. Reading Test

Literature: 10 questions

1) How does Pip initially fail to recognize Estella?

- **Answer: B) She is much more beautiful and womanly**
- **Explanation:** Pip does not immediately recognize Estella because she has changed significantly, becoming more beautiful and womanly.

2) What qualities had Pip always known Estella to have?

- **Answer: B) Pride, moodiness, and capriciousness**
- **Explanation:** Pip describes Estella as having a rich luxurious nature, being proud, moody, and capricious.

3) How does Pip feel when he sees Estella again?

- **Answer: B) Overwhelmed by admiration and love**

- **Explanation:** Pip is overwhelmed by admiration and love, as he finds Estella even more beautiful and feels a rush of emotions.

4) What is Estella's reaction to seeing Pip grown up?

- **Answer: B) She is sad and critical of his lack of wisdom**
- **Explanation:** Estella expresses that it is a sad sight to see Pip grown up but still not wiser than before.

5) What metaphor does Estella use to describe Pip's progress in life?

- **Answer: B) A ship that gets away from a wharf**
- **Explanation:** Estella uses the metaphor of a ship that does not control its own voyage to any port, implying that Pip does not control his destiny.

6) How does Estella describe her feelings toward Pip and others?

- **Answer: C) She has no heart, tenderness, or sentiment**
- **Explanation:** Estella declares that she has no heart and is incapable of tenderness or sentiment.

7) What does Pip confess about his feelings for Estella?

- **Answer: B) She is part of his existence and has influenced every aspect of his life**
- **Explanation:** Pip confesses that Estella has been a part of his existence, influencing every aspect of his life deeply.

8) What does Estella ask Pip to do regarding his feelings for her?

- **Answer: B) To dismiss them from his thoughts**
- **Explanation:** Estella asks Pip to dismiss his feelings for her from his

thoughts, indicating she cannot reciprocate them.

9) What does Pip believe about Estella's capacity for affection?

- **Answer: A) That she is capable of deep love and sympathy**
- **Explanation:** Pip had believed in the possibility of Estella's affection and the existence of her sympathies, though Estella denies having such capacities.

10) What imagery does Pip use to describe Estella's presence in his life?

- **Answer: C) She is part of every aspect of his existence, as real and immovable as the strongest buildings in London**
- **Explanation:** Pip uses imagery of Estella being a part of every aspect of his existence, as real and immovable as the strongest buildings in London, to express how deeply she has impacted his life.

Historical Documents: 10 questions

11) What event is Abraham Lincoln referring to when he says "Fourscore and seven years ago"?

- **Answer: A) The signing of the Declaration of Independence**
- **Explanation:** Lincoln is referencing the Declaration of Independence, which was signed 87 years prior (a "score" being 20 years).

12) What proposition was the new nation dedicated to according to Lincoln?

- **Answer: C) Equality of all men**
- **Explanation:** Lincoln states that the nation was "dedicated to the proposition that all men are created equal."

13) What is the main purpose of Lincoln's speech?

- **Answer: B) To dedicate a portion of the battlefield as a cemetery**
- **Explanation:** The speech was given to dedicate the Gettysburg battlefield as a cemetery for soldiers who died there.

14) According to Lincoln, who has already consecrated the ground of the battlefield?

- **Answer: C) The brave men, living and dead, who struggled there**
- **Explanation:** Lincoln asserts that the soldiers, through their actions, have already consecrated the ground beyond the power of the speakers to do so.

15) What does Lincoln suggest about the words spoken at the dedication compared to the actions taken by the soldiers?

- **Answer: B) The actions of the soldiers are more important than the words spoken**
- **Explanation:** Lincoln emphasizes that the world will not remember the words spoken as much as the actions taken by the soldiers.

16) What does Lincoln believe is the "unfinished work" that the living must dedicate themselves to?

- **Answer: B) Advancing the cause for which the soldiers gave their lives**
- **Explanation:** Lincoln refers to the cause of freedom and equality that the soldiers fought for as the "unfinished work."

17) What does Lincoln hope for the nation as a result of the sacrifices made by the soldiers?

- **Answer: A) A new birth of freedom**
- **Explanation:** Lincoln expresses the hope that the nation will experience a new birth of freedom as a result of the sacrifices made.

18) What does Lincoln mean by "that government of the people, by the people, for the people, shall not perish from the earth"?

- **Answer: C) The democratic government should continue to exist**
- **Explanation:** Lincoln is affirming the importance of democracy and expressing the hope that it will endure.

19) How does Lincoln describe the dedication of the battlefield in a "larger sense"?

- **Answer: B) As something that the living cannot truly accomplish because the ground is already consecrated by the soldiers' actions**
- **Explanation:** Lincoln suggests that the ground has already been consecrated by the sacrifices of the soldiers, making the formal dedication by the living somewhat secondary.

20) What emotion does Lincoln primarily express in this address?

- **Answer: C) Solemnity and dedication**
- **Explanation:** The tone of the speech is solemn and dedicated, as Lincoln honors the fallen and emphasizes the importance of continuing their work.

Social Sciences: 10 questions

21) According to the passage, what is often celebrated in society?

- **Answer: B) Extroversion**
- **Explanation:** The passage begins by noting that society often cele-

brates extroversion, implying that it is more commonly valued than introversion.

22) What unique strength do introverts possess regarding decision-making?

- **Answer: C) They think before they speak and consider potential outcomes thoroughly**
- **Explanation:** Introverts are described as being reflective and deliberate, thinking carefully before speaking and considering potential outcomes.

23) How are introverts described in their approach to tasks?

- **Answer: B) Deeply focused and often working independently**
- **Explanation:** The passage highlights introverts' ability to focus deeply on tasks and work independently with great concentration.

24) What is one significant strength of introverts in conversations?

- **Answer: B) They listen actively and process information before responding**
- **Explanation:** Introverts are noted for their ability to listen attentively and respond thoughtfully, which fosters better communication.

25) What type of relationships do introverts tend to form?

- **Answer: B) Deep and meaningful**
- **Explanation:** The passage states that introverts often form deep, meaningful relationships, preferring quality over quantity in social interactions.

26) In what type of environments do introverts particularly excel?

- **Answer: B) Environments that require solitude and independence**
- **Explanation:** Introverts are described as excelling in environments that require solitude and independence, such as those often found in artistic and scientific fields.

27) Which professions are mentioned as having significant contributions from introverts?

- **Answer: B) Artists, writers, and scientists**
- **Explanation:** The passage mentions that many artists, writers, and scientists who have made significant contributions to their fields have been introverts.

28) What challenges do introverts face in certain work environments?

- **Answer: B) They face difficulties in open-plan offices and group brainstorming sessions**
- **Explanation:** The passage notes that introverts may struggle in environments that favor extroverted behaviors, such as open-plan offices and group brainstorming sessions.

29) What can organizations do to accommodate different working styles?

- **Answer: B) Provide quiet spaces for focused work and allow for written contributions in meetings**
- **Explanation:** The passage suggests that organizations should recognize different working styles and provide quiet spaces and opportunities for written contributions to accommodate introverts.

30) What does understanding the value of introverts challenge?

- **Answer: A) The cultural bias towards extroversion**

· **Explanation:** The passage concludes by stating that recognizing the value of introverts challenges the cultural bias towards extroversion, highlighting the importance of diverse personality types.

Natural Sciences: 10 questions

31) What was Henrietta Lacks diagnosed with when she visited Johns Hopkins Hospital?

- · **Answer: C) Cervical cancer**
- · **Explanation:** The passage states that Henrietta Lacks was diagnosed with cervical cancer.

32) What was taken from Henrietta Lacks without her knowledge or consent?

- · **Answer: B) Tumor biopsy**
- · **Explanation:** The passage indicates that doctors took a biopsy of her tumor without her knowledge or consent.

33) What unique property do HeLa cells possess?

- · **Answer: C) They are immortal and can divide indefinitely under the right conditions**
- · **Explanation:** HeLa cells are described as immortal because they can divide indefinitely under the right conditions.

34) How were HeLa cells instrumental in the development of the polio vaccine?

- · **Answer: B) They helped researchers grow and study the poliovirus**
- · **Explanation:** HeLa cells were used to grow and study the poliovirus, which was crucial in developing the polio vaccine.

35) In what area of research have HeLa cells provided significant insights due to their cancerous nature?

- **Answer: C) Cancer research**
- **Explanation:** The passage explains that HeLa cells have been instrumental in cancer research.

36) Which of the following medical breakthroughs have HeLa cells contributed to?

- **Answer: B) Cloning, gene mapping, and in vitro fertilization**
- **Explanation:** The passage lists these breakthroughs as areas where HeLa cells have played a significant role.

37) What ethical issues are raised by the story of HeLa cells?

- **Answer: C) Patients' rights, informed consent, and the commercialization of human tissues**
- **Explanation:** The passage raises concerns about these ethical issues due to the use of HeLa cells without consent.

38) What did the Lacks family not receive in relation to the use of HeLa cells?

- **Answer: A) Information and compensation**
- **Explanation:** The passage mentions that the Lacks family was not informed about the use of Henrietta's cells nor compensated.

39) What does Skloot's account of Henrietta Lacks emphasize about medical research?

- **Answer: B) The need for ethical standards to respect and acknowledge individual contributions**

· **Explanation:** The account emphasizes the importance of ethical standards in medical research.

40) What has been one of the uses of HeLa cells outside of direct medical research?

· **Answer: A) Testing the effects of zero gravity in space**
· **Explanation:** The passage notes that HeLa cells have been used to study the effects of zero gravity in space.

Dual Passages (Literature, Social Science, or Science): 10 questions

41) What does Tocqueville identify as a measure of the health of a democratic society in Passage 1?

· **Answer: B) The quality of functions performed by private citizens**
· **Explanation:** Tocqueville suggests that the health of a democratic society can be measured by the quality of functions performed by private citizens.

42) What is the main concern discussed in Passage 2 by Robert D. Putnam?

· **Answer: B) The decline of social capital and civic engagement in America**
· **Explanation:** Putnam discusses the decline of social capital and civic engagement in America.

43) According to Passage 1, how do Americans typically form associations?

· **Answer: B) They seek mutual assistance and combine once they**

669

find like-minded individuals

· **Explanation:** According to Passage 1, Americans form associations by seeking mutual assistance and combining once they find like-minded individuals.

44) What is one major indicator of the decline in social capital mentioned in Passage 2?

· **Answer: B) The decrease in membership in traditional civic organizations**
· **Explanation:** The decline in social capital is indicated by the decrease in membership in traditional civic organizations.

45) How does Tocqueville in Passage 1 describe the principle that guides many American actions?

· **Answer: A) Self-interest rightly understood**
· **Explanation:** Tocqueville describes the principle guiding many American actions as "self-interest rightly understood."

46) What are some of the consequences of declining social capital mentioned in Passage 2?

· **Answer: B) Higher crime rates, lower educational achievement, and poorer health outcomes**
· **Explanation:** The decline in social capital leads to higher crime rates, lower educational achievement, and poorer health outcomes, according to Passage 2.

47) How do both passages view the role of community engagement?

· **Answer: B) As essential for the health and function of society**
· **Explanation:** Both passages view community engagement as essen-

tial for the health and function of society.

48) What solution does Putnam propose in Passage 2 to address the decline in social capital?

- **Answer: B) Encouraging people to participate in community activities and join organizations**
- **Explanation:** Putnam suggests that encouraging participation in community activities and joining organizations can help address the decline in social capital.

49) What similarity exists between the views of Tocqueville in Passage 1 and Putnam in Passage 2 regarding associations?

- **Answer: B) Both see the formation of associations as critical to the functioning of a democratic society**
- **Explanation:** Tocqueville and Putnam both view the formation of associations as critical to the functioning of a democratic society.

50) How does Tocqueville's view of American associations compare to Putnam's observations about civic engagement?

- **Answer: A) Tocqueville views them as thriving and essential, while Putnam notes a decline in civic engagement**
- **Explanation:** Tocqueville sees American associations as thriving and essential, while Putnam observes a decline.

B. Writing and Language Test

Careers: 11 questions

51) Which choice best describes what happens in the passage?

- · **Answer: B) The passage describes the roles and responsibilities of urban planners and the importance of their work**
- · **Explanation:** The passage outlines the various duties of urban planners, such as developing land use plans, conducting public meetings, and focusing on zoning, transportation, and environmental sustainability.

52) Which choice best expresses the main idea of the passage?

- · **Answer: A) Urban planners are essential for creating sustainable, functional, and attractive urban environments**
- · **Explanation:** The passage emphasizes the vital role of urban planners in designing and managing urban areas to meet community needs and promote sustainability.

53) In context, what does the phrase "public meetings to gather input and build consensus" in sentence 8 most nearly mean?

- · **Answer: B) Official sessions to collect feedback and reach an agreement**
- · **Explanation:** Public meetings involve gathering feedback from community members and stakeholders to build consensus on urban planning projects.

54) Which sentence, if added after sentence 6, would best support the main idea of the paragraph?

- · **Answer: B) These factors help ensure that urban areas remain livable and efficient**

· **Explanation:** This sentence supports the idea that considering various factors in land use planning helps maintain livable and efficient urban areas.

55) In sentence 10, the term "zoning" refers to:

· **Answer: B) The regulation of land use to promote orderly development**
· **Explanation:** Zoning involves designating specific areas for different uses, such as residential, commercial, and industrial, to ensure orderly development.

56) Which choice provides the most accurate interpretation of the information in sentence 11?

· **Answer: B) Zoning helps to balance the needs of different sectors in a community**
· **Explanation:** Zoning ensures that different sectors, such as residential and commercial, have designated areas, promoting a balanced and well-planned community.

57) In sentence 17, what does the mention of "green building practices" contribute to the passage?

· **Answer: A) It highlights a specific method urban planners use to reduce environmental impact**
· **Explanation:** Green building practices are mentioned as a method for minimizing the environmental impact of urban development.

58) The author wants to add the following sentence to the third paragraph:
"Their input is essential to creating development plans that serve the community's best interests." Where would this sentence best fit?

- **Answer: B) After sentence 8**
- **Explanation:** Placing the sentence after sentence 8 emphasizes the importance of gathering community input during public meetings to create plans that benefit the community.

59) In context, the word "resilient" in sentence 18 most nearly means:

- **Answer: B) Adaptable**
- **Explanation:** The term "resilient" refers to the ability of urban areas to adapt to challenges such as climate change.

60) Which choice best concludes the passage?

- **Answer: A) Urban planners face numerous challenges, but their work is crucial for community development**
- **Explanation:** This conclusion summarizes the challenges and importance of urban planners in developing communities.

61) Which choice most effectively combines sentences 24 and 25?

- **Answer: D) To become an urban planner, a strong educational background in urban planning, geography, or a related field is essential, and the career of an urban planner is both challenging and rewarding**
- **Explanation:** This combination maintains the original meaning and flow, effectively linking the educational requirements with the nature of the career.

History/Social Studies: 11 questions

62) Which choice best describes what happens in the passage?

- **Answer: B) The passage describes the causes, impacts, and legacy

of the Industrial Revolution

· **Explanation:** The passage discusses the factors that led to the Industrial Revolution, its various impacts, and its lasting legacy.

63) Which choice best expresses the main idea of the passage?

· **Answer: B) The Industrial Revolution transformed society and economy, leading to significant technological and social changes**

· **Explanation:** The passage highlights the comprehensive changes brought about by the Industrial Revolution, affecting various aspects of society and economy.

64) In context, what does the phrase "development of new machinery and technology" in sentence 4 most nearly mean?

· **Answer: C) Introduction of advanced industrial equipment**

· **Explanation:** The passage refers to the introduction of new machinery like the steam engine and innovations in textile production, which revolutionized industrial processes.

65) Which sentence, if added after sentence 6, would best support the main idea of the paragraph?

· **Answer: C) This technological advancement marked a significant turning point in industrial production**

· **Explanation:** This sentence reinforces the idea that the steam engine and other technological innovations were crucial in advancing industrial production.

66) In sentence 12, the term "urbanization" refers to:

· **Answer: C) The development and growth of cities**

· **Explanation:** Urbanization refers to the movement of people from rural areas to cities, leading to the growth of urban areas.

67) Which choice provides the most accurate interpretation of the information in sentence 13?

- **Answer: B) Factory work was characterized by poor working conditions, prompting the need for labor reforms**
- **Explanation:** The passage describes factory work as grueling and dangerous, with low wages and long hours, highlighting the need for labor reforms.

68) In sentence 18, what does the mention of "environmental degradation" contribute to the passage?

- **Answer: C) It points out a negative consequence of the Industrial Revolution**
- **Explanation:** The passage mentions environmental degradation as one of the adverse effects of industrialization, highlighting the pollution and resource exploitation caused by factories.

69) The author wants to add the following sentence to the fourth paragraph:
"This led to an unprecedented movement of goods and people."
Where would this sentence best fit?

- **Answer: B) After sentence 15**
- **Explanation:** Placing this sentence after sentence 15 helps connect the improvements in transportation infrastructure with the increased movement of goods and people.

70) In context, the word "grueling" in sentence 13 most nearly means:

- **Answer: C) Exhausting**

· **Explanation:** The term "grueling" describes the physically and mentally exhausting nature of factory work during the Industrial Revolution.

71) Which choice best concludes the passage?

· **Answer: B) The Industrial Revolution's legacy of innovation and industrial development continues to shape contemporary society**
· **Explanation:** This conclusion emphasizes the lasting impact of the Industrial Revolution on modern society, particularly in terms of innovation and industrialization.

72) Which choice most effectively combines sentences 24 and 25?

· **Answer: B) The Industrial Revolution was not confined to Britain; it spread to other parts of Europe and North America, and eventually to the rest of the world, with each region experiencing industrialization in its own way**
· **Explanation:** This option clearly and concisely combines the two sentences, indicating the global spread of industrialization and the unique experiences of different regions.

Humanities: 11 questions

73) Which choice best describes what happens in the passage?

· **Answer: B) The passage outlines key figures and ideas of the Enlightenment and their impact on modern thought.**
· **Explanation:** The passage discusses significant Enlightenment thinkers and their contributions to modern concepts like democracy, science, and human rights.

74) Which choice best expresses the main idea of the passage?

- **Answer: B) The Enlightenment's emphasis on reason and individualism significantly shaped modern thought and institutions.**
- **Explanation:** The passage emphasizes the Enlightenment's influence on various modern institutions and thought, highlighting its foundational role.

75) In context, what does the phrase "intellectual and philosophical movement" in sentence 1 most nearly mean?

- **Answer: C) A change in thinking and ideas**
- **Explanation:** The phrase describes a period characterized by a shift in ideas, emphasizing reason and questioning established norms.

76) Which sentence best supports the idea that the Enlightenment challenged established norms?

- **Answer: B) Sentence 5: "Known for his wit and advocacy of civil liberties, Voltaire criticized the Catholic Church and absolute monarchy, promoting freedom of speech and religious tolerance."**
- **Explanation:** This sentence highlights Voltaire's challenge to traditional authorities like the Church and monarchy, advocating for civil liberties instead.

77) In sentence 6, the term "established norms" most likely refers to:

- **Answer: A) Traditional religious beliefs and monarchical authority.**
- **Explanation:** The passage mentions Voltaire challenging the Catholic Church and monarchy, indicating these were the "established norms" being questioned.

78) Which choice best describes the function of sentence 7 in the passage?

- **Answer: B) It provides an example of a key Enlightenment thinker.**
- **Explanation:** Sentence 7 introduces John Locke as another central figure of the Enlightenment, illustrating his influence on political thought.

79) Which choice provides the most accurate interpretation of the information in sentence 9?

- **Answer: C) Locke asserted that government should be based on the consent of the governed and that citizens have the right to overthrow a government that fails to protect their rights.**
- **Explanation:** This accurately reflects Locke's argument for a government that is accountable to its people and protects their natural rights.

80) In sentence 11, what does the mention of "empirical investigation" contribute to the passage?

- **Answer: B) It emphasizes the Enlightenment's focus on observation and reason in understanding the natural world.**
- **Explanation:** The mention of "empirical investigation" highlights the Enlightenment's emphasis on scientific observation and rational analysis.

81) Which choice most effectively combines sentences 13 and 14?

- **Answer: D) Montesquieu, a French philosopher, articulated the concept of separation of powers in his work "The Spirit of the Laws," which became a cornerstone of modern democratic systems and argued that political power should be divided among different branches of government to prevent tyranny and protect individual freedoms.**
- **Explanation:** This option seamlessly combines the sentences, clearly

attributing the concept to Montesquieu and explaining its significance.

82) Which choice best concludes the passage?

- **Answer: B) The Enlightenment's legacy of reason and individualism continues to shape contemporary society.**
- **Explanation:** This conclusion aligns with the passage's discussion of the lasting influence of Enlightenment ideas on modern thought and institutions.

83) The author wants to add the following sentence to the fifth paragraph:
"This belief laid the foundation for modern democratic institutions."
Where would this sentence best fit?

- **Answer: C) After sentence 15**
- **Explanation:** This placement follows the discussion of Montesquieu's ideas on the separation of powers, which indeed laid the foundation for modern democratic systems.

Science: 11 questions

84) Which choice best describes what happens in the passage?

- **Answer: A) The passage explains the basic principles of quantum computing and highlights its potential applications and challenges.**
- **Explanation:** The passage provides an overview of quantum computing, including its foundational concepts, potential applications, and the challenges it faces.

85) Which choice best expresses the main idea of the passage?

- **Answer: B) Quantum computing has significant potential but faces substantial challenges before it can be widely adopted.**
- **Explanation:** The passage emphasizes the promise of quantum computing while also discussing the significant obstacles that need to be overcome.

86) In context, what does the term "superposition" in sentence 2 most nearly mean?

- **Answer: B) The ability of qubits to exist in multiple states simultaneously**
- **Explanation:** Superposition refers to the quantum property that allows qubits to exist in multiple states (both 0 and 1) at the same time.

87) Which sentence best supports the idea that quantum computing could revolutionize certain fields?

- **Answer: A) Sentence 8: "Quantum computers have the potential to transform various fields, including cryptography, materials science, and artificial intelligence."**
- **Explanation:** This sentence explicitly mentions the transformative potential of quantum computing in several key fields.

88) In sentence 9, the phrase "quantum-resistant encryption techniques" most likely refers to:

- **Answer: B) New encryption methods that can withstand attacks from quantum computers**
- **Explanation:** The phrase describes encryption methods designed to be secure against the advanced computational abilities of quantum computers.

89) Which choice best describes the function of sentence 12 in the passage?

- **Answer: B) It acknowledges the challenges that need to be overcome for quantum computing to become practical.**
- **Explanation:** This sentence introduces the discussion of the various challenges quantum computing must address.

90) Which choice provides the most accurate interpretation of the information in sentence 13?

- **Answer: B) Qubit coherence refers to the duration a qubit can maintain its quantum state.**
- **Explanation:** This correctly explains that qubit coherence is about how long a qubit can maintain its quantum state without decoherence.

91) In sentence 21, what does the mention of "precise control and stabilization of numerous qubits" contribute to the passage?

- **Answer: B) It emphasizes the complexity and resource-intensive nature of building large-scale quantum systems.**
- **Explanation:** This mention highlights the technical difficulty and complexity involved in scaling up quantum computers.

92) Which choice most effectively combines sentences 16 and 17?

- **Answer: C) Another challenge is error correction; qubits are prone to errors due to their quantum nature, and implementing robust quantum error correction techniques is essential to ensure the reliability and accuracy of quantum computations.**
- **Explanation:** This option combines the sentences smoothly and provides a clear explanation of the need for error correction in

quantum computing.

93) Which choice best concludes the passage?

- **Answer: C) Quantum computing has immense potential, and overcoming its challenges will require continued collaboration and innovation.**
- **Explanation:** This conclusion reiterates the passage's focus on the potential of quantum computing while acknowledging the need for further research and innovation.

94) The author wants to add the following sentence to the paragraph discussing quantum algorithms:
"This requires rethinking traditional approaches to problem-solving." Where would this sentence best fit?

- **Answer: C) After sentence 24**
- **Explanation:** This placement connects the sentence to the discussion on the development of quantum algorithms, which requires new ways of thinking about problem-solving compared to classical methods.

2. Math

A. Math Test - No Calculator

Heart of Algebra: 8 questions

Question 95:

Problem: Solve for x in the equation:

$$3x - 4 - 5x + 6$$

Solution:

First, move all terms involving x to one side of the equation:

$$3x - 5x - 6 + 4$$

Simplify:

$$-2x = 10$$

Divide by -2:

$$x - -5$$

Answer:

A) -5

Question 96:

Problem: If $3x + 2y - 12$ and $y - 2x - 3$, what is the value of y?

Solution:

Substitute the expression for y from the second equation into the first equation:

$3x + 2(2x - 3) - 12$

Expand and solve for x:

$3x + 4x - 6 - 12$

$7x - 6 - 12$

$7x - 18$

$x - \frac{18}{7}$

Now, find y using the value of x:

$y - 2\left(\frac{18}{7}\right) - 3$

$y - \frac{36}{7} - 3$

$y - \frac{36}{7} - \frac{21}{7}$

$y - \frac{15}{7}$

Answer: D) 7

Question 97:

Problem: What is the solution to the system of equations:

$$x + y = 6$$
$$x - y = 2$$

Solution:

Add the equations to eliminate y:

$$(x + y) + (x - y) = 6 + 2$$

Simplify:

$$2x = 8$$

Divide by 2:

$$x = 4$$

Substitute $x = 4$ back into the first equation:

$$4 + y = 6$$

Solve for y:

$$y = 2$$

Answer:

C) $(4, 2)$

Question 98:

Problem: Solve the inequality:

$$5 - 3x > 2$$

Solution:

Subtract 5 from both sides:

$$-3x > -3$$

Divide by -3, and reverse the inequality:

$$x < 1$$

Answer:

A) $x < 1$

Question 99:

Problem: If $y - 3x + 2$ and $y - -x + 6$, what is the value of x?

Solution:

1. Set the two expressions for y equal to each other:

$$3x + 2 - -x + 6$$

2. Add x to both sides:

$$4x + 2 - 6$$

3. Subtract 2 from both sides:

$$4x - 4$$

4. Divide both sides by 4:

$$x - 1$$

Answer: A) 1

Question 100:

Problem: The sum of two numbers is 12. If one number is three times the other, what are the numbers?

Solution:

Let the smaller number be x, and the larger number be $3x$. We have the equation:

$$x + 3x = 12$$

Combine like terms:

$$4x = 12$$

Divide by 4:

$$x = 3$$

The numbers are 3 and 9.

Answer: A) 3 and 9

Question 101:

Problem: Find the value of x if $6x + 2 = 4x + 10$.

Solution:

Subtract $4x$ from both sides:

$$2x + 2 = 10$$

Subtract 2 from both sides:

$$2x = 8$$

Divide by 2:

$$x = 4$$

Answer: B) 4

Question 102:

Problem: What is the solution to the equation $2(3x + 5) - 4x + 16$?

Solution:

Expand the left side:

$$6x + 10 - 4x + 16$$

Subtract $4x$ from both sides:

$$2x + 10 - 16$$

Subtract 10 from both sides:

$$2x - 6$$

Divide by 2:

$$x - 3$$

Answer: $x - 3$

Correct Answer: C) 3

Problem Solving and Data Analysis: 3 questions

Question 103:

Problem: A bakery sells cupcakes for $2.50 each and cookies for $1.75 each. If a customer buys 4 cupcakes and 5 cookies, what is the total cost?

Solution:

The total cost of 4 cupcakes is:

$$4 \times 2.50 - 10.00$$

The total cost of 5 cookies is:

$$5 \times 1.75 - 8.75$$

The total cost is:

$$10.00 + 8.75 - 18.75$$

Answer: D) $18.75

Question 104:

Problem: The following data represents the number of hours worked by employees in a week:

Employee	Hours Worked
A	35
B	40
C	28
D	32
E	38

Solution:

The total cost of 4 cupcakes is:

$$4 \times 2.50 - 10.00$$

The total cost of 5 cookies is:

$$5 \times 1.75 - 8.75$$

The total cost is:

$$10.00 + 8.75 - 18.75$$

Answer: D) $18.75

Question 105:

Problem: A survey of 400 people found that 60% prefer watching movies at home, while the rest prefer watching movies at the theater. How many people prefer watching movies at the theater?

Solution:

If 60% of the 400 people prefer watching movies at home, then 40% prefer watching movies at the theater:

$$\text{Number of people} - 0.40 \times 400 - 160$$

Answer: B) 160

Passport to Advanced Math: 6 questions

Question 106:

Problem: If $f(x) - 2x^2 - 3x + 5$ and $g(x) - x - 4$, what is $f(g(x))$?

Solution:

Substitute $g(x) - x - 4$ into $f(x)$:

$$f(g(x)) - 2(x - 4)^2 - 3(x - 4) + 5$$

First, calculate $(x - 4)^2$:

$$(x - 4)^2 - x^2 - 8x + 16$$

Now substitute:

$$f(g(x)) - 2(x^2 - 8x + 16) - 3(x - 4) + 5$$

Expand:

$$- 2x^2 - 16x + 32 - 3x + 12 + 5$$

Combine like terms:

$$- 2x^2 - 19x + 49$$

Answer: B) $2x^2 - 3x - 11$

Question 107:

Problem: Solve for x: $4^{2x+1} = 32$.

Solution:

First, express 32 as a power of 4:

$$32 = 4^{5/2}$$

So:

$$4^{2x+1} = 4^{5/2}$$

Equate the exponents:

$$2x + 1 = \frac{5}{2}$$

Solve for x:

$$2x = \frac{5}{2} - 1 = \frac{3}{2}$$

$$x = \frac{3}{4}$$

Answer: C) $\frac{3}{2}$

Question 108:

Problem: The function $h(x)$ is defined as $h(x) = x^3 - 6x^2 + 9x$. What are the zeros of $h(x)$?

Solution:

Factor the equation:

$$h(x) = x(x^2 - 6x + 9)$$

Factor the quadratic:

$$h(x) = x(x - 3)^2$$

Set each factor equal to zero:

$$x = 0 \quad \text{or} \quad x - 3 = 0$$

$$x = 0, 3$$

Answer: A) $x = 0, 3, 3$

Question 109:

Problem: If $y = \frac{3x-1}{x+2}$, which of the following is true about the vertical asymptote of the function?

Solution:

The vertical asymptote occurs where the denominator is zero:

$$x + 2 = 0$$

$$x = -2$$

Answer: A) $x = -2$

693

Question 110:

Problem: Solve for x: $\sqrt{2x + 9} - 3 = 0$.

Solution:

Add 3 to both sides:

$$\sqrt{2x + 9} = 3$$

Square both sides:

$$2x + 9 = 9$$

Subtract 9 from both sides:

$$2x = 0$$

Solve for x:

$$x = 0$$

Answer: A) $x = 0$

Question 111:

Problem: If $(x + 2)^2 = 16$, what are the possible values of x?

Solution:

Take the square root of both sides:

$$x + 2 = \pm 4$$

Solve for x:

$$x = -2 + 4 = 2 \quad \text{or} \quad x = -2 - 4 = -6$$

Answer: B) $x = 2$ or $x = -6$

Additional Topics in Math (geometry, trigonometry, etc.): 3 questions

Question 112:

Problem: In a right triangle, the lengths of the legs are 6 units and 8 units. What is the length of the hypotenuse?

Solution:

Use the Pythagorean theorem:

$$c - \sqrt{a^2 + b^2}$$

Substitute $a - 6$ and $b - 8$:

$$c - \sqrt{6^2 + 8^2} - \sqrt{36 + 64} - \sqrt{100} - 10 \text{ units}$$

Answer: A) 10 units

Question 113:

Problem: If the area of a circle is 36π square units, what is the circumference of the circle?

Solution:

The formula for the area of a circle is:

$$A - \pi r^2$$

Set the area equal to 36π:

$$\pi r^2 = 36\pi$$

Solve for r:

$$r^2 - 36 \quad \Rightarrow \quad r - 6$$

The formula for the circumference is:

$$C - 2\pi r - 2\pi(6) - 12\pi \text{ units}$$

Answer: B) 12pi units

Question 114:

Problem: What is the value of $\cos(45^\circ)\sin(45^\circ)$?

Solution:

We know that:

$$\cos(45^\circ) - \sin(45^\circ) - \frac{\sqrt{2}}{2}$$

Thus:

$$\cos(45^\circ)\sin(45^\circ) - \frac{\sqrt{2}}{2} \times \frac{\sqrt{2}}{2} - \frac{2}{4} - \frac{1}{2}$$

Answer: B) $\frac{1}{2}$

B. Math Test - Calculator

Heart of Algebra: 16 questions

Question 115:

Problem: Solve for x in the equation $5x - 4 - 3x + 10$.

Solution:

First, move the $3x$ from the right side to the left side:

$$5x - 3x - 4 - 10$$

Simplify:

$$2x - 4 - 10$$

Add 4 to both sides:

$$2x - 14$$

Divide by 2:

$$x - 7$$

Answer: C) 7

Question 116:

Problem: If $3y + 2 - 4y - 6$, what is the value of y?

Solution:

Move the $3y$ from the left side to the right side:

$$2 - y - 6$$

Add 6 to both sides:

$$y - 8$$

Answer: A) 8

Question 117:

Problem: Solve for x: $2(x + 3) - x - 5$.

Solution:

First, distribute the 2:

$$2x + 6 - x - 5$$

Move the x from the right side to the left side:

$$x + 6 - -5$$

Subtract 6 from both sides:

$$x - -11$$

Answer: A) -11

Question 118:

Problem: The equation $y - 4x - 8$ represents a line. What is the slope of this line?

Solution:

The equation $y - mx + b$ is in slope-intercept form, where m is the slope.

In $y - 4x - 8$, the slope m is 4.

Answer: B) 4

Question 119:

Problem: If $y - 5x + 2$ and $y - 2x + 11$, what is the value of x?

Solution:

Set the two equations equal to each other:

$$5x + 2 - 2x + 11$$

Move the $2x$ from the right side to the left side:

$$3x + 2 - 11$$

Subtract 2 from both sides:

$$3x - 9$$

Divide by 3:

$$x - 3$$

Answer: A) 3

Question 120:

Problem: Solve for y: $6y - 5 - 4y + 7$.

Solution:

Move the $4y$ from the right side to the left side:

$$2y - 5 - 7$$

Add 5 to both sides:

$$2y - 12$$

Divide by 2:

$$y - 6$$

Answer: A) 6

Question 121:

Problem: What is the value of x in the equation $8(x + 1) = 4x + 20$?

Solution:

Distribute the 8 on the left side:

$$8x + 8 = 4x + 20$$

Move the $4x$ from the right side to the left side:

$$4x + 8 = 20$$

Subtract 8 from both sides:

$$4x = 12$$

Divide by 4:

$$x = 3$$

Answer: B) 3

Question 122:

Problem: If $y - -2x + 8$ and $y - 3x - 7$, what is the value of y?

Solution:

Set the two equations equal to each other:

$$-2x + 8 - 3x - 7$$

Move the $2x$ from the left side to the right side:

$$8 - 5x - 7$$

Add 7 to both sides:

$$15 - 5x$$

Divide by 5:

$$x - 3$$

Substitute $x - 3$ into the first equation:

$$y - -2(3) + 8 - -6 + 8 - 2$$

Answer: B) 2

Question 123:

Problem: Solve for x: $3(x - 4) - 2(x + 2)$.

Solution:

Distribute both sides:

$$3x - 12 - 2x + 4$$

Move the $2x$ from the right side to the left side:

$$x - 12 - 4$$

Add 12 to both sides:

$$x - 16$$

Answer: A) 16

Question 124:

Problem: The line $y - 6x - 15$ passes through the point $(a, 9)$. What is the value of a?

Solution:

Substitute $y - 9$ into the equation:

$$9 - 6a - 15$$

Add 15 to both sides:

$$24 - 6a$$

Divide by 6:

$$a - 4$$

Answer: A) 4

Question 125:

Problem: What is the solution to the system of equations: $2x + y - 10$ and $x - y - 2$?

Solution:

First, solve the second equation for y:

$$y - x - 2$$

Substitute this into the first equation:

$$2x + (x - 2) - 10$$

Combine like terms:

$$3x - 2 - 10$$

Add 2 to both sides:

$$3x - 12$$

Divide by 3:

$$x - 4$$

Now, substitute $x - 4$ into the equation $y - x - 2$:

$$y - 4 - 2 - 2$$

Answer: A) (4, 2)

Question 126:

Problem: If $9x + 3 - 6x + 12$, what is the value of x?

Solution:

First, move the $6x$ from the right side to the left side:

$$3x + 3 - 12$$

Subtract 3 from both sides:

$$3x - 9$$

Divide by 3:

$$x - 3$$

Answer: A) 3

Question 127:

Problem: Solve for y: $4(3y - 2) - 5(y + 3)$.

Solution:

Distribute both sides:

$$12y - 8 - 5y + 15$$

Move the $5y$ from the right side to the left side:

$$7y - 8 - 15$$

Add 8 to both sides:

$$7y - 23$$

Divide by 7:

$$y - \frac{23}{7}$$

Answer: B) $\frac{23}{7}$

Question 128:

Problem: If $y - 4x + 5$ and $y - -x + 20$, what is the value of y?

Solution:

Set the two equations equal to each other:

$$4x + 5 - -x + 20$$

Move the x term from the right side to the left side:

$$5x + 5 - 20$$

Subtract 5 from both sides:

$$5x - 15$$

Divide by 5:

$$x - 3$$

Substitute $x - 3$ into either equation (let's use the first):

$$y - 4(3) + 5 - 12 + 5 - 17$$

Answer: A) 17

Question 129:

Problem: Solve for x: $7(x - 3) = 4(x + 2)$.

Solution:

Distribute both sides:

$$7x - 21 - 4x + 8$$

Move the $4x$ term from the right side to the left side:

$$3x - 21 - 8$$

Add 21 to both sides:

$$3x - 29$$

Divide by 3:

$$x - \frac{29}{3}$$

Answer: C) $\frac{29}{3}$

Question 130:

Problem: If $5x - 3y - 21$ and $x - 4$, what is the value of y?

Solution:

Substitute $x - 4$ into the equation:

$$5(4) - 3y - 21$$

Simplify:

$$20 - 3y - 21$$

Subtract 20 from both sides:

$$-3y - 1$$

Divide by -3:

$$y - -\frac{1}{3}$$

Answer: A) $-\frac{1}{3}$

Problem Solving and Data Analysis: 8 questions

Question 131:

Problem: A store sells a pack of 12 batteries for $15. What is the cost per battery?

Solution:

To find the cost per battery, divide the total cost by the number of batteries:

$$\text{Cost per battery} = \frac{15}{12} = 1.25$$

Answer: C) $1.25

Question 132:

Problem: A student scored 88, 92, 79, and 85 on four math tests. What score must the student get on the fifth test to have an average score of 85?

Solution:

Let the score on the fifth test be x. The average score of 5 tests is given by:

$$\frac{88 + 92 + 79 + 85 + x}{5} = 85$$

First, calculate the sum of the known scores:

$$88 + 92 + 79 + 85 = 344$$

Now, solve for x:

$$\frac{344 + x}{5} = 85$$

Multiply both sides by 5:

$$344 + x = 425$$

Subtract 344 from both sides:

$$x = 81$$

Answer: A) 81

Question 133:

Problem: If a rectangle has a length of 10 meters and a width of 6 meters, what is the perimeter of the rectangle?

Solution:

The perimeter of a rectangle is given by:

$$\text{Perimeter} - 2 \times (\text{Length} + \text{Width})$$

Substitute the given values:

$$\text{Perimeter} - 2 \times (10 + 6) - 2 \times 16 - 32 \text{ meters}$$

Answer: D) 32 meters

Question 134:

Problem: A person invests $2000 at an annual interest rate of 5% compounded annually. What will be the total amount after 3 years? (Use the formula $A - P(1 + r)^t$)

Solution:

Substitute the given values into the formula:

$$A - 2000 \times (1 + 0.05)^3 - 2000 \times 1.157625 - 2315.25$$

Answer: A) $2315.25

Question 135:

Problem: In a class of 30 students, 18 are girls. What is the percentage of boys in the class?

Solution:

First, find the number of boys:

$$\text{Number of boys} - 30 - 18 - 12$$

Then, calculate the percentage of boys:

$$\text{Percentage of boys} - \frac{12}{30} \times 100 - 40\%$$

Answer: A) 40%

Question 136:

Problem: A shop sells 3 types of fruits: apples, oranges, and bananas. If the ratio of apples to oranges to bananas sold is 3:4:5 and the shop sold 120 fruits in total, how many bananas were sold?

Solution:

The total ratio is $3 + 4 + 5 - 12$.

To find the number of bananas sold, use the proportion:

$$\text{Bananas sold} - \frac{5}{12} \times 120 - 50$$

Answer: D) 50

Question 137:

Problem: A car rental company charges a flat fee of $30 plus $0.20 per mile driven. If a customer pays $50, how many miles did they drive?

Solution:

Let the number of miles driven be x.

The total cost equation is:

$$30 + 0.20x - 50$$

Subtract 30 from both sides:

$$0.20x - 20$$

Divide by 0.20:

$$x - 100$$

Answer: B) 100

Question 138:

Problem: If 8% of a number is 32, what is the number?

Solution:

Let the number be x. Then:

$$0.08x - 32$$

Divide both sides by 0.08:

$$x - \frac{32}{0.08} - 400$$

Answer: D) 400

Passport to Advanced Math: 11 questions

Question 139:

Problem: Solve for x in the equation $x^2 - 4x - 21 = 0$.

Solution:

We solve the quadratic equation by factoring:

$$x^2 - 4x - 21 = (x - 7)(x + 3) = 0$$

This gives us:

$$x - 7 = 0 \quad \text{or} \quad x + 3 = 0$$

$$x = 7 \quad \text{or} \quad x = -3$$

Answer: C) 7, -3

Question 140:

Problem: What is the value of k if the polynomial $x^2 - 6x + k$ has a double root?

Solution:

For a quadratic equation to have a double root, the discriminant must be zero:

$$b^2 - 4ac = 0$$

Here, $a = 1, b = -6$, and $c = k$:

$$(-6)^2 - 4(1)(k) = 0$$

$$36 - 4k = 0$$

$$4k = 36$$

$$k = 9$$

Answer: A) 9

Question 141:

Problem: If $f(x) = 3x^2 - 12x + 5$, what is the vertex of the parabola?

Solution:

The x-coordinate of the vertex for a quadratic function $ax^2 + bx + c$ is given by:

$$x = -\frac{b}{2a}$$

For $f(x) = 3x^2 - 12x + 5$:

$$x = -\frac{-12}{2(3)} = \frac{12}{6} = 2$$

Substitute $x = 2$ back into the equation to find the y-coordinate:

$$f(2) = 3(2)^2 - 12(2) + 5 = 12 - 24 + 5 = -7$$

The vertex is:

$$(2, -7)$$

Answer: A) (2, -7)

Question 142:

Problem: Solve for x in the equation $\log_2(x + 3) = 4$.

Solution:

Convert the logarithmic equation to exponential form:

$$x + 3 = 2^4$$

$$x + 3 = 16$$

$$x = 16 - 3 = 13$$

Answer: A) 13

713

Question 143:

Problem: If $g(x) - x^2 + 4x + c$ has only one solution, what is the value of c?

Solution:

For the quadratic equation to have one solution, the discriminant must be zero:

$$\Delta - b^2 - 4ac - 0$$

Here, $a - 1, b - 4$, and $c - c$:

$$4^2 - 4(1)(c) - 0$$

$$16 - 4c - 0$$

Solve for c:

$$4c - 16$$

$$c - 4$$

Answer: B) 4

Question 144:

Problem: What is the inverse function of $f(x) - 2x + 5$?

Solution:

To find the inverse, swap x and y and solve for y:

$$y - 2x + 5$$

Swap:

$$x - 2y + 5$$

Solve for y:

$$x - 5 - 2y$$

$$y = \frac{x - 5}{2}$$

So, the inverse is:

$$f^{-1}(x) - \frac{x - 5}{2}$$

Answer: A) $f^{-1}(x) - \frac{x-5}{2}$

Question 145:

Problem: If $g(x) - \sqrt{x-1} + 3$, for what value of x does $g(x) - 7$?

Solution:

Set $g(x) - 7$ and solve for x:

$$\sqrt{x-1} + 3 - 7$$

Subtract 3 from both sides:

$$\sqrt{x-1} - 4$$

Square both sides:

$$x - 1 - 16$$

Add 1 to both sides:

$$x - 17$$

Answer: A) 17

Question 146:

Problem: Simplify the expression $(2x^2 - 3x + 1) - (x^2 + x - 2)$.

Solution:

Distribute the negative sign and then combine like terms:

$$(2x^2 - 3x + 1) - (x^2 + x - 2) = 2x^2 - 3x + 1 - x^2 - x + 2$$

Combine like terms:

$$x^2 - 4x + 3$$

Answer: A) $x^2 - 4x + 3$

Question 147:

Problem: Solve for x in the inequality $\frac{x+1}{x-2} > 3$.

Solution:

First, rewrite the inequality:

$$\frac{x+1}{x-2} - 3 > 0$$

Combine into a single fraction:

$$\frac{x+1-3(x-2)}{x-2} > 0$$

Simplify:

$$\frac{x+1-3x+6}{x-2} > 0$$

$$\frac{-2x+7}{x-2} > 0$$

To find the critical points, solve:

$$-2x + 7 = 0 \quad \text{and} \quad x - 2 = 0$$

$$x = \frac{7}{2} = 3.5 \quad \text{and} \quad x = 2$$

These critical points divide the number line into intervals. Test the inequality in each interval:

1. $x < 2$: Choose $x = 0$, $\frac{-2(0)+7}{0-2} = \frac{7}{-2} = -3.5$ (Negative)
2. $2 < x < 3.5$: Choose $x = 3$, $\frac{-2(3)+7}{3-2} = \frac{-6+7}{1} = 1$ (Positive)
3. $x > 3.5$: Choose $x = 4$, $\frac{-2(4)+7}{4-2} = \frac{-8+7}{2} = -\frac{1}{2}$ (Negative)

Since we're looking for where the expression is greater than 0, the solution is:

$$x > 3.5$$

Answer: A) $x = 3.5$

Question 148:

Problem: If $f(x) = x^2 + kx + 4$ has a minimum value at $x = -3$, what is the value of k?

Solution:

The x-coordinate of the vertex of a parabola $y = ax^2 + bx + c$ is given by:

$$x = -\frac{b}{2a}$$

Here, $a = 1$, $b = k$, and the minimum occurs at $x = -3$:

$$-3 = -\frac{k}{2(1)}$$

Solve for k:

$$k = 6$$

Answer: A) 6

Question 149:

Problem: Solve for x in the inequality $3x - 7 > 5x + 1$.

Solution:

Subtract $3x$ from both sides:

$$-7 > 2x + 1$$

Subtract 1 from both sides:

$$-8 > 2x$$

Divide by 2:

$$x < -4$$

Answer: C) $x < -4$

Additional Topics in Math (geometry, trigonometry, etc.): 3 questions

Question 150:

Problem: In a right triangle, the lengths of the legs are 6 units and 8 units. What is the length of the hypotenuse?

Solution:

Use the Pythagorean theorem:

$$c - \sqrt{a^2 + b^2}$$

Substitute $a - 6$ and $b - 8$:

$$c - \sqrt{6^2 + 8^2} - \sqrt{36 + 64} - \sqrt{100} - 10$$

Correct Answer: C) 10

Question 151:

Problem: If $\sin \theta - \frac{3}{5}$ and θ is an acute angle, what is $\cos \theta$?

Solution:

Using the Pythagorean identity:

$$\sin^2 \theta + \cos^2 \theta - 1$$

Substitute $\sin \theta - \frac{3}{5}$:

$$\left(\frac{3}{5}\right)^2 + \cos^2 \theta - 1 \implies \frac{9}{25} + \cos^2 \theta - 1$$

Subtract $\frac{9}{25}$ from 1:

$$\cos^2 \theta - \frac{16}{25}$$

Taking the square root:

$$\cos \theta - \frac{4}{5}$$

Correct Answer: A) $\frac{4}{5}$

Question 152:

Problem: What is the area of a sector of a circle with a radius of 10 units and a central angle of $45°$?

Solution:

The area of a sector is given by:

$$\text{Area} - \frac{\theta}{360°} \times \pi r^2$$

Substitute $\theta - 45°$ and $r - 10$:

$$\text{Area} - \frac{45°}{360°} \times \pi(10)^2 - \frac{1}{8} \times 100\pi - 12.5\pi$$

Correct Answer: A) 12.5π

3. Essay (Optional) - Example Answer

In the passage "The Case for Universal Basic Income," Samuel Grey constructs a compelling argument advocating for Universal Basic Income (UBI) by skillfully employing evidence, logical reasoning, and persuasive language. Grey's approach effectively strengthens the persuasiveness of his argument, making a strong case for UBI as a beneficial policy.

One of Grey's primary strategies is his use of evidence to substantiate the claims supporting UBI. Throughout the passage, Grey references data and studies to demonstrate the positive impacts of UBI. For instance, he cites a pilot program in Kenya conducted by the organization GiveDirectly, which found that recipients of a basic income experienced improvements in health, education, and economic productivity. By providing concrete examples of successful UBI programs, Grey bolsters his argument with real-world evidence, lending credibility to his claims and helping to convince his audience that UBI can have tangible benefits. Additionally, he references Finland's UBI experiment to counter a common criticism that UBI might disincentivize work, noting that participants reported higher levels of well-being without a significant reduction in work activity. This strategic use of evidence helps Grey address potential objections while reinforcing the effectiveness of UBI.

Grey also employs logical reasoning to connect his claims with supporting evidence and to structure his argument cohesively. He begins by outlining the economic challenges of rising inequality and job insecurity, framing UBI as a solution to these issues. Grey then logically progresses through the benefits of UBI, such as providing a financial safety net, reducing poverty and inequality, and simplifying the welfare system. Each of these points is supported by evidence or examples, creating a logical flow that strengthens the overall argument. For example, after discussing the instability in today's job market due to automation and globalization, Grey logically connects this to the need for UBI to provide financial security for all citizens. This clear and logical structure makes the argument easier for the audience to follow and understand, enhancing its persuasiveness.

In addition to evidence and reasoning, Grey utilizes persuasive language and stylistic elements to add power to his argument. His choice of words conveys urgency and importance, emphasizing the transformative potential of UBI. Phrases like "pressing issues," "transformative force," and "promising solution" underscore the significance of UBI as a policy that can address some of the most critical challenges facing society today. Grey also appeals to the audience's emotions by highlighting the human impact of economic insecurity and the potential for UBI to improve well-being. For instance, he mentions that the financial stability provided by UBI can reduce stress and enable individuals to pursue education or entrepreneurial ventures without the constant fear of financial ruin. This appeal to emotion helps to engage the audience on a deeper level, making the argument more relatable and compelling.

Furthermore, Grey's argument is strengthened by his balanced approach, in which he acknowledges and addresses potential counterarguments. By recognizing the criticism that UBI might disincentivize work and providing evidence to refute it, Grey demonstrates a thorough understanding of the issue and presents a well-rounded argument. This approach not only enhances his credibility but also makes his argument more persuasive by preemptively addressing concerns that the audience might have.

In conclusion, Samuel Grey effectively builds a persuasive argument in favor of Universal Basic Income by using evidence, logical reasoning, and persuasive language. His strategic use of data and examples, combined with a clear and logical structure, strengthens the credibility of his claims and makes the argument more convincing. Additionally, Grey's use of emotionally resonant language and his balanced approach further enhance the persuasiveness of his argument, making a strong case for UBI as a policy that can address critical economic and social challenges.

Made in United States
Troutdale, OR
10/04/2024

23423611R00405